Ancient Masonry

Course 4

ANCIENT MASONRY

The Spiritual Significance of Masonic Rituals,
Degrees and Symbols

C. C. Zain

The Church of Light
Los Angeles

Published in the United States in 1994 by
The Church of Light
2341 Coral Street, Los Angeles, CA 90031-2916

©1994 by The Church of Light. All rights reserved

Individual chapters originally copyrighted in 1938 and 1939 by Elbert Benjamine.

Library of Congress Cataloging-in-Publication Data
Benjamine, Elbert.
    Ancient Masonry : The spiritual meaning of Masonic degrees, rituals and symbols / C.C. Zain.
    (Course 4)
    p. cm.
    Includes index.
    ISBN 0-87887-374-0 (acid-free paper) : $16.95
    1. Freemasonry—Religious aspects.   2. Freemasonry—History.   3. Freemasons—Rituals.   4. Freemasonry—Symbolism.   I. Title.
HS495.B43 1998   94-11999
366'.12—dc20   CIP

Ancient Masonry, an exposition of the occult principles and spiritual ideas originally associated with Masonic symbols and rituals, with history dating back to ancient Egyptian mystery schools, may be obtained through your local bookstore or you may order it from The Church of Light, 2341 Coral Street, Los Angeles, CA 90031-2916, (323)226-0453.

Portions of this book not exceeding a total of 2,000 words may be freely quoted or reprinted without permission, provided credit is given in the following form:

Reprinted from *Ancient Masonry* by C. C. Zain, copyright 1994, The Church of Light— Rev. 2 ed.

Contents

List of Horoscopes	vii
1 Introduction	1
2 Entered Apprentice and the Planets	21
3 Entered Apprentice and the Signs	41
4 Numbers and Opening the Lodge	61
5 Initiating a Member	81
6 Fellowcraft	101
7 Lodge Emblems	121
8 Master Mason	141
9 Mark Master Mason	161
10 Royal Arch	181
11 Degrees of the Cross	201
12 Ineffable Degrees	221
13 Historical Degrees	241
Study Questions	262
Appendix	279
Index	302
Other Brotherhood of Light Books	319

List of Horoscopes

Governor Frank Murphy	280
George Westinghouse	281
Albert Dyer	282
Daniel C. Roper	283
James Branch Cabell	284
Leopold Stokowski	285
John Henry Nash	286
Edgar Bergen	287
Hugo L. Black	288
Thomas E. Dewey	289
Lenora Conwell	290
Greta Garbo	291
W. H. Chaney	292
John Leslie (Jackie) Coogan	293
John F. Kennedy	294
Richard M. Nixon	295
Jessie Woodson James	296
King of the Hobos (Jeff Davis)	297
Major Edward Bowes	298
Arturo Toscanini	299
The Church of Light	300
The Brotherhood of Light Research Department	301

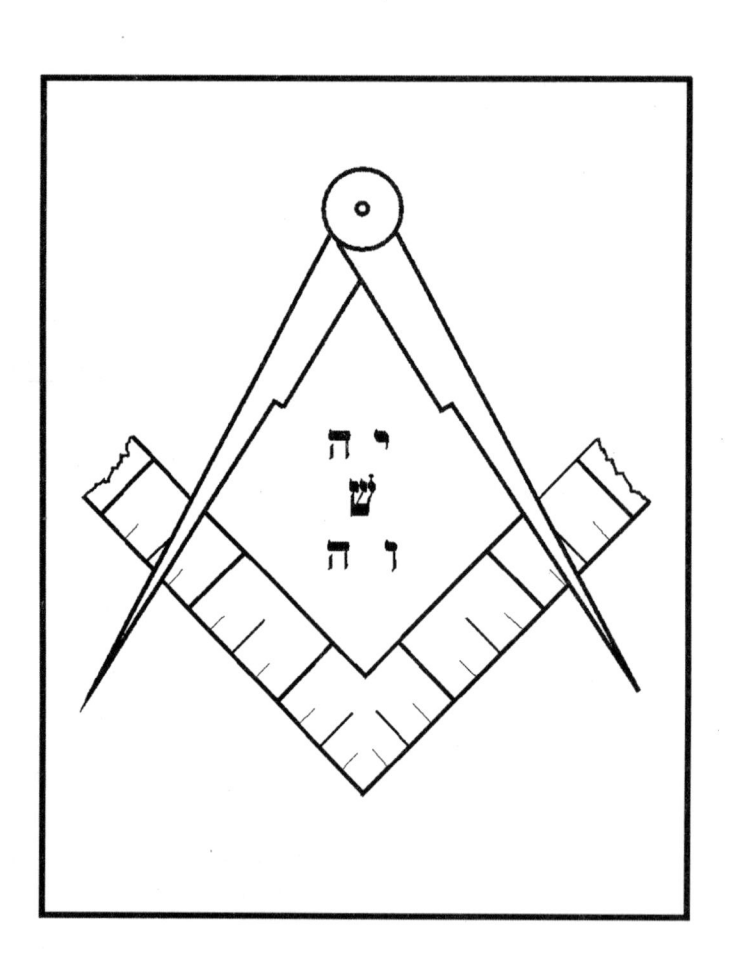

Chapter 1

Ancient Masonry Introduction

FOR MANY YEARS it has been my desire to place before students a concise exposition of those occult principles which form the framework about which are woven the symbolism and ritual of Modern Freemasonry.

The antiquity of its venerable emblems is unquestionable, and it is now generally accepted by Freemasons and occult students alike, that they conceal mystic verities. These rites and pictorial representations that have seemed significant to an important nucleus in the social system of every ancient nation boasting even a degree of civilization, are so widely disseminated that their remnants may be found in remote Tartary and Tibet, among the almond-eyed children of the Flowery Kingdom and Japan, on the slopes of the snow-capped Himalayas, beside the turbid Ganges, amid the desert sands that cover the buried cities of Gobi, and by the revered Tigris and Euphrates. They are found also at the foot of Caucasian passes, by the shores of the Red Sea, in the fertile valley of the Nile, and amid the ruins of classic Greece and Rome, ancient Gaul and primitive Ireland and, crossing the restless expanse where the wide Atlantic rolls, we confront the same hoary emblems in Peru, in the Mississippi Valley, and in the Yucatan.

Certainly the most enlightened inhabitants of our globe, even in what we are egotistic enough to call the barbaric ages, did not spend so much time and energy elaborating and preserving a will-o'-the-wisp devoid of meaning and significance! This divine symbolic language, which has successfully weathered the cataclysms of nature, that has been preserved though all else contemporary crumbled into ruins and returned to the dust from whence it came; the very memory of whose originators is lost in the dim night of time; which of all the childhood possessions of the human race, alone has escaped the Lethean waters of oblivion; though subsequently it may have degenerated into empty soulless forms, hieroglyphics uninterpretable; it is preposterous to suppose had no substance in truth, no foundation in fact, no correspondence in the starlit realms of Urania.

The Ancient Secret Doctrine, now preserved in the symbolic forms of Masonry, gave to the old pagodas of China their peculiar shape. It commanded the erection of the eight-volved tower of Babel on Shinar's plain, prompted the laborious building of the pyramids in Egypt and Mexico, constituted the motive force that scattered huge lithic monuments over the fair face of Europe, and bade the construction of elaborate temples that yet remain but partly discovered amid the tangled vegetation of the American tropics. Consequently, whatever our opinion of the truth or falsity of its tenets, we cannot doubt that it conveyed ideas of moment to the minds of our remote forefathers.

Through the varied web of human history, woven from the odds and ends of half-forgotten traditions, runs an unbroken strand of gold. Nations have risen and fallen, empires have been welded and severed again, continents have been lifted and then submerged; yet through all time since man has made his home upon this mundane sphere, the golden thread of Masonic Symbolism has stretched unsevered through the warp and woof of racial destiny. There have been periods when the glittering strand has almost been lost to view amid the coarser fabric woven by statecraft and priestcraft; but ever it reappeared, scintillating in the foreground of evolutionary progress. Again and again has it strengthened the tone of human moral fiber in times of national decadence, again and again has it constituted the power behind the throne, a lifeline at critical periods to which a superior few could cling and struggle for racial advancement; working silently, secretly, yet effectively.

Modern savants may, or may not, according to the bias of their minds, place confidence in the verity of the esoteric teachings held by the most spiritual of our early progenitors, such as are elaborated and preserved in symbolic rites and hieroglyphics; but no student worthy of the name will fail to investigate ideas which, perhaps more than any others, have shaped the course of man's intellectual and spiritual development, and have ever constituted the mold of his noblest endeavors.

He who would become the possessor of true knowledge must never rest content with theories only, but must be able to prove or disprove them in nature's laboratory. And where a set of ideas has been held by a number of men, or such ideas have exerted an important influence in mundane affairs, if he proves them erroneous his task is but partly completed; for he has yet to ascertain why those opinions were held, why they seemed plausible to others, and in what proportions the false and the true are intermingled. It is most difficult for men to formulate a conception that has not some slight foundation of fact upon which to rest.

Masonic symbolism being the garment worn by a doctrine which has exerted so powerful an influence in human affairs, a mantle still preserved by Freemasons—an organization whose motive is lofty and whose practical endeavors are far-reaching and beneficent—it behooves all students of philosophy and religion to investigate these ancient forms and tenets, to trace them to their original source, and finally, to compare them with Mother Nature.

Yet not until we know the meaning attached to these symbols by the originators are we capable of testing their truth or falsity. And not until we have placed them under the microscope of the soul, and illuminated them by the sunlight of reason and the x-ray of intuition—making at the same time careful comparisons with Nature—are we warranted in passing judgment upon the truth or falsity of the Secret Doctrine they clothe.

A much repeated, and too oft unheeded admonition in Masonry is: "Study the Book of Nature brother, it bears the stamp of Deity."

Such wise council is alone sufficient to mark the integrity of the august body in whose ritual it appears, making a wide distinction between its underlying principles and those of many another religious or social body. These others all too often curtail original investigation, and cramp and shackle their members by imposing a belief in some individual, or company of them, who poses as the special interpreter of the Will of Deity.

Yet in times past, as the history of his activities amply proves, the Masonic Brother has had to pay dearly for the privilege of being Free to build the edifice of his soul conformable to the dictates of his reason and the promptings of his conscience. His option of being a Freemason has sometimes been purchased with his life's blood; for the oppressors of humanity have ever feared and hated those whom they could neither cajole nor bribe into servility, and who resisted all temptation knowingly to become enlisted in an unjust cause.

If Masonic Symbolism is of such paramount importance, the casual thinker will ask, why is it that others have not ere now drunk at the fountain of its enlightenment and offered the cup of its virtues to the whole parched world.

In a measure this has been done, but in a measure only. The labors of Albert Pike are of great value, and those of such worthies as Oliver and Mackey should not be slighted. But the investigator who would discover the conceptions originally underlying Masonry and make them public is confronted with peculiarly obstinate difficulties. Chief among these obstacles is the circumstance that only one having developed his psychic senses and thus able to read from the scroll preserved in the astral light can trace the origin of these prehistoric emblems. And having traced them to their source, their meaning will still remain opaque, or at best but translucent, unless by virtue of having passed his Initiation in the astral spaces, he is firmly grounded in the fundamental principles of the Mission of the Soul.

Once he has discovered their meaning, his difficulties are not yet ended; for the ignorance and prejudice of his race may make their exposition unadvisable. Some church may be in power with whose pet tenets his revelations of Nature's mysteries may conflict, and thus precipitate upon his head the wrath of the clergy. Yet again, he may be hemmed in by obligations that prevent him from revealing what he has learned, or, as happened to one member of the Brotherhood of Light who was also a high degree Freemason—Brother Henry Melville, in the publication of his valuable masonic work, "Veritas," he may be uncomprehended and misunderstood.

The writer of the present series of lessons has cultivated his soul faculties and speaks from the vantage ground of Initiation. Free from his body he has sent his soul through the wide spaces in search of the precious jewels of wisdom, seldom returning without some treasure; and he has studied the Tablets of Aeth, and read from the records of racial memory preserved in the astral light. In these Masonic lessons, however, he claims no originality. He is merely acting as amanuensis, writing down, and imperfectly, facts that are the common property of the venerable order of which he has the honor at present to be the president on this external panel. Not only so, but it is through the permission of the body, The Brotherhood of Light, that he is able to speak, and by them he is limited within what is considered the bounds of discretion.

This work will not be rejected, as was that of Melville, because the time now is ripe for it. Yet it must not be considered the last word upon the subject, as the time even now restricts and curtails what it is wise to place before the public.

In preparing these lessons, there has been some hesitancy as to the best method to employ to convey the basic truths incorporated in Masonry to the mind of the student, and at the same time not seem presumptuously to be treading upon ground held inviolable by the Masonic Fraternity. It is far from the purpose of the author to reveal any secrets of the Brethren to the outside world, or to attempt any so-called exposé of the methods used in their lodgerooms. Whatever the faults of individual members may be, I have a genuine respect for the Order, and brand as travesties the accusations of their enemies; for if true to their principles, there can be no more exalted souls upon this planet than are to be found among Freemasons.

Let it be understood, therefore, that I am not trying to teach Modern Freemasonry. I am teaching Ancient Masonry, upon which all the rites and usages of Modern Freemasonry rest. My object in no wise includes revealing such matters as Modern Freemasons desire should remain secret. Instead, it is to expound the occult principles and spiritual ideas originally associated with Masonic symbols, usages, and gestures, in such a manner that the public will understand these all-important doctrines; and to enable the Modern Freemason instantly to perceive the esoteric and spiritual significance, not only of his symbols, but of everything he does in the lodgeroom.

With this in view, I have selected a little book that is not so recent in its usages as to enable an unworthy person to gain entrance to a modern working Masonic Lodge and successfully pass himself off as a high-degree Mason; yet which is nonetheless Masonic in character. It is to be found in public libraries and upon the shelves of important book stores. It is entitled *Richardson's Masonic Monitor,* and was used for guidance by members of the Fraternity a generation or two ago, containing as it does a detailed description of the rites of initiation into the different degrees of the Fraternity, and picturing some of the ancient emblems of the Lodge.

As this work is easily accessible to the reading public, I deem it will be considered no breach of propriety to cite as a textbook to those who would sufficiently familiarize themselves with Masonic ritual, and I have taken the liberty to use it as a background for these lessons. This will serve a double purpose: First, it will enable us consistently to follow the symbolism of Modern Freemasonry and draw our comparisons between it and Ancient Masonry in a manner intelligible to students; the Masonic Brethren in particular. Secondly, it will enable me to check my work and keep it within the bounds and reasonable limits of what I consider wise to make public, and what I feel confident the Masonic Brethren will have no reason for desiring me to keep secret.

As I have said, my object is to teach Ancient Masonry, not Modern Freemasonry. And I trust in no case to trespass upon the private property of the Modern Fraternity. If, unwittingly, I do overstep the bounds, I plead as my excuse the desire to give those capable of appreciating and using them, truths of utmost importance to humanity, potent for good, vital to human uplift. And I implicitly rely upon the broad mantle of charity, which the Masonic Brethren are more ready to extend than others, to cover any transgression.

The First Masons

The first problem that naturally confronts us in our present quest is: Who were the original Masons?

Here etymology comes to the rescue. The old Sumerians who lived in the valley of the Euphrates, and who were succeeded by the Semites, the fusion between the two producing the famed Chaldeans, used the word "imga" meaning wise, holy, and learned, to denote their wisest sages, priests and philosophers. The Semites, who succeeded the older race, transformed the work "imga" into "mag" to suit their articulation. From this root-word, "mag" belonging to the Assyrian branch of the great Semitic race, has come to us through various transformations the words: Mason, Magic, and Imagination. Therefore, in whatever era of the dim prehistoric past the first Masons lived, it follows from the very meaning of the word that they were the wisest, holiest, most revered of men.

A mason now is considered to be a builder—one who constructs. Likewise were those Wise Men of the East; but in their work the sound of neither hammer nor saw was heard; for they were mental builders. Their labor was construction wrought by the imagery of thought, as the word imagination, coming from the same root as does the word mason, clearly implies. Magic is the skillful use of the imaginative faculty, and the original Masons undoubtedly were magicians. The Magi of Egypt, Chaldea, and even more ancient times unquestionably were Masons.

The Masonic Temple

Having determined that the original Masons were the Magi, and that they were mental builders, let us inquire into the nature of the edifice upon which these wisest of all men bestowed so much constructive effort. Tradition informs us that the Masonic Brethren labored in the erection of Solomon's Temple. Sol is the Latin name of the Sun-God, Phoebus. Om is the Hindu name of Deity. On is the Sun-God of Heliopolis, Egypt. And while combining these words from different languages undoubtedly is far-fetched, yet nevertheless, as will be shown in detail later, Sol-Om-On certainly represents the Grand Master of the Universe, whose most fitting symbol is the majestic and all-commanding Sun, from Whom comes all Life, Love, Energy, and Power. The Masonic Temple thus is the mansion of the Sun; the universe itself; a spangled canopy of blue, so situated and so arranged as to prove the most suitable lodgeroom for the initiation of the candidate: the Human Soul.

But how? We are led to inquire, could anybody of men, howsoever wise, work to build the jeweled mansion of the Sun, seeing that the very stars shining at their birth sang before the dawn of life upon the earth, and will join in the funeral requiem when the world is cold and gray, wrapped in the icy mantle of death? Certainly no earthly hands ever placed those blazing diamonds in the sky.

In what manner, then, could the early Masons have assisted in the construction of the Temple? Now remembering that Mason and Imagination are derived from the same root-word, a little light begins to dawn upon our perplexity. The early Mason was not a worker in stone, but a mental builder, in whose work Imagination played the most important part.

With the first glimmer of intelligence, man's mind, elevating itself above those of lower forms of life, must have been attracted to celestial phenomena. He watched the blazing orb of day peep over the eastern rim of the world, then soaring upward traverse the azure arch, and later sink, declining into the darkening west. He learned that night followed day, and that day followed night; necessity teaching him to start his labors with the rising Sun, and to seek shelter at the approach of night. Thus became he an observer of time.

Still wider experience brought the conviction that there was an orderly succession of the seasons. The rains of winter were followed by the droughts of summer. Cold followed heat, and heat followed cold. To the huntsman these were periods when game was scarce or plentiful, and he must learn to obtain enough food in the times of abundance to nourish him during those of famine. And how eagerly he looked forward to the return of the more fruitful days, and thus he became an observer of seasons.

As a herdsman, our early forefather watched the shortening and the lengthening of the days; and when the Sun in its annual pilgrimage entered a certain cluster of starts, he knew from experience that the green grass soon would be starting on the mountain side, and he drove his flocks from the valley to those more luxurious pastures. So, also, the farmer learned to till the ground and sow his grain when certain starts rose with the morning sun. The time of harvest was at hand when certain other groups were seen, and winter's bleak scarcity was heralded by the wending southward of the orb of day. Thus, early man became the astronomer, his sustenance depending in great measure upon his ability to interpret, upon climate and the denizens of the earth, the effects of celestial phenomena.

Having seen what powerful influences were exerted by the heavenly bodies upon all things external to himself, it was only natural that those studiously inclined should wish to ascertain their influence upon man himself. As a general rule, it was found that people born in the spring, just after the days and nights became of equal length, were more energetic and had more initiative than people born at some other times of the year. People born with the same group of stars rising upon the horizon were observed to possess characteristics in common. Likewise, the portion of the heavens occupied by the Moon was found to influence the brain capacity. From these observations, covering immense periods of time, whose aim was to ascertain the relation existing between man and the stars, arose the sublime science of Astrology. Astronomy was studied, and observations were carefully and systematically recorded, only as factors in determining the effects of celestial influence upon man. And as a factor necessary in the study of astronomy, there was developed the science of Mathematics.

Astrology Also is a Sacred Science

Astrology was not studied merely as a means whereby man might profit materially, but as a Sacred Science. The material universe, even as man's physical body is his material expression, was considered to be the manifestation of an All-Wise Intelligence. Man manifests his will through acts; so were the heavenly motions thought to be manifestations of the Will of Deity.

As year rolled into year, and century into century, a class of men developed who were peculiarly fitted by natural endowments to pursue the study of the starry heavens and formulate the result of their observations of celestial and mundane phenomena into a scientific system. These were the Magi, the original Masons. Just as at the same time a distinct military class separated itself from the mass of the people by virtue of their superior physical prowess, their love of power, their aggressiveness and disregard of all save might, and became the temporal rulers of the people—the Kings and their immediate associates—so, by virtue of their superior mental and spiritual endowments, the Masons, as a class, separated from the populace and become the sages, philosophers, scientists, the spiritual advisers and priests; dictators in matters religious.

And as persistent culture developed mighty warriors, so the rigid discipline from childhood to which the priests were subjected developed mental and spiritual giants whose keen minds and lucid soul faculties penetrated the innermost recesses of nature. These Masons early perceived a sympathetic relation existing between the organism of man and the fiery points in the firmament above, a definite correspondence between certain sections of Solomon's Temple and the human body. They found that there are certain principles pervading nature that express themselves in the influence of the stars, on the earth, in the sea, in the air, and in the body of man.

Slowly, by degrees, and with infinite patience, these correspondences were sought out between the things representing a given principle on the earth and that portion of the celestial sphere having the same influence. As these correspondences were ascertained it became the duty of the Mason to inscribe them in the sky, that their meaning might not be lost to future generations.

In this work of building the Temple of the Sun, his imagination played an important part. With it he wove fanciful pictures among the stars; for often the actual outlines of the constellations bears no resemblance to the animals or objects they are designed to represent. They do, however, invariably signify an influence in mundane affairs well denoted by the things so pictured. To be more precise, the signs of the zodiac and the decanates of the zodiac, of the same names as the constellations have such influences; for the constellations but picture the various reactions of sections of the zodiac. Thus, gem by gem, that which was found imbedded in the soul of man had its corresponding jewel added to the dome above; the whole being formulated by the early Masons into the famed Science of the Soul and the Stars.

How King Solomon's Temple Was Built.

Astrology was studied not merely for its material profit, but also as a religion. The early Mason cast about for an explanation of the visible universe. In his experience he had found no higher type of active agent than the mind. It was the one thing in his experience that could voluntarily create. The mind of man could build a house in imagination, then cause its construction of wood and stone. Yet what was finite mind? It was an invisible, intangible cause about which he could only think in abstract terms; an unknowable director of human actions.

Having found each visible portion of man, each organ and each physical function, to have a correspondence in the sky, what was more natural than to conclude that there must also be a correspondence to his invisible estate! And as finite mind is the most potent of all agents to create below, it logically follows that Infinite Mind is the most potent creative agent in the whole universe. Carrying this line of reasoning a step further, he was forced to conclude that as man is composed of an invisible mind and a visible body, so God likewise has an invisible and a visible domain; the invisible portion being Infinite Mind and the visible portion being the Material Universe, infinite both in extent and in complexity.

Being convinced that the universe, including man, is the result of creative design, it became the endeavor of the Magi to fathom its purport, or at least so much of it as relates to man, that he might conform his life and efforts harmoniously to that purpose. Man's actions are symbolic of his will and purpose. Thus was it legitimate to conclude that God's Will is revealed in the movements of nature to those who have sufficient penetration to grasp the meaning of their symbology.

Therefore, the early Masons sought out the correspondences in nature, and built their pictured symbols into the sky, as the Temple of Solomon, Grand Architect of the Universe. And this grand edifice, erected by the Ancient Masons; is of most perfect design, revealing as it does to the discerning, the Will of Deity; for what wiser thing could man do than to imitate the building of this ancient structure, and build for his own indwelling soul a mansion as perfect in its proportions, and as harmonious in its arrangements, as the Temple of King Solomon!

In time the Mason, as a priest, became only an interpreter of the ideas symbolically built into the Temple by his wiser forefathers. The word "religion" is derived from the Latin "re" (back), and "ligare" (to bind), and means literally, to bind back. This, then, became the work of later Masons: to collect truths discovered in times past and bind them together in such a manner that they might be preserved for future generations. These truths, in their symbolic form, are found woven more or less into all important religion the world has ever known. The earliest religions were purely astronomical, and it is safe to say that every important religion that ever has been entertained by the mind of man has had an astrological foundation.

Man's body is not the real man, nor is the material universe God. The real man is the invisible controlling ego, and God is the invisible and unknowable Infinite Mind that directs and controls the mighty Cosmos. The Ancient Masons ever sought to find a fitting symbol to represent each principle and function of nature, and to build it into the Temple. What more fitting symbol could be found to represent the Infinite Ego, the true King, than the glorious orb of day!

Sol, therefore, was elected as the symbol of the controlling power of the universe—Deity—it being recognized by those of inner vision that the physical orb was but the external covering for the grander and more ethereal Spiritual Sun Who stands exactly in the same relation to the Solar System as does the human ego to its body. Thus originated Solar Worship, one of the most ancient forms of religion.

To the mind of the Ancient Mason, the physical Sun, the center of our system, from which the earth receives the requisite grade of force necessary for every terrestrial manifestation of power, organic and inorganic, vital and physical; was but the emblem of the Spiritual Sun which exerts that degree of celestial energy, which in matter becomes occult force, and in man becomes Will and Mental Power.

Why Two Pillars Were Erected

The studious mind cannot fail to perceive all nature to be divided into attributes: the one positive, the other negative; the one active, the other receptive. Polarity, or Sex, is the One Great Law of the Universe. This One Law manifests as centrifugal and centripetal forces, as repulsion and attraction as spirit and matter. Life in all its infinitely varied forms is but the interaction between positive and negative forces, there being no life apart from sex. Where sex manifests in greatest perfection, there life most abounds. The fire seen when the flint strikes steel is sexual energy; so is the heat of vegetable life. Passion is the prime mover of the animal kingdom. Man destitute of virility soon succumbs. Man's and woman's possibilities, according to the teachings of the Ancient Masons, when harmoniously united are only limited by their sexual powers, and the ability to control and wisely direct them.

The Ancient Masons, realizing that life depends upon these two attributes, wisely erected two columns in the porch of the Temple; one on either side of the great Eastern Gateway. The pillar on the right is called in Hebrew; Jachin; meaning, "He that Strengthens." And it is the Royal Sun returning from the right, or southern, declination, and rising through the eastern horizon that brings renewed strength after the winter season.

The pillar on the left is called, Boaz; meaning, "Source of Strength." It represents the passive and inert north. It is the left side of the Gateway of the rising Sun, which attracts the Sun northward. Truly, the feminine in nature by its attractive power is the Source of Strength, Boaz; and the ever-active masculine, Jachin, seeking that source of strength becomes the Strengthener.

Tracing backward the history of man's religious beliefs, we find interwoven with solar worship, sex worship, which in its original conception was pure, being the recognition of the mighty power of sex as the most sacred attribute of Deity—Creative Ability.

Serpent worship, another important ancient religion arose from sex worship and solar worship, the serpent being considered sacred to the

Sun, and revered on account of its reproductive significance. Solar religion, Sex worship, and Serpent worship, thus had their foundations directly in Astrology.

The builders of Solomon's Temple, ever seeking to embody their discoveries of natural principles in most appropriate symbology, turned to the sky for some object whose quality was pronouncedly virile, creative, fecundative, and masculine. The Sun thus became the symbol of masculine creative energy, the Father of the Universe. And the Moon, typifying the feminine, fructifying principle, became the nourishing Mother. Further, it will be found today, even as then, in starry science, that the Sun is the source of all power, and the Moon is the Mother of its manifestation.

The Masculine Symbol

Turning to the earth, it was found that the Sun exerts its greatest power when its rays fall vertically. Thus, in choosing some common implement of labor by which to express this masculine creative energy implied by the vertical Sun, the Plumb was selected as the embodiment of that idea. Therefore is the Masonic Plumb the symbol of the masculine principle in nature; the vertical line being used as an abbreviation of the same symbol.

The Feminine Symbol

The plumb and vertical line having been chosen to represent the positive element, it was natural that the level and horizontal line should be chosen as the most suitable emblems of the passive, negative, inert principle.

The Symbol of Union

The earth being considered as the womb of nature; the point where the masculine, electric rays of the Sun are embraced by the feminine, magnetic, rays of the Moon; it was represented by the union of the vertical line and the horizontal line; by a cross.

Astrological Significance of the Square

The angle at which the rays of the Sun, Moon and Planets meet were found to have an influence upon life and mundane affairs. Thus in astrological calculations it is necessary to measure and record these angles. And it is found that two different sets of measurements must be taken.

The first set is measured entirely in the plane of the Ecliptic, regardless of the latitude of the orbs. In this manner, the Celestial Longitudes of the heavenly bodies are found. With the exception of "Parallel of Declination," those most potent influences upon mundane life for good and evil called in astrological terminology "Aspects," are due to the angles formed by the difference in longitude between the orbs. So, as these angles are measured entirely within one plane, the Ancient Masons, seeking to indicate this measurement, selected Euclid's Square.

The square, being an instrument suited to the measurement of plane surfaces, embodies the idea of a vertical line, or positive force, meeting a horizontal line, or negative force at an angle which is measured in a single plane. And in practical astrology this is the first step, for the zodiacal positions of the Sun, Moon and planets are found, and their aspects calculated, as if they all moved in the plane of the Ecliptic. Strange as it may seem to the uninitiated, with but one exception, it is these aspects, disregarding latitude, that are found potent in the affairs of life.

Astrological Significance of the Compass

But as a matter of fact, the Sun, Moon and planets do not move in the same plane, but describe orbits that are inclined to one another. To trace such curved orbits and measure their inclination to each other, another implement is required—the Compass. Owing to the fact that the planes of their orbits are at an inclination to each other, the Sun, Moon and planets at different points in their journeys form different angles to the Celestial Equator. This angle at any given time is called the planet's Declination. Orbs having the same Declination either north or south of the Celestial Equator form an aspect called "Parallel of Declination," and are found to Intensify the influence of each other, and thus exert a very powerful influence in the affairs of life.

The Compass, being an instrument used to draw circles, embodies the idea of a male force meeting a female force at an angle, this angle being measured in different planes. The right hand of man is the executive, so the right leg of the compass was taken to signify the positive force. The left hand of man is receptive, so the left leg of the compass was taken to represent a negative force. Thus when the compass is seen with the right leg superimposed at their juncture, it indicates masculine supremacy; while when the left leg is uppermost, the feminine principle is shown to be dominant.

Each year, the Sun apparently performs a pilgrimage through the 360 degrees of the zodiac, and in longer or shorter periods the Moon and planets make a similar journey. At the same time, owing to the obliquity of the Ecliptic when considering the Sun, and to the angle of inclination of their orbits when considering the planets—the various inclinations of their orbits to one another that I have just mentioned, and particularly their inclination to the plane of the earth's equator—the vertical rays of these orbs form a spiral path upon the surface of the earth. Thus as the earth turns upon its axis each day, one day following another, the Sun apparently moves north in summer and south in winter, its vertical rays falling each day a little north or a little south of their former path. This is the cause of the Seasons.

Where the Ritual Places Emphasis

Early in this lesson I traced the word Mason back to the early inhabitants of the valley of the Tigris and Euphrates, yet the world wide dissemination of the doctrines taught by Ancient Masonry makes it certain that these teachings had their origin in times still more remote. Expressed in forms which convince they were but modifications of an identical original, they were fully developed at the very beginning of the seven ancient centers of civilization—Egypt, India, Crete, Peru, Mexico, China and, as I have indicated, Chaldea.

We may be sure, therefore, that these ideas had their origin in a single region of dispersal. And as there is ample scientific evidence now that both Atlantis and Mu—the former in the Atlantic and the latter in the Pacific—once had an existence, there is little reason to doubt that these ancient continents each was inhabited, as legend holds, by several races, one of which had reached a high degree of scientific knowledge and spiritual attainment. Thus from a still more ancient region which became submerged beneath the waves, was the Secret Doctrine embodied in Ancient Masonry carried by the colonists from that land before it sank, to other shores. And when the old continent of Atlantis, which perhaps in turn had derived much of its insight from the Pacific land of Mu, finally sank, its spiritual ideas already were thriftily growing in each of the mentioned seven centers of civilization where colonists had planted them.

The four chief tenets of these spiritual doctrines were embodied in huge monuments of stone that yet, because succeeding peoples have been powerless to destroy them, are to be found in numbers in many important areas of the globe. More details of the spiritual wisdom were set forth in those symbolical pictographs which we call the constellations, traced by the Ancient Masons in the sky. Still further explanations, also in the language of symbolical pictograph, were traced upon plates, and come down to us through Egypt in the Egyptian tarot cards. Many of the doctrines also found their way as allegorical stories in the various sacred books of the world; and many also, as this series of lessons will make certain, were preserved in the ritual and symbolism of later Masonry.

The explanations traced by the Ancient Masons on the tarot cards and in the constellations among the stars set forth at great length how the signs and planets influence human life and destiny. They give practical instructions in a wide variety of matters, and place emphasis on things different than those given most attention in Masonry.

The Ancient Masonic ritual and its symbols, while acknowledging that the planets in their courses have an influence on human life, and that knowledge is an essential to human progress—two of the chief doctrines preserved in the monuments of stone—more strongly emphasize the other two of the outstanding doctrines preserved in the huge lithic monuments they left. Throughout, the attention is called to assurances that life persists after the dissolution of the physical, and instructions are given in much detail relative to building a spiritual form for happy and successful survival, not merely on the astral plane, but in realms still higher which are truly spiritual.

And throughout there is persistent emphasis on love and the domestic relation as instruments through which the highest, noblest and most spiritual qualities possible to mankind can be developed; qualities which build the spiritual body and insure harmonious and self-conscious immortality.

Astrological Significance of United Square and Compass

Now the word Spiral and the word Spirit are both derived from the Latin word "spira," meaning, to breathe. The spiral, indeed, is the breath of life. From this spiral motion of the orbs, which, as I previously indicated, causes the succession of the seasons and the various results which follow, comes forth all terrestrial life manifestations. The spiral return of the Sun in spring banishes the ice and snow of winter and germinates the dormant seeds of vegetation. Later it warms them with its genial rays into luxuriant foliage, grains and fruits, and these in turn become the support of higher forms of life.

In Ancient Masonry this union of zodiacal motion and declination was symbolized by the union of the compass and the square. And to indicate the germination of physical life generated by this motion an additional symbol was placed in the center between them. A serpent in the form of the letter S was originally used; typifying the generative act. Later, the third Hebrew letter, Gimel, was used with the same significance. This letter is the hieroglyph for the zodiacal sign Libra. Its symbolical meaning is exemplified in the third Arcanum of the Egyptian Tarot. This picture represents a pregnant woman. The Sun is surrounding her head, the Moon is at her feet, and there are twelve stars that represent the twelve zodiacal signs that rule over the processes of gestation. By its form, the symbol of the sign Libra also suggests union resulting in pregnancy. At the present time, the English equivalent of the Hebrew, Gimel, the letter G, is placed in the center of the joined compass and square.

Remembering that the Ancient Masons, building the Temple of Solomon, erected it as a model for the building of the human tenement, and that each truth represented above has its corresponding truth relating to man and his possibilities, we now search for the terrestrial meaning of the joined compass and square.

The square placed below is typical of the purely physical union of the sexes. In astrology, the inharmonious aspects each constitute a portion of the square, or angle of 90 degrees—Semi-Square, Square, Sesqui-Square, and Double Square, or Opposition—and the right angle has been used from time immemorial as the symbol of discord and strife. It becomes a fitting emblem, therefore, of man and woman when united from purely selfish and carnal motives; and it thus represents the result of the ignorance so prevalent in the present-day matrimonial system.

The compass placed above is typical of that higher union of souls in which reciprocal love is the chief factor, and in which thought of gain form no part. The angle formed by the male and female portions of the compass is less than a right angle, and should approximate 60 degrees, the astrological sextile. The benefic astrological aspects each constitute a portion of the sextile—Semi-Sextile, Sextile, and Double Sextile or Trine. The sextile is used to denote harmony and joy. It is a fitting symbol of the union of those rare individuals "whom God hath joined together."

The Letter G, typifies the Generation of offspring as the result of physical union. But in order that these progeny shall be endowed with soundness of body and mind, and thus become a blessing to their parents and the human race, the Ancient Masons taught that there must be a higher union in addition to the physical, as indicated by the compass above; and the Spiritual as well as Physical Laws must be obeyed.

The union of the compass and the square form a diamond, the hardest and most precious of stones. With the G in the center, it is the diamond in the rough. When ground and polished it becomes the priceless jewel of the soul. Only by removing the G does it become a diamond without blemish. The God within then becomes manifest, a condition symbolically represented by the Hebrew letters Jod-He-Vau-He within the compass and square.

"Search then," said the Ancient Masons, "to remove the G, that the diamond may be clear and reflect the light of the Divine Sun in the full glory of the Holy Shekinah." This perfect condition is fittingly symbolized in Ancient Masonry by the Hebrew letter Shin in the compass and square and between the positive and the negative halves of the Divine Word. Shin, corresponding to the Twenty-first Egyptian Tarot, indicates the completion of the Great Work, the full realization of the Holy Shekinah on all three planes of being.

"Yet remember," said the Ancient Masons, "that before the polished jewel there must be the stone in the rough, nor reject it because of the G. Accept it as it is found, but seek ye to learn the laws of workmanship governing its transformation from an unsightly pebble into a shining gem."

Chapter 2

Entered Apprentice and the Planets

THE ANCIENT MASONS, ever striving to solve the mysteries of God and man, seeking to peer beneath the veil of the Virgin Isis, working to wrest from nature the secrets of life and immortality; labored long and diligently in the construction of the royal temple of the sun. The blazing gems of heaven were made the subjects of wearisome observation and study. And as their toil and research was gradually rewarded by establishing definite correspondences between the orbs above and objects below, link after link was added to that majestic chain which binds to men on the one hand terrestrial life entire, and on the other serves to unite with his soul the radiant stars.

Unlike the brilliants of apparently immovable station, it was found that a few of the heavenly bodies rapidly change their relative positions. At a much later date they were named planets, meaning wanderers. These wandering orbs, with the exception of the newly discovered Pluto, all keep within the boundary of a path some 18 degrees in width that encircles the celestial sphere. Furthermore, each has an influence and an individuality of its own. Yet this influence, observation disclosed, is greatly modified by the particular section of the starry highway in which the nomad chances to be found.

Keep penetrative minds, as time moved on, discovered that the pathway of the moving orbs has twelve natural divisions, each division coloring in its own peculiar way, the power of the planet within its bounds. The attributes and qualities of each of these twelve divisions, the Ancient Masons carefully noted, and then set to work to find among terrestrial things such objects as embody the same principles and properties. When these were found, it became the Mason's task to inlay with gems of light, each in its appointed space, the designs of these objects in the firmament above. Thus it is that while the groups of stars in the constellations often bear no resemblance whatever to the animals and other objects pictured among them, yet so enduring was the imaginative construction of a bygone time, that today there is presented to our eyes the same accurate symbolic picture of celestial influences, which whisper in our ears the same divine messages, having the same purport, as in the day when flourished at its zenith, the famed Chaldean lore.

In this manner, the belt through which the planets perform their luminous pilgrimage became the abode of starry-formed denizens, mostly animals. And although, due to the slow precession of the equinoxes, the unequally spaced constellations no longer cover, each in its appointed order, the regularly spaced zodiacal signs, yet as monumental proof of how well the Masons builded, today each pictured celestial object stands in relation to the section of the zodiac it was then used to represent as a perfect symbol of its influence. These twelve zodiacal signs are twelve letters in the divine alphabet. They are the consonants used in the language of the stars.

The vowels, ten in number, are the planets. This may seem strange to those conversant with modern opinion that the ancients, having no optical instruments, could have known only those planets visible to the unaided eye. It must seem they could not have known of Uranus, Neptune and Pluto. Yet at least the attributes of these three wayward planets are presented in their mythology in clear cut and unmistakable terms. The modern astrologer, after painstaking study of Neptune, Uranus and Pluto, writes down their attributes; and these attributes, experimentally demonstrated, are in detail just such as are ascribed to the mythological characters Uranus, Neptune and Pluto. This, I am sure, is more than mere coincidence.

New Planets Usher in New Periods in World Affairs

Perhaps, also, beyond the orbit of Pluto,—which marks the present day frontier, lie other yet to be discovered orbs. When they are discovered, provided they exist, our observation of the affairs of the world coincident with the finding of Uranus, Neptune and Pluto, suggests that each will usher in a new era in the progress of the world.

Uranus, the planet of invention and of independence, was discovered in 1781, and may rightly be said to have ushered in the machine Period, and the Period of republics. It was then that the looms of England rapidly transformed her from an agricultural into an industrial nation. Engines of all kinds came into use, one invention following another. Still later electricity added its power to this Period of manufacture.

In 1782, the Peace of Versailles and Paris granted independent existence to the United States. This set a precedent to be followed by most of the countries of the New World. The Republican form of government came to be a dominant factor in all the Western Hemisphere.

Neptune was discovered in 1846, ushering in the Period of oil and gas; which prepared the way for our present industrial system and our present means of locomotion. Also it brought into the world a new religious conception; that of modern spiritualism. Before the Fox Sisters and their rappings, in 1848, similar phenomena were recognized, but they were called witchcraft and deemed the work of the devil. Modern spiritualism had its birth in 1848, and gave to the world scientific proof that the soul survives the dissolution of the body.

Also in 1848, there were revolutions in France, Germany, Italy and Austria-Hungary. And gold was discovered in California, which opened up a quite new section of the world.

The Period of oil also ushered in a new method of financing business, the method by which many individuals could pool their resources. Instead of individual enterprise, and partnerships, with their limited ability to raise capital, Corporations, composed of share holders, came to be the dominant factor in the business and industrial world.

And then on March 13, 1930, only a few months after the collapse of the stock market in 1929 and the commencement of the greatest financial depression the world has ever known, the discovery of the planet Pluto was officially announced. This then started the Pluto Period.

Kidnapping came to be the most lucrative crime, and large scale racketeering, bred of prohibition days, reached its zenith. The New Deal thrust itself into politics, the sit-down strike pervaded industry, and the whole world became divided into two camps, one dominated by militant and predatory dictators and the other a defensive cooperation of democracies.

As to the influence of the discoveries of these planets on astrological practice; it is true that after the Period ruled by a planet began, environmental conditions made its influence in the lives of individuals far more important than previously. Yet the work of the Church of Light Research Department on the charts of those who lived before the Periods of each of the upper-octave planets began, shows conclusively that, despite astrological ignorance of their existence, these planets were then profoundly affecting people's lives through such conditions as already were at hand.

Astrologers are not omniscient, no more so than are chemists. At the turn of this century chemistry had only atoms and molecules. Then it found within the atom the electron and the proton, and became satisfied it had all the building blocks. But this family of two had expanded by 1938 to embrace no less than six fundamental particles within the atom. Yet the world would have been vastly poorer had it been without chemists in 1900.

Astrology, like chemistry, is a progressive science; and it is as foolish for astrologers now to claim they know all about astrology, as it would be for chemists to insist there is no more to learn about chemistry. Nevertheless, both even in their present state are practical and highly useful sciences.

Ten Constitutes a Chain of Planets

However many planets there may be, the Ancient Masons held that ten completes one chain, and that of these ten only seven are completely active at one time, the other three to the extent seven are energetic, being latent. As one of these active potencies grows dormant, its octave expression takes up the work and becomes more active. Thus when the influence of Uranus becomes more pronounced in human life, its octave expression, Mercury—for both Mercury and Uranus express through intellectual powers—wanes in influence. As man becomes capable of receiving the subtle infiltrations of ideal love from utopian Neptune, he cares that much less for the Venus kind. And as he expands his domestic interests to a protective care for all the members of society under the influence of Pluto, he cares not less for his own home and children, but this Moon influence loses its restrictions and is held in abeyance sufficiently to permit its upper-octave to express.

An alphabet of twelve consonants and ten vowels, however, was not sufficient for the purposes of the sages. Their researches pointed to the fact that the power and trend of any celestial group or orb upon human life depends upon its position relative to other groups or orbs at that time. To express such relations, and to calculate such positions, past, present, and future, the science of mathematics was developed. This made necessary the use of numbers.

Whether these numerals be represented, as in the Chaldean, Hebrew, and Coptic, by giving each letter of the alphabet a numerical value, or by using separate characters as did the Romans and at a still later date the Arabians, the effect is to add to those expressed alone by letters another distinct set of ideas. The twenty-two letters of the ancient alphabet added to the ten characters expressing number gives the complete set of thirty-two primitive ideas—thirty-two kinds of material with which they worked—used by the Ancient Masons.

Origin of Symbols for Planets, Signs and Numerals

After having carefully ascertained the nature and qualities of each of the twenty-two heavenly potencies, having also ascertained its terrestrial correspondence, and having quarried the latter and transported it to become a panel in the vault of Solomon's Temple, there to look down with immortal vision upon countless generations of humanity, the next step was to condense, or abbreviate, the image pictured above, that it could with convenience and celerity be used in writing. In this later work the emblems were not chosen arbitrarily, but with great care that the brief notation should express clearly by its symbolic import both the individuality and the influence of the heavenly orb or zodiacal sign.

Quite naturally, the disc was chosen to represent the sun. Not less easily mistaken, the crescent was selected to signify the moon. And the earth, where solar forces and lunar rays meet and cross, was designated by a cross. Nothing easily mistaken here, even a thousand generations hence! The attributes symbolized by the sun, moon, and earth, are present also, in diverse combinations, in the other planets. So to indicate the latter, the disc, the crescent, and the cross, are combined in manners appropriate to indicate the attributes of each. Such an arrangement could not be misunderstood in its import by anyone in any age who should be familiar with planetary influence.

In designating the signs of the zodiac, the same method was employed. That is, as the disc so well pictures the sun, and a crescent, the moon; each zodiacal sign has a definite picture among the constellations, and it was sought to so abridge this picture that it could quickly and easily be written, and at the same time suggest the picture of which it is the abbreviation.

The numerals were also developed after a somewhat similar manner, but as there are different systems in existence the exact method must be traced in the language of the people employing them. Thus the Roman numerals were evolved from simple marks, or tallies, of the same number as the objects to be counted. Later on X, representing two paths crossing at a harmonious angle, and so signifying man and woman joined in marriage, was taken to signify ten. Man and woman together, like the number ten, it was considered, closed and completed the cycle. The number of mankind as a whole has always been considered in sacred science to be ten. The V of Roman notation was obtained by dividing the X into two equal portions, symbolizing man or woman alone. Man from time immemorial has been designated by the number five.

The Arabic numerals, developed at a much later date, at a time when Arabia was the scientific center of the world, are more abstract in character, and include certain advanced scientific observations relating to cell division which were used rather arbitrarily, which can yet be traced. This will be discussed more in detail in Chapter 4.

The symbols that commonly are employed to designate the planets, the zodiacal signs, and the numerals, are each replete with meanings known only to the initiated. These meanings relate to mundane life and endeavor. But the Ancient Masons did not rest here; they were not content to confine their researches to this world. They also extended their investigations to the spirit zones, to the homes of the dead, and to the activities of the discarnate as well as the incarnate human soul. As a result they found that astrological principles have a meaning in other than earthly realms and that they have a relation both here and hereafter to the development of the powers of the soul. Thus the zodiacal signs, planets, and numerals came to have an esoteric, as well as a common, significance; and this esoteric meaning, instead of being available to all, was conveyed only to those deemed worthy, by means of carefully selected symbols.

Origin of the Thirty-Three Degrees of Masonry

In fact, the policy of the Ancient Masons was to mark every discovery of importance relative to the development of human character and the attainment of immortality with an appropriate symbol. Thus if the

Ancient Masonry

symbol should be perpetuated the discovery would not be lost, even though generations unable to read it passed; for to nature's initiates a symbol is both a diagram and a description of the fact it was selected to represent. Though a universal symbol, such as the Ancient Masons employed, should be lost to sight for a thousand years, the first keen student of Nature's laws to stumble upon it would be able to comprehend its meaning as well as those who used it first. The study of Ancient Masonry, then, becomes a study of such universal symbols.

In addition, therefore, to the common symbols employed for signs, planets, and numbers, the esoteric interpretation of each was engraved on a separate tablet. In Egypt these thirty-two tablets were called, from "Tar," meaning Path, and "Ro," meaning Royal, the Tarot, or Royal Path of Life. Each of these tablets relates to a distinct potency of the human soul, and to one of the essential steps that the neophyte must take to reach the climax of human possibilities and become the exalted adept, heir elect of the angels, who may realize while yet in the flesh his Self-Conscious Immortality.

To denote that all thirty-two steps had been ascended, that all human victories had been won, it was common to add a thirty-third symbol, the seal of the adept, Master of Destinies. The oldest philosophical treatise to be found in the Hebrew language, the Sephir Yetzirah, or Book of Formation, contains thirty-three paragraphs, each descriptive after the code system of the kabala of one of the thirty-three tablets of the tarot. And as a commentary to it, also in kabalistical code, is another ancient Hebrew treatise, the Thirty-Two Paths of Wisdom, containing thirty-two paragraphs which are each an exposition of one of the steps to be taken on the Royal Path of Life.

Then again, although expanded at a later date, the alphabets of the then western nations, Chaldea, Arabia, and Greece, were originally composed of twenty-two characters. Likewise the Hebrew, and the Coptic of Egypt, derived from Chaldean sources, were alphabets having twenty-two characters. And it is believed that these early alphabets of twenty-two letters were derived from the tablets symbolizing the esoteric significance of the heavenly influences, each being a conventionalized abbreviation of the significance of one of the twelve zodiacal signs or one of the ten planets.

I believe enough now has been said to show that there is no chance in the circumstance that there are thirty-three degrees in Ancient Masonry. Each of the first thirty-two degrees is founded upon one of the thirty-two most important principles in nature, the thirty-third degree being a seal showing that earth's mission has been accomplished. Each degree in its ritual, therefore, is also an elaboration of one of the tablets of the tarot. It is one important step in the progress of the soul, a step that to be correctly taken must correspond in its nature to one of the ten numerals, to one of the ten planets, or to one of the twelve zodiacal signs.

Why Symbols Were Used

As Masonry is a study of symbols, let us now get a clearer conception of their nature. A symbol is that which stands for something. Material objects cannot be present in our minds, therefore when we think of them we substitute our impressions concerning them. Such impressions as enable us to distinguish one thing from another become symbols by which we recognize them. Thus if we think of a dog, or of a star, the image of a dog or a star may present itself to our minds. This image is a symbol.

But it is only when we give the dog or star a name that we are able really to think about it; for complex thinking is impossible apart from language. Language is composed of a special class of symbols. These symbols are usually arbitrary, that is, they require special education to recognize them. They are thus in a different group—although there is no hard and fast line of demarcation—from universal symbols. Universal symbols, such as those employed in Ancient Masonry, are those that so conform to man's customary experience with nature that their import may be recognized by any studious mind.

Thus, according to the philologists, when primitive man felt an emotion he accompanied it with a gesture or a sound. Then through repetition of the emotion and its accompanying expression, the sound or gesture came to be associated in the mind as representing a distinct emotion. A cry became the symbol of pain, laughter the symbol of mirth; and because of the wide application of these symbols—everywhere in our experience finding laughter representing mirth and a cry representing suffering—we may consider these typical universal symbols. But the terms commonly used in the arts and sciences, having been coined merely as conveniences, and adopted through usage, are much more arbitrary.

As ideas can only be communicated from one mind to another by means of symbols, these are employed to an extent even by creatures lower in life's scale than man. Thus in the animal kingdom, a mother may not see danger to her young, but if she hears it cry she recognizes the symbol as one of distress, and rushes to its rescue. Birds, such as the raven and the jay, post sentinels, and when a lookout sees an intruder approaching a warning call is recognized by the whole flock, and conduces to their safety. So also the barnyard aristocrat, proud chanticleer, announces the approach of day with a warning call; or on other occasions imparts the information to his admiring harem, by affectionate clucks, that he has found a choice morsel; nor is one of these symbols apt to be mistaken for the other. In the human species a smile certainly is a symbol of amity and a frown a symbol of displeasure. And while there are places where people do not kiss, I am inclined to believe that the ebony maiden of darkest Africa would recognize the kiss as a symbol of love quite as readily as would the latest debutante whose polished manners grace the most exclusive circles of effete society.

As thought is impossible without the use of symbols, it will be seen that the study of symbolism is the study of the counters of thought. The study of Masonic Symbolism, then, becomes the study of the thoughts and ideas of the ancient Master Minds as expressed by them in the language of universal symbolism. Well knowing the transitory nature of arbitrary language, the words of one generation often having an opposite meaning in the next, these sages spoke and wrote in a language the words of which never change their import, thus preserving their thoughts in their original purity for all time. They discerned truly that so long as human minds abide upon this terrestrial globe there will be some, from time to time, who will discard arbitrary methods of interpretation and turn to nature for the clew. These, and these only, are able to read the message of the Ancient Masons as it was first taught in the secret schools of long, long ago.

The Entered Apprentice Lodge

In reading this message, then, let us commence at the beginning, at the Entered Apprentice degree. An apprentice is one whose services are rendered that he may gain knowledge through experience. As the object of all ancient mysteries was to impart information about the origin, proper culture, and final destiny of the human soul, it will be seen that an

Entered Apprentice is a candidate for soul knowledge. He typifies any man or woman who resolutely sets his foot upon the path leading to the spiritual height of complete initiation.

Now in opening a lodge of Entered Apprentices there must be present one Past Master and at least six apprentices. What, then, does this mean?

The room in which these seven assemble is said to represent a ground plan of King Solomon's Temple. King Sol, as we have noticed, is the sun, and his temple is in the arching sky. The ground plan, of course, refers to the earth, with the walls of heaven coming down on all sides to meet it at the horizon. And those who gather here, the various apprentices on the lodge of life, occupy physical bodies and are subject to material laws.

In the Grand Lodge above, the sun, as Past Master, together with the six lower-octave planets, form the seven types of celestial power, all of which must be present that life on earth may find complete expression; for each exerts an influence peculiar to itself and necessary for the fullness of life's expression. Sunlight is not complete unless it contains the seven rays of the solar spectrum, nor is the musical gamut as it should be unless there are seven tones within the octave. Thus also, a little study of astrology will demonstrate, there are seven lower-octave planets the influences from which are felt by every living being. Together they tend to mould the course of each human life, and so, after a manner, constitute the initiators of all.

In the heavens, then, the seven Masons required to open an Entered Apprentice lodge are the seven lower-octave planets. And according to the laws by which the Ancient Masons worked—which are also the famed laws of the Medes and Persians—that which is above has an exact correspondence to that which is below, and Solomon's Temple was actually constructed to serve as a model after the design of which each apprentice should strive to erect his own physical tenement. Consequently, as there are seven chief planets in the heavens above, there must be, and are, exact correspondences to these in man's domain. These embrace man's seven-fold constitution.

We have before us, then, the problem, though not a difficult one, of ascertaining the office in the lodgeroom corresponding to each of man's seven chief components. Such a problem is most easily approached by first studying the correspondence between the sections of man's constitution and celestial influences, and the correspondences between the officers of the lodge and celestial influences; and then, from this knowledge, arriving at the correspondences and their meaning between the officers and the sections of man's domain. This method of approach may best be started by gaining some knowledge of the influences of the various planets.

The sun is symbolized by its disc, in which appears, like a nucleus, a dot. It is the source of all life, even as the simple cell in which appears a nucleus is the source, or parent, of all organic life. This solar disc containing a nucleus typifies the vital, creative, positive, controlling attributes in nature. The vibrations of the sun are electric, and they rule the vital force in man. It may be considered the father of all within the solar system.

The moon is symbolized by its familiar crescent. It is the power that fructifies, nourishes, and rules the magnetic life currents. It represents the moulding, formative attributes of the astral world. The moon gives form to all life, her vibrations are magnetic, and she may be considered as the mother of all manifestation within the solar system.

The earth is symbolized by a cross. It is the place where active forces meet and cross one another. Negative and mediumistic, it has no power of its own, being but the matrix in which other forces develop. Electric and magnetic forces often meet here at cross purposes; therefore, in a sense, it signifies by its abrupt angles, discord, as well as stagnation and inertia.

In natal astrology we find that the sun actually rules the individuality, the moon the mentality, and the ascendant the personality. That is, in actual astrological practice the sun is considered as ruling the ego, or spirit, the moon as ruling the mind, or soul, and the ascendant, or cross, as ruling the body. Thus the disc becomes symbol of the spirit, the crescent the symbol of the soul, and the cross the symbol of the body. And the symbols of all the other planets are formed from these three, joined in such combinations as accurately to portray the observed influence of these planets in the manner in which they express physical, mental, and spiritual qualities.

Origin of Saturn's Symbol

Saturn is symbolized by the crescent of the soul surmounted by the cross of matter. This signifies that the emotions, aspirations, and ideals, are made subservient to material and self centered ambitions. Temporal power is the motive, and all the feelings are repressed that action may result solely from deliberate consideration after due time for meditation. In natal astrology we find that individuals dominated by Saturn are careful, deliberate, subtle, cautious, prudent, and practical. Their chief characteristic is the persistence with which they labor for their own selfish interests. The cross above, typifying forces in antagonism, expresses the thought that all things are subject to change, that all terrestrial life ends in death, and that the tomb is the leveler of all earthly rank and distinction. Thus the cross above the crescent became the scythe held in the hands of Old Father Time. This is but one of the ancient conceptions relating to the planet Saturn as the orb of old age and dissolution.

Saturn is the planet expressing that one of the seven principles of nature the qualities of which are coldness, contraction, and concreteness. He corresponds to the Blue ray of the solar spectrum and has rule over the bones, teeth, and spleen in the human body. This should give us the clue to his correspondence both in the lodgeroom and in the human constitution. The physical body is the most gross and concrete section of man's constitution. The treasurer in the lodge well typifies the acquisitiveness of Saturn, as does his place in the lodge, which is north of the Master, in a region, therefore, of coldness, misery, and death. As the treasurer and the physical body (although no one planet can be said to rule the physical body of man) both correspond to the planet Saturn, we are justified in concluding that the treasurer, in the initiation of the soul, represents man's material form.

Origin of Jupiter's Symbol

Jupiter is symbolized by the cross of matter surmounted by the crescent of soul. This is just the reverse of the Saturnine emblem, so we need not be surprised that in practical astrology Jupiter expresses qualities the antithesis of those expressed by Saturn. Feeling preponderates, and gives rise to genial warmth, noble aspirations, generosity, expansion, and good will toward all. Those dominated by Jupiter often became philanthropists, or take an active part in work having for its object social welfare and moral uplift. Lovers of fair play and benevolence, it is their constant delight to make others happy. The magnanimity of the Greek Jove and the Scandinavian Thor, and the Jupiter quality of giving, are well expressed as arising from soul emotion by the dominant crescent.

Jupiter is the planet expressing that one of the seven principles of nature the qualities of which are warmth, expansion, and geniality. He corresponds to the Purple ray of the solar spectrum and has rule over the liver and the arterial system of the body. This should give us the clue to his correspondences. Warmth and geniality as felt by others are largely due to the radiations of personal magnetism, and these as well as the strength of the will upon the physical plane, depend upon the strength of the etheric body, or aura. This etheric form of man vitalizes the physical body, and during life is inseparable from it. By it impressions from the outside world are registered on the consciousness. Jupiter corresponds well (although astrologically the planet Uranus has specific rulership over it) to this etheric body, and also to the secretary of the apprentice lodge, who sits at the south of the Master, in a region of warmth and radiation. Consequently, in the initiation of the soul, the secretary represents the etheric form of man.

Origin of Venus' Symbol

Venus is symbolized by the circle of spirit surmounting the cross of matter. It indicates inspiration which expresses itself as blind love and art. Grace, exquisiteness, and beauty in all its forms are typified; but the soul being absent, impulse preponderates, and there is submission to more positive natures. Lovers of society, innocent and refined, the natives of Venus are mirthful, pleasure seeking, and convivial; but because reason is absent, they posses little moral power. Aphrodite, springing from the ocean foam, expresses her lightness and grace.

Venus is the planet expressing that one of the seven principles of nature the qualities of which are lightness, joy, mirthfulness, and clinging affection. She corresponds to the Yellow ray of the solar spectrum, and has rule over the internal sex functions and the venus system of the body. The readiness with which she yields to impulse and desire without thought of consequences or moral reflection, acting upon the strongest momentary whim, establishes her correspondence with (although astrologically it is specifically ruled by Neptune) the astral body of man. This astral form is easily separated from the physical body, is molded in its shape and texture by the desires, and blindly obeying the will of the intelligence controlling it, is peculiarly susceptible to suggestion.

Now if correspondences are strictly observed, the point of sunrise being positive, those Masons sitting in the east always represent masculine potencies. As the place of sunset is negative, those Masons sitting in the west must represent feminine potencies. Furthermore, as the south is the region from which the sun comes to overcome the evil powers of winter in the spring of the year, and as the blighting cold comes from the north as the sun moves southward in autumn, those Masons sitting in the south represent benefic influences, and those sitting in the north represent malefic influences.

Venus is both a benefic and a feminine potency; therefore she represents a position in the lodgeroom both south and west. A diagram of the lodgeroom of Entered Apprentices shows that the Senior Warden sits in the West, and the Junior Deacon sits south of him. The Junior Deacon, then, who sits both south and west represents Venus, and because Venus corresponds to the astral body, the Junior Deacon also corresponds to man's astral form.

Origin of Mars' Symbol

Mars is symbolized by the circle of spirit surmounted by the cross of matter. He is just the reverse of Venus, and expresses matter overpowering spirit as a force for destruction. Instead of love we find passion, instead of grace we find strength, instead of art we find war. There is nothing submissive about Mars. He will dominate or die.

Strife is his joy, and conquest his religion. His desires are insatiable, and he knows no right but might. Those dominated by Mars are selfish, aggressive, cruel, and will brook no interference from anyone. Their selfishness, however, is very different from that of Saturn; for they are lavish of their substance, it being used chiefly as a means to gratify their passions and appetites. Vulcan is the planet Mars in its most constructive aspect.

Mars is the planet expressing that one of the seven principles of nature the qualities of which are combativeness, aggression, fiery impulse, and passion. He corresponds to the Red ray of the solar spectrum and has rule over the muscles, sinews, and external sexual organs of the human body. His inflammable passions, cruel selfishness, and coarse appetites (although no one planet can be said astrologically to rule it), establish his correspondence with man's animal soul. This animal soul is very necessary to man so long as he must struggle for survival on the physical plane, but while it makes a good slave it makes also a tyrannical master. It is the demon within that each must conquer through a transmutation of its energies. As Mars is positive and malefic, his position is represented in the lodgeroom by the east and north. In the Apprentice lodgeroom it is the Senior Deacon who sits in the eastern portion of the room and to the north of the Master. That he is not so far north as the Treasurer indicates the recognition that in astrology Mars has less power for evil than Saturn. The Senior Deacon corresponds to Mars, and likewise represents the animal soul of man.

Origin of Mercury's Symbol

Mercury is symbolized by the crescent of soul, surmounting the circle of spirit, and this surmounting the cross of matter. This indicates that soul and spirit have triumphed over sensation. It conveys the thought that wisdom has been garnered in both physical and superphysical realms, and that this has resulted in an equilibrium between the practical and the ideal, that the aspirations have been realized through the union of inspiration and concrete experience. The natives of Mercury live and move largely on the mental plane. They are studious, seekers of knowledge, finding delight in science, conversation, and literature. Mercury is the messenger of the gods.

Mercury is the planet expressing that one of the seven principles of nature the qualities of which are restless activity, intellectuality, volatileness, and changeableness. He corresponds to the Violet ray of the solar spectrum, and has rule over the tongue, brain, and nervous system of the human body. The brain and nervous system are the most refined of man's physical structures, and the spiritual body is the most refined of all his possessions. Likewise, similar to the intelligence which Mercury rules, it is but little developed in the majority. Its delicate structure is only built up by man's intense unselfish emotions, his love for others, and his soul's longing for, and effort to gain, esoteric wisdom. The spiritual body corresponds (although astrologically it is specifically ruled by Pluto) to Mercury. Mercury is convertible in sex, also in its nature through its associations, although easily made benefic. To represent the convertibility of sex the Junior Warden sits in the lodgeroom midway between east and west, and to denote that Mercury should be benefic he sits in the south. The Junior Warden corresponds to Mercury, and also to the spiritual body of man's domain.

Origin of the Moon's Symbol

The Moon is symbolized by the crescent of soul. This signifies the dominance of the plastic, emotional, and enfolding qualities. She is the mother who clothes the ideals of her more positive lord. She is the mould of all that was, that is, or that ever will be, expressing the formative powers of the astral world. Those dominated by the Moon are mediumistic and greatly influenced by their surroundings. They are changeable, submissive, and inoffensive. Luna is the goddess Isis.

The Moon is the planet expressing that one of the seven principles of nature the qualities of which are purely magnetic and formative. She corresponds to the Green ray of the Solar spectrum, and has rule over the breasts, stomach, and fluidic system of the body. The Moon is feminine in nature, tending to be kind and gentle. She thus corresponds (although no one planet can be said specifically to rule) to the divine soul of man's multiple constitution. The divine soul is the good genius, from which spring noble impulses and unselfish aspirations. It is the inner voice of the conscience, the guardian angel whose admonitions when heard and heeded will not fail to direct the steps aright. A potency so feminine is rightly symbolized in the Apprentice lodgeroom by the west, where sits the Senior Warden facing the Master. The Senior Warden, therefore, represents the divine soul of man.

Origin of the Sun's Symbol

The Sun is symbolized by the disc of spirit within which is a dot, or nucleus. Even as all physical life has its origin in a single cell, so the circle within which is a dot indicates limitless powers and possibilities. Power, dominion, vitality, strength, and radiant energy are represented. The Sun is the father of all life, the source of all energy, the controlling potency of our solar system. Those dominated by his influence are proud, majestic, combative, discreet, magnanimous, self-confident, kind, and benign. The Sun is the Egyptian Osiris.

The Sun is the planet expressing that one of the seven principles of nature the qualities of which are power and royal dignity. He corresponds to the Orange ray of the solar spectrum, and has rule over the heart of man. His central controlling station establishes his correspondence with the ego (which astrologically he also rules) of man's septenary constitution. That is, the ego in man's universe is the eternal controlling spirit power. The controlling power in the Apprentice lodgeroom is the Worshipful Master, who sits in the positive region of the rising Sun and rules the lodge. Therefore, the Worshipful Master corresponds to the ego in man's hermetic constitution.

Why Seven Must Be Present to Open an Apprentice Lodgeroom

It should now be plain why a lodge of Apprentices can only be opened when one Past Master and six Apprentices are present. The lodgeroom being a ground plan of Solomon's Temple indicates the material plane where all receive their first human initiation—where they encounter the tests and trials of everyday life. And as man is a seven-fold creature, being incomplete and incompetent when any of the seven are absent, so the lodgeroom, typifying man on the physical plane also is incomplete and incompetent unless the seven officers are all present.

To be capable of successful endeavor it is quite as necessary that man shall be possessed of his seven constituent factors as it is that to function successfully on the physical plane his chief physical organs—heart, brain, stomach, lungs, etc.—shall be present. Such is the information the Ancient Masons sought to convey by their tradition that the Apprentice lodgeroom may be opened only by a Past Master—for the ego is the oldest member of man's constitution—and six Apprentices.

Though they have no part to play in the work of the Apprentice Lodge, there are three other planets as follows:

Origin of Uranus' Symbol

Uranus is symbolized by two crescents joined by the cross of matter surmounting the circle of spirit. This indicates two souls in union dominating the sensations of the flesh. Spirit is beneath, however, showing that the union is of body and mind, and not of spirit. The union is not that of soul mates, therefore they are not able to reach the highest spiritual states. Nevertheless, there is penetration, intuition, and occult insight. Those dominated by Uranus are independent, inventive, and lovers of occult science. The form of the symbol conveys the idea of a union not made in heaven, and Uranus in his influence over life is notorious for estrangement. Uranian people seek the true counterpart, yet when their keen intuitions impress them of a mistaken choice, they break the bond asunder. Uranus rules the etheric body of man.

Origin of Neptune's Symbol

Neptune is symbolized by two crescents joined by the cross of matter which is surmounted by the circle of spirit. This indicates soul-mates occupying one blended astral form and controlled by one ego which is common to both. Neptune, the octave of Venus, typifies the realization of the highest love, which alone gives united souls the power to soar into the highest celestial realms. Those dominated by Neptune are idealistic, psychic, and given to mystical investigation. They seek fair utopia, and when inspired by love are capable of rising to the pinnacle of human genius and attainment. Neptune rules the astral body of man.

Origin of Pluto's Symbol

Not only the 1939 NAUTICAL ALMANAC, from which the ephemerides makers obtain their astrological data, but other scientific works have adopted the symbol for Pluto THE CHURCH OF LIGHT has been using. Van Nostrand's Scientific Encyclopedia, copyright 1938, has this to say: "The name Pluto was selected for the new planet and the first two letters of the name, combined in monogram form are used as the symbol of the planet."

The influence of the planet is either the highest or the lowest of any, and tends to divide the qualities of the animal soul from those of the divine soul; groups each striving for supremacy. The symbol represents the cross of earth below, which is significant of the materialistic trend of the planet's lower influence. Above is the lunar crescent of soul.

But it is not such a crescent as is used in forming the symbols of Mercury, Jupiter, Saturn, Uranus and Neptune. These crescents, like that of the Moon, are open. Yet while this upper part of the symbol of Pluto is clearly a crescent, its union with the cross of matter is such as completely to close one side, and make it also resemble an imperfect circle. Or to state it another way: the upper significance of the symbol is to portray the transition, or change, of the soul to a higher form of expression, which is more nearly that of the circle of spirit. Pluto rules the spiritual body of man.

The Charter Under Which a Lodge Must Act

Now we are informed that a lodge of Entered Apprentices can act only under a charter, or warrant, from the Grand Lodge. Man, therefore, as a copy of the Apprentice Lodge with its seven members, also must act under a warrant, or charter, from the Grand Lodge of the solar system. This warrant, or chart of birth, is a map of the soul's need for expression, and outlines unerringly the course it should follow. This chart(er) indicates just the work the candidate must perform to make progress and receive initiation within the lodge of life.

It is only when man becomes familiar with the chart and conforms his life and efforts to its mandates that he is able to escape the disapproval, and the consequent pain and suffering, from the Grand Stellar Lodge. It is only when he conforms his life to the music of the spheres as sounded at his birth, and either avoids the discords then sounded, or transmutes them into harmonies, that he lives to his best and reaches the highest degree of soul initiation.

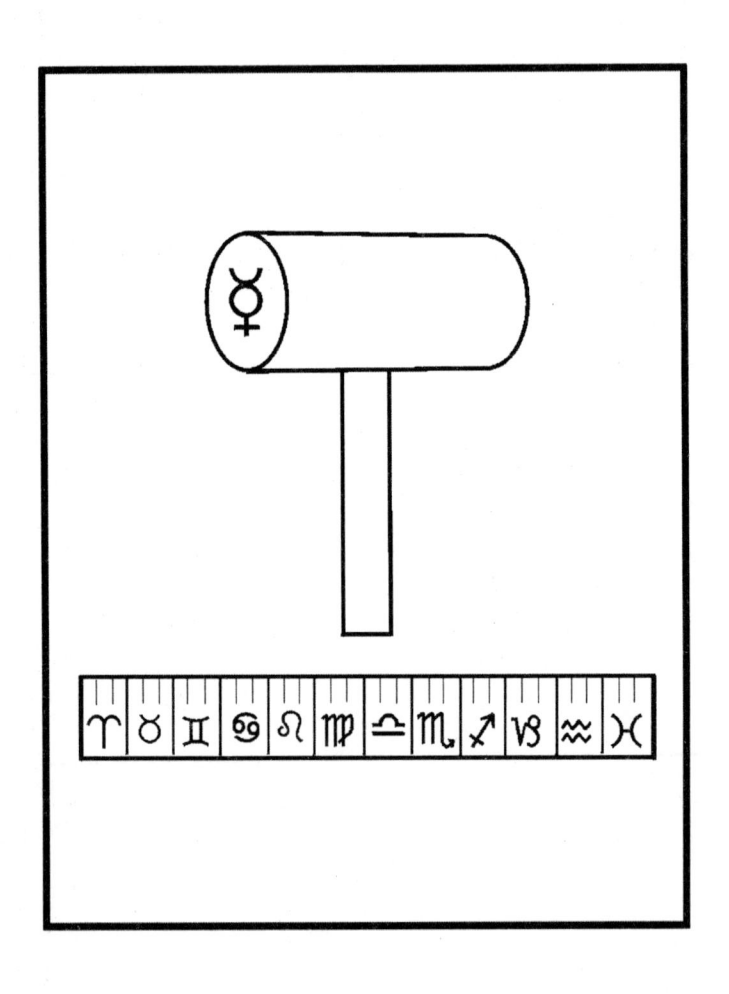

Chapter 3

Entered Apprentice and the Signs

AS THE Entered Apprentice lodge represents a ground plan of the temple of the sun, it must relate chiefly to physical functions and the physical plane of life. One of the objects early brought to the attention of the candidate, not merely in the Entered Apprentice degree, but also in those higher, is the common gavel. What, then, did the common gavel signify to the Original Masons?

Tradition informs us that the ancients summed up the whole of existence, past, present, and future, in one word. This ineffable name, in the Bible translated as Jehovah, was expressed in Hebrew by the four letters, Jod-He-Vau-He. Elsewhere a sphinx of four-fold form was used to express the same idea. Rendered into English it signifies that there is but One Principle, but One Law, but One agent, and but One Word. The One Principle is symbolized by the form of the common gavel.

This common gavel, which is the first implement used in a Masonic lodge, derived its form astrologically by removing one of the four bars that divide the universe into four quadrants by the cross formed from the intersection of the equinoctial colure with the solstitial colure. The removal of one arm of the cross leaves the ancient Tau Cross, which has been used universally as the sign of the linga, which is reverenced today by hundreds of millions in India alone with no thought of shame; for it is the symbol of masculine virility.

The gavel, inherited from a past that placed no shame on man's body and its holy natural functions, due to its form, is the symbol of the Universal Creative Principle; the supreme attribute of Deity. Its form, it is true, is phallic; but merely because the ancient sages used the physical object the import of which is most easily recognized to represent universal principles. This gavel is the sledge with which Vulcan shaped the instruments of war. It is likewise the mighty hammer with which Thor forged his powerful thunderbolts. To be more explicit, every force and movement in the universe contains the expression of this One Principle.

That such is the case might be illustrated by analyzing any movement or energy with which we are familiar. A few examples will probably suffice for our purpose. But to understand the One Universal Principle, symbolized by the form of the common gavel, we must recognize the One Universal Law. This great cosmic law, that governs every conceivable action, is the Law of Sex.

As I look about me in search of examples, the first thing I observe is the fire in the grate that warms my room. Now chemistry teaches me that relative to each other atoms are sexed. These atoms that exhibit the widest difference in polarity, are more strongly sexed; experience the strongest attraction toward each other. Where opportunity is favorable the result of this attraction is the marriage between atoms. If the difference in sex is small, but little attraction is manifested, and the result of this chemical marriage, as the old alchemists would call it, is a feeble offspring. But if the difference in sex is great, as in the case between the oxygen in the atmosphere and the carbon fuel in my grate, the attraction is violent, and the product of the union is energetic. The heat and light radiated by the fire in front of me, according to the alchemist's view, is but the energy radiated by the intensity of the sexual combination of atoms of carbon with atoms of oxygen.

If next I contemplate my own actions, I discern them also to be the result of Chemical Marriages. Muscular movement is due to the combustion of fuel within the body of an animal. Furthermore, actions not chemical are quite as much due to the law of sex. The earth is held in its orbit about the sun, which I see through my window, by the equilibrium of masculine centrifugal force and feminine centripetal force. And every mechanical force may in like manner be shown to result from the union, or tendency toward union, of a positive and a negative factor.

Etheric energies, of which electricity is the best recognized example, are so commonly regarded as the interaction of positive and negative forces that extensive comment would be superfluous. Everyone is aware that it is the attraction of the feminine polarity for the masculine polarity that causes the electric current to speed along the wires, perhaps performing much work on the way. And mental action also, as a perusal of Course 5, *Esoteric Psychology* reveals, is quite as much due to the attraction and union of factors of different polarity within the mind. All mechanical force, all chemical activity, all etheric energy, and all mental effort; in fact, all action in the universe, is due to sex.

Now the modern reader is all too apt to narrow the meaning of the word sex, and limit it to the more obvious examples. But it was the object of the Ancient Masons to discover the comparatively few principles that pervade all nature, yet manifest in diverse forms. Sex, to them, then, was a principle that pertains to inanimate objects, as well as to those animate. It divides the universe into two qualities, one positive and controlling, and the other negative and receptive. The positive, controlling, creative half of the universe is symbolized by the form of the common gavel.

Of course, nothing is created in the sense that something is made from nothing. Substance of some kind, energy of some form, and intelligence in some degree, have always existed (see Course 3, *Spiritual Alchemy*). The exercise of the creative attribute on the part of man, then, is the utilization of energies already in existence. It is the turning of them into different channels of expression.

Not only is energy universal, but the ancient Masters taught that intelligence is universal also. When Camille Flammarion, after a half century of psychic research, says that intelligence is always present wherever there is an organism through which it can express, he states the same general idea. Anyone, I believe, who has much experience with psychic phenomena in its various phases will concur in this, that if the means be at hand through which intelligence may readily express, there is always an intelligent force present to take advantage of the opportunity. That is, intelligence, like substance and energy, is a universal attribute.

The Source of Will Power

The one universal principle, or energy, when directed by intelligence, becomes Will. Man's only source of will power lies in his ability to receive energy and then persistently direct it into channels of his own choosing. Lower species of animals also transmit universal energies. But they have a texture and organization that permits only the less complex vibrations to express through them; while man, whose substance is more refined and highly organized, receives, utilizes and again projects in manners of his own selection, finer and more potent rates of energy.

Man thus is capable of transmitting the one universal principle in a manner of which lower animals are incapable. Man also uses a gavel in his work of building. He uses it with force and directs it intelligently to the accomplishment of a predetermined purpose. The gavel, then, while by its form typical of virility and creative energy, has come to have an added significance. It signifies that energy is directed by intelligence. And as energy directed by intelligence persistently to a predetermined end is will, the gavel has come to be recognized by its use as the symbol of the human will.

If we are in doubt as to the relation between the significance of the form of the gavel as indicating sexual virility, and the significance of its use as indicating will, a little observation will reveal the association. Those animals, for instance, that in the full vigor of their sexual life are energetic, alert, and combative, when altered by man become dull, listless, lazy, and cowardly. The bull is the lord and protector of his herd, while the steer is a lazy coward. The stallion is high spirited and independent, while the gelding is meek and submissive. The cock energetically scratches to provide food for this flock, while the capon cares for nothing but ease. And if we look to the most attractive and the most successful among our human acquaintances, we find they are without exception markedly feminine women and strongly masculine men.

The gavel being the first implement of Masonry indicates that the Ancient Masons believed the first thing the candidate should do is to cultivate his will power. In fact, the continued use of the gavel even in the higher lodges indicates their opinion that the culture and use of the will is necessary on all planes of existence. How, then, may the will be cultivated?

We often hear the remark that a certain person could do a specific thing if he but willed to do so. This no doubt is sometimes true, but as it is often the case that the person is notoriously weak and wavering in will, how can he exercise that which he does not possess? It is as great a fallacy to think that all men can use their wills successfully, as it is to think that all men can, without previous practice or experience, play a good game of golf. To play a decent game of golf requires long and arduous practice; and to use the will successfully requires at least as persistent training.

This brings us back to the one universal principle symbolized by the form of the gavel. Energy is universal. It is present in the sunshine we feel, in the food we eat, in the air we breathe, and as still finer currents that radiated from the stars flow through our astral bodies. That we may be energetic, physically, mentally, or spiritually, requires that we tap some existing source of energy and adapt it to our needs. The energy used in spiritual activity, quite as much as that used in physical effort, requires that we first receive energy from some outside source. One cannot exercise a spiritual force unless one has at hand a supply of energy of such refinement as to be spiritual.

Electrical Source of Energy to be Used by the Will

The first thing, then, in the exercise of will power is to have at hand an adequate supply of energy. The kind of energy consumed in the exercise of will on the physical plane is etheric (electric) energy. It is the kind of energy that constitutes the nerve currents, the kind that is recognized as personal magnetism. The source of this electric energy—and how the physical cells, acting as miniature batteries—generate it, is explained in full detail in Course 5, *Esoteric Psychology,* Chapter 9. It is present, associated with the human body in normal quantities in all healthy persons. Well sexed persons have an abundant supply of it, but under sexed persons are deficient in it; for the former are recognized to be magnetic, while the latter are always deficient in personal magnetism, that is, in etheric energy. A normal healthy sexual nature, as the gavel suggests, seems to be requisite for a normal supply of etheric energy.

The amount of this energy may be greatly increased, and the amount thus available for the use of the will greatly augmented, by tension exercises and by rhythmic breathing. Rhythmic breathing, while the mind is firmly fixed on indrawing and utilizing the imponderable forces from the atmosphere, is the method most commonly employed to supply the requisite amount of etheric energy for unusual efforts of the will. It was the method employed by the Ancient Masons, and has for centuries been thus employed by the Hindu Yogis. The latter term the invisible electromagnetic energy so obtained, prana. Instead of being subtracted from the atmosphere, in reality it is chiefly generated in the nervous system. But from whatever source it is obtained, or whatever the method employed to secure it, man can only exercise will power on the physical plane when supplied with it, on the same principle that a motor will only run when supplied with electricity.

There is still another important consideration in connection with this etheric energy. It has a wide range of vibratory rates. Some are of high frequency and very fine and powerful, and some are of low frequency, coarse and of less power. And like other energies, the higher the frequency, that is, the finer they are, the more powerful they become. This seems to be a general law, that the higher an energy is in rate of vibration, the more powerful it is, providing its energy is properly utilized.

This brings us to another observation of the old Magi. They held that in strict ratio and proportion to the refinement of substance is it vitalized by spirit. That is, the more refined an organism, the higher the frequency of vibrations it will transmit. And as the higher rates of energy are more powerful, the more refined the organism, the more capable it becomes to exercise a powerful influence on other organisms and things. In other words, other things being equal, the higher refined organism is capable of exercising a stronger will power than one more gross.

Intelligence, like energy, being a universal attribute, we perceive why it is that often persons of small cranial capacity have more intelligence than those of larger capacity. Their whole physical make-up is finer, and more complex in texture; hence they are capable of receiving and transmitting finer forces than those less refined. Fine rates of energy, true spiritual powers, can find no point of contact in a gross body. Therefore, for spiritual power, and also for will power, there should be a progressive refinement of the body.

The Proper Culture of the Will

The mere transmission of energy, even if refined, however, does not constitute will power. Will power, as indicated by the use of the gavel, is energy directed persistently to some purpose.

How then can we develop will power? How can we develop the first implement of a Mason? Only by practice. There is no other way. One learns to play golf or tennis by keeping doggedly at it, and one develops will power in the same way. In the first place, to avoid discouragement, one should never attempt doing something until careful reflection has shown that it is both possible and advisable. But once having come to a decision to do something, it should be carried through to complete accomplishment in spite of all obstacles. This system should be tried at first on the inconsequential things, as one in golf first tries the easier strokes. Little by little, the plan should be enlarged to embrace larger undertakings, until finally the exercise of a powerful will becomes a permanent habit in the life.

Such a development of the will is, therefore, according to the ancient sages, the first implement of a Mason. Any person will find such an implement most useful. But to one who intends to practice magic it is quite indispensable. All the asceticism, self-torture, harsh discipline, and self-mortification of the oriental fakirs and certain of the yogis has for its sole object the building up of an inflexible will. Once a thing is decided upon it is always carried through in spite of obstacles, pain, or sorrow. Yet a useful and normal life affords quite as much opportunity for rigid will development.

The habit and mood of inflexible will in time becomes so impressed upon the astral organization, or unconscious mind, that all energies are focused to the accomplishment of the desired result. Therefore, in the practice of magic, when a thought is formulated and projected by such a person, all the etheric energy available is concentrated in the projection of the thought, and the astral form of the person continues, even after the matter is no longer present in objective consciousness, to utilize every effort to bring the formulated event to pass.

Nothing worth while, either in magic or in more prosaic endeavor, can be accomplished without the development of a strong will. In this development, as we have seen, there are three factors. There must be an energy supply. Such energy is available to the naturally virile person who practices dynamic breathing for the purpose of generating etheric energy. This energy supply must be of high frequency. That it may be so the body is refined through careful diet, through high aspirations, and through the cultivation of pure and lofty emotions.

This energy must be directed with an inflexible purpose. Such inflexibility may be gained through practice with the normal affairs of life. To use the methods of oriental ascetics is to develop the will at the expense of the divine soul. The divine soul is built up by the nobler impulses and finer emotions. To crush all feeling from the life is to starve and perhaps destroy the immortal part of one's nature. Cold intellect alone is not high enough in vibration to penetrate the higher spiritual realms. The animal soul, like any animal, yields to firm treatment, but if treated harshly it either becomes savage and vengeful, or loses all heart and becomes a quailing coward. It should be transmuted until all its energies are utilized by the divine soul, not beaten or slain. People, animals, and the animal soul of man, all respond to kind yet firm treatment.

Every man, according to the Ancient Masons, has a definite constructive work in the world. When this work is discerned, the culture of his will requires the absolute adherence to carefully weighed resolutions that have been formed irrespective of impulse and momentary desire, having for their end progress toward the One Great Aim of the individual's life; and the vitalization of the organism with energy sufficient in quality and quantity to carry out the dictates of these resolutions.

Significance of the 12-inch Gauge and the 24-inch Rule

Now in Modern Masonry, as well as in that more ancient, we find closely associated with the common gavel the 12-inch gauge and the 24-inch rule. The factors that gauge the tone quality of the forces reaching man and expressing through his organism are the twelve zodiacal signs. They are the chief gauges of his life, character, and efforts. The sign the sun is in at birth is the gauge of his individuality, the sign the moon is in at birth is the gauge of his mentality, and the sign on the ascendant at his birth is the gauge of his personality. They gauge his thoughts, his speech, his actions, and the events which enter his life. They gauge the strength and the harmony of the influence of such planets as may be within their bounds.

But the particular department of life influenced by each zodiacal sign, by each section of the twelve-inch gauge, must be ascertained by the application of the 24-inch rule. This rule embraces the 24 hours of the day. All the zodiacal signs rise, culminate, and set, within the limit of this 24-inch rule. Only by determining the time of an event, or of a birth only by applying the 24-inch rule—can the astrological influences affecting it be learned. Furthermore, this rule of 24 sections measures out to man the time when each of the important events of his life will take place; for each 24-hour cycle after birth, according to the most approved astrological practice, actually releases forces that bring to pass the major events that transpire during the corresponding year of life.

The 24-inch rule, then, is the 24-hour day, during which the signs of the zodiac, bearing with them all the planets, rise and set. By its proper use as a time measuring instrument the exact position of all the signs and planets at any moment of time may be known. Such a chart, erected for the moment of birth, is the best possible road map to a successful life, and to the goal of complete initiation.

As to the 12-inch gauge, each section is one of the consonants of celestial language. The observations of the Ancient Masons convinced them that Solomon's Temple was actually divided into twelve such equal sections. They consequently sought for those things on earth, and within their own bodies, that vibrate to the same tone quality as each of these signs. Having selected some familiar object on earth that best summarized the influence of a zodiacal sign on human life, they traced the outlines of this object in its appropriate place among the stars. And then, at a later date, to express the same thing quickly in writing, the object's form was merely greatly abbreviated and conventionalized. Let us, therefore, trace this process with each section of the 12-inch gauge.

Origin of the Aries Symbol

In the Ram the Ancient Masons discerned the primitive fighting instinct, the desire for leadership, the headstrong aggressiveness, the fiery temper, and the impetuosity, that they observed in people born when Aries is the ruling sign. These people are ambitious, intrepid, despotic, often quarrelsome, pugnacious, and passionate. Yet in their work of construction or destruction they are noted for creative power and original thought, always using their brains in all they do. The Ram also is combative, and uses its head in offensive work. Thus the Ram, typical of the influence of Aries, which rules the head of man, was given first place in the arch of Solomon's Temple. To denote the Ram in writing they used a conventional form of the face of a sheep surmounted by its curling horns.

Origin of the Taurus Symbol

Those born under the influence of the sign Taurus are careful, plodding, and self-reliant. They are quiet and thoughtful, patiently awaiting for plans to mature. Remarkable for endurance, industry, and application, they sometimes become sullen and reserved. They are virile, with strong procreative instincts, are slow to anger, yet when once aroused are furious and violent; are warm friends and relentless foes. The sages of old noted similar qualities in the Bull, a similarity that can be observed also today, and they chose the Bull to occupy second place among the starry constellations in the sky. The Bull is remarkable for the strength of his neck, and the sign Taurus is found to rule the neck and throat of man.

The Bull was denoted in writing by the conventionalized face of a bull with the two horns readily recognized.

Origin of the Gemini Symbol

Duality is the most marked characteristic of those born under the third division of the zodiac. They have both intuition and reason well developed, are fond of all kinds of knowledge, are restless, changeable, energetic, enterprising, and good teachers. They are dexterous and quickly acquire skill with their hands, often following more than one occupation at the same time. Their chief difficulty is to concentrate their energies long enough in one channel to make it a great success. This marked duality led the ancients to picture the sign Gemini in the sky as the Twins, Castor and Pollux. Gemini rules the hands and arms in the body of man, and to express the Twins quickly in writing two perpendicular marks were used.

Origin of the Cancer Symbol

People born under the sign Cancer are tenacious, sensitive to their surroundings, retiring, timid, and desirous of carrying out their own ideas in their own way. They are mediumistic, possess good reflective powers, and are true conservers of force. In these things they are like the crab, and further, when the sun in its annual journey enters this first of the watery signs it starts back toward the south from the north, suggesting the backward method of locomotion common to the crab. So the Crab, influenced by the tides and the moon as are Cancer people by their moods, was selected to represent the sign Cancer. Water is the mother and nourisher that carries food to the united sperm and germ enabling them to grow. The sign Cancer also rules the home and family, the sperm and germ moving toward union well showing the foundation of domestic ties. Cancer rules the breasts and stomach of man. And to represent this chief of the domestic signs quickly in writing, the Wise Ones used the claws of the crab as emblems of the two cells moving toward each other.

Origin of the Leo Symbol

Those born under the sign Leo are marked for their courage, for the strength of the physical constitution, and for recuperative power. They are honest, fearless, magnanimous, generous to their friends, impulsive, passionate, faithful, sympathetic, and ambitious. They are lovers of their offspring and will defend them regardless of cost; are majestic, proud, and become natural rulers of others. Their ideas are usually on a large scale, seldom stooping to pettiness or meanness. These qualities were also discerned in the lion, therefore, the Masons of Old traced a lion in the sky to mark the fifth division of the zodiac. Leo, ruler of the heart in man, is the sign ruled by the sun, which is typical of creative power. And because the deadly cobra has the power of raising itself and expanding its hood in fancied resemblance to the procreative organ, it was, and is, venerated in many countries of the world as sacred to the sun. Therefore, to represent the sign briefly, in writing, the cobra, much conventionalized, was used.

Origin of the Virgo Symbol

Virgo people are thoughtful, serious, contemplative, modest, ingenious, careful, cautious, and industrious. They often become scholars and scientists, repositories of information, with the ability to assimilate experience in such a way as to yield a rich harvest of knowledge. They are thus always ready to suggest improvements in existing methods. To the Ancient Masons, the human body is the womb of the universe, from which after its period of gestation, through the travail of death, the son of God is born into the spiritual world. Death to them was but the freeing of the soul from the restricting envelope of matter, a passing from darkness into light. This is the mystery of the immaculate conception: Man, as the uterus of Isis, is impregnated with the Holy Spirit, to develop within himself Christ Consciousness. When this mystical atonement is made he can truly say: "I and the Father are One." In the sky this thought is depicted as a gleaning maid, immaculate and pure. She holds in her hands two ears of wheat, typifying the harvest of love and wisdom which constitutes the mission of the soul gestating in human form. This harvest well expresses the discriminative function of the bowels, that part of the human anatomy ruled by Virgo, and also the discriminative powers of Virgo people. It was expressed hieroglyphically by a sheaf of wheat.

Origin of the Libra Symbol

Those who are ruled by the sign Libra are lovers of peace and harmony, are amiable, even tempered, affectionate, sympathetic, and inclined toward marriage. They are fond of art, refined pleasures, and amusements, dislike unclean work intensely, have a deep love of justice, and feel the need of a companion to share their lot in life. For a moment they are easily carried away by their emotions, but quickly regain their balance. This mental equilibrium, and the instinct for justice, was pictured in the sky by the Scales. Libra rules the veins, the internal sexual organs, and the reproductive fluids in man. It is the sign of marriage, and was represented in writing briefly by the union of a feminine, or crooked, line, with a masculine, or straight, line.

Origin of the Scorpio Symbol

Those born under the sign Scorpio have strong sexual desires and possess an inexhaustible fund of ideas. They are thoughtful, contemplative, ingenious, scientific; and where others are concerned can be cold, calculating, unsympathetic, deceitful, and cruel. Suspicious, determined, secretive, energetic, shrewd, they possess fine mechanical ability, and often have a strong life-giving magnetism that enables them to become successful healers as well as good surgeons. The intensity of the sexual nature, the subtlety, cruelty, fighting instincts, and underhanded methods by which they attack opponents, suggested to the minds of the Ancient Masons the Scorpion, whose chief weapon of offense is the least suspected part of his anatomy, at the end of his tail. Scorpio rules the external sexual organs in the anatomy of man. Like Virgo people, those ruled by Scorpio are harvesters of knowledge, but unlike Virgo people, whose sheaf of wheat is closed at the bottom to indicate conservation, the sheaf denoting Scorpio is left open at the bottom to indicate wasteful expenditure of precious energy. And to indicate the retaliating pangs of remorse for such loss, as well as to suggest the Scorpion, in denoting the sign briefly in writing the sheaf of wheat was provided with a scorpion's tail.

Origin of the Sagittarius Symbol

The Centaur, half animal and half man, was chosen by the Sages of Old to picture in the sky the sign Sagittarius. It well represents the dual nature of those born under this sign; for their animal propensities are strong, yet they are also well supplied with the higher, nobler, more generous impulses. The body and legs of a horse indicate restlessness, physical activity, and migratory tendencies; while the upper and human part indicates conservatism, self control, and executive ability. They are free, energetic, ambitious of worldly position, are loyal, patriotic, and charitable to others. Their love of hunting and all outdoor sports is shown by the full drawn bow, which also expresses retribution; for Sagittarius people are quick to fight for the rights of others. They are prompt and decisive in action, can command others, are frank and candid, and when they speak their remarks go straight to the mark like an arrow to the bull's eye. Sagittarius rules the thighs, which are the seat of man's locomotion. To write the sign quickly, the arrow from the archer's bow was used.

Origin of the Capricorn Symbol

Those born under the sign Capricorn are quiet, thoughtful, reserved, serious, economical, prudent, cautious, good reasoners, decidedly practical, and ambitious of wealth and position. They are born diplomats, and quick to see and use the weaknesses of others for their own advantage. Thus as a goat ascends a mountain, taking advantage of every possible foothold, so these people climb to their ambitions by grasping every possible opportunity, great or small, to advance themselves. Suppliantly they bow to the reigning authority, seeking by sundry and devious ways to gain the good will of others, that they may partake in power, much as the goat must bend his knees and devise many a clever method to crop the foliage among the precipitous rocks of his upland pastures. These people are patient and persistent, and by concentrated effort and skillful maneuvering butt their way through, or climb their way around, all but insurmountable obstacles. In the body of man Capricorn rules the knees. It is pictured in the sky as the Goat. And to write it quickly a twisted devious line was used, twisted to suggest the spiraled horns of the goat, but in its pattern a still better representation of the circuitous path by which goats and people reach the heights of material ambition.

Origin of the Aquarius Symbol

The chief characteristics of those born under the sign Aquarius are the predominance of humanitarian instincts and the desire for a scientific verification of all theories. This intellectual trend is represented by the Man of the zodiac, while the sympathies and emotions that bind him to his fellowman are pictured by water flowing from the urn. It is the baptismal urn, the water representing the pure emotions that prompt man to reform and lead a new life. These people are kind, amiable, witty, fond of refinement and society, and are keen students of human nature. As Leo is symbolized hieroglyphically by one serpent, Aquarius, where Reason and Intuition balance, where man and woman have learned the significance of sex, have partaken of the tree of knowledge of good and evil, was anciently symbolized by two serpents moving in opposite directions. Aquarius rules the legs of man. It is written briefly as two wavy lines, a conventionalized form for the two serpents, and also suggesting the water that flows from the Waterbearer's urn.

Origin of the Pisces Symbol

Pisces people are amiable, very sympathetic, kind, neat, and particular, yet are often timid and lacking in self-confidence. They are greatly influenced by their environment, are restless, emotional, highly imaginative, and capable of high intellectual development. In their ideals they are utopian. They long for universal brotherhood, for the highest expression of love, and for peace on earth good will to men. Sensitive, mediumistic, capable of psychic lucidity, romantic and lovers of mystery, they are apt to become too negative and dreamy to practice their ideals. They take an interest in psychic investigation, have a strong desire for the ideal in marriage, and when this ideal is not realized become restless and discontented. Pisces rules the feet of man. Fish, due to their reproductive ability, are ancient symbols of sex, and water is the symbol of the emotions. To represent the ideal love and marriage for which Pisces people long—that union referred to in the Bible as the tree of life and in the Kabala as the Holy Shekinah, or perfect way of nuptials—the Ancient Masons placed in the sky two fish and united them by a cord of love. To write the sign quickly they used two crescents, symbolizing two souls, likewise united by a connecting line.

Significance of the Signs in the E. A. Degree

Now having defined the 12-inch gauge, let us revert to the first implement of a Mason, the common gavel. In the Entered Apprentice lodge the Master gives one rap with his gavel. The Master, as has previously been explained, represents the human ego. The gavel represents the human will. The table, against which the gavel is struck, is a plane surface, and thus represents a plane, any plane, of existence upon which the soul may sojourn. One blow on the table, of course, represents the first plane, that is, the physical plane. Two raps signify the second plane, that is, the astral realm. Three raps indicate the third or spiritual plane. But in the E. A. degree but one rap is necessary, because the mysteries of this degree all pertain primarily to the physical plane. In fact, if we are to be able to check our information concerning other planes of existence adequately, we must first thoroughly understand all the laws and facts, in so far as possible, relative to the physical plane. How can we understand higher mathematics unless we first learn to add, subtract, multiply, and divide? Therefore, the Ancient Masons insisted that the candidate should, before investigating higher realms, thoroughly understand his physical functions and the physical plane of life.

As soon as the lodge is opened, the Master asks the Junior Warden, representing the planet Mercury, if all are E. A. Masons in the South. The South is the place where all the planets reach their highest position. He then asks the Senior Warden, representing the Moon, if all are E. A. Masons in the West. The West is where all the planets sink from sight beneath the horizon. Having been answered in the affirmative, he, representing the Sun, then vouches for those in the East. The east is where all the planets rise into view. But the North is left unmentioned, for to us of the northern hemisphere there are no planets to our north. The North, where water freezes, is the symbol of crystallization and of strictly material motives. These latter are left unmentioned, for material achievement based on purely material motives, has no part to play in soul advancement.

The Junior Deacon, representing the planet Venus, is next called up to the Master, and gives a sign by which he may be identified. It is quite fitting that Venus, the planet of love and affection, should be the one to give this sign. It consists of placing the open fingers of the right hand upon the open fingers of the left hand.

Venus, in astrology, rules the sign Libra, the sign that governs both marriage and open enemies. Therefore, it is quite fitting also that the Master should appoint Venus, the Junior Deacon, to station outside the door, the Tyler with drawn sword. This door is the barrier between the seeming and the real, the exoteric appearances and the esoteric verity. Venus, the planet of love, affection, and marriage, knocks three times on the inside of this door, signifying the esoteric and real knowledge concerning marriage as applied to all three planes. The Tyler, symbolizing man's thoughts, then answers by three knocks on the outside of the door, signifying those exoteric and unworthy opinions about marriage on all three planes that guard the real truth from the uninitiated.

Finally, the Junior Deacon knocks once and is answered by one rap, indicating that in the Entered Apprentice degree the candidate is expected to master the laws governing physical marriage only. That the study of such laws, and the attempt to apply them in the production of a nobler race of mankind, as well as the attempt to apply them in the elevation of the soul to higher states of spiritual attainment, was one of the chief objects of the Ancient Masons in the E.A. degree is plainly shown by the sign given by the Junior Deacon to the Master. Five is, and as far back as such things can be traced always has been, the symbol of man or woman alone. The five fingers of the right hand represent man, the five of the left hand represent woman. The right and the left hand joined, in universal symbolism, represents the marriage of man and woman.

Contrast of Ancient Masonry Teachings With Those of Present Day Orient

However moderns may regard marriage, the Ancient Sages attached no sense of shame, immorality, or degradation to it. They looked upon it as one of life's noblest privileges, and by deep study sought to learn how through it better offspring might be brought into the world; how the noblest sentiments possible to man might be strengthened, how life might be prolonged, disease avoided, and a greater amount of happiness brought into the world.

If we are to believe tradition they in a measure succeeded in all these things. The Bible gives repeated accounts of man living far beyond the allotted three score and ten years. But irrespective of the literal veracity of these stories, the Ancient Sages believed that their lives were prolonged and that they attained higher powers through their understanding of love in the sacred precincts of marriage.

Nowhere are these teachings and beliefs more plain to discern than in Ancient Masonry. But let no one be led astray by the thought that any so-called sex practices were taught. Neither was asceticism and celibacy taught. The Sages of Chaldea, the Priesthood of Egypt, and the Ancient Masons, were married people. They believed in marriage, believed it was a holy and sacred institution, believed in purity, in kindness, in love. In India, it is true, asceticism developed, and also sex-magic such as is found among the Tantrics today. But I find no hint of such extremes in Ancient Masonry.

Dozens of sects flourish today throughout America teaching suppression of the love nature. Other dozens of sects, usually as sworn-to-secrecy inner circles of cults, teach sex practices as the means of gaining supernormal powers. If the teachings of the Ancient Masons, as revealed by their symbolism, are true, both these ideas are a delusion and a snare. In fact, it is my belief that if those doctrines were permitted full public discussion they would soon have no adherents, because the medical profession alone would present such an array of actual pathological cases caused by such ideas that it would discourage others. Such beliefs thrive on secrecy.

If I may be pardoned for mentioning personal observations, I may say that I have been in occult work since 1898, and have contacted, directly or indirectly, most of the cults, colonies, and beliefs of any consequence throughout the world. In that time I have known of centers and colonies devoted to some special sex practices, but while I have known of many cases of physical and mental derangement to result, up to the present day I have not known of a single person that has been in any way benefitted. Also, I have known of many centers and cults that teach repression, and while I have observed much psychism to result from this, it has always been an unreliable and often obnoxious form of psychism.

Such personal remarks are relevant because to explain Ancient Masonry it is impossible to avoid reference to sex; and a plain statement may prevent hasty conclusions. The teachings of Ancient Masonry in such regards are very simple, very plain, and such that they would be endorsed by medical men of high standing, quite coincide with the legal requirements of our land, and set a high moral code. Their doctrines relative to sex are concerned with marriage, and teach man not to starve his animal nature, but to transmute the animal into the divine. They teach man how he can cease being a brute and become an angel.

Oriental doctrines which are in all essential respects the very opposite of those of Ancient Masonry are prevalent today. First of all, they advocate that the individual shall eat only the most negative of foods. Yet his ability to control himself and to exercise will power, depends upon, not the volume of electricity generated in his body and nervous systems, but upon its voltage, or potential. As explained fully in Course 5, *Esoteric Psychology,* Chapter 9, it is the protein molecules of the body which are able to release the high-frequency energy of the lightning which fixed the nitrogen that plant life took from the soil. And most people cannot thus release high potential enough or in any manner develop high voltage in the gray matter of their brains, while living on the negative foods advocated in this Oriental training.

The action of the endocrine secretions of the gonads on the nervous system is to cause it to generate electrical charges in greater volume. Celibacy, therefore, tends to have the effect of charging the individual with much surplus electromagnetic, or etheric energy.

Rhythmic breathing also is advocated, and exercises prescribed which tend to generate still greater excesses of etheric energy.

Thus sex repression and dynamic breathing are employed to generate a great excess of etheric energy which floods the system; but, because of the diet and the practices in meditation, no ability to control this low potential etheric excess is developed. On the contrary, the dreamy fantasy kind of thinking called meditation is cultivated, which breaks down whatever power the individual already had to direct his thoughts concisely and clearly into channels of control.

As a perusal of Course 5, *Esoteric Psychology,* Chapter 9 will make plain, control of one's thoughts or control of one's body depends upon being able to mobilize in the brain cells used for such control, an electrical energy not merely strong enough to gain recognition, but with a potential sufficiently high that it can overcome, and displace, other electrical energies which compete with it.

If the brain cells employed for control can not acquire a higher electrical potential than potentials generated in other regions of the body—in the sympathetic nervous system, for instance—it can not control, but is controlled by, these electrical energies thus elsewhere generated. Yet the various meditations and concentrations employed in the Oriental teachings mentioned, have as a direct result the discouragement of positive clear cut intellectual thinking, and they break down the power of the brain to generate electrical energies high enough in voltage to exercise control. Instead the control comes from the sympathetic nervous system.

Etheric energy, having a velocity when in motion approximately that of light, is the bridge between the physical world and the astral world. According to Einstein's General Theory of Relativity, no material thing can have a velocity greater than light. Therefore, that which has a velocity greater than about 186,284 miles per second no longer belongs to the physical, but is an object on the astral plane.

And an excess of this boundary line etheric energy makes it easy for motions from the physical plane to be communicated to the astral plane, or for motions on the astral plane to be communicated to the physical.

The excess of etheric energy developed by breathing and sex repression, therefore, is favorable for enabling astral entities, either in the flesh or on the astral plane, to contact the individual and use him and his electrical forces to produce phenomena, to impress him with their wishes, or to exert an influence upon others at a distance.

But the training has been careful to discourage, both by the negative diet and the mental exercises, the development of ability on the part of the individual to use these etheric energies he generates. The whole system is designed to develop volumes of low potential electrical energy such as most readily can be used by a distant Mahatma in the flesh, or by some astral entity, in spite of any attempted resistance on the part of the poor dupe thus trained; when he realizes that he is being controlled for purposes about which he knows nothing.

Instead of the opposite process, which the Ancient Masons taught, in which pains are taken to develop Intellect and Will, so that the individual always may be master of himself, this Oriental training furnishes plastic individuals quite incapable of directing their own forces, but who generate great quantities of etheric energy which can, and is, used, whether or not there is consent, by cunning and dominant minds working from the inner plane for their own selfish purposes.

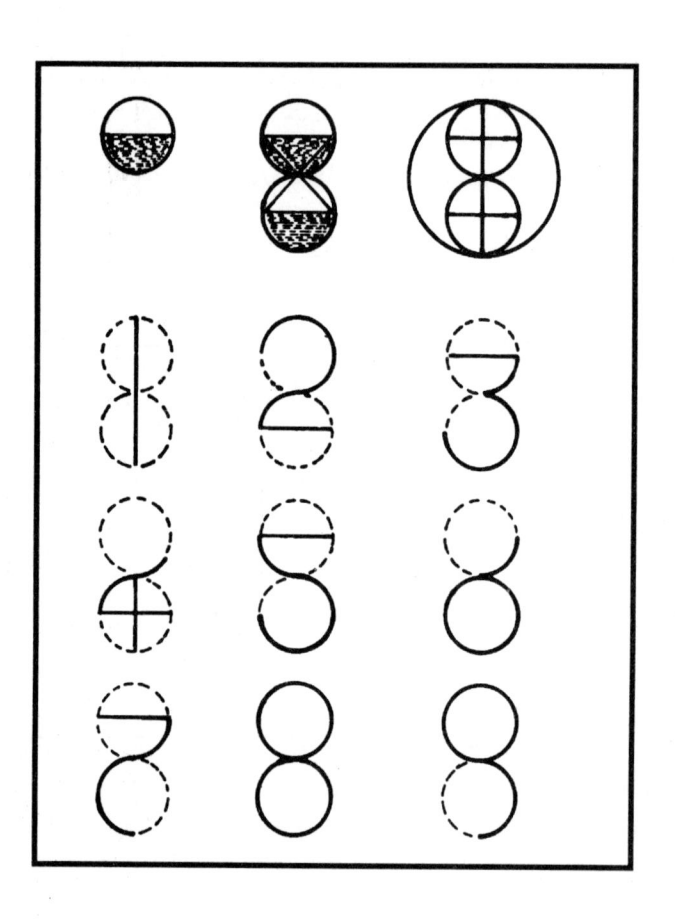

Chapter 4

Numbers and Opening the Lodge

MODERN FREEMASONRY is the traditional remnants of Ancient Masonry. It retains the older forms of the ritual imperfectly; yet in spite of the modifying influence of time, and the alterations that are inevitably the outcome of passing through countless generations, it still presents to our vision the essential elements of truth as they were found when first gleaned from the starlit realms of Urania.

Following the modern ritual we learn that the Master—representing, as we have found, the sun in the solar system and the ego of man—ascertains that all present are E.A. Masons, and thus duly qualified for the work to be done. He next instructs the Junior Deacon—representing the planet Venus, and the astral body of man—to have the lodge properly tyled, or guarded; and then commands the brethren to be clothed, to don their aprons and jewels.

Within the astral body of man, corresponding to the Junior Deacon, reside thought-cells, the mental elements of which embrace all the experiences the soul has had. These mental elements, built into thought-cells and thought structures, constitute his unconscious mind. All his external perceptions, actions, and thoughts are recorded here, and when raised into the region of objective consciousness constitute memory. And there are other trains of thought, and perceptions relating to the astral world, also here residing that never reach the level of objective consciousness. The astral body, therefore, is the great reservoir of consciousness.

The Important Duty of the Tyler

The duty of the Tyler is said to be to keep off all cowans and eavesdroppers, and to see that none pass and repass except such as are duly qualified and have permission from the Master. This Tyler represents objective consciousness, chiefly the reason, that guards the threshold of the mind and determines what thoughts shall, and what thoughts shall not, be allowed entrance to man's domain. Reason only becomes alert to its duties when there is a determination on the part of the unconscious mind, in other words a strong desire, that it shall do so. Such desire, as explained in detail in Course 5, *Esoteric Psychology,* Chapter 4, arises from the astral form, the Junior Deacon.

Very few people realize how very important this work of the Tyler is. As the thought-cells which comprise the unconscious mind, or character, are derived from experiences and the thinking that is done about them, it is the Tyler who determines what is added to the character and what alterations in the character are made.

These thought-cells, constituting the membership of the unconscious mind, in turn determine what the individual does, and what events are attracted into his life. It is only when certain groups of them acquire unusual additional energy that events of a specific nature come to pass. And not only do these thought-cells, which are thought formed, determine when the events in his life come to pass, but they also determine to what extent these events are such as he desires, or such as he deems to be misfortunes.

Thus is it, that the only way man can change his destiny, and make it better than it otherwise would be, is through cultivating appropriate thoughts and emotions, which implies that he must be able effectively to guard his domain and prevent the entrance of those thoughts and emotions which he has decided are inimical to the life and fortune which he desires to attain.

But effectively to tyle his lodge, to prevent the eavesdroppers and cowans, which are the unworthy thoughts and inharmonious attitudes toward life, from entering his constitution, requires much more than merely desiring to prevent their entrance. They have a most insistent way of forcing themselves on the attention of consciousness, and to prevent them from so doing requires a proper technique and much practice. In fact, it is one of the most difficult and important tasks which man is called upon to undertake.

Ancient Masonry 64

One first, of course should determine just which thoughts are worthy of entrance to his constitution, or lodgeroom, and then keep alert to note the approach of those which it has been decided should be excluded.

That which gains the attention of objective consciousness must do so through the use of electric energies generated within the body, chiefly by the nervous system. How these energies are generated is explained in Course 5, *Esoteric Psychology,* Chapter 9. And there also is explained that the thoughts which hold the attention, and thus shoulder all other thoughts from the consciousness, are those which can command the highest electrical potential. Thus if an individual is to predetermine the kind of thoughts which are to gain the attention of his objective consciousness and consequently enter his lodgeroom, the gray thought-cells of his brain must be able to command a higher voltage of electric energy than can be commanded by the thought-cells of his unconscious mind which have insistent desires, and higher than those generated by other portions of his body, such as by portions of his sympathetic nervous system.

Constant training to use his brain thus to control his thoughts is essential to this work of guarding the lodgeroom. But in spite of such Conditioning of the brain cells to develop high potential electricity and direct it into channels of control, various factors may lower the output of electrical energy upon the part of his body in such a way as to make thought control difficult. These things he should understand.

Overwork may lead to physical exhaustion. And physical exhaustion normally is accompanied by a decrease in the amount of electrical energy available for the use of control. That is, vitality is electrical in nature, and lowered vitality indicates a low generation of electrical forces.

High tensions of the nervous system, on the other hand, or over stimulation of any kind, such as through the release of adrenalin in the blood stream in response to a real or imagined emergency, may so increase the voltage of the nerves other than the brain that these are able to dictate to the brain and control the thinking.

Also, especially when they receive great volumes of astral energy from the planets forming progressed aspects, certain groups of thought-cells within the unconscious mind may be able to impart their energy so strongly through the ether to the brain or nervous system, as temporarily to dominate the mind. Their desires, or the images which they project on the objective consciousness, may be able to generate so much electrical potential as to hold the attention in spite of previous resolves that they shall not.

And the thoughts of others, incarnate or discarnate, through impinging powerfully upon the unconscious mind, and through etheric forces imparting energies to the brain or nervous system, may become insistent or at times almost obsessive, in the same way.

Under such conditions one should not become introspective, but have something outside of oneself, something which in itself is very pleasant, to think about. The consciousness then should be extended to this thing—not directed to how it causes one to feel. This will result in the energies being radiated outward toward that which is the object of attention. Under this process, unless the electrical power has been permitted to get too low, any thought or emotion—eavesdropper or cowan—can be excluded.

These eavesdroppers and cowans that should thus be kept from the lodgeroom, or human constitution, are all unworthy thoughts and inharmonious attitudes toward life. Only thoughts that are constructive in quality, and emotions that are harmonious, are duly qualified, and only to such does the Master, the human ego, if he performs his duties properly, grant permission to enter.

When the brethren don their aprons and jewels they consistently represent the Grand Man of the skies. The apron indicates them to be virile and in full possession of their natural functions. The jewels show them to be in full possession of their mental and moral faculties, even as the jewels, the plumb, the level, and the square were shown in chapter 1 to be the methods by which the mandates of Deity are carried out. Each congregated Mason, then, when so clothed, as well as the lodge as a whole, represents both the Temple of King Solomon, the home of the glorious orb of day, and the mansion of the indwelling human ego.

Function of the Junior Deacon

When the brethren are clothed the Worshipful Master asks the Junior Deacon—Venus, and the astral body—his place in the lodge and his business. The Junior Deacon answers that his function is to wait on the Worshipful Master and Wardens, act as their proxy in the active duties of the lodge, and take care of the door.

As the astral body functions there, it is quite evident why it should be placed in charge of the door to the inner recesses of man's constitution. As a matter of fact, the astral body does have charge, not merely of what enters the mind, but through its direction of the involuntary functions of the body, also of what enters the physical makeup. The astral governs the whole human constitution, physical and mental, in regard to what shall enter it.

The Worshipful Master and the Wardens, as has been explained, represent the human ego, the divine soul, and the spiritual body—the trinity that survives even after the second death on the astral plane. It seems, then, that the Ancient Masons considered it the duty of the astral body to serve this higher trinity of man's constitution. That is, instead of serving the animal soul, or pandering to the physical senses, as it so commonly does, it was thought that the astral form should serve and act as proxy for the noble, immortal part of man, and thus assist in the work of successful initiation. Likewise in the Grand Man of the skies, and in the individual birth-chart, we find Venus, the planet of love, the most useful assistant to the Sun, the Moon, and Mercury; for love is the refining influence, and lies at the foundation of all true progress.

Function of the Senior Deacon

The Senior Deacon's place in the lodge being ascertained, the Master asks him his duties there. The Senior Deacon—Mars, and the animal soul—replies that he must wait on the Worshipful Master and Wardens, act as their proxy in the active duties of the lodge, attend to the preparation and introduction of candidates, and welcome and clothe all visiting brethren. The proper function of the animal soul, as well as that of the astral body, is to serve the higher trinity of man. Some would have it that the animal soul should be killed; but the Ancient Masons clearly held that it has a very useful function in man's constitution, and that instead of ruling the lodge, as it sometimes does, and instead of being chained and crushed, or killed as some advocate, it should be taught to serve man's immortal nature.

Certainly the animal soul prepares the candidate for its human initiation; for the soul evolving upward through mineral, vegetable, and animal is under the dominance of it and builds it up through struggle and strife. The animal soul thus developed gives the initiative to work for that which is still higher, until finally the soul is introduced through the animal kingdom, which is the preparatory stage next below, to the human plane of existence.

The welcoming and clothing of visiting brethren refers to the circumstance that while man occupies a physical body he must subsist to an extent on other forms of organic life. Man's animal soul and physical requirements demand the co-operation of these cosmic brethren, and they are welcomed as food to build up the physique of man. This organic life is itself undergoing a cycle of development, evolving toward greater perfection. But this ruthless sacrifice is not without compensation; for while these entities form the conditions necessary for the progress of the human soul, they are given additional opportunities for progression. They partake, by their association, of the qualities and experiences of the organisms they inhabit temporarily, and thus are hastened in their evolutionary development.

Function of the Secretary

The Secretary's place in the lodge being ascertained, he is required to explain his duties there. He replies that he must observe the Worshipful Master's will and pleasure, record the proceedings of the lodge, transmit a copy of the same to the Grand Lodge if required; receive all moneys and money bills from the hands of the brethren, pay them over to the Treasurer, and take receipts for the same. The Secretary—Jupiter, and the etheric body—should ever be ready to obey the commands of the Master, or ego. It is also the etheric body that transmits all states of consciousness from the physical to the astral form. The record of every experience of life, every thought, every sensation, every emotion, is retained in the astral body as modes of motion in astral substance. It is the etheric part of man's constitution that makes this record. And when anything thus recorded—a memory, a resolve, or an emotion—is to be brought up into the region of objective consciousness and expressed either in thought or physical action, it is through electricity (ether vibrations) that the energies constituting the astral record are transmitted to the physical, and thus to the Grand Lodge, or universe, by which man is surrounded.

The moneys and money bills represent values, and the only values in life are our attitudes toward events. Our attitude toward any given event may be constructive or destructive, and thus according to the mental attitude taken, each event is recorded in the astral body either as a credit or debit. And as every thought and emotion is accompanied by a change in the physical body, these values, either as assets or as liabilities, are actually turned over to the Treasurer, or physical body. The physical body then gives a receipt for these harmonies and discords; for in turn the condition of the physical body reacts upon the nerve currents and other portions of the etheric form.

Function of the Treasurer

The Treasurer's place in the lodge being ascertained, he is requested by the Master to tell his duties there. His duty is to observe the Worshipful Master's will and pleasure; receive all moneys and money bills from the hands of the Secretary, keep a just and true account of the same, and pay them out by order of the Worshipful Master and the consent of the brethren. Of course the Treasurer—Saturn, and the physical body—should serve the will and pleasure of the ego. Likewise the chemical and other changes that occur in the physical body as accompaniments of all thoughts and emotions constitute a true account of the harmonies and discords—the moneys and money bills—transmitted by the etheric body. These values so received are then paid out, that is, they are transformed into mental and physical actions; for all actions depend upon what has first been received from the environment. They should be paid out, that is, action should be taken, only on orders from the ego and with the consent of the brethren. In fact, action to be effective, must have the support of all the various portions of man's complex constitution.

Function of the Junior Warden

The business of the Junior Warden—Mercury, and the spiritual body—is said to be observing time, calling the craft from labor to refreshment, watching them through this period that they may not give way to intemperance and excess, and calling them at the right time, that the Worshipful Master may have honor, and that they may have profit and pleasure.

Man's most vital refreshment is the period of sleep. As explained in detail in Course 5, *Esoteric Psychology,* Chapter 9, the cells of the gray matter of the brain are the most effective batteries of the body. And like any electric battery if the circuit is kept closed, as it is by thinking, it tends to run down. But if, before the battery is dead, the circuit is broken, as it is in sleep, the battery recharges itself. Furthermore, in sleep the soul carries on exploration in the inner plane. And if the spiritual body has had proper growth, it will guard the consciousness from entering lower astral realms where dwell excess and dissipation; and at the proper time it will cause the consciousness, to whatever region extended, to return to the physical, and awaken to commence another day of activity on the material plane.

Function of the Senior Warden

The duties of the Senior Warden are to assist the Worshipful Master in opening his lodge, to take care of the implements and jewels that none may be lost, to pay the craft their wages if any be due; and to see that none go away dissatisfied. The Senior Warden—Moon and divine soul—does assist the ego in its work, even as the moon assists the sun in bringing forth life on earth, or as in a birth-chart she assists him in governing the life forces. As the seat of the higher, imperishable consciousness, the divine soul has charge of the jewels and implements, that is, of man's mental and moral faculties and natural functions. Some have taught that man would be more perfect without some of his natural functions, but if the still small voice of the divine soul be heeded, she will direct that none should be misplaced or lost. The divine soul also recognizes, if its admonitions be but heeded, that there are physical necessities and spiritual necessities. It is thus able to mete out just compensation unto all, permitting no part of man's constitution to be neglected, or underpaid, but rendering unto Caesar the things that are Caesar's, and unto God the things that are God's.

Function of the Master

The duties of the Master in the lodge are to open and adorn it and to set the craft to work with good and wholesome instructions, or to cause it to be done. As the sun is the center and controlling power of the solar system, so the ego is the inward source of power, and should be the controlling power of man. It should direct all his efforts. Through devout aspirations its promptings may be recognized. The Master adorns the lodge as the sun adorns the day, and the temple of man is glorified only when dominated by, and under the instructions of, the indwelling spiritual ego.

The Lodge Opens

After the duties of the seven officers in the lodge have been stated the Master gives three raps with his gavel, indicating that the will is to be exercised on all three planes. He then states that in opening the lodge he forbids the use of all profane language, or any disorderly conduct whereby peace and harmony may be interrupted.

Language refers not only to man's utterances but also to his thoughts. The temple in which he dwells must not be profaned by vicious thoughts or unseemly fantasies. Constructive work in the human edifice demands only pure and elevated thinking. In this edifice there are many workmen—organs, cells, and thought-cells. Little progress can be made if there is antagonism between them. Disorderly conduct upon the part of one of these is like a small rebellion. All must perform their tasks in harmony, and in obedience to the true Master, the deific ego.

The Master, declaring it his will and pleasure that a lodge of E.A. Masons be opened for the dispatch of business asks the Senior Warden to communicate his pleasure to the Junior Warden, who gives three raps with his gavel and communicates the will of the Master to the brethren. This signifies that the dictates of the ego are transmitted through the divine soul to the spiritual body, and from thence, through the medium of astral vibrations to other sections of man's constitution. In a similar manner natal astrology teaches that the influence of the sun, ruling the individuality, is transmitted to the moon, ruling the mentality, and thence to find expression is directed by Mercury, the messenger of the gods.

The Sign of Distress

Next, the signs of this degree are attended to. They consist of right angles, horizontals, and perpendiculars. The horizontal sign is made at the level of the neck, that part of man ruled by the feminine planet Venus, the planet of love. It is a quick horizontal motion from left to right with the five fingers open. These five open fingers indicate humanity, and the horizontal line that section of it represented by woman. At the same time as this motion, the left hand drops vertically at the side, giving the perpendicular sign. This perpendicular sign with the five open fingers represents man. The hand is then at the level of the region of the body ruled by the masculine planet Mars, the planet of desire and strife.

The horizontal and perpendicular signs thus given simultaneously indicate woman's pure and unsullied affections, represented by Venus; which have been violated by man's inconsiderate passions, represented by Mars. The result is that woman, instead of embracing, shrinks from him, as pantomimed by the due-guard or horizontal motion.

That there may be no mistaking the teachings of this degree that the nuptial union is recognized as commonly abused, it is still further portrayed in terms of universal symbolism by the right angle. This is made by holding open the left hand and crossing the palm of it with the open palm of the right hand at right angles. Here the lower, or negative, five fingers represent woman, and the superimposed, or dominant, five represent man. In astrology all the discordant aspects are portions, or multiples, of right angles. The right angle, therefore, is the universal symbol of discord; and the two hands are crossed at this angle to indicate the all too prevalent discord arising out of the nuptial union. To still further emphasize the significance of the sign, in the E.A. degree it is termed the sign of distress. This sign of distress is called the first sign of a Mason.

It would seem from this, that the Ancient Masons placed much importance upon the relations between husband and wife. Such relations might be considered, by the unthinking, to be not merely a matter which good taste forbids should be discussed; but of so little moment in the more important effort of soul development as to entirely unwarrant being given so much attention. But the Ancient Masons knew that soul development consists of transforming existing mental factors, and adding new constructive mental factors to the astral and spiritual bodies. The development of the soul to a state of Self-Conscious Immortality is the work of the Masonic candidate; and his building is not fictitious. He builds with thoughts which are vitalized by emotion. And not only does his marital partner stimulate the thoughts with which he builds, in a considerable measure, but the emotions aroused through their association build these thoughts into his finer bodies, either as harmonious, or as discordant, thought-cells.

A thought to be effective, from a magical standpoint, must be clear cut and strongly energized. The carrying power of a thought and the amount of work it can accomplish depend upon the energy associated with it. A thought which is associated with any emotion whatever has considerable ability to perform work. It has, as one might say, horsepower. A thought associated with a very strong emotion has a very high horsepower. Ordinarily, strong emotions habitually aroused are those of the nuptial relations. That is, whether man is aware of it or not, in this relation he is giving his thoughts a tremendous energy to go forth and accomplish, either constructively or destructively.

Under such circumstances, however, we have not one set of thoughts and emotions, but two. And because the astral bodies at this time tend to become fused, whatever thoughts and emotions are held by one finds unusually ready access to the astral body of the other. In other words, not only are the dynamic powers of thought raised to the highest degree, but due to their vibratory proximity, each is particularly open to receive the thoughts of the other. Thus the thoughts held at this time, more than any other thoughts that may be held—the emotions of intense religious fervor being next in dynamic strength—tend, because of their unusual dynamic strength, to build their harmonies or discords both into the astral body of the thinker and into the astral body of the other.

The Ancient Masons were well versed in magic; and here is a very real and extremely potent form of magic that husband and wife constantly, and usually unwittingly, practice on each other. If this relation, therefore, be discordant, the participating parties are practicing upon each other a very destructive form of magic. For that which is attracted from the outside world is determined by the activities of the thought-cells built into the astral form. If discordant thoughts are built into the astral body, discordant events will be attracted. Disease, financial failure, and all the evils that may befall man, may very well be attracted if through the years he forces his attentions upon an unwilling and loathing wife. Is it to be wondered, then, that the symbol of such an unfortunate state of affairs should, by the Ancient Masons, be called the sign of distress?

The laws of the land may demand that husband and wife must yield even unwillingly to the desire of the other. But such yielding, if thought has any power to heal or injure, if such a thing as mental magic exists, must inevitably bring to both a train of physical woes. And because the soul itself is built by states of consciousness—is, in fact, the sum total of the states of consciousness organized in the finer forms—such relations have a powerful influence over the soul's progress. If degrading thoughts, thoughts of loathing, thoughts that are associated in any manner with decidedly strong inharmonious emotions, are being engendered by oneself, or being received from another through such close association, the power of the soul for progress is lessened.

To remedy a fault, it must first be recognized to exist. The first sign of a Mason, therefore, is a recognition of the state and the cause of distress.

These signs being given, the Master, Senior Warden, and Junior Warden, each give one rap with the gavel; indicating that there is complete unity of the higher trinity of man's constitution in exercising the will to overcome the problems of the physical plane. The Master then declares the lodge open.

In Course 2, *Astrological Signatures,* Chapter 2, I have explained at length the Written Law and the Oral Law. The Oral Law in general is traditional knowledge, and as applied to individual man is his knowledge of natural law. The Written Law is that law written in the stars; it is in general, astronomy, and as applied to individual man is the various vibrations that reach him from celestial sources as mapped by his birth-chart and progressed chart. I mention these two laws here because both are a part of any correct Masonic lodge.

Having declared the lodge open, the Master reads from a book, representing the Oral Law, the following passages:

"Behold how good and pleasant it is for the brethren to dwell together in unity! It is like the precious ointment upon the head that ran down upon the beard, even Aaron's beard, that went down to the skirts of his garments; as the dew of Hermon, as the dew that descended upon the mountain of Zion, for there the Lord commanded the blessing, evermore. Amen. So mote it be."

This passage following immediately after the sign of distress, which calls the attention to the cause of a great amount of misery and failure in the world, is evidently intended to call the attention to the great benefits that may be derived from harmony in marriage. And right here is a good place to emphasize that I do not find in Ancient Masonry any teaching which upholds the tendency repeatedly to divorce simply because for some reason the ideals are not at once realized. I do find that the Ancient Masons emphasized the importance of selecting a mate that is physically, mentally, and spiritually harmonious, when entering into marriage. That is, marriage was considered to be worthy of careful thought, and not to be entered into haphazard. But once the marriage took place, it seems to have been their belief that no stone should be left unturned by either to make it a successful, constructive, and harmonious union.

While there is a higher phase of marriage to be striven for, as will be noticed in detail later, the Ancient Masons did not view the physical relations between husband and wife as something abhorrent. On the contrary, while recognizing the existence of still higher phases, they taught that even the physical relation within moderation could be made an instrument of soul growth and physical construction.

In this doctrine sensualism played no part. For it was with the unconscious magic exercised by the participating parties that they were concerned, and not with physical gratification. These Ancient Masons were Master Magicians, and they recognized that even the physical relation between husband and wife, in addition to being the means by which superior offspring could be brought into the world, might also be the means for the highest form of white magic. A thought associated with the emotion of love is the most powerful constructive agent known. The more intense the emotion the greater the volume of constructive energy with which the thought is empowered. And where there is perfect agreement and sympathy between the two, the united thoughts are energized manifold.

That such ideal conditions might obtain, according to this ancient teaching, it is first necessary that there be the utmost harmony of desire and sympathy of understanding. Little acts of consideration and kindness in the daily life prepare for this. Both should have their energies aroused to the highest degree, and both should find complete expression. And above all, each should feel toward the other the loftiest, kindest, and most sympathetic emotions. The rapport established through mutual desires, fuses the astral bodies, and as the thoughts and feelings are all harmonious, hence constructive, each builds in himself, and in the other, thought-cells in the astral form that are constructive. And because the emotions are so intense, these constructive energies are given a powerful dynamic force, entering permanently into the makeup of the astral and spiritual bodies of each, thus becoming powerful harmonious thought structures that build up the soul's power for progression, and tend to attract harmonious conditions, hence success, in the environment.

At a further stage a still higher union is advisable because the power of a thought depends not merely upon the volume of energy with which it is energized, but also upon the quality of the energy. Physical relations, although they may be emotionally spiritualized and refined to a degree, yet usually retain enough of physical desire to lower their vibratory rate.

They have not, therefore, the power to produce results in the physical world, nor the power to affect the constitution of the spiritual body, that strong emotions have that spring from a still loftier plane. However, it is evident—judging from the vast literature on psychoanalysis that has recently come into existence, and the cure of so many patients by releasing their repressions—most without some training, are not ready for regeneration.

Such a harmonious marriage as has been suggested in the ritual is first referred to as ointment—which is the symbol of sanctity—being upon the head. In other words, in such a holy union the thoughts—for the head is where thinking is done—are lifted up to God and sanctified. The beard is typically an emblem of masculinity, and the priestly robe, or garment, is purposely feminine. Its enfolding form suggests woman. Aaron typifies those who have consecrated their lives to higher service, who know the law, and who enter into marriage with the object of endeavoring to assist each other evolve their divine attributes. The ointment running down upon both the beard and the skirts of the garment symbolizes the opening of the doors of the inner spaces upon such a man and woman.

The next comparison is to the dew of Hermon that descended upon the mountain of Zion. Water is the symbol of the emotions, air is the symbol of aspiration, fire is the symbol of creative energy, and earth is the symbol of practical results. Dew is the product of heat—creative energy—acting upon water—the emotions. Carried up by the air—aspirations—it is finally precipitated on the mountain of Zion; that is, yields the very highest practical results. This dew that falls on Zion, therefore, indicates those unusual spiritual energies that are only contacted when intense love enables the soul to soar to the heights; and even as mountains are the highest portions of the earth, these energies enable work of the highest type for the benefit of mankind to be accomplished.

The ideas meant to be conveyed by the verses quoted were given in the 7th, and further explained in the 14th degree. In this system of degrees of Ancient Masonry the 7th degree revealed the mysteries of generation, the 14th degree revealed the mysteries of regeneration, and the 21st degree revealed the mysteries of the great work. David, no doubt was a high degree Mason.

Therefore, we need not be surprised to find the original of these verses to be the 133rd—1 plus 3 plus 3 equals 7—Psalm. This Psalm is

The Song of Degrees, being the 14th song. The number 7 in the Hermetic System of Names and Numbers (see Course 6, *The Sacred Tarot*), relates to perfect physical union, and the number 14 to complete regeneration, as revealed by the Major Arcana of the tarot.

After the recital of the 133rd Psalm as a prayer, the Master raps once with his gavel, indicating that the will must dominate the first, or physical, plane; whereupon the members are seated.

And now, before taking up the work of a lodge after it has been opened, let us complete our brief survey of the 32 primitive ideas that form the counters of universal language by considering the numerals.

Origin of Arabic Numerals

The Arabic numerals which we commonly employ bear a rough correspondence to cell division after the union of sperm and germ. If this resemblance is more than accidental, it may be questioned how those who originated them, without the aid of a microscope, could know about cell division. The same query arises in reference to their knowledge of the attributes of the planets Uranus, Neptune and Pluto, in the absence of telescopes. They had ESP (Extra-Sensory Perception) well enough developed accurately to describe the influence of these planets, as we now find through research. This being the case, there is no inconsistency involved in believing they might have known, through ESP, of cell division and many other things.

The fertilized cell is itself unity. But a cell possesses polarity, possesses a positive and a negative portion, this constitutes a duality; even as a duality results from the first cell division.

Now in all things possessing life there is a trinity; substance, energy, intelligence. The cell itself may well be represented by a circle; for the circle is the most perfect form, containing within its circumference the greatest possible area within a boundary of a given length. The trinity may be expressed diagrammatically by a triangle inscribed within the half circle representing the dominant polarity. Thus if the sperm is represented, instead of the fertilized cell, the triangle will be found in the positive, or light half; while if the germ is represented, the triangle will be found in the shaded, or negative, half. Reproduction is thus seen to be the union of a positive trinity, the sperm, with a negative trinity, the germ. Where the two trines have their point of contact gives the 7th factor, 7 being perfection of form. But at this point of contact a new trinity, the offspring, is developed, which may be expressed diagrammatically as three trines, or the number 9, the highest digit, the perfect number. The new trinity of substance, energy, and intelligence may then separate itself from its parents to commence an independent cycle or existence. This cycle, or orbit, is expressed by a cypher, which enclosing the whole group as a unity, adds the thought of a new era to the whole unity, giving the number 10.

I shall not go further into these symbolic diagrams, nor shall I try to trace in detail, for they have been greatly conventionalized, the axial divisions and other processes of cell development that may have suggested to the unconscious minds of the Arabian Sages the numerals we now use. Instead I shall now consider the functions of the numbers themselves:

One

The number One expresses the absolute, and suggests infinite possibilities. It is that from which all proceed, which contains all, and to which all finally return. It is evidently a synthesis; for nothing can be imagined not composed of parts. It represents the universal principle, the creative intelligence of Deity, that force which is the motive power of the universe and in man becomes intellect and will. In science it is the law of conservation of energy. In the macrocosm it indicates unlimited potentiality, in man it indicates relative potentiality.

Two

The number Two expresses polarity. It suggests night and day, inhalation and exhalation, heat and cold. The most evident of all things is duality, even truth being dual, esoteric and exoteric, the real and the appearance. Two represents the universal law of sex; attraction and repulsion, love and hate, centripetal force and centrifugal force. In science it is the law that every action is accompanied by an equal and opposite reaction. In the macrocosm it is the positive and the negative; and in man it is represented by reason and intuition, and by his differentiation into the polar opposites, man and woman.

Three

The number Three expresses the union of polar opposites. It is the reaction between forces generating vibration and change. It represents the universal agent, action, or word, and is typical of fecundity. It is the union of forces that is the basis of all life and motion. There is no such thing as freedom from change; for all existence is in motion. In science three represents the laws of dynamics, those that pertain to the generation and control of energy. In the macrocosm it is action, and in humanity it is generation.

Four

The number Four expresses the result of action, the fruit of two interacting forces. It thus represents the practical, the concrete, that which has form and substance; hence is typical of the universal truth of reality. In science it represents the laws of statics, those that pertain to bodies at rest or in equilibrium. In the macrocosm it is the result of action; and in man it is the offspring of experience.

Five

The number Five unites the first four digits, or principles, into a harmonious unity, and thus explains the apparent contradictions in nature. The One Principle, One Law, One Agent, and One Truth do not contradict each other, but imply each other's existence. These four factors are pictured in the sky by the four animals that symbolize the four quadrants of the zodiac. All were synthesized as a fifth in the ancient four fold sphinx; which explains all nature to converge in man. Man has passed through the four elemental realms of life, has triumphed over all submundane degrees of existence, and by virtue of his spiritual supremacy gained their allegiance as obedient servitors. Man, symbolized by five, maintains his health when his magnetic forces are radiated equally by each of the five main points of projection: the hands, feet, and head. In man, and as composed of one and four, it represents the realization that is the outcome of intelligently directed willpower. In the macrocosm, and as composed of two and three, it signifies polarity in action.

Six

The number Six signifies two actions: two times three. But as such it does not represent forces in equilibrium, but forces in a state of vacillation, in a state of action and reaction. It is thus typical of virtue that may be misapplied. As such it signifies weakness and indecision, hesitancy and timidity. As composed of two and four it signifies the realization of polarity. As composed of one and five it represents man dominated by the will of another. In the macrocosm six is force uncontrolled, and in man it is temptation.

Seven

The number Seven as composed of three and four expresses action and realization, and is thus the number of completion of form. Things on the physical plane which have perfection of form are constituted of three active elements and four passive, or formative elements. Seven as composed of two and five signifies man having within his power the law of polarity. As composed of one and six, it signifies indecision overcome, and hitherto uncontrolled forces dominated by intelligent will. As composed of twice three plus one it denotes body, soul, and spirit, united to body, soul, and spirit, guided by intelligence and controlled by will. In the macrocosm it indicates the seven principles of nature, and in man those whom, "God hath joined together," as well as the dominion of intelligence over action, hence victory over temptation.

Eight

The number Eight as composed of two fours expresses two opposite realizations, hence equilibrium, crystallization, stagnation, and possibly death. It is thus the antithesis of progress. It is ultra-conservatism. As composed of three and five it represents man succumbing to action. As composed of two and six it signifies temptation polarized. As consisting of seven and one it denotes the victory over intelligence and will. In the macrocosm eight is the number of inertia, in man it is the number of justice, and also the number of dissolution.

Nine

The number Nine is the Deific number. It is the highest digit, and has many unusual properties. Thus it may be multiplied by any number and the digits repeatedly added together will give 9 as their sum. All numbers above 9, in their last analysis, consist of a root number to which multiples of nine have been added, this root number being always the sum of the digits repeatedly added together. Because of its extraordinary properties, nine was held sacred by the ancients, and is the key by which all their cryptic cycles may be unlocked. As composed of five and four it signifies man realizing all that earth can teach. As consisting of three and six it indicates temptation overcome by action. As composed of two and seven it indicates intuition and reason added to perfectly united body, soul, and spirit with body, soul, and spirit. As being one and eight it signifies that inertia has been overcome by intelligently directed will. In the macrocosm it signifies, by being three times three, action on all three planes, and in man it becomes the number of wisdom.

Ten

The number Ten expresses the same as number one, except that a cypher, symbolizing a complete cycle, has been added. It therefore shows that one round of experience has been completed, and that another cycle of experience is being commenced. Vibrations on the inner plane repeat their chief characteristics in decaves, instead of in octaves. One shows infinite possibilities only, nine shows that all the possibilities of one plane have been experienced, and ten indicates the transition to a new plane where other possibilities await. Ten, then, in the macrocosm indicates the commencement of a new cycle, and in man, as composed of two fives, it indicates man and woman together, humanity at large.

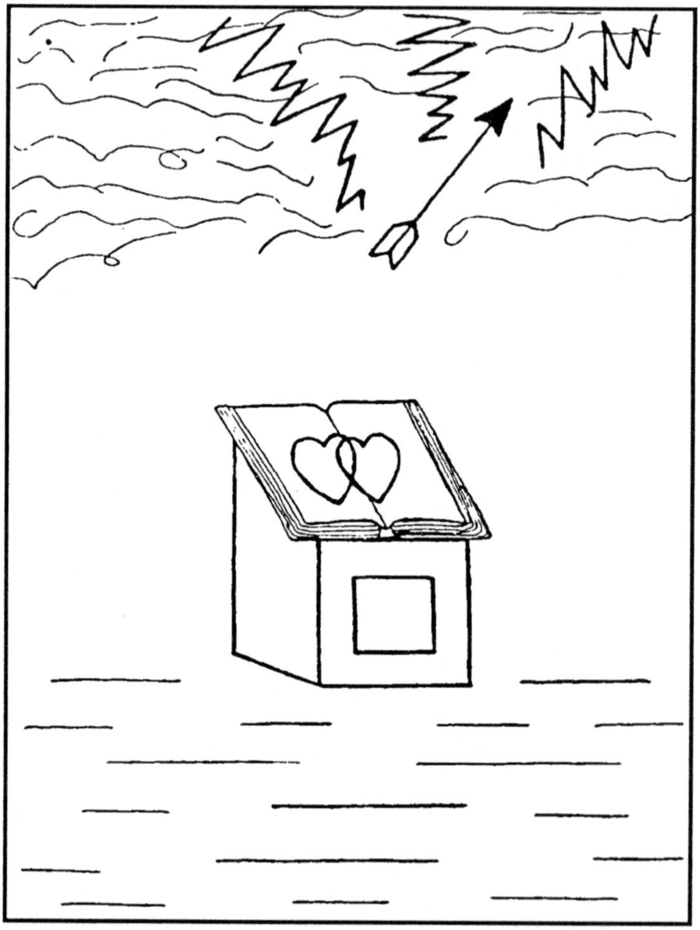

Chapter 5

Initiating a Member

SINCE THE DAY when the spiritual children of the Golden Age, wandering in an earthly paradise were instructed in the arcane laws of life by visitants from celestial worlds, even down to present-day orthodoxy with its fantastic and misunderstood ritual, the Mysteries have been conducted in every land and clime. Their primary object has ever been the same: to impress upon the soul the vital truths of man's past history and future destiny. Their rightful purpose is to enlighten the participant concerning his divine source, the nature of his deific attributes and potentialities, the sublime angelic goal toward which he struggles, and the manner in which he best can hasten his journey to the heights, and thus, no longer bound and shackled by sense and environment, come into full possession of his spiritual heritage.

The ease with which a thing can be remembered depends upon its associations and the vividness of its impression; a psychological law that ever has been made use of to implant important truths indelibly in the mind of the candidate. In the first place, the difficulty of obtaining permission to undergo initiation conveys the impression that something of tremendous importance is to be revealed in the Mysteries, an impression subsequently strengthened by the administration of terrible vows and the acceptance of solemn obligations. Then, with the initiation under way, the situations are so intense, often terrifying, that their impress is left graven unerasably upon the tablets of the memory. Thus did the ancients as well as moderns perpetuate their ideas in never-to-be-forgotten symbolism.

Those whose physical natures were dominant and whose inner perceptions were yet latent had this symbolism seared on their minds with such vividness as easily to be recalled and meditated upon at will. Thus the meaning would filter through from the inner spaces as their soul powers slowly unfolded. To others, of a more sensitive nature, the stress of the trials, and the mystery surrounding the ritual, frequently produced a psychic awakening in which there was true illumination. In this higher consciousness the full meaning and spiritual purport of each symbol was clearly recognized, and their more acute perceptions opened to them new worlds and a realm of undreamed of possibilities.

Now Modern Masonry, no less than Ancient Masonry, explains by its symbolic ritual that the soul descended from a spiritual Eden into material conditions of toil and suffering for the sake of experience. Only through experience are Love, Wisdom, and Self-Consciousness acquired; and only through the conscious application of love, guided by wisdom, is the soul able to win its way homeward again to realms of infinite light, a self-conscious, immortal being. There, in full possession of matured Wisdom and realized Love, it becomes an Angel of the Blest, a Deific Being, the arbiter and creator of a future universe. Such is the glorious destiny of man as taught by seers and sages and as revealed by the ritual of Ancient Masonry.

Each Soul Is Responsible for Its Own Destiny

Though man is now a pilgrim in a vale of tears, far from his native land, besieged by perils and hampered by a thousand difficulties, the road to redemption lies straight ahead. Not salvation by the sacrifice of others! Not a vicarious atonement! Not by the blood of the innocent! No! Such is not the message of Ancient Masonry handed down through a million generations. Instead, it teaches the sacrifice of man's animal nature on the altar of love's devotion, the consecration of the lamb, or creative principle, to a nobler purpose; to the purpose of building an enduring temple for King Sol, the indwelling Ego. Such sacrifices alone enable man to atone for past mistakes, and thus attain salvation, a salvation which frees him from blind fatality and the restrictions of matter.

Ancient Masonry teaches that each soul is a responsible entity working out its own deliverance from a voluntary and purposeful incarceration in matter. Freedom can be obtained only through knowledge of the laws of nature, and conformity in thought and deed to them. It is the exemplification of these laws relating to the development of the body, intellect, and soul, that constitutes the paramount message of Ancient

Masonry to the Twentieth Century world. Those who in the long forgotten past learned in the Mysteries who and what man really is, and the sublime height to which he may attain, bethought themselves of other souls that in the future would attempt to climb the same rugged path their feet had trod. When they gained one victory after another in the struggle for mastery, finally attaining freedom, they therefore left an outline of the work to be done, of methods to be used in surmounting obstacles, of laws to be obeyed in order to triumph. This outline of incomparable value is the ritual of Masonry.

The candidate seeking admittance is called upon to state that his desire for the rites of initiation is entirely voluntary, free from compulsion, and actuated by a favorable opinion of the institution. Now in the Bible story, the serpent in the Garden of Eden represents the wisdom which tempts the soul to leave its spiritual paradise and descend into matter. The soul realizes that only through partaking of the fruit of good and evil, partaking of material experiences, can it develop self-consciousness. This fruit of its experiences in relative conditions brings to it life, wisdom, and love. The candidate, therefore, by his statement of voluntary choice, indicates that the soul, when entering the Cycle of Necessity which constitutes its initiation, is not under compulsion, but acts through the desire to reap the benefit of material incarnation.

Furthermore, the soul entering upon this cyclic pilgrimage, must abide by the laws of nature, even though at times this means toil and suffering. Such is indicated by the candidate's declaration that he promises to conform to all the ancient and established usages and customs of the Fraternity.

The black and white balls used in balloting to determine if the candidate is acceptable represent the soul's experiences in material environment preceding its birth into human form; for before the human state is reached the unconscious mind must traverse the whole scale of life from mineral upward, subjecting each in turn. Through the dual powers of attraction, represented by white balls, and repulsion, represented by black balls, it evolves through all the lower forms of life, in each progressive organism annexing to its domain the attributes and functions inherent to that state. Consequently, in the supreme form of man the scale of life is complete, and he has within his own constitution all types of life, forms, powers, and functions, expressed upon the planet earth, and likewise the germs of every state in the infinite realms above.

Having conquered all states below the human, by the law of affinity he is drawn into the fiery vortex of his parents during their union. The particular soul whose need for expression most closely corresponds to the polarity and spiritual state of the parents becomes magnetically attached to the ovum of the mother. One or more black balls among the white ones indicates the affinity at the time considered is insufficient to make incarnation possible; but if the ballot is clear, it indicates that no strong repulsive forces are present, and that conception takes place.

The ballot boxes are passed by the two Deacons, representing Venus and Mars, the planets of love and passion, of attraction and repulsion. It is the vibrations of love and passion that attract the soul to its future parents. The ballot box is passed three times to indicate that the vibrations making conception possible may spring from one or more of three distinct planes. When vibrations from one plane preponderate a soul of a very different character is attracted than if the vibrations are chiefly those of another plane.

If the union is purely physical, the interplay of animal magnetism attracts a soul whose need for expression is largely physical. If in the union there is love based on mutual admiration, trust, esteem, and kindred mental qualities, a higher type of entity will be drawn into the magnetic current. And should there be marked harmony between the parents on all three planes, engendering soul love as well as magnetic affinity and mutual mental interests, the conditions will be fulfilled for bringing into the world the highest type of mental and moral genius, endowed with a physique capable of sustaining him in his untiring efforts for the benefit of mankind. From such unions have sprung the noble philosophers, the inspired reformers, and the truly great men of all times.

Significance of the Manner in Which the Candidate Is Clothed

When the candidate has been accepted he is led into a small room adjoining the main lodge, where he is prepared by the Senior Deacon for his entrance into the lodgeroom proper. This small room, or antechamber, represents the womb of woman, where each soul ushered into mundane existence is prepared for its final earthly initiation. During the period of gestation the fetus briefly passes through the various stages that correspond to the lower forms of life by which it has ascended to its present estate, lastly, of course, having passed through and subjected the realms of animal life. As the Senior Deacon represents the animal soul, the organization of which in the animal kingdom paved the way to incarnation in human form, we find him rightly chosen as the one to prepare the candidate for human experience, to lead him symbolically through the avenue of physical birth into the realm of self-consciousness.

The animal soul, corresponding to the Senior Deacon, supervises the various automatic functions of the body. Thus it is that the heart beats, the lungs breathe, and the processes of digestion, assimilation, and secretion are carried on, largely independent of conscious thought and direction. When conception takes place, it is also the animal soul that directs the building of the embryo, the clothing with a material form the soul soon to see in human form the light of day. Therefore, in the antechamber of the lodge, first making him remove all his garments but his shirt, the candidate is clothed by the Senior Deacon.

Covering the upper portion of his body, and thus representing the astral form in which the soul functions just before incarnation, the shirt is not removed. The astral form, whether in or out of matter, covers the soul through all the various transformations by which it scales the cyclic rounds of evolutionary life on earth.

His lower garments are removed, and in their stead he is clad in red flannel drawers. Flannel is made from the wool of sheep, and is therefore under the dominion of the astrological sign Aries. Aries is the sign of creative energy, and when the Ancient Masons wished to denote virility, they used as symbol a sheep, a ram, a lamb, or some garment made from them. Aries rules the head of man, and thus signifies mental creative energy as well as that physical, but in this instance the color is red, denoting blood, lust, and carnal desires; the physical aspect of the planet Mars. The shirt, which the candidate still wears, indicates that the soul has not evolved high enough to be free from its astral body. It is still bound and limited by an astral raiment largely organized by the grosser desires and impulses of the animal realms through which it has just ascended; the red drawers indicating animal passion and the use of creative energy for sensual gratification.

To represent the soul's inability to see and comprehend either physical facts or spiritual truths when first born into human form, the candidate is blindfolded. This condition is also typical of the masses of humanity who have no knowledge either of physical science or of esoteric wisdom. They grope through life swayed by every wind that blows, accepting as fact the assertions of others who pose as repositories of wisdom, yet who are as destitute of the true light as they themselves.

Such understanding as they have is negative, based upon the authority of others. This is symbolized by the left, or negative foot alone being unshod, free for action, while the right is hampered by a shoe made from the skin of an animal. Right understanding is as yet restricted by, immersed in, the animal propensities. In this stage of development, as well as at birth, man's emotions and aspirations spring from material motives. This is shown by the candidate's left breast being bare. Furthermore, man's works at this stage are executed upon the physical plane. This is signified by one arm being hampered by clothing, while the left, or negative arm, to be free to work, is left bare.

Now the ego, or spiritual potentiality, is incapable of descending into material conditions, which the soul alone can enter; but at all times there is a faint vibratory line of communication between the two. Thus the soul is vitalized and sustained, receiving energy from the ego to enable it ever to struggle upward. This line of rapport, by which the soul at all times is connected with the ego, is represented by the cable-tow.

This cable-tow is placed around the neck and left arm of the candidate. The neck is ruled by Venus, the planet of love. The cable-tow placed around the neck, therefore, points to the power of affection to strengthen the line of communication between the soul and ego. The arm is the agent of service, and the cable-tow around the left arm indicates the paramount value, as an agent for strengthening the bond between soul and ego, of being of greatest possible service to others on the physical plane. The power of love to lead the soul from the lower to the higher is further emphasized; for it is the duty of the Junior Deacon, representing Venus, the planet of love, to lead the candidate to the door of the lodge.

As the candidate enters the lodge, the Senior Deacon, representing Mars, the planet of strife, presses a compass in a painful manner against his naked left breast. The mother's love for her unborn child conducts it up to the period of parturition, where stern and cruel Mars takes charge of affairs. In so far as the higher laws of life have been violated by passion and sensualism, in that much does the offspring inherit a body and mind tortured by emotions and desires that conflict with those laws. It is only when man's desires are not contrary to the spiritual laws of his being that he is able to escape misery and suffering, sickness and failure, and the thousand and one ills to which the flesh is heir. The higher laws are represented by the compass, and the purely physical desires and emotions that sometimes conflict with these laws to cause suffering are symbolized by the left breast.

Inside the lodge the candidate kneels while a prayer to the Father of the universe is offered asking that his life may be consecrated to service, and that wisdom may come to him. When asked in whom he places his trust, he answers: "In God." It is only when the neophyte consecrates his life to Deity and places his faith in divine providence that he may expect the assistance of unseen helpers who will conduct his initiation and will lead him to the light. Man's inward yearning for something higher than the purely physical, his devout aspirations and unselfish resolutions, are prayers that ascend to the upper spheres and attract forces and intelligences that unknown to himself lead him to the fulfillment of his hopes. It has been truly said that nothing is impossible to a good and determined man; for faith is the avenue to the soul world.

The candidate is led three times around the room while the Master reads the 133rd Psalm, which has already been explained. This indicates that man must evolve through three planes: the physical, the astral and the spiritual. The Junior Warden represents the spiritual body. Therefore, to convey the thought that on the third, or spiritual plane, man functions in a spiritual body, the candidate is halted in front of the Junior Warden. Furthermore, as the Senior Warden represents the divine soul, and the Master represents the ego, both of which are also present on the spiritual plane, he is next led to the Senior Warden and finally, as representing the most interior of all, to the Master.

The Master demands to know from whence he comes and whither he travels. To which he replies that he comes from the west and travels to the east in search of light. The answer is entirely correct; for the west, astrologically considered, is feminine, and thus symbolizes matter, while the east is masculine, and symbolizes spirit. The soul involved from spirit into matter, but is now on the ascending arc, evolving from matter to spirit. It therefore is traveling eastward, toward the source of light, toward spirituality.

The First Step Toward the Light

Spirituality, however, is not gained by haphazard effort. Its attainment requires systematic endeavor based upon a full understanding of just what is sought and the various steps by which it may be reached. The candidate, therefore, is next instructed in the proper manner of approaching the east. He is taken back to the west, or material plane, and caused to advance by one upright regular step, to the first step, his feet forming the right angle of an oblong square, his body erect at the altar.

This oblong square is made by the candidate stepping forward with his left foot and drawing the heel of the right foot into the hollow of it, making the feet stand at right angles. The feet symbolize understanding, and thus placed represent the union of male and female. The upright body symbolizes will. The first step toward the light, therefore, according to the Ancient Masons, is the will to understand the mysteries of generation. This symbolic attitude implies that man should always keep his desires and passions under the control of a resolute will. He should never be inconsiderate of the finer feelings and delicate sensitiveness of woman, should never force unwelcome attentions upon her, but permit her to abide her own pleasure; for in forming the oblong square it is the left, or feminine foot, that makes the first advance.

The teachings of the Ancient Masons in this respect, as revealed by symbolism, seem to be this: They regarded marriage as a sacred institution, in which man and woman should assist each other through arousing tender and sympathetic emotions, noble aspirations, and spiritual ideals. Undue aggressiveness on the part of either is sure to defeat this end, because love is not subject to demand, but must be won. The man who forces attentions upon a woman, even though she be his wife, quickly turns affection into disgust and love into loathing. Nor should the woman who, as soon as the legal knot is tied, ceases to put forth an effort to retain the love and admiration of her husband, expect to arouse in him those higher feelings and emotions that give to marriage its constructive power.

Love thrives upon kindness and tender consideration. Little attentions, thoughtfulness for the welfare of the other, and sympathetic understanding, tend to sustain the warmth of affection between man and wife. Unless the desire for marriage is mutual there is no fusion of the magnetic forces, and the energies set in motion by one, meeting with no energies of opposite polarity with which to blend, act as unbalanced forces that set up discords within the astral constitution. But when desires are mutual, and the energies aroused are of approximately equal intensity, finding complete expression by each, there is a fusion of forces that sets up harmonies within the astral constitution, and these have great constructive power.

Perhaps it should be emphasized, as the symbolism indicates such emphasis, that both should find complete expression if the energies set in motion are to conduce to health, happiness, and attainment. But such emphasis may be found in much detail in the works on psychoanalysis in which the pathological condition that may arise from such lack of expression is termed the incompletion complex. The advantage of marriage, from a purely physical standpoint, may also be left to the vital statisticians; who show that spinsters are much more subject to disease than married women, and that bachelors are markedly less long lived than married men.

That magnetic forces, then, may act constructively, and not destructively, it is necessary that there should be kindred feelings which establish a rapport between husband and wife. Through this rapport there is an exchange of energies, and a complete blend that causes the forces to act, not divergently, but in unison. This principle—that there must be unity of desires, unity of thought, and unity of emotions—according to Ancient Masonry, is important not alone on the physical plane of endeavor, but also on the plane of purely mental union and the plane of purely spiritual marriage.

Aside from this unity, the grade of feeling aroused is the important thing. Like attracts like. If thoughts are high, if the heart is filled with pure love and sacred devotion, if the soul outpours in tender blessings, invisible energies are attracted of like quality. They are attracted at such times even more readily than at any other; because when the soul is aroused to great intensity it contacts more fully the inner worlds. The intensity that has the power to contact the astral and draw a soul and provide for its incarnation is an intensity that at the time places the person directly in touch with astral forces. If the thoughts be evil, evil energies are attracted; but if the thoughts be noble, and the aspirations lofty, the higher spheres are contacted and the energies attracted are spiritually constructive.

Jachin and Boaz are United by Electromagnetic Boundary-Line Energy

The two pillars, Jachin and Boaz, one at the right and the other at the left of the great Eastern Gateway, divide the zodiac, even as the earth is divided into two polarities. Extending from one polarity on the earth to the other are lines of force, constituting a magnetic field, which exerts the commonly observed influence upon the needle of a compass.

Likewise between Jachin and Boaz, when they are considered as the inner plane and the outer plane—as well as between man and woman—there are lines of force and exchanges of energy. And the character of these energies—their trend and rate of vibration—are pronouncedly influenced by the relations between husband and wife, as set forth to the candidate in the symbolism of his FIRST STEP TOWARD THE LIGHT.

Whether or not Einstein's General Theory of Relativity is correct in other particulars need not here concern us. But according to that theory, and according to theories of other scientists, the ordinary ideas about time, space and gravitation are applicable to things which move with the more commonly observed velocities; but when the velocity of light is approached, the classical laws of gravitation no longer apply, space no longer has the relations commonly assigned to it, and time slows down.

In reference to time having different characteristics on the inner plane (the structure and vibrations of which are fully explained in Course 1, *Laws of Occultism*), on April 25 of this year (1938) experiments were described to the National Academy of Science at Washington, which are supposed to prove the reality of the ether (which we term the BOUNDARY-LINE SUBSTANCE) and to verify the assumption of Einstein's Theory of Relativity that time slows down as high velocities are acquired. The experiments were conducted by Dr. Herbert E. Ives. To quote from the report:

> The newest (experiment), concerning one of the great mysteries of science, involved timing events in a vacuum tube. It showed that a moving clock keeps slower time than one standing still. It gave an inkling to the nature of 'ether' as probably a sea of energy, stationary and filling all known space.

In considering the realms of Jachin and Boaz it should be kept in mind that time relations, conditions affecting space, and the influence of gravitation which so commonly limit activity on the outer plane of Boaz, do not thus limit activity and the range of perception and consciousness on the inner plane of Jachin; and that the only communication which can be established between the two planes is through utilizing the BOUNDARY-LINE ENERGY which has a velocity similar to that of light.

As the soul of man is an organization on the inner plane, while man is on the earth he can affect it in any way only through utilizing the boundary-line energy. This boundary-line energy is generated by the cells of the physical body. These constitute miniature electric batteries, of which the nerve cells are most potent. It is utilized as the nerve currents which direct the physical activity, and as the energy which enables all types of objective thinking. Through this boundary-line energy thought and states of consciousness experienced on the physical plane build the structure of the soul on the inner plane.

Emotion of any kind is due to the presence of an unusual amount of this boundary-line electrical energy in the nervous system. It is this excess of boundary-line energy which enables certain experiences of life so powerfully to impress themselves upon the unconscious mind (which occupies the inner plane) that they form complexes, fixations, or other mental difficulties. And it is through an excess of this boundary-line energy that the inner plane is consciously contacted either negatively or positively; negatively if the potential is low, and positively if the potential is high and thus subject to the individual's control.

As in affectional relations of any type there is also generated an excess of this boundary-line energy, the thoughts and emotions then present in the mind, or during the period in which electromagnetic forces are present in unusual volume, have a tremendous power to cross from the plane of Boaz to the plane of Jachin and do work there. That is, they then, because of the volume of boundary-line energy available for their use, become powerful agents to build or destroy.

They enable the level of the astral plane to be contacted which corresponds to the thoughts with which they are charged at the time. And not only does this enable the intelligence of this level to be contacted, but there is indrawn, to feed the soul, substance of that vibratory level.

Nutrition on the Inner Plane

On the physical plane we partake of food by eating. About 72 percent of all protoplasm, however, is oxygen, a large portion of which is partaken of through breathing. We partake of food through breathing quite as truly as through eating; and as a relative measure of the importance of the two methods of food gaining it is known that we can go without eating or drinking considerable time, but can only survive a short time without breathing. On the higher astral, and on the spiritual plane, man no longer must eat organic substance to live, he no longer eats his fellows—for even plants are his lowly kin. In these higher realms he is nourished entirely through a process similar to breathing.

Furthermore, even while yet occupying a physical body, his astral body to some extent, and his spiritual body entirely, is nourished by a process similar to breathing. Every mental state adds its energies to the astral body. Every mental state also has an attractive power. Deep thought, or depressive thoughts, cause a person on the physical plane markedly to lessen his breathing. Surprise, good news, or excitement causes a person to take a deep breath, or to breathe deeply. Acting on principles not dissimilar, every emotion, every mental state, affects the breathing on the inner plane. It affects it not merely as to quantity, but also as to quality. The refinement of the substance built into the astral body depends upon the refinement of the thoughts and feelings. And it is only when the feelings and emotions are up to a certain refinement that they can influence spiritual substance in any way. But if the emotions are intense, and at the same time lofty, tender, and unselfish, as they are when true refined love is in the ascendant, they cause a respiration of spiritual substance. They contact this inner plane and draw to the spiritual body spiritual nourishment which builds up and strengthens it. Lofty, noble, tender, aspiring emotions build up the spiritual form by supplying it with spiritual food.

Possessing an understanding of the mysteries of generation, and keeping his desires under the control of a resolute will, the next step of the candidate symbolizes wedlock. It is made before the altar, to indicate that of all the acts possible to man, this is the most holy, sacred, and ennobling, when actuated by love, and its inner laws are obeyed. It is then that the inner spaces open and the germs of divine power are contacted. This is the mystery of the Holy Shekinah, so carefully guarded by the Jewish Kabalists. The candidate steps off with his right foot, and kneels on his left knee, the knees forming right angles. This position gives the appearance of a hollow square, or room, above which the body is virtually perpendicular. He then places his left hand, palm up, under the Holy

Bible, and his right hand on the compass and square that are on the Bible. In this position he is required to take the oath.

The Bible is the "Oral Law," the compass and square symbolize the "Written Law," and the position of his hands symbolize union. His attitude before the altar signifies his willingness to sacrifice his lower nature to the higher self. Symbolically, he thus swears strictly to obey both the spiritual laws and the physical laws of generation; and in token of his sincerity he is required to kiss the book twice.

As the result of obedience to these laws, and the realization of the higher love, his soul aspires to wisdom and awakens to a knowledge of higher truths. This aspiration and knowledge draw to him those who are able further to enlighten him. To indicate this, the brethren clap their hands and stamp their feet on the floor, whereupon the bandage drops from his eyes. The clapping of hands signifies the work of those who strive to spread the light, the stamping of feet signifies their understanding, and the bandage dropping from the eyes indicates the illumination that results from noble sentiments inspired by pure love.

When love has removed the scales from his eyes the candidate perceives Three Great Lights which are revealed by Three Lesser Lights. The Three Great Lights of Masonry, so the Master explains to him, are the Holy Bible, the Square, and the Compass. The Bible, or Oral Law, contains in its symbolism the knowledge gained by investigating nature's laws in the remote past. The Compass and Square, or written Law, represent the actual forces of nature. The square relates to the physical world, to the realm of effects, and the compass relates to the inner planes, the realm of causes. Together they embrace all natural law, and exemplify the Hermetic Axiom: "As it is above, so it is below."

The Three Lesser Lights of Masonry are three burning tapers placed on candlesticks, standing in a triangular group. They typify man's reason, his physical senses, and his psychic senses. Man perceives with his physical senses the physical universe. With his psychic senses he perceives the inner worlds. With his reason he gathers together the separate strands of experience, outer and inner, and thus gains knowledge of both exoteric and esoteric law. He can both read the records left in books by men, and read the records left in the astral world, as well as make independent investigation.

In the universal temple the three greater lights are the Sun, Moon, and Venus; and the three lesser lights are their corresponding qualities of

Life, Light, and Love, that give purpose to existence, serve as beacons to light the pilgrim on his lonely way, and beckon him encouragingly to struggle ever upward.

The grip of an E.A. Mason is a pressure of the thumb at the base of the other's index finger. In palmistry the thumb denotes power of will. The base of the first finger is ruled by the planet Jupiter, as are also the phrenological faculties of veneration, benevolence, hope, spirituality, and those impulses that spring from generosity and the feeling of good fellowship. When, then, the Master says, "I now present you my right hand in token of friendship and brotherly love," he indicates the paramount importance of unselfishness and good will in spiritual attainment. The grip symbolizes the will to be kind and benevolent. Its name is Boaz, and in naming it the word is halved, the candidate saying the letters "B-O," and the Master saying, "A-Z."

Boaz is the left hand pillar of the porch of Solomon's Temple. In the cosmic lodge it typifies the southern half of the ecliptic; for when the sun enters this half the nights are longer than the days and winter gains victory over summer. In humanity, Boaz represents the formative powers of woman; in the individual man it represents his left side and his negative attributes. Even as man and woman each contain within themselves both positive and negative qualities, so each half of the ecliptic contains a positive and a negative season, the two being divided by the solstice. Thus the signs Libra, Scorpio, and Sagittarius, belong to B-O, and Capricorn, Aquarius, and Pisces, to A-Z.

Around the Zodiac Through Boaz and Jachin

Now as the sun, typifying the soul, reaches the sixth sign, which is an earthy sign, or six pots of stone, it turns, by means of the vineyard, water into wine. Wine is symbolic of the creative energy of the Lamb, but as the sun is in the sign of the Virgin and at the commencement of the feminine season, it here must symbolize the creative function particularly of woman. The cross upon which the sun is crucified is that where summer and winter meet, the cross of Libra where the sun crosses the celestial equator. By this crucifixion the sun is drawn down into the signs of winter, even as the soul is drawn from a spiritual state into matter, thus entering the region of Boaz. Consequently, the wine pressed in autumn from the grape, and the blood flowing from wounds of a crucified sun as his forces wane, both express the redemptive power of woman's creative periods which make possible the weaving of a material garment, or shroud, for the incarnating soul.

The sun reaches its lowest point, or place of the soul's birth into matter, at the time it enters the earthy sign Capricorn, thus being born in the manger of the goat. Capricorn is ruled by the planet Saturn, therefore, he is persecuted by the ruler of the country, by Herod. Egypt is the land of darkness and privation, and this is the time of year marked by dearth and famine, hence the sun flees into Egypt. Nevertheless, the twelfth day after birth at Christmas, the sun may be perceived to be gaining in power. This twelfth day is called the Epiphany, meaning appearance; and so we learn that the Christos, when twelve years old, put in an appearance at the temple and manifested his true character. During the remainder of his youth, due to the clouds that obscure the sky at this time of year, although gradually conquering this region of sin as he moves northward, he is lost to view.

By the Hermetic System of Astrology, one day's movement in the sky measures out the influence for one year in the life of man. The sun's movement through the 30 degrees of Capricorn equals thirty years of life—thirty years of age before it enters the sign of the Man, Aquarius. From the urn of Aquarius flow forth the baptismal rains of winter that melt the snow and ice and purify the earth; and as soon as the sun is thirty degrees of age, the baptism takes place. Furthermore, as soon as he has left the sign of Satan behind him—the sign Capricorn—we find him tempted, but saying; "Get thee behind me Satan." In Aquarius, the sign of wisdom, of knowledge of good and evil, his true work begins. The emotions—shown by the water from the Aquarian urn—lifts his soul to a spiritual baptism, and the Holy Ghost descends in the form of a dove, sacred to Venus the planet of love, and lights upon him.

As the result of wisdom and inspiration, intuition and reason, the personal love engendered in Aquarius expands as the sun moves northward toward the region of Jachin, or spirit, until it becomes the teaching of brotherly love, or love for all mankind, the utopian ideal of the sign Pisces. From this sign of the fish, then, he draws his disciples to become anglers of men.

After delivering to the world his spiritual message, as indicated by light predominating over darkness, the days being longer than the nights while the sun is in the northern half of the zodiac, the sun again approaches the autumnal cross to enter Boaz. Judas is there, represented by the sign of death, Scorpio, thirty degrees—thirty pieces of silver—from the cross of Libra. After the crucifixion the sun descends into the tomb of Capricorn, the lowest point in its cycle, where it enters this earthy sign. At this point, which is the winter solstice, the sun in so far as north and south movement is concerned apparently is stationary. But after three days in the tomb, the stone is rolled away by the angel of the Lord—the angle of the Law—in this case the southern angle of the ecliptic. His ascension into the spiritual region of Jachin, into the summer zodiacal signs, takes place on Easter, which is the first Sunday after the First Full Moon after the sun crosses the vernal equinox.

Man immersed in frigid materialism has as little genial warmth as the sun after it dies on the autumnal cross. To be rejuvenated he must experience a higher love, a higher union, even as the sun is resurrected and rejuvenated on the rosy cross of the vernal equinox. Union, like that of the autumnal equinox, may result in death and destruction, the icy selfishness of winter; or, like that of the vernal cross, bring warmth, affection, and the blush of dawn of a new era. The sun, resurrected by the virile powers of the Lamb, or Aries, typifies the soul drawn by pure affections from material winter into Jachin, the realm of spirituality. The true ascension does not take place in the case of the sun, however, without the assistance of the moon, for Easter depends upon Full Moon. Likewise, the noblest efforts and highest ideals of man depend upon the refining influence of woman, and he ascends into the truly spiritual realms only with her co-operation.

As to the word Boaz, we find in the tarot that the letter "B" is "The Gate to the Sanctuary," and the letter "O" is "The Lightning Struck Tower." The former pictures a woman at the gate to the holy of holies, and the latter indicates the destructive use of the creative forces. The letter "A" is "The Magus," typical of intelligence and will; and the letter "Z" is "The Chariot of Triumph," illustrating victory over temptation and sovereignty of mind over matter.

The letters thus represent the progress of the sun through the negative half of the year, first descending into darkness, and later ascending in triumph over it. They also sign-board the way by which the discerning may triumph over physical limitations and reach spiritual illumination.

Significance of the Lamb-Skin Apron

The candidate is told that the lamb-skin apron has been worn by the great men of earth; and as typifying the virility that must sustain all worthy effort this is undoubtedly true. It is said to be more ancient than the Golden Fleece or the Roman Eagle, and more honorable than the Star and Garter. The Golden Fleece is symbol of the sun's virile powers in the sign of the Ram. The Roman Eagle is symbol of the sun's fruitfulness in the sign Scorpio; for the eagle is one symbol used for this zodiacal sign of sex. The five-pointed star typifies intelligent man. The garter, upon which the Star and Garter order is founded, was originally a girder used by women at their creative periods. The order thus honors woman's power to mold the destiny of the human race, and consecrates itself to use its creative energies intelligently.

The shape of the apron is a square surmounted by a triangle. The lower portion is the passive square, Boaz, typifying the four elemental realms, the four lower sections of man's constitution, the formative powers of woman, and matter as distinct from spirit. The trine above, with its point tapering toward heaven, symbolizes the active Jachin, typical of the higher trinity of man's constitution, the creative attribute of man, spirit as distinct from matter, and the divine fire of heaven.

The strings of the apron tied about the candidate's waist, the region ruled by the sign Libra; corresponding to the autumnal cross, divides his body into two halves as the zodiac is divided by the equinoctial colure. The portion of the body below the waist is ruled by those signs in which the sun is found in winter. The body also naturally is divided into right and left halves, this dividing line corresponding to the solstitial colure, which divides both Jachin and Boaz into positive and negative portions. The apron strings crossing this vertical division divide the body into four sections. The candidate thus accurately represents the universe above divided into the four quadrants that give rise to the four seasons. The apron, a trine above and a square below, or a full complement of seven, symbolizes the seven planets which move ceaselessly through the four quadrants of heaven. The point of the apron, representing the sun, is worn exactly over the solar, or sun, plexus.

In this degree, typical of the material plane of effort, the square only covers the region of Scorpio. This indicates that the creative energy is expended on the physical plane. The rapport between body, soul, and spirit, therefore, is imperfect, and the higher trinity of man's constitution has but little influence over the lower quaternary. The raising of the creative forces to a higher plane of expression, the process of regeneration, is indicated by turning up one corner of the apron. To indicate that the forces have been so completely spiritualized that the lower quaternary is completely controlled and directed by the higher trinity, the flap of the apron is permitted to fall down over the square. This signifies that the ego manifests completely through the body.

The Candidate Tries to Borrow Money

In concluding the initiation the candidate is asked for a piece of money, or for something metallic. As he has nothing of the kind with him he tries, but in vain, to borrow. Money represents value, but to the soul the thing of value is wisdom. Knowledge is earned through experience. Man is born into the world in ignorance, and by his own efforts he must earn wisdom. He cannot borrow wisdom from another nor can another learn his lessons for him. Experiences on the physical plane are of various kinds, and even as metal is of more value than common earth, so are certain experiences, symbolized by metal, of higher quality and greater value than others. These finer experiences, though still of the physical plane, are not to be slighted, for they are necessary steps in progression.

By the same symbol is also conveyed the information that knowledge of the higher mysteries can never be purchased for material considerations. The candidate's effort to purchase his way into initiation fails, as it must always fail; for the real truths of nature are revealed only to the worthy, and without price.

"Knock and it will be opened unto you."

♉

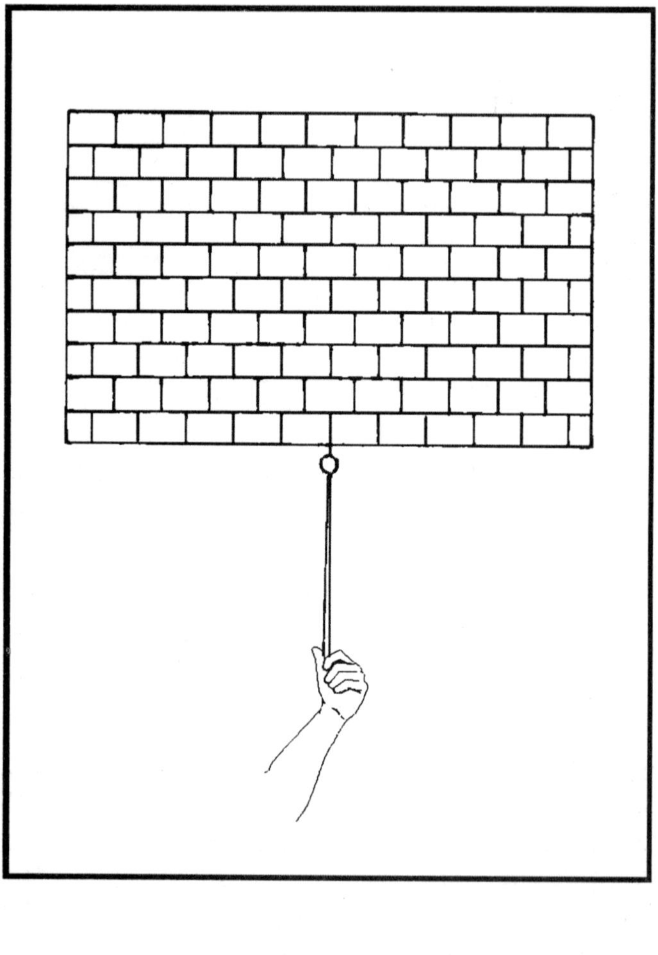

Chapter 6

Fellowcraft

THE RITUAL of Freemasonry is a symbolic exposition of man's functions and possibilities. It illustrates the correspondence between the macrocosm and the microcosm at the important points in the soul's cyclic journey, and thus serves as a road map to spiritual attainment. We find, therefore, that the Entered Apprentice degree treats of man on the physical plane. The Master Mason's degree treats of man on the spiritual plane of existence. And the Fellowcraft degree, which we are now considering, treats of man in association with the astral plane.

Now upon the physical plane man has a seven-fold constitution. But at the death of the physical body both the physical form and the etheric body are lost. Physical substance and etheric substance, as most physicists now agree due to experiments conducted in the effort to prove or disprove Einstein's Theory of Relativity, cannot have a velocity greater than that of light, which in a vacuum is 186,271 miles per second. And astral substance cannot have a velocity less than that of light. That is, velocities in the ether approximating that of light are the Boundary-Line between the two planes of existence. And as the physical body and the etheric body cannot exist on the astral plane, which is the region where the soul functions immediately after death until it has evolved sufficiently to pass to the spiritual plane, man on the astral plane has a five-fold constitution.

Those parts of man corresponding to the Treasurer and the Secretary, even when man functions voluntarily on the astral plane before death, are left behind. Consequently we find that a lodge of Fellowcraft Masons may be opened by five officers; a Master, two Wardens, and two

Deacons. And, instead of being a ground plan of King Solomon's Temple, the F.C. lodgeroom is said to represent a middle chamber of the temple; that is, it corresponds to the middle, or astral plane.

The password of the Fellowcraft degree is Shibboleth. This word means plenty, and refers to the abundance and high vibratory rate of etheric energy generated in the human nervous system by those striving to attain regeneration. This super-vitalization is a great aid to one who desires to pass from the physical body and travel consciously on the astral plane without a break in consciousness. In fact, so essential was it considered by the Ancient Masons that no one is permitted to remain in the F.C. lodge who has not, in some measure, accomplished this; that is, who has not the proper password. To state it plainly, generation in the physical sense pertains solely to the physical plane, and when man reaches the astral, either through the avenue of death, or through voluntary sojourn while yet possessing a physical body, marriage becomes a higher, yet less specialized, fusion.

The Masonic ritual states that this pass was instituted in remembrance of a quarrel between a Jewish judge and the Ephraimites, that resulted in a battle. The Ephraimites were routed, and guards were placed along the River Jordan that they might not pass. All passing the river were required to pronounce the name Shibboleth. The Ephraimites, being of another tribe, were unable to pronounce it thus, saying Sibboleth, which revealed their identity, and they were slain to the number of forty and two thousand.

According to the Hermetic System of Names and Numbers (see Course 6, *The Sacred Tarot*), the fifth Hebrew letter, which was omitted from the password by the Ephraimites, denotes the feminine principle in nature, and applied to humanity it denotes woman. Its omission from the word signifying the process of regeneration typifies those who attempt regeneration while living lives that are isolated from the opposite sex.

Let no one think that the Ancient Masons taught there is any danger in a chaste life. Chastity, under normal circumstances is quite consonant with physical health and physical balance; for nature has adequately provided for such a contingency. In fact, when nature is not violently tampered with she usually keeps her children from disaster.

But there are those who make great virtue of the celibate life. Numerous sects today quote scriptural passages to prove that wonderful advantages result from sex repression, in spite of the very obvious circumstance that those making such claims, as well as their followers, have not made any great attainment, and usually have the psychic faculties opened in a way that gives erroneous visions and distorted notions. One of the favorite quotations is from I John; 4;9: "Whosoever is born of God doth not commit sin; for his seed remaineth in him; and he cannot sin, because he is born of God."

A reading of the passage in the Bible preceding this one shows that the seed referred to is the seed of righteousness implanted by the Son of God. But this, and other passages, are misconstrued to mean that in some way man is greatly benefited and spiritualized by never losing his physical seed. There is undoubtedly a great amount of nonsense afloat in regard to this.

Among other things, it is quite commonly taught that the seed is reabsorbed into the blood stream and thus confers magnetic strength and psychic power. Yet a fuller knowledge of the nature of the seed indicates that such absorption does not take place, and that if it did it would be a detriment to the physical body. The spermatozoon, which is the male seed, for instance, is to all intents and purposes a flagellate cell. That is, it is an independent one-celled organism provided with a whip-like tail by which it lashes itself through whatever fluid it is in. If such a cell should enter the blood stream it would be, while it still lived, a parasite; as much a parasite as the protozoon microbes—certain ones of which cause malaria and sleeping sickness—which it greatly resembles. It is very doubtful, however, that the seed does thus enter the blood. At least it does not unless forcibly retained; for nature has her safety valves, and under normal conditions the seed when so abundant as to cause danger passes from the body with other secretions.

It is quite likely that the basis of this notion lies in a misunderstanding. For the glands associated with the seed, the gonads, have been found by physiologists to be the most important of all agents for restoring youthfulness and vigor of body and mind. Gland transplantation, in many cases, has produced marvelous results in this respect. Both old men and old women have been restored, at least for a time, to youth, vigor, and the functions of earlier life. But this regenerating substance is the endocrine secretion—which enters the blood stream under any sexual excitement, and does not pass from the body in sexual union—and not the seed.

Therefore, let those who wish to retain youth and vigor study how to keep their various glands, particularly the gonads, from wearing out; and how to keep these glands vigorous and healthful, and they will be on the way to an actual accomplishment of that which some imagine may be attained through mere retention of the physical seed. The teachings of the Ancient Masons, while making no mention of endocrine glands, are such as to indicate that they had studied and mastered methods of preserving and strengthening these glands, and thus not only lived in full vigor to a greater age than people live today, but also arrived at a much greater spiritual power.

Forced Celibacy

Before turning from the subject of forced celibacy still another fallacy should be mentioned. It is often stated that because the sex fluids contain the very quintessence of life that their loss results in great depletion, and that their retention leads to great vitality and power. Now there is no denying that excess in this direction is devitalizing. Nevertheless we must bear in mind that nature has provided for the expenditure of a normal amount of energy in reproduction. That is, a normal quantity of such fluids are manufactured by the body, and if not used in reproduction will find a way to leave the body. Also, man has normal muscular strength and normal mental strength.

It might be supposed that if man did not use up his muscular energy in exercise that he would retain his strength. But the facts are that if he fails to take the normal amount of physical exercise, not only his body weakens and his health fails, but his mental powers deteriorate also. And it might be thought that if man did not exercise his mind that it would be strong and vigorous; but lack of exercise weakens the mind. And as the sexual function is an essential portion of man's constitution, we can hardly help drawing the conclusion that prohibiting sexual expression is bound to weaken the sexual nature and that this in turn will react upon the body and mind in a manner to lessen their vigor.

This is not a brief in favor of indulgence. It is an attempt to explain the real nature of regeneration, in which physical union is no longer necessary, as taught by the Ancient Masons. But before being able to understand regeneration we must know something about generation. A whole school of psychoanalytic doctors have sprung into existence and have a widespread practice today, because they are able to correct and heal thousands of cases of serious maladies caused by repressed sex desires. Freudian literature is now known to almost everyone. And the first step in the treatment of those afflicted through repression is to get them to recognize that there is nothing ungodly in normal sexual desire and expression.

There is, however, according to the teachings of the Ancient Masons, a higher expression of sex than the physical. Regeneration is the sublimation of desires into aspirations. Physical unions are no longer necessary because there is a higher, finer, magnetic union that satisfies. Desires are not repressed, they are transmuted. No effort is made to retain the sexual fluids, because, to a great extent the energy that previously was consumed in their manufacture now is used in the manufacture of etheric energy. In other words, instead of forcing a condition upon the physical, there is no longer a desire for physical expression because the energies are expressing themselves in a more refined manner.

When the thoughts enthusiastically turn to a higher, better, more spiritual mode of expressing the love nature, there need be no concern about the physical; for the energies go where the thoughts are directed. Under such circumstances, the physical will take care of itself, and no attention need be given to it.

In regeneration, as taught by the Ancient Masons, lust, passion, and carnal desire are entirely unknown, having been transmuted into a higher expression. Sexual union as commonly recognized has no existence, but has become blended gradually into a glorious, harmonious, transcendent, responsive reverberation of soul to soul. Man, as we know, has an etheric body, an astral body, and a spiritual body. Regenerate union may relate to any one, or to all three, of these finer bodies. It may be but the harmonious blending and mutual exchange of magnetism between husband and wife, an interchange of vital energy beneficial to health and accompanied by exalted feelings. It may mean the complete fusion of their astral bodies in a symphony of concord, strengthening their mental ability, and arousing their psychic perceptions. It may consist of a blending of their spiritual bodies that unless their spiritual faculties are very acute they will fail to comprehend; a blend that is realized as a sense of sweet peace and moral uplift when they are in each other's company. Or it may be all three of these. It is not, however, on any plane, a union of sexual organs; it is a complete blend. At least in so far as I am able to interpret it, this is the regeneration of Ancient Masonry.

The Ephraimites, who are stated to be a stubborn, rebellious people, represent those who through asceticism crush out the finer qualities, and renounce association with, or thought of, the opposite sex. The Jordan is the boundary between the physical and the higher astral plane—the region of earth-bound spirits—which those who have crushed out the feminine part of themselves are unable to cross.

The 42,000 who perished—4 plus 2 equal 6, and 6 represents forces in a state of unbalance—signify not only those unbalanced through asceticism, but because 6 is also the number of Venus, the love planet, it applies to those who are unwise in union. This unbalance of energy is the cause of immeasurable misery; for one of the psychological laws of great importance relating to physical and to higher unions alike, is that there must be a balance in intensity, and complete expression by both. Lack of complete expression by one results in the release of mental forces lacking in proper stability and equilibrium, and the one failing completely to express develops the symptoms well known to psychoanalysis as the incompletion complex, which may result in a variety of troubles. It would seem that the 42,000 who perished are mentioned as a warning that the best results, either on the physical or on higher planes, are obtained when there is complete co-operation.

The River Jordan Is the Dense Etheric-Astral Belt Separating the Physical from the Upper Astral

Velocities which are less than those approximating that of light belong to the physical plane. Velocities which are in excess of those approximating light belong to the astral plane. But the velocities of etheric substance, such as radiations, light and electromagnetic waves belong to a transition region. And energy from one plane (bank of the Jordan) can be transmitted to the other plane (other bank of the Jordan) only through first communicating its motions to this belt of etheric rates having approximately the velocity of light.

Vibrations of the ether may be of comparatively low-frequency or high-frequency. Vibrations of physical substance can be produced of far higher frequency than the lower frequencies of electromagnetic waves. Likewise, etheric vibrations can be produced which are far higher than the more commonly encountered astral frequencies (not to be confused with velocities). But most of the etheric frequencies set in motion by thoughts are on the animal level of existence, and thus communicate their energies to the level of the astral plane which contains animals, other intelligences, and discarnate human beings whose motives and feelings are those common to animals.

Shrewdness, intelligence and knowledge, or lack of them, is no gauge of the vibratory level of a person or creature on earth, or of a person or creature in the astral realm. Some of the brainiest men of earth are the greatest scoundrels. And animals which have an intelligence no greater than limited instinct, survive on the astral plane after their physical deaths, and occupy the vibratory level corresponding to their feelings and motives.

In other words, intelligent human beings dominated by the animal propensities, regardless of their cunning, may still be beasts of prey in their basic vibratory rate, and when they pass to the next life occupy a vibratory level on which beasts of prey also are to be encountered. Not that they necessarily associate with such beasts; but they and the beasts occupy the same stratum, even as men and beasts are both to be encountered on the earth.

On earth the struggle for survival is so intense, that a large portion of the thoughts of men, and a large portion of their emotions and feelings, relate to the animal level of existence. Only a portion of the thoughts of humanity are accompanied by feelings of tenderness, are actuated by willing self-sacrifice for the welfare of another, are charged with noble sentiment, or lift the soul in aspiration, and thus set up etheric vibrations on a higher-than-animal level. And only etheric vibrations of a higher-than-animal level can impart their motions, and thus make the contact with, an astral level above that where animals and discarnate souls with animal-like propensities reside.

Thus it is about the earth there is a dense belt of etheric energy the vibrations of which have been set in motion by the feelings of animals, and the thoughts and feelings of men when they were actuated by animal propensities. Most of these men have a far higher basic vibratory rate, and when they pass from earth life consequently will move to a much higher level. But their temporary bursts of passion, their momentary greeds, and their transitory periods of base selfishness, radiate etheric vibrations on a corresponding low vibratory level.

And astral entities that permanently reside, due to their basic vibratory rates, on a similar vibratory level, find it easy to use the energies of this dense etheric belt to influence those still on earth who become negative.

As this Lower-Pluto astral realm, where motives are still those of the beasts, possesses velocities exceeding those of light; space, time and gravitation do not restrict as they do on earth. Consequently ESP (Extra Sensory Perception) can be exercised on this level. More spiritual types of information can be acquired only on more spiritual levels of the astral world. Yet information of value, especially that relating to the affairs of earth, can be acquired in the Lower-Pluto realm.

However, this dense belt, where lower astral levels and the etheric energies derived from the animal thoughts of men and the emotions of animals so closely blend as to make it difficult to determine just where the astral begins and the ether leaves off, is a poor place to tarry. Many of the denizens of this River Jordan are dangerous.

Consequently either in contacting the inner planes through EXTENSION OF CONSCIOUSNESS, or in ASTRAL TRAVEL, it is wise quickly to pass through this etheric-lower-astral belt. To do this, the etheric vibrations at the time must be of sufficient potential to carry the consciousness through to the astral plane, and of a vibratory frequency higher than this River Jordan Belt. One who has developed sufficient electrical potential and a high vibratory rate—can pronounce the password, Shibboleth—can pop through this belt so swiftly as not to notice it is there, just as one can turn the dial on a radio from one program, past a frequency over which one knows a disagreeable program is being broadcast, and to a desirable program with no perceptible interference.

Preparing the Candidate

In preparing the candidate for initiation into the Fellowcraft degree, all his clothing is removed except his shirt. This is symbolical of the astral raiment in which the soul functions after it leaves the physical body. He is then provided with a pair of woolen drawers, still typifying creative energy, but as they are no longer red they indicate that he has overcome and transmuted his purely animal and physical desires. Instead of his left breast being bare, his right is now bared, indicating that instead of selfish and physical desires and emotions he is actuated by unselfish aspirations.

The right foot and right arm are bare, showing by the former that he has arrived at right understanding, and by the latter that his present work is largely upon the positive, or astral, plane. His left foot and left arm are yet clad, indicating that he is yet hampered both in understanding and in execution by physical requirements. And the right eye is blindfolded to signify that he is yet unable to perceive higher truths, while the left eye is uncovered to show that through experience he has learned properly to view the things of the physical world.

The candidate approaches his new initiation by giving two knocks upon the door of the lodge, which signifies his intention to seek admittance to the second, or astral, plane. This rapping is called the Alarm, and arouses the brethren within. Such a neophyte attempting to enter the astral plane not only arouses those friendly to his visit, but also may arouse certain classes of astral beings who have a violent antipathy to man. There is, therefore, cause for alarm, both to the neophyte and to his brethren and teachers on the inner plane, when he attempts first to enter voluntarily the astral realms. In addition to the positive electrical potential and high vibratory rate assured by the password, his only other sure protection is to possess a soul radiating unselfishness; one purified of sensuality and grossness. Against such a purified soul the fiends of hell may rage in vain.

At this point he must give the password. This password, Shibboleth, indicates that he at least has made some progress in regeneration. He is then called upon to enter the lodge—the astral plane—in the name of the Lord (law). That is, he is asked to enter it in obedience to the various laws governing voluntary travel on the astral plane. As he enters the room the angle of a square is pressed against his naked right breast. The square is the symbol of physical union, and the right breast of spiritual aspirations. This signifies that the candidate at this stage, while aspiring to regeneration, has not yet discarded more physical union. He realizes that his physical organism has adapted itself to its present mode of life over a long period of habit forming, on his own part, and on the part of innumerable ancestors from whom his physical body is inherited. To suspend or suppress any natural function is a violent shock to the astral body that will usually react unfavorably on the physical body also. The animal soul is not to be destroyed, but transformed, and this is usually a gradual process of training.

Eastern mystics say to kill out desire, but they really mean its transmutation, not its death. Desire is one of the finest steeds, but it is yet wild and unbroken. A horse can be killed with a knife. So may desire be slain with the will. A horse can be tethered, starved, and beaten. Desire can be treated likewise. It is true that an unbroken mount may unseat and if unchecked even destroy his rider. But if ridden with skill, curbed and guided, the rider will travel many, many times as far as a man without a mount.

If the animal part of man is fought, starved, and otherwise mistreated, it will not have the strength to carry the soul to higher realms. But if treated kindly, yet firmly, its wildness will disappear, and it will become gentle. It will then be desire no longer, but aspiration, the trusty mount of the soul. Had desire been killed there would have been no aspiration, for they are one and the same in different stages of development.

Entering the astral plane with the square against the right breast is quite different from entering the physical world with the point of the compass pressing against the left breast, as in the E.A. degree. The latter is called Torture; for it indicates that the physical desires, symbolized by the left breast, must be made subservient to the law of higher union, in order that birth on the physical plane may be accomplished under the best of circumstances.

Entering the Astral Plane

Entering the lodgeroom the Fellowcraft candidate is led twice around the room, indicating that he has evolved through one plane, the physical, and is now evolving on the next, or astral plane. He is then led first to the Junior Warden (spiritual body), then to the Senior Warden (divine soul), and finally to the Worshipful Master (ego). This is to indicate the members of the higher trinity of his constitution which influence his progress on the astral plane. While being conducted around the room, representing his astral evolution as mentioned, the Master reads the following passages, which consist of the seventh and eighth verses of the seventh chapter of Amos: "Thus he shewed me; and behold, the Lord stood upon a wall made by a plumbline, with a plumbline in his hand. And the Lord said unto me, Amos, what seest thou? And I said a plumbline. Then said the Lord, Behold, I will set a plumbline in the midst of my people Israel. I will not again pass them by anymore."

The number 7—this is the seventh chapter of Amos—as applied to human life signifies the perfect nuptial union; and the number 8 signifies death. The word Lord, here, as elsewhere, is interpreted by initiates to mean Law. The wall, by its horizontal position, symbolizes the feminine principle. This principle is here signified to be a foundation and a protection. The plumbline, by its position, signifies the masculine principle. The hand signifies human work. That the Lord will not pass by them anymore, indicates that the law is changeless. Israel signifies a chosen people. Therefore, these verses as here applied may be interpreted as the changeless law that love lies at the foundation of all, and that those who are chosen to defy death work in accordance to this law.

The candidate is next led to the west—the material plane—and instructed to approach the east, the place of light—the spiritual plane, by advancing upon two upright steps to the second step. The first step has been explained in the E.A. degree to symbolize the will to understand the mysteries of generation. The oblong square of that degree is made by the heel of the right foot being placed in the hollow of the left foot. This is the first step. The two steps are taken by stepping off first with the left foot and then with the right and bringing the heel of the left foot into the hollow of the right. On the astral the feminine, emotional, becomes the more positive in its effects. That is, woman more naturally acts from the subjective, or astral plane; and man more naturally from the physical. The left foot within the hollow of the right, then, indicates the will—shown by the standing position—to understand the mysteries of regeneration.

The candidate now kneels on his right knee before the altar, making his left knee form a square. The left arm is held horizontal as far as the elbow, the forearm vertical to it making another square. The elbow also rests upon a square. He is required to take the oath of a F.C. Mason in this position. In this degree the right knee is suppliant, indicating the subservience of masculine forces to feminine upon the astral plane; being the reverse of the symbol of the E.A. degree. The left arm forming the upper square denotes that the feminine, or subjective, forces are employed in execution upon the astral plane. The square supporting the arm that symbolizes execution imparts the information that its strength at this stage of initiation is sustained by physical co-operation.

After the oath has been taken the Bible is kissed twice. This indicates willingness to abide by the laws of union on both planes as taught to him by his instructors. The moment of transition from the physical to the astral plane is signified by the bandage being lowered until it covers both eyes. This typifies the momentary unconsciousness that takes place as the astral body separates itself from the physical. The magnetic union that assists in generating the force necessary for this volitional transition is shown by the brethren forming on the square. They stretch forth their hands to assist the new brother, as a token of the service rendered by union, and also to represent the unseen helpers who respond to the devout aspirations of the worthy neophyte who obeys the law of progress. Then the Master says, "And God said, Let there be light, and there was light." Whereupon the bandage is snatched from the candidate's eyes and the brethren give the grand shock as in the E.A. degree, the meaning of which has previously been given. Thus is the soul in "search of more light" awakened to the new truths of a different plane of existence.

The candidate's attention is next called to the fact that in the E.A. degree, or on the physical plane, both points of the compass are beneath the square, while in the present degree one point of the compass is elevated above the square as they lie upon the altar. He is also informed that while he now possesses more light upon Masonry, he yet remains in darkness regarding one material point. This conveys the idea that he has partly removed the shackles of sense and seeming by obedience to the laws of both generation and regeneration, but has not yet entirely freed himself from material limitations.

The one point of the compass beneath the square symbolizes that the higher laws of union are yet in a measure subservient to demands for physical expression. The one point of the compass above the square indicates that the neophyte has partially overcome the physical impulses and made them obedient to the laws of regenerate union. This is typical of the transitional stage between the purely physical life and the truly spiritual life. It represents a stage of growth in the candidate's development, usually of long duration, in which the demands of both natures must be heeded, and physical requirements gradually eliminated by being transmuted into those spiritual. These symbols of the present state of his unfoldment are upon the altar, indicating that he should approach the mysteries of his creative nature in a reverent manner, and make them the altar of his most devout prayers and unselfish aspirations.

Strengthening the Rapport Between the Soul and the Ego

To represent the strengthening of the rapport between the soul and the ego, due to living a life of greater spirituality, the cable-tow in the F.C. degree is placed twice around the neck. This is the region ruled by the planet of love. No longer is the cable-tow passed under the arm as in the

E.A. degree, and it is passed twice around instead of once. The higher love, and its importance in spiritual progress is thus emphasized.

Significance of Grips and Passwords

The sign of a F.C. Mason is made by taking hold of the left breast with the right hand as though to tear a piece out of it, then the hand is drawn with the fingers partly closed, quickly to the right and dropped to the side. The breast is the seat of emotion, and the right breast indicates the higher aspirations and longings. The left breast symbolizes the more physical emotions; and as the region of the heart, ruled by the sun, is also the center of vital life.

The hand grasping the left breast as if to convey a portion of it to the right breast, signifies that the material emotions are to be transmuted into those more spiritual, and that the life is to be transferred to a higher plane. The hand dropping perpendicular at the side indicates that the creative life is to be raised to the region of the breast. In the E.A. degree the sign is made from the pharyngeal plexus, the seat of amative desires, the region ruled by Venus; and the hands are open to indicate repulsion. In the F.C. degree, however, the sign is made at the cardiacal plexus, the seat of emotion; and the hand is partly closed, indicating an attractive force that binds man and woman more securely together. It is thus representative of the attraction between man and woman resulting from congeniality in temperament and the harmonies aroused through sympathetic emotional response, rather than the attraction of a more physical nature.

In giving the due-guard the left arm is raised until that part between the shoulder and the elbow is horizontal, and the forearm is vertical to it. It symbolizes the union of husband and wife upon the astral plane. The horizontal part typifies woman, the vertical represents man; and the elevated position indicates them on a plane above the physical. It being the left arm indicates it is the negative, or astral plane. The sign and due-guard are given together to symbolize that the raising of the energies from the plane of generation to the plane of regeneration results in union in the astral realm.

The name of the pass-grip of a F.C. Mason is Shibboleth. It is given in the following manner: The right hands are clasped as in shaking hands, and each presses his thumb between the base of the first and second fingers of the other's hand. The thumb in palmistry denotes will. The first finger is ruled by Jupiter, and governs the feeling of fellowship. The second finger is ruled by Saturn, and has dominion over labor and secrecy. In giving this grip the Master says, "I now present you with my right hand in token of brotherly love and confidence." The pressure of the will finger is made between the finger of brotherly love and the finger of caution, thus denoting the will to be both benevolent and silent.

The real grip of a F.C. Mason is made in shaking hands by pressing the thumb on the base of the second finger where it joins the hand. The thumb is crooked in such a manner as to stick the nail into the joint of the other. As the second finger is the Saturn finger, the grip signifies; the will to labor diligently and in silence. The pressure of the thumb nail is symbolical of the painfulness of the endeavors that lead to any worthwhile realization. "Sloth is the eighth deadly sin," and the Masons of all ages have realized the paramount value of work; and as their ideas often differed widely from those held by a reigning authority who had power to deprive them of life and liberty, discretion imposed silence.

The name of the grip is Jachin. Jachin is the right pillar of Solomon's Temple, and in the cosmic lodge signifies the Northern half of the ecliptic. While the sun passes through this half of its annual cycle the days are longer than the nights, producing the genial warmth of summer. In humanity Jachin represents the virile powers of man, and in the individual the positive and executive attributes. Its more specific significance is phallic, typifying the creative principle. As every plane of existence is negative to the plane interior to it, the physical world being moulded by the astral, the astral may be termed the world of Jachin, that is, the world of creative action.

When the grip has been given, the Worshipful Master says, "Arise, brother Jachin, from a square to a perpendicular; go and salute the Junior and the Senior Wardens, and convince them you have been regularly passed into the degree of Fellowcraft." This speech intimates both the method of transit, and the passage, from the physical plane, Boaz, to the astral plane, Jachin. From the square, or co-operation, by which the force is generated, to the perpendicular, or attribute by which it is positively directed, the neophyte ascends to the astral, or region of Jachin. This brings him more closely in touch with his spiritual body and divine soul, which are symbolized by the two wardens.

The candidate is told that at the building of Solomon's Temple the workmen were distinguished by the manner in which they wore their aprons. Then an apron is tied on him in a fashion to denote that he belongs to the F.C. degree. The significance and correspondence of the apron were given in chapter 5. It is tied on in the same manner in the F.C. degree as in the E.A. degree, except that one corner is turned up and tucked under the apron strings. As the square covering the Libra-Scorpio region typifies their purely physical functions, a portion of this square being raised in the form of a triangle indicates a partial transmutation has taken place. It thus symbolizes that to enter the F.C. degree it is assumed that a portion of the physical energies have been transmuted into etheric energies of such refinement that they are potent to affect results on the astral plane.

The Master then says, "As you are now dressed, it is necessary you should have the tools to work with." Thereupon, the candidate is presented with a plumb, a square, and a level. The significance of these tools has been previously explained, and it only remains to be added that they are here presented to the F.C. in exemplification of the Hermetic Axiom: "As it is below, so it is above, as on the earth, so in the sky;" indicating that progress on the astral is made by methods analogous to those employed on the physical plane.

Thus at death man passes to the astral plane, permanently leaving behind him the physical body and the etheric body, which correspond to the planets Saturn and Jupiter, and in the lodge to the Treasurer and Secretary. The physical body and etheric body then gradually disintegrate, and man functions on the astral plane with a five-fold constitution.

I have already mentioned two dangerous extremes that the Ancient Masons warn against: forced celibacy in the hope of gaining selfish ends, and sex practices for selfish aims. Either extreme, according to these Ancient Masonic teachings, is dangerous; and as bearing this out, we find that practically all the mystical manias of history have arisen among forced celibates, or were accompanied by orgies of licentiousness. Where love and marriage are given their rightful place there is little danger of fanaticism.

Jewels and Check-Words

Therefore, to admonish the neophyte not to jump to hasty conclusions in regard to these and other matters, the Entered Apprentice was given three jewels: A listening ear, a silent tongue, and a faithful heart.

The listening ear indicates that strict attention should be paid to all instructions from within as well as to those from without. The silent tongue signifies that the voice of the silence may be heard only when external thoughts and sensations are inhibited. The faithful heart reveals that there should be strict obedience to the mandates received from within, and perseverance and discipline in its execution.

These three jewels have correspondences above and below. Thus in natal astrology an individual's mental capacity is gauged by the moon; and the moon also rules the quality of receptivity, which is symbolized by the listening ear. It corresponds to the divine soul, from whence proceeds the voice of the silence. In natal astrology the mental expression, the inactivity of which is symbolized by the silent tongue, is ruled by Mercury. Mercury rules speech, and corresponds to the spiritual body. The sun in natal astrology indicates the individuality, and rules the heart of man. It corresponds to the ego. True faith is from the inner recesses, and a faithful heart results when the actions are governed by the ego.

The Entered Apprentice was also given two check-words and a new name. The first is called the Grand Master's check-word. It is TRUTH. Thus before accepting any practice or accepting any doctrine, the Mason should exhaust every means to prove its verity. This check against error is as indispensable to the adept as to the acolyte, to the Grand Master as to the E.A. Hence it is called the Grand Master's check-word.

The second word is UNION. This emphasizes the importance of co-operation between husband and wife. Such intelligent co-operation is a check against fanaticism.

The new name assigned the E.A. is CAUTION. Caution is most necessary; for impatience and hasty conclusions in regard to the use of the forces revealed by Masonic Symbolism is very dangerous. Strength lies in Union; but unwise union leads to disaster. To leave the physical and "travel in foreign countries" opens the door to knowledge, but to depart without due preparation may mean inability to return. Hence while the candidate still is concerned with the physical plane he is given the name Caution.

In the Fellowcraft degree also, the candidate is given three precious jewels. They are Faith, Hope, and Charity. Faith to follow unhesitatingly the dictates of the inner voice. Hope to buoy up the soul during its period of anguish while in spiritual travail. Charity towards those who perceive not the light and struggle yet in outer darkness.

When the F.C. has finished the first stage of his initiation, as outlined, he is led back to the outer room to be reinvested with his clothing, even as he returns to his physical raiment after his first pilgrimage into the spheres of the astral.

Lights, Points and Dedications

The ritual states that there are three lights in the lodge; one in the east, one in the west, and one in the south; but that being a true representation of King Solomon's Temple there is none in the north. This means that the sun rises in the east, culminates in the south, and sets in the west; at which stations it can be plainly seen. But when it is at the nadir, or northern point, at midnight, it is hidden from view, and consequently no light is apparent in the north of the lodge.

It is asked to whom the Ancient Masons dedicated their lodges. The answer is given, "to King Solomon." But Modern Masons dedicate their lodges to St. John the Baptist and to St. John the Evangel, "Because they were the two most eminent Christian patrons of Masonry, and since their time, in every well regulated and governed lodge, there has been a certain point within the circle, which circle is bounded on the east and west by two perpendicular parallel lines, representing the anniversary of John the Baptist and John the Evangelist, who were perfect parallels, as well in Masonry as in Christianity; on the vertex of which rests the Book of the Holy Scriptures supporting Jacob's ladder, which is said to reach the watery clouds; and passing round the circle, we naturally touch on both these perpendicular parallel lines, as well as the Book of the Holy Scriptures; and while a Mason keeps himself thus circumscribed, he can not materially err."

Masonry applies the correspondences existing between the soul and the stars. In astrology the heavens are measured in three different planes. The Mundane Houses correspond to the physical realm, and to the E.A. degree of Masonry. The Zodiacal Signs correspond to the astral plane, and to the F.C. degree of Masonry. And the Constellations correspond to the spiritual world, for, like the Master Mason's degree, their realm of influence pertains strictly to man's spiritual nature.

The point within the circle is the world upon which we live, which is bounded by the circle of the zodiac. The two parallel lines are formed by the solstitial colure, cutting the zodiacal circle at opposite points; one point being where the sun reaches its greatest northern declination, and the other point being where the sun reaches its greatest southern declination. When the sun is at either of these two points and rises or sets, these lines are east and west from the observer, and actually bound by lines running north and south, what may be seen of the zodiacal circle. The sun reaches one of these lines when it passes into the watery sign Cancer on the 22nd of June. That is, the Son of God is immersed in a watery sign on that day, and two days later, June 24th, is the day given by the Church to St. John the Baptist.

Evangel, means to bring good news; and after the sun has gone to its extreme southern point, giving the least light and heat of any time in the year, it is certainly good news when he is observed to turn back to be resurrected from his wintry tomb. He reaches this latter line on December 23rd, and soon thereafter is seen moving north again, bringing the tidings of another period of warmth and growth. Therefore, even as the opposite point, where he first begins to submerge, was dedicated to St. John the Baptist, so this point, where he begins to emerge, is dedicated to St. John the Evangelist; and the day given to St. John the Evangelist by the Church is four days after this line is crossed, or the 27th of December.

These two points, because easily determined by observation, are important points in all Masonic reckoning, and are thus also the supports of the Oral Law which has its foundation in astro-traditions. Hence the Bible, symbol of the Oral Law, rests upon them. And above the Bible, reaching to the watery clouds is Jacob's ladder. This ladder symbolizes the involutionary descent and evolutionary ascent of the soul, each rung being a form of life in which it lives, yet ever within the zodiacal circle and under the influence of planetary forces. The watery clouds above, that is, water and air, symbolize the emotions and aspirations that have led the soul upward on its toilsome ascent.

The two lines where the solstitial colure cuts the ecliptic, are perpendicular to this zodiacal circle, and the sun cannot travel around the zodiac without touching both; nor can it do so without making an impress upon the Oral Law. Neither can man travel the orbit of his life without being influenced by the astrological energies bounded by these lines, nor without, if he is a Mason, coming in contact with the Oral Law as handed down by the Magi from the past. And he who can conform his efforts to the boundary of his possibilities as shown by the stars, and adapt his life to the Oral Law as handed down by the sages, will be as free from error and the chain of blind fatality, as it is possible for man to be. No truer guide exists than that circumscribed by the zodiac as mapped in the jeweled canopy of heaven.

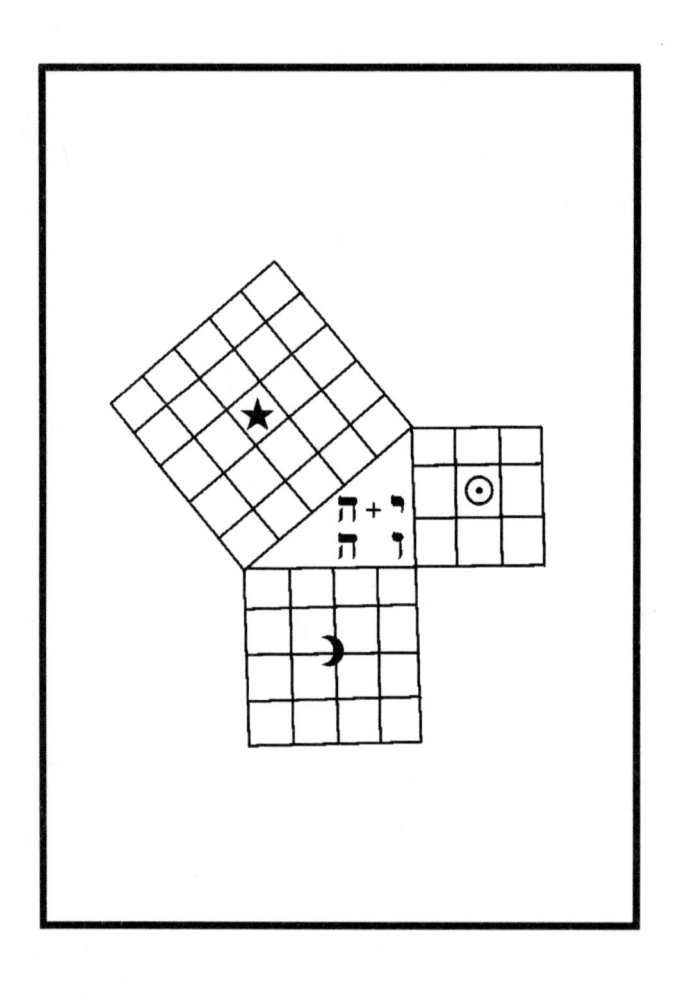

Chapter 7

Lodge Emblems

THE EMBLEMS of Masonry, no less than the pictured starry constellations, the designs of the tarot cards, and the allegorical stories of the world's sacred books, bespeak an ancient language whose terms are intelligible to peoples widely separated both in space and time. It is the language of the unconscious mind, the language even to a small degree understood by the creatures of the wild as well as by man, the language which derives from common associations, and which, therefore, is the language of dreams.

In this peculiar transmission of ideas it is assumed that people have had certain experiences in common, and that, therefore, the Law of Association will readily suggest to them the outstanding qualities of things seen or heard. It is assumed that people the world over who have had any experience with horses are familiar with the idea that horses commonly are used to carry riders to their destination. This association of ideas is then made use of to suggest by means of a horse that which carries man to his goal. Horses thus become the symbol of thoughts, and especially of thoughts which are expressed, and thus is derived part of the symbol of Sagittarius, which is natural ruler of the house of expressed thought in a chart of birth.

That which is seen and experienced in dreams is not without significance. All of it—except that which consists of witnessing some actual event, past, present or future—is a portrayal to the consciousness in this language of symbolism, which derived its terms from Association of experiences and ideas, of something of significance to the mind of the individual.

But the significance of the symbolism of dreams is far more complicated than the symbolism we here consider, not because the meaning of the symbols is more difficult to discern, but because in the dream state we are more or less conscious of the astral plane in which there are new properties present as if it embraced still another dimension.

In dreams, for instance, there are images derived from sensory stimuli, there are fantasy images induced by desire, and desire may cause condensation or expansion of the symbolism. On the astral plane, and in dreams, not only objects, but people's thoughts may be seen as definite images. And occurrences that happen on various astral levels may be witnessed, as contrasted with events on a single level that may be witnessed on the earth.

But this is only the beginning of the possible multitude of things that it is possible to see in sleep, or on the astral plane; for, due to the lack of restriction of time, space and gravitation, it is possible to witness one's own past experiences and thoughts, and one's probability line of future experiences and thoughts as if they were realities in the now, and to witness other people's past experiences and thoughts, and their probability lines of future experiences and thoughts as if they were happening in the now.

Thus the problem confronting us in discerning the significance of things seen in sleep or on the astral plane, is not so much that of interpreting the symbolism, as it is in untangling the past and future from the present, discriminating that which is merely a thought from that which represents an occurrence involving individuals, and in otherwise unscrambling images and impressions and giving each its proper place. The infant taken on a drive through a great city has the same difficulty. But with experience and training the infant grows to recognize the relative value and significance of its impressions. And man also, in due course of time if he trains himself diligently, can while still on the physical plane, learn properly to appraise what he sees in dreams, and what he sees without dreaming on the astral plane.

The Masonic Lodgeroom

It is said that the Masonic lodgeroom is as long as from east to west; as wide as from north to south; as high as from the surface of the earth to the highest heaven; and as deep as from the surface of the earth to the earth's center. Only one thing has such dimensions. That thing is the universe as mapped by the Mundane Houses of a horoscope. Therefore, the lodgeroom is the universe considered from the point on the earth where the candidate stands (see Course 2, *Astrological Signatures,* Chapter 3).

From east to west is considered the length, and north and south the width, because the planets in their orbits about this celestial lodge move fewer degrees north and south than they move east and west. The limit of their movement by declination—the north and south movement—is less than 60 degrees; but they move through the zodiac, and also by their diurnal travel about the earth from east to west, the entire circle of 360 degrees. The third dimension of a horoscope is always considered to reach from the center of the earth beneath the observer's feet to the zenith directly over his head. From the standpoint of astrology it would be difficult to give a better definition of the dimensions of the stellar universe than this one formulated by the Ancient Masons.

The Three Pillars

It is further asserted that there are three columns, or pillars, that support the lodge. These are the equinoctial colure, the solstitial colure, and the meridian. They are the support of the lodge because the lodge is the vault of heaven and all calculations relating to it are referred to one or more of these three lines, or pillars. Thus the celestial longitude of a stellar body is always calculated as so many degrees, or hours, from one end of the equinoctial colure, which is called the first point of Aries. Celestial latitude is reckoned as so many degrees north or south of the ecliptic; the ecliptic being a circle passing over both ends of the equinoctial colure, and also over both ends of the solstitial colure; the latter line, or pillar, being necessary to determine the plane of the ecliptic. Yet astronomical calculations to be of value on the earth must not stop with defining the position of a celestial body in terms of latitude and longitude, but must designate the position with reference to a given spot on the earth. This third necessary element is calculated from the third Masonic pillar, the meridian. Thus if we say a planet is 12 degrees of Sagittarius, has 3 degrees south latitude, and that 9 degrees of Sagittarius is on the meridian, its position is completely defined. Without these three elements precise definition of celestial positions is impossible. Therefore, the Meridian, the Solstitial Colure, and the Equinoctial Colure, are truly the supports of the celestial lodge.

When the sun rests upon the equinoctial colure the days and nights are equal, masculine and feminine forces are united by the colure in equilibrium, as pictured in the zodiac by the Scales of Libra, the zodiacal sign of marriage. And because proper marriage is considered a constructive function, the Ancient Masons named the pillar Wisdom.

When the sun rests upon the top, or northern end, of the solstitial colure, the days are longest and the masculine forces are dominant; when it rests upon the bottom, or southern end of the solstitial colure, the nights are longest and feminine forces are dominant. Because that man is strongest who is dominantly masculine, and that woman is strongest who is dominantly feminine, the Ancient Masons named this pillar Strength.

When the sun rests upon the meridian it is noon and there is the maximum sunshine for that day. This light makes more plainly visible the innumerable beauties of nature. Because of this the Ancient Masons named this pillar Beauty.

Furthermore, to make the identity of the lodge unmistakable, Masons assert that it has a clouded canopy, or starry decked heaven, where all good Masons hope to arrive.

The Northeast Corner

Any complete map of this lodgeroom divides it into the Mundane Houses commonly employed in erecting a birth-chart. Such a map, or birth-chart, has the directions well defined, each house ruling certain departments of life. The First House of the celestial map, the place where the sun is each day at dawn when it awakens the sleepy world into a fresh period of activity, in natal astrology rules birth. This house of birth is the northeast portion of the birth-chart. Therefore, in absolute conformity to astrological correspondences, when the candidate for the E.A. degree, that is, the candidate for initiation on the physical plane, has been reinvested with his clothing he is placed in the northeast corner of the lodgeroom and caused to stand upright like a man. He represents the soul that has evolved far enough to be born into human form. He also, by his position in the house of birth, indicates that through the knowledge imparted to him in initiation, he has been reborn and is now ready to commence a new life. Even as the sun after its daily birth ascends to a vertical position, so does the candidate stand upright like a man, by his position indicating the will to strive for higher things.

Not only is the First House, or northeast corner, of a celestial chart, the house of birth of man, but it marks the birth, or commencement, of each new enterprise. This explains why, "The first stone in every Masonic edifice is, or ought to be, placed at the northeast corner, that being the place where an E.A. Mason receives his first instructions to build his future Masonic edifice upon."

No Metal Tool Was Heard

In the building of the original Masonic edifice, Solomon's Temple, the sound of ax, hammer, or other tool of metal, was not heard: "All the stones were hewed, squared, and numbered in the quarries where they were raised; all the timbers felled and prepared in the forests of Lebanon, and carried down to Joppa on floats, and taken thence up to Jerusalem, and set up with wooden malls, prepared for that purpose; which, when complete, every part thereof fitted with the exact nicety, that it had more resemblance of the handiworkmanship of the Supreme Architect of the universe, than of human hands."

Because inorganic substances possess the lowest degree of life expressed on the earth they symbolize human experiences that are viewed solely from the standpoint of material loss or gain. But organic substances, possessing a higher degree of life, and a more complex organization, symbolize human experiences that are viewed from the standpoint of spiritual alchemy, from the standpoint of their effect upon character. Tools composed of inorganic substance, then, represent such mental activities as are concerned with the physical welfare; and an edifice built with metallic tools signifies an environment that has been constructed through selfish ambition. Such an edifice is bound, sooner or later, to fall into decay.

But the temple built upon true spiritual principles, built upon a recognition that the important function of each experience is its effect upon the character, does not decay; but becomes a glorious and permanent habitation for the immortal soul. Nor is this entirely figurative; for it is the attitude toward events, and the motive behind actions, that determine whether states of consciousness are evolved of sufficient intensity, and of such polarity that they combine, to affect spiritual substances. Only mental factors of proper intensity affect the spiritual body and have power to organize it as a vehicle for the immortal soul (see Course 3, *Spiritual Alchemy*, Chapter 4).

Because thoughts prompted by material motives have not intensity of vibration sufficient to affect the spiritual body, in the construction of Solomon's Temple, the spiritual body, the sound of no metal tool—thoughts based upon purely material motives—was heard. And the malls of wood were specially prepared because it takes special preparation and training to give the thoughts the viewpoint and spirituality that they may be used to build up the spiritual body.

The stones indicate the external experiences of mankind. They were hewed, squared, and numbered in the quarries where they were raised. That is, they were classified as the various sciences. The timbers, being of organic substance, represent the experiences of life that organize the character. They have their origin in the forests of Lebanon, the material plane. But they are floated by the emotional reactions toward them to Joppa, the astral plane. And from thence—if fit for the purpose, if of sufficient spirituality—up to Jerusalem, the spiritual plane.

And the spiritual body of man—organized by constructive thoughts that are largely motivated by the desire to benefit society, yet based upon a wide variety of experiences that are viewed as opportunities to build character—because it corresponds in its various parts to the universe—is a microcosm—resembles, therefore, the handiwork of Deity.

Three Movable Jewels

Now the three movable jewels of a lodge are, the rough ashlar, the perfect ashlar, and the trestleboard. The rough ashlar represents man's character unmodified by spiritual aspirations and occult training. The perfect ashlar represents man's character after it has been perfected by applying the keen chisel of discrimination, driven by the hammer of will and intellect; and after it has been polished by persistent aspirations to be of greatest possible service to mankind. It thus becomes fit to be used in the construction of the permanent, or spiritual, human edifice.

The trestleboard is man's consciousness, where the soul drafts the plans for the actions of life.

Ornaments

The ornaments of the lodge are: the checkered pavement, or mosaic; the blazing star in its center; and the indented tassel, or beautiful tessellated border that surrounds the pavement.

The blazing star has five points, and is thus the symbol of man. The one point above the other four indicates that man's head is uppermost, that his intellect has dominion over the four elementary realms, and should have dominion over the instincts of the flesh. In the heavens above, this Masonic star is Polaris, the Pole Star, which, because apparently it is the only point in the sky that does not move—for it represents the extension of the earth's axis—has throughout the ages been the emblem of that other thing which changes not, Truth. "Upon this rock will I build my church." Had it actually been founded on this rock the church need not have changed. The King, Cepheus—a word meaning rock—among the constellations, rests his foot on the Polar Star, which is a part of the constellation. This—Truth—is not merely the Rock of Ages, but it is also, "The rock that is higher than I," a recognition not merely of the permanence of truth, but that it is the highest religion. Therefore, when it is said that this star should appear conspicuously in the conduct of every Mason, we are informed that a conspicuous feature of Masonic conduct is adherence to Truth.

About this star, which on earth represents man and in the sky represents Polaris, is a mosaic of black and white checks. The movement of the planets through the zodiac causes their rays to converge to form squares, trines, sextiles, semi-squares, and other geometrical figures. The influence of some of these is harmonious, corresponding to the white checks. The influence of others is discordant, corresponding to the black checks. These checks, therefore, considered as planetary influences converging on man's astral body in regular geometrical patterns, attract to man, through stimulating certain unconscious trains of thought, periods of good fortune and periods of adverse fortune. That is, they well represent not only the geometrical designs of the birth-chart, which predisposes him to certain experiences, but they also represent the progressed aspects which add energy and thus bring certain types of events to him at times that may be predetermined.

The recognition of these influences, symbolized by the checkered pavements, is important; but of still more importance is the advice given, that brethren may walk together upon this pavement without stumbling. In other words, adverse planetary influences cannot be avoided, but it is quite possible to avoid the adverse events that are threatened by planetary positions; and because mental vibrations may be reinforced by emotion, and because planetary influence operates through stimulating discordant mental states, that which can be used to engender specific constructive emotions may be used to annul adverse planetary influence. The Ancient Masons counseled, for this purpose, harmonies engendered through close cooperation.

Chalk, Charcoal and Clay

The next thought requires some preliminary explanation. Life in association with the earth is embraced in seven stages, the seventh stage of consciousness summing up the other six and providing a point of transition to higher spheres. The incarnating soul first undergoes experiences in the mineral realm, then a cycle of experience on the astral plane where the mineral experiences are reorganized to fit it for vegetable life. It then incarnates repeatedly in the vegetable kingdom; following which it undergoes another cycle in the astral, gestating these experiences before incarnating as an animal. The fifth stage is its various incarnations in the animal kingdom; the sixth being a cycle in the astral realm where it synthesizes these experiences to a point where human incarnation is possible.

Now when the Senior Warden (corresponding to the soul) in the E.A. degree is asked whom he served, he answers, "My Master," meaning, the ego. When asked how long, he replies, "Six days." These six days are the six states through which the soul serves the ego, the six states from the mineral up to the point where human incarnation is possible. It thus represents the labors of the impersonal soul, impelled by the ego, to reach the human plane and thus come into possession of self-consciousness.

To the question with what he served him he replies, with Freedom, Fervency, and Zeal, and that these are present in Chalk, Charcoal, and Clay. That is, charcoal, which is used for fuel, is a symbol of fire, and hence of the fervency of creative energy. Clay is igneous rock that has been eroded by ice, and thus represents the union of fire and water, male and female principles, and it is stated that nothing is more zealous than clay to bring forth. Chalk is chiefly composed of the minute shells of Foraminifera, being deposited in the shallow water of the sea. It is thus of animal origin, and well symbolizes the offspring, or life, resulting from the union of male and female principles. And in addition, its common use as a means of facilitating expression suggests the freedom with which the soul, in its evolutionary ascent, expressed itself through incarnating in one form of life after another.

When the state of man is reached, from the lowest human state up to the perfect man, or adept, there is another series of seven states. These states are indicated in the F.C. degree where it is said that the Masons working on Solomon's Temple wrought six days, but on the seventh day they rested. That is, in perfecting the human temple, seven states of consciousness are developed (see Course 3, *Spiritual Alchemy*, Chapter 5 for detailed discussion of these states of consciousness). The ego only becomes incarnated and the man perfect when the seventh state of manhood is reached. He is then a Master Mason, has developed seven states of consciousness, and is at the point of transition where he is ready to function on the spiritual plane of life.

Furthermore, in the spiritual realms there is still another series of seven states by which man passes from spiritual life into angelic form. These are also each marked by a definite development of consciousness. In the seventh state of the spiritual world, due to the permanent union of the two souls that are the expression of one divine ego, the angelic form is attained and the next step is transition to the celestial sphere.

The Red Sea

The statement is made that the lodgeroom is situated due east and west, not only because it is a model of Solomon's Temple, but also because Moses, after conducting the Children of Israel through the Red Sea, by divine command, erected a tabernacle to God, and placed it due east and west, which was to commemorate to the latest posterity that miraculous east wind that wrought their mighty deliverance.

Now red is the color ruled by the planet Mars, and a sea typifies the emotions. The Red Sea, therefore, symbolizes a condition of sensuality. Sensations, by those who listen to the dictates of the divine soul, are utilized to build a fit tabernacle to God; but to those less worthy they become a snare, and such persons are flooded and drowned in the sea of their own animal propensities. Wind symbolizes aspirations, and the east is the region of light. Therefore, the candidate is informed that through aspiration for spiritual wisdom he may cross the sea of sensuality dry shod, but that those who foolishly enter this sea with unworthy motives are doomed to destruction.

Dimensions and Ornaments of the Columns

In the F.C. degree we also have a complete description of the two columns, Jachin and Boaz. On the earth Jachin is the region of heat and warmth, the South; but because it is summer when the sun is in the northern half of the zodiac, Jachin in the sky is the northern section of the zodiac. Likewise, Boaz, on earth is the region of cold, the North; but in the sky represents the southern half of the zodiac; for it is coldest when the sun is so situated. These columns are said to be eighteen cubits high, twelve in circumference, and four in diameter; they are adorned with two large chapiters, one on each, and, so the description continues, these chapiters are ornamented with net-work, lily-work, and pomegranates.

That is, the Ancient Masons, as do modern astrologers, considered the zodiac as a belt about the heavens extending 9 degrees each side of the sun's apparent annual path, or 18 degrees high. As there are twelve signs in the zodiacal belt, they are 12 in circumference. The belt is further divided into four quadrants, each quadrant representing the station of the sun during one of the four seasons. It is thus 4 in diameter. And the two halves of the zodiac, representing the sun's station during summer and winter, show Jachin and Boaz united.

These pillars, or sections of the zodiac, are surmounted and adorned by the various starry constellations, the northern constellations forming one chapiter, and the southern constellations forming another. These constellations, as any star map will show, are a net-work of lines connecting various stars. Their exalted and spiritual meaning can only be read by those of pure heart, symbolized by the lily; and as indicated by the pomegranate, which is mostly seeds, their interpretations are the seeds of all valuable esoteric knowledge. In human life these two chapiters signify those crowning attributes by which true men and true women differ. The net-work signifies the noble ties that bind together man and woman, the lily-work the purity of their relations, and the pomegranates the fruitfulness of their endeavors on all planes of action when thus united by an exalted love.

The Globes on the Columns

On these columns are two globes, one on each. They are balls containing on their convex surfaces all the maps and charts of the celestial and terrestrial bodies. In composition they are molten, or cast, brass; and were cast on the banks of the River Jordan, in clay ground between Succoth and Zaradatha, where King Solomon ordered these and all other holy vessels to be cast. They were four inches, or a hand's breadth, thick, and were cast hollow the better to withstand inundations and conflagrations. They were the Archives of Masonry, and contained the constitution, rolls, and records.

The two globes are the celestial sphere, or globe mapping the constellations, and the terrestrial sphere, or globe mapping the earth. For astrological purposes it is necessary to map the heavens at any instant of time in reference to any specific point on the surface of the earth. The latitude and longitude of birth must be known before a birth-chart may be erected, and the longitude and declination of the planets must be calculated. The former data are obtained from a map of the earth, or terrestrial globe, and the latter data are obtained from a map of the heavens, or the celestial globe. The whole of Masonry, as well as the whole of human life, is contained within these two spheres; for they symbolize astrology. They are Archives of Masonry in which the records are kept written in the divine language of celestial correspondence.

The River Jordan represents the boundary between the physical world and the astral world; between Succoth and Zaradatha. On the banks of the River these globes were cast; and because the various planetary energies that stimulate man converge, or unite, on the earth at the point where he stands; that is, the astral vibrations from both heaven and earth meet where he stands to influence him, these spheres are said to be cast in clay-ground; the latter being the symbol of united forces. These forces that converge in man's astral body are from the heaven and from the earth, thus being positive and negative like brass which is a union of two metals, and they are ever on the move, fluxing like the molten brass to which they are compared.

The celestial globe is divided into four quadrants, and by the law of correspondence the terrestrial globe has also four natural quadrants.

They are thus four in thickness. And to indicate that they have an influence over man's life and destiny they are said to be a hand's breadth in thickness. The hand is not only the symbol of work done, of the executive attribute, but because of its five fingers it also symbolizes man. The inundations and conflagrations which threaten these precious maps, which threaten this knowledge of the religion of sky and earth, which alone constitutes the true constitution, rolls and records of Ancient Masonry, are the unreasoning emotions and violent passions of man.

The Long Winding Staircase

The long winding Masonic stairway, which it is said has three, five, seven, or more steps, refers to the annual journey of the sun. At the winter solstice, for three days before its birth on Christmas, the sun is stationary, moving neither north or south. Then as there are 365 days in a year, and only 360 degrees in the sun's annual cycle, it was customary in ancient times to cross off five days after Christmas. These days were given over to a festival in honor of the sun's birth in the manger of the Goat, Capricorn. And because the sun is then in the sign ruled by Saturn, the festival period was called the Saturnalia. Following these five days, there were yet another seven days before the ephiphany, on which the new born sun was said to first put in an appearance; just as Jesus was said to be twelve years of age before appearing in learned discussion. These seven days, or Masonic steps, in practical magic, are of great importance; for at this time of the year the magnetic forces are peculiarly susceptible and plastic to the will of man.

In human life, according to numerology, the three steps symbolize marriage, the five steps represent intelligence, or enlightenment, and the seven steps the perfect union of body, soul, and spirit with body, soul, and spirit to triumph over physical limitations.

In the F.C. Degree the candidate is admitted into the middle chamber of the temple for the sake of the letter G. G in Ancient Masonry stands for generation, and this ceremony indicates that because the candidate has mastered the mysteries of generation, he is now ready for initiation into the mysteries of regeneration.

Emblems of the Master Mason's degree are of two kinds. Those of the first class are: The Bee-Hive, the Book of Constitutions guarded by the Tyler's sword which points at a naked Heart, the All-Seeing Eye, the Anchor, the Ark, the Forty-Seventh Problem of Euclid, the Hour-Glass, the Scythe, and the Three Steps on the Master's Carpet.

Bee-Hive

The Bee-Hive is a triple emblem. The hive proper denotes man's physical body. The honeycomb signifies that which is interior to the physical, the astral body. And the honey is symbolical of the spiritual body, which is composed of the choicest nectars and aromas of earthly experience. The bee, which makes the honey, is symbol of industry and creative energy. Both its warlike spirit and its constructive ability indicate that it is ruled by the planet Mars. It thus typifies constructive ability, not merely to multiply the species, but through taking a constructive attitude toward all events of life to gather material experiences and build up the physical form and the astral body to a higher state of perfection, and to incorporate the finer essences, the higher emotions, into the spiritual body of man. As the bee exercises industry and prudence in gathering honey while it may, storing it for use during the long winter, so should man industriously gather experiences, and through a constructive attitude toward them store them properly to serve as spiritual nourishment when the summer of physical life is supplanted by the icy winter of death.

Book of Constitutions

The Book of the Constitutions symbolizes the Oral Law. The Sword is but an inverted cross; and history proclaims that those who have most ardently adored the cross have been those who most readily took up the sword. Perhaps it was the realization that this would be the case that inspired the great teacher of Peace on Earth to say, "I came not to send peace, but a sword." As a cross is the symbol of matter, so also is a sword, with the added implication of dire affliction. It thus becomes also a menace and a threat of retribution. As the Tyler is man's objective consciousness, or reason, his sword guarding the Book of Constitutions represents the consciousness that any violation of the Oral Law will be followed by unfailing punishment.

The All-Seeing Eye

The All-Seeing Eye typifies the omniscience of Deity, and the limitless powers of the soul to gain knowledge. It also conveys the thought that though there are times when all is dark and dreary for the neophyte, yet he is ever watched over by friendly unseen intelligences, who but await opportunity to convey to him words of comfort and wisdom.

The Anchor

The Anchor combines in its form the solar circle of spirit, the cross of earth, and the lunar crescent of soul. The ring above, indicates that the body and soul, represented by the cross and crescent, are under the dominion and control of the ego. The crescent and the circle are united by the cross, indicating spirit and soul united in one physical form.

The Anchor thus also symbolizes the Lost Word, Jod-He-Vau-He, which embraces all possibilities within the universe. The circle represents the positive divine fire, the one principle, the creative Jod, or alchemical sulphur. The crescent signifies the receptive plastic water, the feminine He, the alchemical mercury, the universal law of sex. The cross of the anchor represents the union of the two, the Vau, the manifestation of the divine Word, alchemical salt. The figure as a whole represents the product of the union, the final He, the whole divine truth, alchemical azoth. That is, the universe as it now exists is the result of evolution brought about by the union of positive and negative forces; and by correspondence the evolution of the human soul may be facilitated by the application of the truths concerning cooperation.

The Ark

To explain the symbolism of the Ark we must refer to the biblical version of Noah's experiences. Noah, the central figure of the story, represents the central figure of our solar system, and in the human constitution the ego. The Ark was built in three stories, corresponding celestially to Mundane Houses, Zodiacal Signs, and Starry Constellations; in man to the physical body, the astral body, and the spiritual body, in which the ego functions.

Besides his own family, which is represented in the heavens by the various planets, and in man by his component parts, Noah took into the Ark specimens of every living thing upon the earth. The latter are depicted in the heavens by the numerous objects and animals that make up the starry constellations, and are represented in man by the various vestigial structures and animal traits that he has inherited from the lower forms of life that are his physical ancestors.

The ego, clouded by the emotions of the physical body, cannot manifest its full glory; nor when the winter rains set in can the sun, hidden by clouds, be seen. These represent the flood. The rains, representing sensualism, shot through with the lightning of passion, tend to destroy all life. But those that dedicate their lives to some noble and unselfish work are safe from sensualism, and even as the sun reappears after triumphing over the storms of winter, they arrive triumphantly at a safe haven. The sensual waters, after a time, are assuaged by the wind of higher aspirations, the gentle zephyrs of spring. The raven, bird of ill omen, is sacred to the planet Saturn, the ruler of the sign Capricorn, through which the sun passes when the winter rains are most severe. It is sent out, but returns not. Selfishness and craft, denoted by this Saturnine bird, will bring no good tidings to the ego, nor will such motives bring rest and content amid the swirling waters of desire. Like the raven, they pass to and fro over the tides of sensation, ever seeking, but not finding, rest and shelter.

The dove is sacred to Venus, the planet of love, the planet ruling the spring sign Taurus. It is sent out once over the turbulent waters of sensation, signifying the action of love upon the plane of generation. But no tidings of much worth are brought to the ego. In the heavens this represents the first action of the sun in spring drying the earth. The second going forth of the dove is the action of love on the plane of regeneration. This brings the tidings of future tranquility and peace, as symbolized by the olive leaf. It also represents in the heavens the growing verdure of spring, under the warmth of the sun. The third time the dove is sent forth represents the accomplishment of the full mission, the complete transmutation of sensations into spiritual emotions. The sun transformed the season of rain into a season of gorgeous bloom.

The golden egg of Braham, the oriental type of the ark, is said to have burst. The shells formed continents, the white became the oceans, and the yolk produced, first vegetable life, then animal life, and finally man. This is the egg of the Orphic Mysteries from which the sun bursts with power to triplicate himself. It is really the earth, functioning as the womb of the universe, from which will be born, after its period of gestation, the divine man. Even Noah was imprisoned nine months in the Ark before the tops of the mountains could be seen. Each human soul is ushered into physical life after such a nine months imprisonment. Furthermore, after birth, the body of man becomes the ark in which human life develops; and only at death is it freed from this prison that tosses on the tide of turbulent desire, to enter a brighter world of infinitely more glorious possibilities. The Ark, therefore, will be seen in its various aspects as the symbol of Gestation.

The Forty-Seventh Problem of Euclid

One of the most important symbols of Masonry is the Forty-Seventh Problem of Euclid. The principles illustrated by it form the foundation of numbers, geometry, and mathematical symbolism. It represents perfectly the Tetragrammaton and the operation of divine law. It is the problem of the right angle triangle. The three sides represent the divine trinity, and the trine as a whole represents the unity of God. The perpendicular line forming one side of the triangle is the Masonic Plumb, corresponding kabalistically to the masculine letter Jod, also to Osiris of Egypt, and to God the Father.

Now nature manifests herself in every septenary by means of three active principles, and four passive forms. The vertical side is consequently divided into three parts representing the three active principles. The number three expresses action, and these three divisions correspond to the three strongest positions of the sun; on the Ascendant, on the Mid-heaven, and on the Descendant. It also corresponds in astrology to the three qualities and the three degrees of emanation, into which the zodiacal signs are divided. Likewise it corresponds to the three active portions of the human constitution; the ego, the divine soul, and the animal soul.

The horizontal side of the triangle is the Masonic Level, corresponding kabalistically to the feminine letter He, also to Isis of Egypt, and to the Virgin Mary of later times. It is divided into four sections to designate the four forms by which the three active principles always manifest. All material things have four relative states—three dimensions and position—and express the active qualities of attraction, repulsion, and motion. The attractive power is represented by gravitation. The repulsive power is illustrated by the cohesion which enables it by repelling other substances to keep its own identity without yielding to their gravitational attraction and fusing with them into a homogeneous mass. Motion is denoted by the change of relative position of every object in the universe.

The number four expresses realization, and corresponds astrologically to the four quadrants of the heavens, and to the four triplicities into which the zodiac is divided. In man it corresponds to the four forms of his constitution; spiritual body, astral body, etheric body, and physical form.

The union of 3 with 4, of a plumb with a level, gives us a Masonic Square of 7, which, properly interpreted reveals the Lost Word of the Master. To become that word, however, it must relinquish the square aspect, and be transformed into two interlaced trines having as a common center the 7th point. As the triangle is presented, however, the third factor of the figure is the meeting point of the 3 and 4, of Sun and Moon, of active and passive, of Jod and He. This right angle is the key to the solution of Euclid's problem, even as it is the symbol of the solution of man's. Astrologically it is the meeting point of planetary energies on the earth, corresponding to the Vau of the word, to the Overshadowing Intelligence of Egypt, to the Holy Ghost of Christianity, to vibration in the natural world, and in human life to union.

Mathematical evolution means the multiplication of a number by itself. The evolution of man is accomplished through the union of the 3 principles with the 4 elements. Their multiplication gives the number of the signs of the zodiac through which the impersonal soul must successively pass, and their union produces 7, the number of component parts of man's constitution.

Evolve the side 3, and the side 4—that is, multiply each by itself—and the sum of these two is equal to the evolution of the third side. This third side, the evolution of which results from the evolution of principles and elements, has the number 5, the symbol of man. This demonstrates, according to the Ancient Hermetic System of Numbers, the evolution of man.

This hypotenuse is the fourth factor of the figure, the product of the union of masculine and feminine forces. It represents, therefore, the climax of evolution on the physical plane. The area of the figure is 6, signifying temptation. This leads to the union of 3 and 4 to evolve man, symbolized by 5, who possesses a 7-fold constitution. The hypotenuse corresponds to the life resulting from the union of solar and lunar rays upon the earth. It also corresponds in man to intellect, kabalistically to the final He of the divine word, to the Egyptian Horus, and in modern religion to the Son of God.

The figure of the 47th problem of Euclid (see illustration at front of chapter) therefore, by its three sides, representing man's principles, and his forms, expresses the cycle of life. This cycle indicates the struggle by the area, 6, which must express through the sides, the sum of which is 12, the number of the zodiacal signs under the influence of which all evolution expresses. By adding together the evolved sides—each side multiplied by itself—we have the number 50, typifying the number of steps that lead man to adeptship, that evolve man into superman. It is said that Moses was able successfully to take 49 of these steps, but failing in the last he was denied entrance into the promised land. He could see this land of plenty, he had the wisdom to see this final step, but was unable to take it. This, perhaps, was not so much the fault of Moses as that of the times in which he lived.

Incense

Incense, which is used at times in Masonic rites, has a practical use in ceremonial magic. All magical work comes under definite planetary vibration, and the forces brought into play also, if the ceremony is to be successful, should come under similar planetary influences. Astral beings, and unseen intelligences of all kinds, degrees, and grades, which sometimes are invoked in magical work, correspond likewise to definite planetary rulership. The nature of the work at hand being ascertained, and its astrological correspondences determined, that incense is used having a like astrological rulership. Its function is dual. Primarily, because odors are the most etheric of material substances, they tend strongly to stimulate the nervous system. Such stimulation causes the generation of electrical energies which tend to strengthen and build up the etheric forces. Secondarily, if chosen with due respect to their astrological vibrations, they act as agents by which man is more easily placed in rapport with invisible entities having astrological vibrations similar to those of the incense.

Symbolically considered, incense represents man's thoughts, and the pot in which it burns represents his body. The fires of passion, or those of aspiration, kindle our thoughts. These, in turn, become burnt offerings either to our lower or to our higher nature. If man's thoughts are kindly and noble they tend to build up his spiritual body; but if they are ignoble and selfish they rise no higher than the astral plane and there distort and disfigure the astral body. When Abel, corresponding astrologically to the moon, and in man to the divine soul, sacrificed his animal passions and creative desires upon the altar, they became an acceptable sacrifice unto the Law. But Cain, corresponding astrologically to Mars, and in man to the animal soul, hoped to propitiate the Law by offers of the fruits of the earth, by offering to buy his way with material things. But the Law of spiritual construction accepts only the highest thoughts and aspirations. These, which incense symbolizes, become a "sweet savor" which build for the ego the spiritual form.

The Scythe

This is the emblem of the planet Saturn, the ruler of old age and dissolution. It thus symbolizes the harvest of earthly endeavors and the end of life; announcing that the purpose of life is the production of spiritual food. Whatsoever is sown will be reaped, the tares as well as the wheat. The crescent blade symbolizes the soul, the handle represents the material body. The function of the soul thus expresses as a means of garnering the harvest of experience in matter. The soul moves on, harvesting as it goes, the end of one life being the beginning of another. Death forces the expiation of every evil, adjusts all apparent inequalities, and in the spheres of the disembodied the keen blade becomes the sword of conscience. Death is the great leveler.

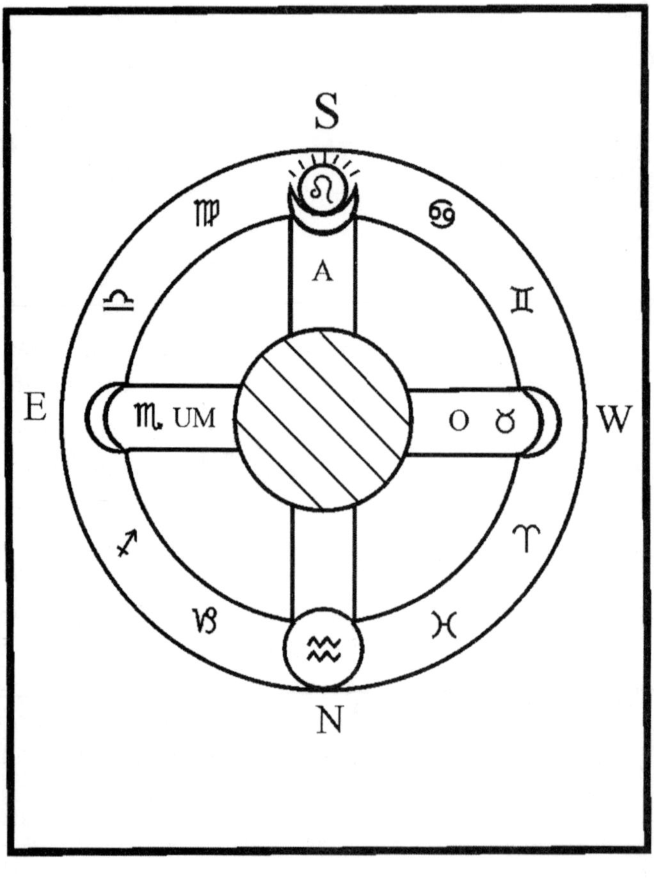

S
A
E
UM
O
W
N

Chapter 8

Master Mason

THE MASTER MASON'S lodge represents the sanctum sanctorum of King Solomon's Temple. That is, it is the inmost, or spiritual plane of the cosmic edifice. Such a lodge, it is said, is composed of three Master Masons—The Master, the Senior Warden, and the Junior Warden—typifying in the constitution of man the ego, the divine soul, and the spiritual body. It will thus be recognized that the Master Mason's lodge typifies existence in the spiritual world.

In the spiritual world the ego and divine soul function in a spiritual body; and the other four factors of man's constitution have been lost. At the death of the physical body both the material form and the etheric form gradually disintegrate. The soul then lives upon the astral plane and functions in an astral body. After its cycle of existence on the astral plane—undergoing first, if gross or materially minded, a period of purification in the lower astral regions corresponding to the purgatory of Roman Catholicism—occurs the second death, in which the astral body and such of the animal soul as had not been transmuted into divine soul, disintegrate; permitting the soul to live unfettered in the spiritual body on the spiritual plane.

The candidate for this degree is prepared by being stripped naked and then furnished with a pair of drawers reaching just above the hips. His drawer legs are both rolled above his knees, and his shirt is slipped down about his body, partly covered by his drawers, the sleeves and collar dangling behind over his waistband. His eyes are bandaged and a cable tow is wound three times around his body.

Both feet and both arms are left bare to indicate that both the understanding and the ability to work are unimpaired on the astral plane and on the spiritual plane. The shirt, symbolizing the astral body, though largely discarded, still clings to the candidate. This indicates that while yet in a physical body he may travel on the spiritual plane in the spiritual body, but that there must also be a connection with the astral body, that through it the connection with the physical may not be entirely severed. That is, a portion of the astral body must be used to preserve communication between the spiritual and the physical.

The woolen drawers are no longer red; for the animal part of man has been lost; yet the presence of this woolen underwear still serves to draw the attention to the importance of creative energy even on the spiritual plane. The candidate is blindfolded; for he is first represented as so newly arrived from the astral plane as to be unable to see things spiritual. Yet he has lost two-thirds of his clothing to indicate the loss of his outer forms. The cable-tow is wound around him, in the region ruled by the sign Libra, three times. Taurus is an earthly sign, and more typical of earthly love; but Libra, the day sign of Venus, typifies the more spiritualized love; such a love as triples the bond between soul and ego.

Tubal-Cain

The candidate desiring to enter the Master's lodge must knock three times; signifying his desire to enter the third, or spiritual plane. The pass word is Tubal-Cain.

Now Cain, according to the Bible, was a murderer; hence symbolizes Mars in its destructive aspect. But Tubal-Cain was an instructor of every artificer in brass and iron; was versed in the constructive use of iron, or Mars, and of brass, which is two metals in union. Cain thus represents the sex sign Scorpio in the aspect pictured by the deadly scorpion; while Tubal-Cain represents the sign in the aspect pictured by the eagle. And as the eagle is the highest flyer among the birds, so Tubal-Cain is the symbol of that complete regenerate marriage by which, according to the doctrine of the Ancient Masons, spiritual realms may be contacted.

As the candidate is permitted to enter, the two extreme points of a compass are pressed against his naked right and left breasts, indicating the subjugation of all the lower desires as well as the nobler aspirations to the spiritual laws, as signified by the compass, that govern regenerate union. He is then led around the room three times in the direction the Sun travels, and as he passes the Junior Warden, the Senior Warden, and the Master, they give him each during the first time around one rap, during the second time around two raps, and during the third time around three raps. This is to indicate that each of his three higher components—spiritual body, divine soul, and ego—have had an influence over him during his progress on the physical plane, on the astral plane, and on the spiritual plane.

Preparation for Life on the Spiritual Plane

While he thus travels about the room the Master reads from the Bible the first seven verses of the twelfth chapter of Ecclesiastes:

Remember now thy Creator in the days of thy youth, while the evil days come not, nor the years draw nigh, when thou shalt say, I have no pleasure in them; while the sun, or moon, or the stars be not darkened; nor the clouds return after the rain; in the day when the keepers of the house shall tremble, and the strong men shall bow themselves, and the grinders cease, because they are few, and those that look out of the windows be darkened, and the doors shall be shut in the streets, when the sound of the grinding is low, and he shall rise up at the voice of the bird, and all the daughters of music shall be brought low: Also when they shall be afraid of that which is high, and fears shall all be in the way, and the almond tree shall flourish, and the grasshoppers shall be a burden, and desire shall fail; because man goeth to his long home, and the mourners go about the streets: Or ever the silver cord be loosed, or the golden bowl be broken at the fountain, or the wheel broken at the cistern. Then shall the dust return to the earth as it was; and the spirit shall return unto God, who gave it.

This whole passage is an exhortation to the candidate to prepare to abide in the spiritual world, pointing out the transitory and unsatisfactory nature of all things below the plane of spirit. The number 12 is the number of sacrifice, the number indicating the end of the cycle of life, the completion of the zodiacal wheel. This twelfth chapter then, quite consistently, warns that the physical must inevitably end and that there should be a sacrifice of the lower nature. The vital forces, symbolized by the sun, the mental forces, symbolized by the moon, and the powers of perception, symbolized by the stars, should be sacrificed to higher things in youth before the years of sterility approach, while the natural forces are undimmed by clouds of emotional storm. The grinders, of course, are the planets which move over the zodiac as mullers in this mill of the gods; and when their ability to vivify man's body ceases, the windows of his soul are darkened, and the doors of his speech close, the vibrations cease their harmony, or music, and he passes as a bird might fly, in his astral body to the astral plane.

In the astral world the memory pictures of his good deeds and his bad deeds are with him, and he that has been guilty of wrong-doing must atone. Hence the fears, and the elements of destruction symbolized by grasshoppers. But the good deeds shall be a joy. Such are symbolized by the almond tree, which, like Aaron's staff that budded, is a symbol of creative power.

The silver cord is the magnetic thread connecting the spiritual body with the astral body. The golden bowl is the vital forces animating the candidate, which become broken at the fountain from which they spring, and the wheel is the birth-chart which is broken at the cistern of emotional expression. Then does the physical return to the physical and the spiritual return to the spiritual.

This all recalls to the candidate the inevitableness of death, and admonishes him to prepare while yet in the flesh, through purification and the sacrifice of his lower nature, for life on the higher plane; also suggesting that such preparation is quite as necessary for one who before death expects to travel on spiritual planes.

Next, the candidate is led to the west, representing the material plane; and is instructed how to approach the east, the place of light, representing the spiritual plane, by advancing upon three upright regular steps, to the third step in Masonry, his feet forming a square, his body erect. This is accomplished by first stepping off with the left foot and bringing the heel of the right into it, signifying the understanding of generation; and then stepping off with the right foot and bringing the heel of the left into it, signifying the understanding of regeneration; and finally stepping off with the left foot and bringing up the other so that the heels are together with the feet at right angles, signifying the understanding of spiritual union. That is, these three steps indicate that the candidate has mastered the knowledge of generation, regeneration, and the great work.

He then kneels before the altar on both naked knees and raises both hands to heaven with the arms bent. This is called the hailing sign. The kneeling position, both knees being bent, signifies obedience upon the part of both to the admonitions of the higher self, and the uplifted bent arms that they join in work upon the higher planes. In this degree both points of the compass are shown above the square, indicating that through obedience to the spiritual laws governing generation and regeneration the candidate has freed himself from the limitations imposed upon him by his physical and astral bodies. At this point, as in other degrees, the bandage is removed from his eyes, signifying here that he perceives clearly the things of the spiritual plane.

The sign of a Master Mason is given by raising both arms as in the hailing sign, letting them fall, and saying, "Is there no help for the widow's son?"

The widow's son is the divine soul of man, who has long been separated from his Father in Heaven, the ego, and dependent upon mother nature. The two hands represent the two divine souls of one ego, and the bent arms signify their desire for reunion. The hands falling to the region of Scorpio, as well as the spoken sentence, indicate the despair of reaching spiritual heights through mere physical means. The dieugard of the degree shows where the hope lies. It is made by drawing the right hand, palm down, from left to right across the abdomen in the region ruled by the sign Libra and letting it fall to the side. Libra, as well as Scorpio, is a sex sign, but being an airy sign it symbolizes unselfish love and spiritual union.

The pass-grip of a Master Mason is given by pressing the thumb of the right hand between the joints of the second and third fingers where they join the hand. The pressure is between the finger ruled in palmistry by Saturn, symbolizing the earth, and the Sun, symbolizing spirit. It thus betokens desire to transmute and refine. Its name is Tubal-Cain, signifying regeneration accomplished; and the word is given in three syllables—Tu-Bal-Cain—to denote that the work has been accomplished on all three planes.

The apron, in this degree, is worn with the triangle down over the square. This indicates that spiritual energies have completely permeated the creative forces, and that the ego has come into full control of the physical form of man.

The Trowel is Especially Significant

The working tools of a Master Mason embrace all the implements of masonry; but particular attention is given to the trowel. The trowel in form is a triangle surmounted by a plumb, representing the higher trinity of man's constitution—ego, divine soul, and spiritual body—receiving and utilizing the divine fire of creative energy. Its significance is that of another symbol, the trine in the center of which is the Hebrew letter, Jod. It is an implement used in joining stones to form a single structure, and is thus symbolical of creative energy used to bind together in consciousness the various experiences of life that build the temple of man.

In the Master's degree, however, which has to do with the spiritual plane, the trowel has an added significance. It signifies the use of creative energies to bind together permanently twin souls. This inseparable union, which according to the ancient doctrine insures joint immortality, takes place on the boundary of the sixth and seventh states of the spiritual world. Henceforth the two divine souls occupy but one spiritual body. These two and the one body they occupy form the triangle of the trowel. The ego which is common to both is signified by the handle. The triangle, in this aspect, thus represents the Lost Word recovered, as elaborated in the death, burial, and resurrection of the Grand Master, Hiram Abiff.

The Tragedy of Hiram Abiff Represents the Cyclic Journey of the Soul

This tradition informs us that at the building of Solomon's Temple there were present three Grand Masters: King Solomon, as instigator of the work, is symbolical of the sun in the sky and the ego of man's constitution. Hiram, King of Tyre, furnished the wood; the mental experiences, or perceptions. He typifies the spiritual body of man, the planet Mercury in the finished macrocosmic structure and, as the most earthly of the three, the mundane angles where the rays of sun and moon meet. Hiram Abiff was the widow's son, employed by King Solomon because he was a cunning artificer, a skillful worker in all kinds of metals, stones, timber, and cloth, and engraving upon them. He, of course, symbolizes the divine soul. Thus the ego instigates the work, the body furnishes the materials, or experiences, and the soul truly builds them into a fitting temple.

"It was the usual custom of the Grand Master, Hiram Abiff, every day at high twelve when the craft went from labor to refreshment, to enter into the sanctorum, or holy of holies, and offer up his adoration to the ever-living God and draw out his plans and designs on his trestle-board for the craft to pursue their labor." The craft are the celestial bodies that are more readily seen at night; for as midday is the period of maximum sunshine the heavenly bodies are then more difficult to see, and may be said to be at refreshment.

Now if we turn for a moment to the Kabala, we find that the holy of holies, called by them the Shekinah, is the place where the devoted retire for communion with higher powers. This Shekinah on earth, by them, also represents a spiritual union of man and woman, a union represented in the sky by the joining of the sun and moon, that is, new moon. And as our narrative relates to the temple of the sun, his holy of holies, his own sign, the sanctum sanctorum of the sun is the sign ruled by it, Leo. Our story starts, then, at noon, with a new moon in the first degree of the sign Leo. Hiram Abiff, symbolizing the divine soul of man, is represented by the moon.

Fifteen (this is the number of Satan and of black magic) Fellow Craft conspired to extort the Master's word from Hiram Abiff, and in case of refusal to kill him. Twelve, representing the twelve zodiacal signs, repented and confessed; but three, representing the three visible angles—Midheaven, Descendant and Ascendant—carried out the crime.

The names of the three ruffians that committed the crime were Jubela, Jubelo, and Jubelum. Now in the Bible Jubal is mentioned as the father of all such as handle the harp and organ. This refers unmistakably to the sign Leo, which rules the house of pleasures and entertainment of all kind in a natural birth-chart. Hence we start the story at the beginning of the sign Leo. In the same passage, but not of significance to this story, the three other signs that each rule one of the four quadrants of the heavens also are mentioned. Thus Jabal was the father of such as dwell in tents and have cattle. This refers to Taurus. Tubal-Cain was an instructor of every artificer in brass and iron. This denotes, as previously mentioned, the sign Scorpio. And Enoch, the perfect man, represents the Man of the zodiac, Aquarius.

Jubel, it is quite clear, is the sign of the sun. The designation of the three ruffians is shown by the suffix. The meaning of the letters used as suffixes to Jubel may be had by referring to Course 6, *The Sacred Tarot*, the

Hermetic System of Names and Numbers. The letter A corresponds to the planet Mercury, and to the attribute of will. The letter O corresponds to the planet Mars, and the attribute of destruction. The letter U corresponds to the planet Venus, and to pliability. The letter M corresponds to the zodiacal sign Aries, signifying transition through death to birth in a new life.

The sun and moon are represented in conjunction in the midheaven in the first degree of the sun's home sign, Leo; and evidently in some manner the Master's Word, which the villains try to obtain, refers to the most spiritual union thus symbolized.

Jubela, so the story goes, is stationed at the southern gate of the temple, or at the midheaven. He grabs the Grand Master and handles him roughly, demanding that he give the password. Hiram replies that if he will wait until the temple is completed and the Grand Lodge assembles at Jerusalem, and he is found worthy, it will be given to him.

Now the "a" as a suffix to Jubel signifies will, in this case the will to obtain the knowledge that confers immortality. The moon is with the sun, indicating that the soul has not yet separated from its divine ego, nor from its counterpart. Nevertheless, there is the will for conscious immortality. But it is only through experiences with external life that the spiritual form of man can be constructed, and only when this form has been completed that the permanent union of the divine counterparts can take place. And this constitutes the Master's Word as applied to the spiritual plane.

Not receiving the word, Jubela strikes the Master a blow across the throat with a twenty-four inch gauge. The twenty-four inch gauge represents the twenty-four hours of the day, hence the diurnal cycle of the sun. The throat is ruled by Venus, the planet of love. Hence the blow on the throat signifies the rupture of the ties of love by time; the separation of the twin souls at the moment of their involutionary descent from the spiritual world to gain experience. In the more personal sense, it signifies the effects of time to alienate the affections of the husband and wife when the sacred rites of love are violated.

The Master rapidly retreats toward the west gate, the Descendant, which is guarded by Jubelo. Thus is the moon, as it separates from the sun, carried by the diurnal rotation of the earth immediately to the western horizon, or Descendant. And thus also is the soul, in its involutionary descent before its first material incarnation, rapidly carried down to the place where it enters the physical realm. So too, the man or woman who violates the sanctity of love tends quickly to sink into the darkness of materialism.

Jubelo—representing the destructive tendency of Mars, the destructive tendencies of unwise unions; for the western horizon in astrology is the place of partnerships and unions, as well as of strife—gives the Master a blow across the breast with a square. This square, while symbol of inharmonious union, also represents the first quarter of the moon as it separates from the sun, and is a destructive astrological aspect. It typifies the soul joined, at last, to a material body. In a more personal sense it indicates inharmonious relations which injure the aspirations, these being symbolized by the breasts.

The Master then goes to the east gate which is guarded by Jubelum. This signifies that the moon, separating from the sun the while, is next carried by the diurnal motion of the earth from the western horizon, where it sinks, to the eastern horizon, where it rises. In relation to the progress of the soul, the period during which the moon is beneath the horizon, and invisible, represents its evolution through the various material forms of life below that of man. The east gate, where the moon rises into view, symbolizes the state where the soul rises from the purely material and incarnates in the intellectual being called man. Applied to humanity at large, this indicates the desire for more knowledge.

Jubelum strikes the Master upon the forehead with a gavel, whereupon the Master falls dead. This signifies that the moon arriving at her second quarter, receives the maximum force of the sun's rays, and is at the furthest point from her heavenly spouse. After this time, according to astrology, vital and magnetic forces begin to decrease, or die. This signifies also that the soul, arriving at the state of manhood in its evolutionary ascent, is tempted by, and becomes a slave to, sensations. The pure unsullied intuitions of the soul as to proper conduct are slain by the use of reason and an unbending will (the gavel). As applied to humanity at large, this indicates that having departed from the true source of light, yet seeking knowledge, it often falls into one of two destructive extremes: dissipation, or the complete annihilation of the emotions and sentiments through the use of an unbending will. Either deadens the soul to things spiritual.

Now the Grand Master having been killed, is carried out the east gate and buried with rubbish at low twelve. We have three thoughts here.

The moon at full passes above the horizon. Twilight obscures it, and as it is waning, instead of growing brighter it grows dimmer, is covered with rubbish. This burial is at low twelve, because at midnight the sun having reached the lowest point in its daily cycle, the moon has reached the highest point overhead, and exactly at low twelve (midnight) descends toward the horizon, descends into the grave. In the soul's progress its first efforts to learn the truth lead it to become buried in the various theories of materialists or the innumerable uncritical fantasies of mysticism, both of which are still further covered with the dust of prejudice. As applied to humanity at large, it represents man and woman seeking light, but blinded by false teaching and covered with the rubbish of illusory doctrines.

The Grand Master is carried at low twelve in a westerly direction, and there buried in a grave on the brow of Mount Moria; the ruffians hurrying, as the Master already begins to smell. That is, the moon after midnight of its full does travel to the west and sink in her grave below the western horizon. The reference to the smell signifies that she has begun to decrease in light, or decompose.

Mount Moria is the region of sacrifice. But it should be remembered that Abraham was finally commanded by the Lord (Law) not to sacrifice his son, not to sacrifice the human qualities as is done in asceticism; but to sacrifice only the Ram, or creative energies, on the altar of his devotion. The soul all too often, slain by false reasoning and covered with dogmatic debris, sinks into the west of materialism, and sacrifices its spirituality on the mountain of material ambition. This spiritual decay is indicated by selfish thoughts. As applied to mankind as a whole, man and woman may be misled by false doctrines and fall into destructive practices or into morbid asceticism, thus to be buried on the mountain of sensual desire, or in the tomb of vain and foolish sacrifices. The vibrations of sensualism and those of asceticism alike are offensive odors to the spiritual senses.

The Grand Master is buried in a grave six feet due east and west, and six feet perpendicular. The grave is marked by a sprig of cassia. This grave, or lowest point in the daily journey of the moon, is the nadir. The grave is as long, therefore, as from the eastern horizon to the western horizon. That is, the moon is invisible while in six mundane houses, or feet. It is buried as deep as from the midheaven to the nadir. That is, six mundane houses, or feet, deep. And it is marked by a sprig of cassia because cassia, always being green, symbolizes immortality. It thus promises resurrection.

This resurrection of the human soul is symbolized in the heavens by the moon being raised through the diurnal rotation of the earth on its axis from the nadir through six houses to the midheaven. All above the horizon symbolizes the spiritual realm, and all below the horizon symbolizes the physical realm. Therefore, the six houses, or feet, east and west symbolize the boundary between the spiritual and physical planes. This boundary marks the region of struggle that precedes the entering of the ego into full control of the physical form, which takes place when the seventh state of manhood, or adeptship, is reached.

Applied to humanity at large, the six feet east and west typify the material horizon, and the struggle to obtain the physical necessities of life and at the same time encourage the spiritual nature. The six feet perpendicular represent the six states of the soul world which the soul must traverse before it can permanently be united to its missing mate. Applied to humanity as a whole it represents the antagonism between the sexes, their misunderstandings of one another, and the temptation to yield to the dictates of the senses. This significance of the number six was given in chapter 4.

The sprig of cassia, in each case offers the hope of redemption through the rejuvenating action of the creative principle. Fire, in the days of the Ancient Masons, was used as a symbol of the sun; and the wood that fed the fire also was considered a creative symbol. Cassia being ever verdant, adds the thought of perpetual youth and life to the symbol of the creative principle signified by its wood.

After the murder of Hiram Abiff the three ruffians try to get a passage to Ethiopia; but they only get as far as Joppa, symbolizing the astral realm. Ethiopia is the land of darkness lying to the south of Jerusalem. While the sun is in Leo and the moon is making this symbolic cycle, the sun moves southward, and the points where he rises, culminates, and sets—the three ruffians—also travel southward. These ruffians are discovered by a wayfaring man—the sign Pisces, which rules the feet of man and is the sign of imprisonment—for the full moon, when the sun is in Leo takes place in Aquarius, and the moon immediately passes into Pisces.

The soul also, in its pilgrimage, may try to escape from the penalty of its folly by seeking oblivion in death, but only reaches the astral realm, where it is imprisoned and must give an accounting in full to the ego, its King Solomon, for its crime. And mankind may seek a like oblivion for itself in the doctrines of materialism; but the absurdities of such a course are quickly revealed by those psychic investigations ruled by the sign Pisces, and it must finally be brought before the throne of spiritual enlightenment.

Hiram Abiff was discovered missing at low six, when as usual King Solomon came up to the temple. He found all in confusion, no plans having been laid out on the trestle-board for the craft to follow. At full moon, which is the period we have been considering, the moon sinks below the horizon, and is discovered missing, and the sun, Solomon, rises in full sight, at 6 a.m. The light of the planets wanes and becomes confused, owing to daylight. The soul of man, reaching the sixth state of manhood, or cosmic consciousness, realizes it is separated from the ego, and that until they become again united its work is not directed from the spiritual plane; the work is not properly laid out. Applied to humanity, man and woman having arrived at a state of antagonism are able to form no efficient plans because of lack of co-operation.

Twelve Fellow Craft Masons, the twelve zodiacal signs, are sent to hunt for Hiram. Three, taking a westerly course—that is, setting—get news from the wayfaring man, Pisces. Finally one of them sitting down to rest on the brow of Mount Moria, the horizon, discovers the sprig of cassia, at the point of union of night and day. This promises the coming resurrection, for the moon will rise again, as will the soul that sinks into the grave. At this point, also, are discovered the three assassins, or visible angles. The three Fellow Craft that discover the assassins, represent the three zodiacal signs through which the moon moves from full to last quarter. They report the discovery to King Solomon, the sun, who sends another to look, that is, the sun during the moon's journey around the cycle has moved forward a sign, so the moon to reach it must, in addition to the twelve, move also through this sign.

When the body is uncovered, an offensive smell arises. The moon is still decreasing, or decomposing, in light. A search is made for the Master's Word, but nothing is found except a faint resemblance to the letter G marked on the left breast. The letter G found on the body is not recognized as a key to the Master's Word; for being on the left breast it signifies generation impelled by material motives. Yet while not the Word itself the discerning will not fail to note that it is the key to the word. The three signs by which the body is discovered represent the explorations of the soul on all three planes. Applied to humanity at large, it signifies material, mental, and spiritual effort.

The Master, finding the Word lost, repeats three times the Master's sign and the words; "O Lord, my God, is there no help for the widow's son?" Unless the word, to which Generation is the lost key, be recovered, there is little help on any of the three planes for the soul, nor as applied to humanity is there much hope of greatly improving the condition of the world.

Twelve Fellow Craft, zodiacal signs, are summoned to go with Solomon, the sun, to raise Hiram Abiff, the moon. They form a circle around the grave—the zodiacal signs form a circle—and the Master offers up a lengthy prayer the purport of which is a plea for immortality. The Master then directs that the body be raised by the E.A. grip, Boaz; but the skin cleaves from the flesh and it cannot be thus raised. Immortality cannot be attained by the application of mere physical methods; for the body is not the man, no more so than the skin is the whole body. It is next proposed to raise the body with the F.C. grip, Jachin; but it cannot be done because the flesh cleaves from the bone. The soul is not assured of immortality when it can work on the astral plane; for the astral body is not the whole man, no more so than the flesh is the whole body.

Finding the grip of the two lower degrees inadequate, the Master raises the candidate for the Master's degree, who represents Hiram Abiff, with the Master Mason's grip, upon the five points of fellowship, uttering in his ear the Word Mah-Hah-Bone, used as a substitute for the lost Master's Word.

This Master's grip is called the Lion's grip, because it is typical of the sun's action in the sign Leo where it exercises its most virile power. It is made in shaking hands by sticking the finger nails of each of the fingers into the joint of the other's wrist where it joins the hand. The five fingers of one hand represent woman, and the five fingers of the other hand represent man. As all portions ruled by the various planets thus come in contact, it represents complete fusion, soul infiltration of soul. Such is the powerful influence of the Sun in the love sign Leo, by which the Moon is again united to it; denoting the eternal union of twin souls through which their united immortality becomes assured. It is called Mah-Hah-Bone, because the word, signifying marrow of the bone, denotes a more complete fusion than that of the physical, symbolized by the skin; or of the astral, symbolized by the flesh; or even of spiritual bodies, symbolized by the bone. It refers to the complete and permanent soul union between natural counterparts, soul of soul, heart of hearts.

The raising on the five points of fellowship is accomplished by taking the candidate, who represents Hiram Abiff, by the Master's grip and lifting him by bracing the right foot against him. When raised, the Master's right foot is inside his right foot, the inside of the Master's knee is against his, the Master's breast against his breast, and their left hands are on each other's backs, each putting the mouth to the ear of the other, in which position alone the Master's word may be given.

In this manner the fullness of the reunion between sun and moon is designated. Being together, both receive the five points, that is, the same aspects from the other five planets. The three attempts at raising account for the three signs through which the moon passes from its last quarter to reach new moon, which is its union with the sun. By this time the sun, having started at the first of Leo, has reached the 28th degree of the sign. According to the Hermetic System of Names and Numbers (see Course 6, *The Sacred Tarot*), 2 plus 8 equals 10, which is the number of man and woman, that is, the union of two 5's, or the five points of fellowship.

The soul also, having taken its cyclic pilgrimage from spirit into matter and from matter back to spirit again, not only arrives at its original state of exaltation in the spiritual world, but the ego, having gained wisdom and love through its soul's experiences, has passed to still higher spheres, and the soul uniting with it is raised to these regions. Applied to humanity as a whole, through the reestablishment of harmonious relations between man and woman, and their united efforts, the misery that has resulted from their strife is banished, and they become efficient agents for building up a better world.

The union of foot to foot (Pisces) represents mutual understanding, which is essential to united effort. It further refers to united effort in spiritual science and psychical research, because these are ruled by the sign Pisces.

The union of knee to knee (Capricorn) typifies the value of mutual service. In this manner co-operation yields the best results. It also indicates that there is united effort in regard to material attainment, for this too is ruled by the sign Capricorn.

Breast to breast (Cancer) signifies that if best results are to be obtained there must be unity of aspiration. It also indicates that the magnetism of each should nourish and sustain the other, and that there should be unity in the home, for these things are ruled by the sign Cancer.

The left hand to the back (Leo) of the other shows that each should work in a physical way to strengthen and support the other. Each should support by his mental endeavors, ruled by Gemini, the ambitions, ruled by Leo, of the other.

Lastly, there should be complete and mutual exchange of confidences between husband and wife, such as is denoted by mouth to ear (Taurus). And the lips should offer encouragement to the other, and both should fulfill their financial obligations, these being ruled by Taurus.

How the Five Points of Fellowship Do Their Work

The number five is the number of Jupiter, the planet of religion. And if the resurrection of the soul, Hiram Abiff, is to take it through the astral realm—the upper regions of which commonly are called the spiritual realm, but are not, as although their vibratory rates are high, the velocities are still those which pertain to astral substance—there must be great devotion, not to piety or any special orthodox belief, but to true religion.

Velocities of substance below that approximating light define the substance as physical in nature, and thus as belonging to the material plane. But when velocities are attained greater than that of light, that defines the substance moved as no longer physical, but as belonging to the inner realms. The planetary vibrations that affect human life and destiny, the thoughts of man, and the unconscious minds, not only of men, but of all other creatures, persist in substance having a velocity greater than the Boundary-Line etheric energy, of which light, radiation and electricity are well known manifestations. That is, they occupy the astral plane, and are not restricted by the limitations imposed upon purely physical existence.

Things, by the mere circumstance of their physical existence, also have astral counterparts in the astral realm; and all life-forms on earth, when the physical is destroyed, tend to persist for some time as astral life-forms in the inner realm. Good and bad, high and low, vicious and saintly; people continue existence after physical death on the astral plane.

But although there are fewer limitations to existence on the astral plane than on the physical, it too has its own restrictions. Life there is not everlasting. Planetary currents and the cycles which affect astral life in time cause the dissolution of the astral form, more slowly, to be sure, than the physical is caused to disintegrate, but none the less surely. Immortality is not static, but depends on eternal progression.

When velocities still higher than those which astral substance can attain are reached, new properties are at hand, and that which is affected is spiritual substance. But while all life-forms on earth have an astral counterpart in which they survive for a time after physical dissolution, none has a spiritual body until that form is built, either from the material plane before death of the physical body, or from the astral plane, where time and opportunity also are present, before the second death dissolves the astral form.

If the individual is to continue to survive he must construct, by the quality of his aspirations, thoughts and feelings, a body in which he can function on the plane of velocities still higher than the astral, the real spiritual plane.

While the range of vibratory rates on one plane often greatly overlaps those of another plane; for molecular vibrations may be more rapid than some vibrations in the Boundary-Line etheric substance; nevertheless, vibratory rates of a particular kind can be used to affect substance on a still higher plane. That is, much as the molecular vibrations of a piece of iron when they become sufficiently rapid through heating, impart energy to etheric substance which we recognize as light, or an electric light filament glows, so aspirations based on definite motives, love of the less selfish kind, and certain combinations of thoughts which act as a flux one with the other, affect spiritual substance directly. That is, the vibrations imparted to astral substance by these mental states have the property of affecting spiritual substance which has velocities that astral substance cannot reach.

And in the Master Mason's degree particular stress is placed upon the higher types of love thus to affect spiritual substance and build a spiritual form. Yet true religion in its practice, although not so easily, also can be utilized for this purpose. This, however, implies much knowledge of Spiritual Alchemy (explained in detail in Course 3, *Spiritual Alchemy*), determined practice in thought control, and devotion to Universal Welfare.

The individual, regardless of his physical environment, who resolutely directs all the acts of his life, including his thoughts and emotions, to those things which after due thought he believes are in the interest of society as a whole, by so doing is being raised on the five points of fellowship. He is gaining in understanding (Pisces), co-operating in attaining (Capricorn) practical benefits for mankind, developing exalted aspirations (Cancer), strengthening (Leo) his will, and mentally exchanging confidences and receiving (Taurus) encouragement from those still further along the path who impress him from the inner plane.

In fact, to be truly a Master Mason implies that through diligent practice one has learned how at all times to maintain a constructive attitude, and to keep the thoughts directed to the accomplishment of those purposes which are of greatest assistance to mankind. It implies that one has so conditioned his emotional nature that anger, fear, hatred, grief, disappointment and jealousy are never felt; and that instead there is at all times, and toward all persons, a feeling of benevolent kindness, which may nevertheless be strict and firm; and that one has acquired the ability to feel, with no great effort exalted love and tender affection.

Mastership, according to Ancient Masonry, thus is seen to be a very different thing from the popular conception that to be a Master one must retire from the world and devote the time to meditation and so-called spiritual practices. In fact, true spiritual practices are now seen to rest upon man's contact with others. It is impossible to acquire spirituality or true Mastership through selfish seeking. Instead, they come only as the result of pronounced effort to assist others.

It is not primarily to gain spirituality that the Master learns to develop a steady, positive and rather high electrical potential, through which he is able to shut from his consciousness thoughts of others or thoughts of his own which he has decided are not constructive, and through which he is able to maintain control of his emotions. He learns to do this, and to extend his consciousness to the inner plane and there acquire information not to be had through other channels, because these abilities enable him to help the people he contacts.

When, depends upon individual circumstances. But one who thus develops the other requisites of a true Master Mason, will not too long have to wait for union with the soul of his soul. For now it will be apparent that the whole tragedy of Hiram Abiff, and his later resurrection, are meant to symbolize the soul's separation from its divine counterpart, its separate journey through the cycle of involution and evolution, and its final attainment of an immortal life through reunion with its lost mate.

In Egyptian tradition Osiris is dismembered, but the fourteen pieces representing the fourteen days from full moon to new moon, are collected and reunited by Isis. The ashes of Hiram, however, are represented as having been buried under the sanctum sanctorum, and a monument erected over them figuring a virgin weeping over a broken column, with a book before her, in her right hand a sprig of cassia, in her left hand an urn; Time standing behind her, with his hands infolded in the ringlets of her hair.

The virgin is Isis weeping over the slain Osiris, her lost mate, signified by the broken column. That immortality be assured, as suggested by the cassia, it becomes necessary under the law, signified by the book, that reunion take place. This has not yet occurred, for the urn, symbol of affections, is still empty. Hair is ruled by the planet Venus, and until the reunion takes place her affections bind her to the realms where time is master. Applied to humanity at large this ensemble signifies the destruction of the better impulses of the soul through the abuse of the creative energies.

The involution of the soul into matter and its evolution back to spirit, is symbolized astrologically by the Sun's journey through the zodiac, as related in chapter 5. But the separation of the two halves of the divine soul and their subsequent reunion after the pilgrimage of zodiacal cycles is symbolized astrologically by the separation of the sun and moon, and their ultimate reunion. It may be thought that the Ancient Masons were somewhat arbitrary in enacting the scene with the sun in Leo, but not so in fact; for in practical magic, at which they were adepts, operations of an electric and repellent nature are more successful if initiated at noon of the day of the first new moon after the sun enters Leo. On the other hand, as any astrologer readily understands, operations of an attractive and magnetic nature are more successful if initiated at midnight of the day of the first full moon after the sun enters Capricorn.

As Isis of Egypt searched for the fourteen fragments of Osiris, and as the moon decreases for fourteen days between full moon and new moon, so we need not be surprised to find it related that Hiram Abiff remained fourteen days in his grave before being resurrected.

In the individual horoscope the tragedy of Hiram corresponds to the revolution of psychic forces within the astral body of man from month to month and from year to year. It is the magical cycle of the soul as measured from one transit of the moon over the radical place of the sun to another such transit; and this is the exact measure of psychic power received by the individual from month to month. It has a most important practical application, for soul powers are found to have their periods of ebb and flood, there being times when it is possible, and there being times when it is not possible, to establish the essential conditions necessary for the successful practice of high magic. This phase of the matter is explained in detail in *Award Manuscript 13*.

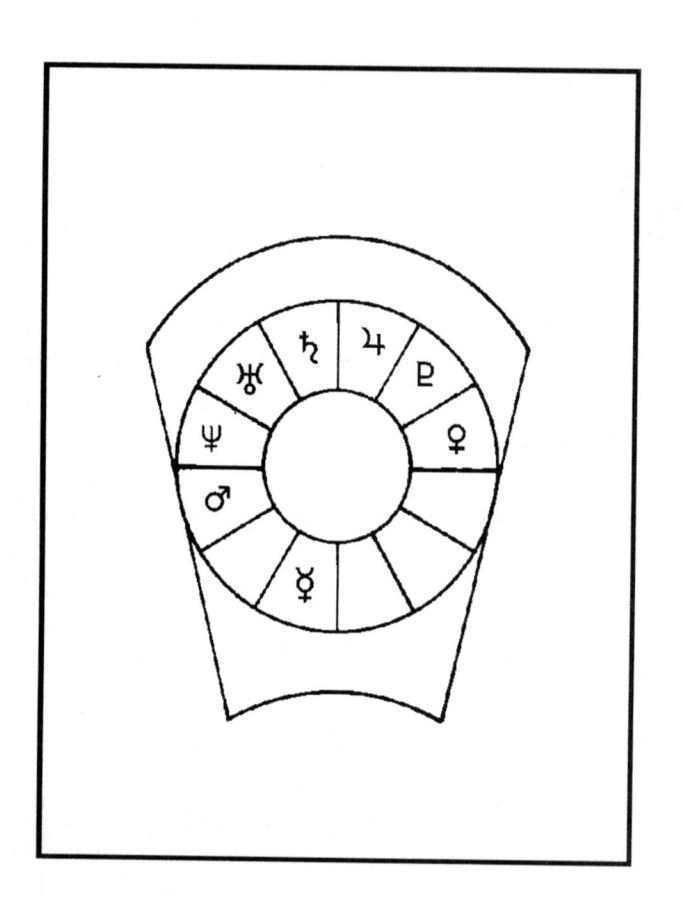

Chapter 9

Mark Master Mason

THE FOURTH DEGREE of Masonry, to be consistent with the science of numbers which associates four with Realization, relates to the realization and utilization of the powers and functions conferred by the first three degrees. Thus does the fourth Major Arcanum of the tarot (see Course 6, *The Sacred Tarot*, Chapter 4) become a commentary, in the language of symbolical pictograph, on the Mark Master degree of Ancient Masonry.

The divine Tetragrammaton of the kabalists summarizes all potencies in a word of four letters. Astrologically, all celestial influences are synthesized in the four-fold form of the sphinx. And in Ancient Masonry the whole of essential Masonic doctrines are compressed within the first four degrees; additional degrees being merely an elaboration of what in its essence may be found in Entered Apprentice, Fellowcraft, Master Mason and Mark Master degrees; Mark Master denoting that the soul has reached maturity and is at the period of its fruition.

To open the Mark Master lodge eight officers are necessary and ten usually are present, corresponding to the seven planets of man's sevenfold constitution, plus the three upper-octave orbs, or overseers. Uranus, Neptune and Pluto are truly overseers in the sense that when injustice and tyranny become rampant on earth, the factors within the unconscious minds of men take a hand and bring, through revolution, a change; and in the sense that it is through utilizing the high-frequency electromagnetic radiations of the nervous system which are ruled by these planets that ESP and other inner plane activities of the soul can effectively be directed, and through which the inner plane intelligence of man can reach and effectively direct the physical brain. Uranus prominent in the birth-chart gives facility in using the Inspirational System of mental activity, Neptune prominent in the birth-chart gives facility in using Feeling ESP, and Pluto prominent in the birth-chart gives facility in employing the Inner Plane System of mental activity. Through these upper-octave faculties man can acquire information and power to direct his own life and destiny which can be acquired in no other way.

The Junior Overseer is located at the South Gate, to indicate the illumination given by the type of Intellectual ESP conferred by the electromagnetic radiations of the nervous system ruled by Uranus; even as at noon, which is the Sun's south point, the illumination is greatest.

The Senior Overseer is placed at the West Gate, to indicate the receptive quality given by the electro-magnetic field of the nervous system ruled by Neptune, which makes of it a receiving set to pick up, radio fashion, the astral vibrations radiated by objects, thoughts and conditions.

The Master Overseer is stationed at the East Gate, to indicate the new life, the conscious inner plane life, bestowed by the highest of all electromagnetic radiations of the nervous system, ruled by Pluto, which when properly active in the individual life can be compared to a rising sun revivifying a slumbering world.

The candidate is represented as having passed initiation on all three planes and returned to his body. Four raps signify the accomplishment resulting from this action on three planes, and the cable-tow is wound four times around his body to represent his realization of the complete union between soul and ego. To indicate that after his travels upon the higher planes he has now returned to physical life, the Senior Warden reads the following passage of Scripture: "Then he brought me back the way of the gate of the outward sanctuary, which looketh toward the East, and it was shut, and the Lord said unto me: Son of man, mark well," etc.

The Mark Master's sign, the Heave-over, is made by interlacing the fingers of both hands, holding them down in front opposite the right hip and then bringing them to the left side of the neck as if to throw a weight over the left shoulder. The E.A. degree, represented by the First Major Arcanum of the tarot, corresponds to the planet Mercury. The F.C. degree, represented by the Second Major Arcanum, corresponds to the sign Virgo. The Master Mason degree, represented by the Third Major Arcanum of the tarot, corresponds to the sign Libra. The Mark Master degree, represented by the Fourth Major Arcanum, corresponds to the sign Scorpio; thus this Heave-over, alluding to the rejection of the Keystone, refers to the sign Scorpio.

The ten locked fingers represent the union of man and woman, and the front of the right hip symbolizes the constructive power of Scorpio, which by most is discarded, or used negatively in Venusian pleasures as indicated by the left side of the neck.

The Keystone of Psychic Development is Proper Electrification

Any control of the thoughts and emotions, by which alone the character and the fortune attracted into the life can be improved, ESP or inner plane work of any kind accomplished, or domestic felicity advanced, depends upon proper electrification; and proper electrification is closely related to the activities of the region ruled by Scorpio, which symbolically are thrown on the rubbish heap in the heave-over.

Love as a mental condition is very real. But to feel love there must be appropriate electrical energies in the nervous system. While we occupy physical bodies we feel with the nerves, and that which gives rise to the feeling is the electric charges which they generate and whose impulses flow to some central station in the brain.

Love is of various kinds and on various levels of expression. The feeling of affection for children, for instance, seems to depend much upon the electrical energies generated through the secretions of the back pituitary gland; and the more refined type of love seems linked with the electrical energies generated through the secretions of the thyroid glands. But for the sake of this illustration let us consider the more common phase of attraction between the sexes.

Man and wife may mentally and spiritually love each other devotedly, but the feeling of physical attraction commonly is subject to wax and wane. Loyalty, devotion and willingness to self-sacrifice may well be constant; but the more physical attraction and responsiveness are largely dependent upon the electrical condition at the time. In spite of willing to do so, neither can have any real passion, or even strong feeling of physical attraction toward the other, if through overwork, illness, or too much sex indulgence, that one is electrically depleted. Feeling depends upon the electrical energies present, and if these are absent and cannot be generated, the feeling cannot be coaxed or willed into existence.

While other glands are involved in lesser degree, it is chiefly the function of the secretions of the gonad glands to develop in the nervous system those particular electrical energies which give the feeling of physical attraction toward the love object. When the high-tension electrical energies are expended there is a lowering of potential, and the feeling which persists, due to the strong lower potential electrical energies present, is of different quality. If harmonious, it may sustain a tender love which is far above mere passion. If the thoughts at the time have been conditioned to consider all expression of sex sinful, or if for a variety of reasons there is inharmony or thoughts of defilement, the low potential electrical energies present will bring and sustain a feeling of degradation. But in any case the violent expenditure of electrical energies which have been generated largely through the action of the secretions of the gonads on the nervous system, for the time being markedly lowers the electrical potential.

Depending upon the health of the individual, the activity of his gonad glands and other factors, in a shorter or longer time the electrical potential due to gonad activity normally rises to a point where it exerts considerable tension; in other words, to a point in which the feeling of physical attraction for the loved one again is quite strong.

Now electrical energy in the nervous system is capable of being diverted, much as the electrical currents flowing over the ordinary power lines are; and those generated through the action of the secretions of the gonads on the nervous system are not only capable of being diverted into different systems of mental activity, but also are capable of being stepped up or stepped down markedly in voltage. They, therefore, are capable of quite a wide range of use to give additional power to the electrical energies developed by the action of other endocrine glands.

It might seem from this that a celibate life is of decided advantage in that it provides electrical energies of high voltage and power which can be used for the production of psychic phenomena, for building up vitality, to use in cerebral thinking, or for such other purposes as require energy. And this is the general idea behind the Oriental training which decrees that a neophyte must renounce marriage and live a celibate life. But here we are confronted with three factors which are subject to a widely variable personal equation.

1. The electrical power normally generated in the nervous system through the action of the gonad secretions by a person who has Mars inconspicuous in his birth-chart and Venus in conjunction with Saturn is but a small fraction of the electrical power generated by the action of these secretions by a person who has Mars conjunction Venus and both very prominent in his birth-chart. Those who do creative work of any kind have active gonad secretions; and it is likely that some creative artists generate daily, in spite of marital excess, more electrical energy of this kind than most other people do even when they live celibate lives.

2. Ordinarily a gland, muscle or nerve which is called upon to do no work tends to reduce its activity, perhaps even atrophy. While under normal conditions of abstinence no such deterioration is likely to take place, the question remains whether or not gonad secretion which is given no opportunity to function normally will continue as well to assist in the development of electrical power in the nervous system as if not too frequently it were called into normal play.

3. The electrical power that can be handled successfully by the nervous system when generated, varies markedly with different persons; and anyone can only handle so much successfully. When the lighting system in your home gets an overload of electric current, there is a fuse which melts and cuts the current off so it will not burn down the house. Now some people put a one cent piece, which will not melt, in the fuse box when a fuse has been blown, and because while they have it there no unusually heavy electrical load is present, no damage occurs. But when an unusually heavy current comes in under such circumstances, there is usually a fire or other catastrophe. And the individual who normally generates much electrical power under the influence of the secretions of his gonad glands, and who through trying to awaken his kundalini or by rhythmic breathing intensifies this current, and at the same times lives a life of enforced celibacy, suffers much damage. He generates more electricity than he can handle and it causes disaster.

That which is related to sex becomes a very delicate subject of discussion, too delicate to go into the details as the importance of the matter warrants. Yet the individual who employs everyday common sense, instead of being led astray by fantastic mysticism or by the opposite extreme, sensualism, will solve its problems without much difficulty. He can do this more readily than anyone can lay down hard and fast rules for him, because he is in a position to observe the actual effect in terms of the volume and potential of electrical energy present as the result of variations in conduct.

Not only do hard and fast rules that work for one person often fail to work well for another, but usually there is a periodic variation of gonad activity during the month, which differs widely in intensity with different persons, so that at one period even though the thoughts are turned exclusively to cerebral pursuits, the electrical power present may be far more than at another period even when the thoughts are not especially guarded.

The condition of electrification to be sought, and to which the sex activity or lack of sex activity may contribute or from which it may detract, is that in which there is not so much electrical power within the nervous system as to place the individual under a strain of pressure, but in which there is ample to do whatever work is at the time required of it. And of course it is understood that this sex factor is only one of a number of things which may assist or detract from thus acquiring the proper electrical power.

Emotion cannot be felt in the absence of electrical energies, and to sustain a Mood there must be available adequate electrical power which can be used for this purpose. Yet, because there is so much nonsense written and talked about sex and the kundalini, I believe I should again emphasize that while electrical energies generated through the action of the gonad secretions are capable of being diverted into widely different channels, or sublimated so that their voltage and trend support noble aspirations and the highest phases of love, it is quite possible to develop more electrical power than can be diverted, or used in a constructive way.

The second sign is made by dropping the right hand again to the region of Scorpio, clenching the last two fingers, and leaving the thumb and first two fingers open. It refers to the method of carrying the keystone, represents the male trinity, and indicates symbolically this process of proper electrification.

The hand is next raised to the right ear and the open thumb and two fingers passed with a circular motion about the ear. This signifies that after proper electrification the electromagnetic energies are used to reinforce astral vibrations which enable the individual to exercise Intellectual ESP and thus receive information from the inner plane. The ear indicates the reception of such information.

The hand is then dropped partially down, the palm open and in a horizontal position, and the left is lifted up and brought down edgewise upon the wrist of the right. This alludes to the penalty of having both the ear and the right hand cut off, meaning that if the wages are not properly received, that is, if they are received negatively instead of through ESP, that the ability to receive anything of value, or to execute anything meritorious, will be cut off.

The Keystone of Attainment is Proper Cooperation Between Husband and Wife

The third sign is made by extending the right arm in front with the hand clenched except the thumb and two fingers. It indicates the method of receiving wages, and the importance of positive virility.

The keystone which the builders rejected is neither oblong nor square, but is composed of both straight and curved—masculine and feminine—lines. It is taken successively by the candidate to the three overseers, who note its singular beauty and form, but finally reject it because it has not the mark of any craft upon it.

It was formed by Hiram Abiff, the divine soul, to be the keystone of the temple; but upon his death was lost, and when later rediscovered and presented to the overseers it was not recognized, but was cast out among the rubbish. It has the mark of no particular craft upon it because it belongs to all souls, and each must be found worthy before he can place his astrological signature upon it. In its highest aspect it is the union of soul mates by which they are enabled to receive the wages of immortality.

On planes less high the keystone refers to proper union, the knowledge of which, as indicated in reference to electrification, for ages has been lost to mankind, and now rediscovered is in danger of being rejected by the overseers; that is by the occultists, mystics and spiritual aspirants; as was the case in the past.

But before the temple is completed a search is made by the Craft for the missing keystone; for the temple cannot be finished without it. It is found amid the rubbish and brought to the Master, who reprimands the overseers, and reads the following passage from the Scripture, which clearly designates its nature: "To him that overcometh will I give to eat of the hidden manna, and I will give him a white stone, and in the stone a new name written, which no man knoweth, saving him that receiveth it." That is, by united regeneration man becomes renewed, or given a new name, even as by soul union man becomes man no longer, but an angel.

The keystone is said to be 4 x 6 inches dimensions, representing 24 hours, or the circumference of united night and day. About its circumference is a circle of 8 letters, given as H-T-W-S-S-T-K-S, the initials of Hiram Tyrian, Widow's Son, sent to King Solomon. This refers to the return of the divine soul to its source, and may be rendered: He That Was Slain Soars to Kindred Spirit. In humanity it also refers to regeneration supplanting generation.

Within this circle of letters every Mark Mason must place his own private mark, which, of course, is his astrological signature. Thus the 8 letters represent the 8 planets—in addition to Sun and Moon, that are not planets and signify masculine and feminine—which circle the heavens daily.

The Keystone as Applied to Natal Astrology

Thus is indicated that one diurnal rotation of the earth measures out to man the astrological energies to be released during one year of life, and that this is the keystone of timing and indicating the major events which are attracted into an individual's life.

The progressed aspects calculated by this day-year system are not merely symbolic; for that which is symbolic only may reveal information of value, but it does not exert a definite and positive force such as progressed aspects do.

Horary astrology certainly to a large extent is only symbolic, and by its aid information of value may be acquired. But horary astrology is a method of divination and thus in a different category than natal astrology, which I am convinced maps actual energies which have an impact upon the person whose birth-chart and progressed aspects are under consideration. No doubt, as there are many methods of divination by using cards and numbers, there are various systems of astrological divination which can be used, even in connection with the birth-chart, through which considerable information can be obtained about that which will happen to the individual in the future. Having tried some of these methods out, I feel confident such is the case. But I am even more firmly convinced that the progressed aspects employed in the Hermetic System are something more than divinatory clues, and actually map invisible forces radiated by the planets which have a definite effect upon man.

I have progressed the charts of many people who knew nothing about astrology and asked them how they felt in reference to various matters as compared to the way they felt about the same matters at other periods in their lives. I have found invariably that at the time a certain strong progressed aspect was operative that the trend of their thoughts and their feelings about the things represented by the houses of their charts affected by the aspect had changed markedly in the direction indicated by the progressed aspect.

Almost any astrologer of experience upon learning of the outstanding conditions and events in another person's life, yet without knowing the birth-chart, can correctly tell the person that a certain specified planet is being heavily aspected by progression at the time. Each planet has its own characteristic manner of affecting events. I have witnessed this picking of the planet responsible for an event, before the birth-chart has been seen or the progressed aspects calculated, innumerable times, and later verified when the progressed aspects were worked out.

On many occasions I have had students, who had not taken the trouble to work up their progressions, or who as yet did not know how to do so, remark that they felt the vibrations of Mars, or Venus, or Uranus, or Saturn; and on working up the progressed aspects I have found that there actually was a progressed aspect to the mentioned planet then operative. And students who know they are coming under a progressed aspect, and keep on the lookout to discern when they first feel it, sometimes feel it distinctly when it is a full one degree from perfect, and sometimes feel it only when within half a degree or less from perfect. Many students report that they always can feel the distinctive influence of any of the planets when it is making a strong progressed aspect. They can name the planet to which they are thus most strongly responding.

More evidence could be cited to indicate that the day-year progressed aspects at the time they are operative exert a well defined and plainly felt force upon the individual. But as many who read this can feel what planet is making a strong progressed aspect in their charts, when they have for a time neglected to look up their progressions, let us consider how that which takes place in one day after birth can spread its influence over 365¼ days of life.

Now I realize that when I again mention Einstein and Relativity that many will feel I am treading upon highly debatable ground. And in so far as Einstein's General Theory of Relativity is concerned, which deals with curved space in relation to gravitation this is true. But in regard to Einstein's Special Theory of Relativity, which was first propounded in 1905, and whose implications alone, I believe, explain the action of progressed aspects, extension of consciousness, ESP and inner plane properties in general, it has now become almost unanimously accepted by those best qualified to prove or disprove it. To quote from an article by H.P. Robertson, Ph.D., Professor of Mathematical Physics, Princeton University, which appeared in the June, 1939, issue of Scientific American Magazine:

> In view of these developments one may say that at present the special theory of relativity is one of the most thoroughly accepted and most firmly established doctrines of modern physics. It has permeated the fields of mechanics, electromagnetism (including optics) and atomic physics; while it may appear desirable to have further direct checks on the validity of its mechanical aspects, a deviation from the predicted effects would constitute a most puzzling—and, at least temporarily, distressing—jolt for modern physics.

An essential factor in the special theory of relativity, which has now become so completely accepted in scientific circles, is the interrelationship between velocity and time. It is held that there is no such thing as absolute time, but that as velocity increases, time slows down, until, at the velocity of light time comes to a standstill. Conversely, as time speeds up, velocity slows down until at the time speed with which we are familiar, objects tend to move at the velocity physical things are observed to do.

Nor is this just a theory, as the experiments of Dr. Herbert E. Ives, mentioned in chapter 5, demonstrate. He reported that observing the Doppler shift in an oncoming hydrogen beam, and at the same time the shift due to the recession of the same beam, shows that, as relativity predicts, a moving clock keeps slower time than one standing still.

If at the velocity of light time stands still, within a single moment of such slow time an infinite number of events could happen. And in a realm, or condition, where velocities were not so great as light, but are greater than that of ordinary physical objects, a large number of events can happen in a single moment of this slower time. In our dreams, for instance, and to some people when they are on the verge of dying, there are numerous experiences which in ordinary time would require days or years, compressed into a few minutes of the slower time of this borderline state of consciousness.

When our consciousness moves from this borderline realm where velocities are far greater than those of physical life, to the realm of physical existence where velocities are much slower, the events which in our dream took but a few moments to happen, spread out in this faster time of normal life to occupy a period which seems to us days, or months or years.

To take another illustration, suppose we walked from Los Angeles to San Francisco at the rate of 25 miles per day, and pass through 30 towns on the way. At this velocity it would take us 18 days to see the 30 towns. But by airplane we can make the trip in 3 hours, seeing the 30 towns. That is, in three hours' movement at airplane velocities we can see as many towns as in 18 days at walking velocities. The amount of experience to be had in a given interval of time—3 hours, for instance—is relative to the velocity with which such events are passed.

According to relativity, as velocities increase there is a definite slowing down of time, the exact amount being determined by the Lorentz transformation. Similarly, as velocities slow down there is a definite speeding up of time, the exact amount being determined by the Lorentz transformation.

We have already seen that a dream, or near death state of consciousness may have a velocity, in so far as the number of events witnessed within a few moments of this slower time of the boundary-line state, such that these same events happening on the physical plane would require days or months to take place. That is, in the boundary-line region between the physical world and the realm having velocities greater than that of light, time so slows down that when brought up into physical consciousness it is similar to bringing all the things witnessed in a 3 hour airplane flight from Los Angeles to San Francisco up into a consciousness that knows no faster velocities than walking, in which time is speedier and movement proportionally slower, so that it requires 18 days for the same amount of experience.

Material science has now proved that the nerve currents are electrical in nature and that man has an electromagnetic form. Electromagnetic waves when radiated move with the velocity of light; but electric currents traveling over wires or over nerves move much slower. In other words, in man's electromagnetic form are velocities greater than those of ordinary physical substance, but which are not as great as the 186,173 miles per second that light travels.

From what already has been said it will be apparent that if a clock slows down relative to the velocity it acquires, as consciousness attains higher and higher velocities it will be able to have more and more experiences within the space of four minutes of this slowed down time. At a certain velocity, which is well within the limit of what can be expected to occur in man's electromagnetic form, the ratio of the number of experiences in four minutes of slower time, to the number of experiences in the faster time of external life, would be 365¼ to 1.

Bear in mind that in the one interval of the slower time of the high velocity region as many events can transpire (remember the airplane trip to San Francisco) as in 365¼ similar intervals (remember the walking trip to San Francisco) of the faster time of the ordinary objective world. The slower the time, the more numerous the events that can happen in any given interval, but as time is speeded up to the tempo of ordinary physical existence, it takes more intervals of this physical time to accommodate a given number of experiences.

In case the ratio between the electromagnetic region of man's body and his physical were 365¼ to one, the occurrences that took place in a little less than four minutes of this slower boundary-line time, when expressed in the faster time of the external world would occupy a duration of twenty-four hours, and what took place in 24 hours in the time of the boundary region, when externalized on the physical plane would take 365¼ days of the ordinary faster time; that is, what took place in one day in the boundary region, when externalized would take place in one year of the faster physical time.

Under such circumstances, just as a dream occupying less than four minutes when brought into objective consciousness may represent a whole day of physical existence, so changes brought about in a portion of the finer body at a certain velocity level, by planetary movement during one day, when transformed into the faster time of objective existence, occupy 365¼ days, or one year of this faster objective time. This represents the time-velocity transformation of energies released by the day-year progressions.

I am confident that the forces thus released by day-year progressions are no more symbolic than is the radiation of high-velocity particles from radioactive matter which takes place in the laboratory of the physicist, and to measure the mass of which he must apply the same relativity transformation I have indicated. These radiations are invisible to the unaided physical eye, but even as do planetary forces, they are capable of producing powerful effects on man.

Wages and the Astral World

At the building of the Temple it was the custom of the craft to assemble at the sixth hour of the sixth day of the week to receive their wages. The members of the lodge, therefore, march two and two to the window where they are paid. As the sixth day is Friday, ruled by Venus, and the sixth planetary hour of Friday is the hour of Mars, they typify these two planets, corresponding to the astral body and animal soul of man. The attraction of these two planets for one another is greater than that between other planets, and it is in the astral world while man possesses an astral body and an animal soul that he receives the reward of his deeds upon earth. The wages are paid by the Senior Warden, or divine soul, who gives each worthy craft a penny. When the candidate puts his hand through the lattice window, it is held fast and the order given to cut it off. This signifies that the soul may incur the penalty of being held captive in the astral world by not knowing how to receive wages, not being able to raise the vibrations of Venus and Mars to the spiritual plane, as typified by the circular coin. The hand being cut off symbolizes that the result is a loss of executive power.

The pass grip is made by grasping the fingers as though to assist another, and refers to the assistance given to each other by the workmen as they climbed the steep banks of the river Joppa when bringing timber from Lebanon. It symbolizes the mutual assistance that may be given in reaching the astral plane, Joppa. Joppa, therefore, is the password.

The true grip is made by passing from the passgrip to the Mark Master's grip, which is given by locking the little fingers of the right hand, turning the backs of the hands together and touching the thumbs. It is called Siroc, or Mark Well; symbolizing that the lower passions and desires have all been conquered and that the spiritual bodies unite in a mutual use of the will. The little finger is ruled by Mercury, emblem of the spiritual body, and the thumbs signify will. The neophyte should Mark Well, therefore, that as he climbs the height of occultism all passion will have gradually to be overcome to enable the soul to direct its will without the aid of passional excitement.

The candidate is received into the Mark Master degree upon the edge of the indenting chisel. This represents vivid formulation of the object to be attained and the constant application of the will to that attainment. He is finally instructed how to receive his wages, and receives a penny. At this the others murmur and throw their coins upon the floor, protesting that one inexperienced should not receive the same wages as an accomplished workman. But the justice of so paying is supported by a passage of Scripture, and the craft are at last satisfied. Thus in life some must toil long and laboriously to become worthy of receiving a spiritual reward, while others make attainment almost immediately, which apparently is an injustice. But time and opportunity, in the course of divine providence, are meted out to all, and only the foolish question divine justice.

A brother in asking a favor pledges his Mark, and so resembles Hiram Abiff, the divine soul, who seeks sustenance from Solomon, the ego, in order to accomplish his destiny. The divine soul receives succor only as it pledges its immortal nature to work in harmony with the universal will. It is symbolized by the Moon seeking the beneficence of the Sun's rays. For a similar reason, a brother receiving a pledge and granting a favor is like King Solomon, who was renowned for his beneficence. He resembles the Sun which sheds its rays upon the Moon, and he is like the ego which sustains and inspires the soul.

5. Past Master Degree

A Master Mason cannot preside over a Master Mason Lodge until he has taken the Past Master degree. It has to do with man's intellectual and religious qualifications, and much light is shed upon it by the Fifth Major Arcanum of the tarot, to which it corresponds. This Arcanum, ruled by the planet Jupiter, represents the hierophant, prince of occult science, who by his knowledge and goodness is enabled to exercise authority and command obedience. Man rules over the four elements of nature by virtue of his intellect. This is expressed by the number five.

The Past Master Lodge is opened by the same officers, and the lodgeroom is the same, as in the E.A. degree. It typifies man in his normal physical state. The only difference is that they all wear hats. This symbolizes their knowledge concerning union; for the head in the hat astrologically represents the sun and moon conjoined.

The step is made by placing the heel of the right foot against the toe of the left to form a right angle. It symbolizes mental union. The first sign is made by placing the thumb of the clenched right hand to the lips, and means the Will to keep Silent regarding knowledge that would prove dangerous to others. The dieugard is made by drawing the right hand from the left side of the neck down diagonally across the breast. It signifies the transference of negative affections into positive aspirations.

The grip of a Past Master is made by first taking the Lion's grip, and then as they say, "from grip to span," slipping their right hands so as to catch each other by the wrist, grasping each other by the right elbow with the left hand. It refers to the interplay of forces between those who have lived together a spiritual life and understand the inner laws.

The other feature of this degree is the abdication of the Master in favor of the candidate. The candidate attempts to conduct the Lodge, but is made the target of witty remarks, the Lodge breaking up in confusion. It is meant to teach the folly of attempting prematurely to control the inhabitants of the astral realm. The elementals that the neophyte attempts to force into his service will turn and rend him unless he has undergone the necessary preparatory training.

6. Most Excellent Master Degree

"When the Temple of Jerusalem was finished, those who had proved themselves worthy by their virtue, skill, and fidelity, were installed as Most Excellent Masters. "This degree is founded upon the Sixth Major Arcanum of the tarot, ruled by Venus and pictured as Temptation. The degree represents the trials surmounted, as indicated by the significance of the Scripture read by the Master: "He that hath clean hands, and a pure heart; who hath not lifted up his soul unto vanity, nor swore deceitfully. He shall receive the blessings from the Lord," etc.

In opening the Lodge the brethren gather round the altar and kneel on the left knee with their arms crossed and holding hands so that each gives his right hand brother his left hand and his left hand brother his right hand. When the scriptural reading is over they lift their hands up and down six times while the Master counts: "One, Two, Three; One, Two, Three." This is called balancing, and refers to the wavering of the soul between good and evil, and to the extreme tendencies that produce disastrous reactions. This also signifies the sexes in antagonism, as well as loss of equilibrium. The crossed arms represent inversion, but more particularly the cross-roads where the neophyte must decide whether he will follow the path of black magic or the path of magic that is white.

After balancing, the brethren lift their hands, now free, above their heads rolling up their eyes in an attitude of astonishment. This indicates that they have been confronted by temptation. They then turn to the right extending their arms, afterwards permitting them to fall nerveless at their sides. It indicates they have yielded to temptation. This sign is said to represent the Queen of Sheba on first viewing Solomon's Temple. It really indicates that man progresses by alternately yielding to and struggling with his animal desires, and that not without repeated effort is the final victory won.

The candidate is received into this degree upon the keystone, which as applied to man is the fundamentals of sex. The password is Raboni, signifying to overcome. The sign is made by placing the two hands, one on each breast, the fingers meeting at the center, and jerking them apart violently. It refers to antagonism that may arise between man and woman, and to triumph over temptation of a sexual nature by the aid of the aspirations. The grip is given by grasping the other's hand and pressing with the thumb the base of the third finger where it joins the hand. This is the Sun finger of palmistry, and presides over worldly honors. The grip signifies the Will to resist the temptation to use psychic powers for temporal advantage. As the candidate receives the grip the Master places the inside of his right foot inside the candidate's right foot and whispers the word, Raboni. This symbolizes that the candidate must understand the necessity for resisting temptation.

Next, an arch is brought out supported by two pillars, Jachin and Boaz, each about five feet high. It consists of ten blocks, five on either side, with a mortice between for the reception of the keystone. The keystone, symbol of union, is placed into the arch between the five blocks representing man and the five symbolizing woman; and is driven down by six raps of the gavel, indicating the use of the Will in overcoming the temptation to abuse the sacred function denoted by the keystone.

The brethren then march around and hang their jewels, sashes, aprons, etc., on the arch to denote their willingness to make sacrifices that the marriage relation may be perfect. The ark, which has been carried around by four brethren, is then brought forward and placed on the altar and a pot of incense is placed on the ark. The symbol of the ark, as well as that of incense, was explained in chapter 7. The four brethren carrying it typify the four quadrants of the heavens, and thus represent a cycle of time in which sought for results are realized.

In closing the Most Excellent Master Lodge, all kneel around the altar while the Master reads out of the Bible, then they balance six times, arise and balance six more, and give the signs from this degree downward to indicate complete mastery of the knowledge received in the past, and that they have finally overcome all indecision, and have surmounted all temptation by obedience to the Law.

8. Royal Master Degree

This degree corresponds to the sign Capricorn, and to the Eighth Major Arcanum of the tarot, the significance of which is Justice and Equilibrium.

At the building of the Temple, King Solomon, Hiram, King of Tyre, and Hiram Abiff decided to award the most skillful and faithful of the Master Masons by imparting to them the Omnific Word. But they took a solemn oath not to impart the Word until the completion of the Temple, and then only when all three were present. As this Omnific word is the immortal union of soul-mates, it is at once apparent that it can only be imparted in the presence of the ego, divine soul, and spiritual body; for if the divine soul, corresponding to Hiram Abiff, be slain, its union with its mate is impossible. Furthermore, it can only be imparted at the completion of the Temple; for man must have completed the construction of his spiritual body before this permanent union can take place.

The candidate impersonates Adoniram, a worthy Master, who symbolizes the twin soul of Hiram Abiff. As Hiram is leaving his sanctuary he is accosted by Adoniram who asks him at what time he shall receive the Omnific Word. Hiram answers: "My worthy friend, it is uncertain when, or whether, you will receive it at all; for the Omnific Word cannot be given until the Temple is completed, and then only by the free consent of the three Grand Masters." Adoniram then asks how he can expect to receive it if one of the three should be removed by death. Hiram answers by tapping the floor three times with his foot, saying: "When I die, they will bury it there."

Thus is imparted the knowledge that in case one of the twin souls sins against his immortal nature and sinks into the Lower-Pluto realm, Pluto ruling the eighth birth-chart house, it will be long ere the other receives the Word. Yet all things being possible in the accomplishment of divine justice, a new monad is budded to take the place of the prodigal, and is sent on its pilgrimage through the three planes alluded to by the taps on the floor. Thus the word is buried between the three planes, but will be recovered at the end of the new monad's cycle of involution and evolution. Justice will finally be meted out unto all.

The Master, representing Hiram Abiff, tapping the floor three times asks the candidate, "Do you know about this?" The candidate replies, referring to the Omnific Word of soul union, "I know something about it." He is then asked what he knows about it, and replies that he knows something of the beginning of it, at the same time tapping the floor three times with his toe. That is, as impersonating one of the twin souls, he knows they were together at the beginning of the cyclic pilgrimage. Asked what was the beginning he answers that it is Alpha, and that the end is Omega. And truly the separation of the twin souls is the beginning of their career, and the reunion is the end of the cycle in which manhood is attained. The next cycle is that of the angel.

Separation and reunion closes the great orbit of the Cycle of Necessity. Reunion is the tree of life, the reward of the faithful, as indicated by the Master reading from the Bible the following: "And behold, I come quickly; and my reward is with me, to give every man according as his work shall be. I am Alpha and Omega, the beginning and the end, the first and the last. Blessed are they that do his commandments, that they may have a right to the tree of life, and may enter in at the gate of the city."

The grip of this degree is given by each taking his left wrist with his right hand, and with his left hand taking hold of the other's right wrist, forming a square seat. It typifies inertia and stability resulting from forces in equilibrium. The Word is given by letting the left hand fall to the side, placing the right toe to the other's right heel, making a triangle, and saying, "Alas, poor Hiram!" This indicates dissolution, and refers to the disintegration of the wicked by the Lower-Pluto forces. The feet forming the triangle refer to understanding that the three parts of man's spiritual being must be present before union of soul mates is possible. The dieugard is made by placing the forefinger of the right hand to the lips. It enjoins silence concerning such sacred things in the presence of the profane.

יהוה

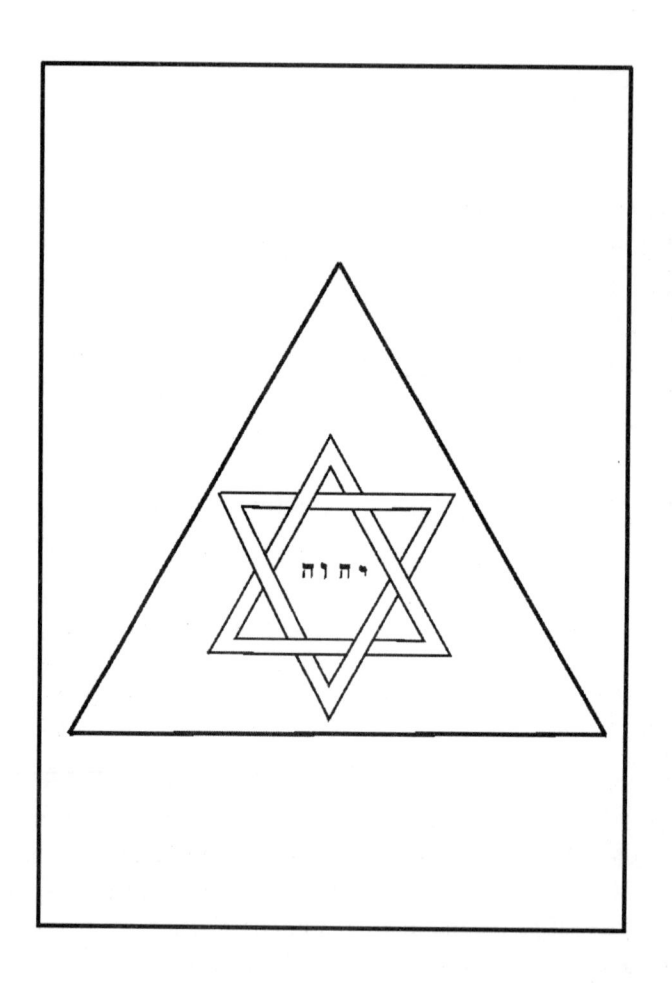

Chapter 10

Royal Arch

THE PHYSICALLY perfect man, or adept, possesses and is master of seven physical senses, seven psychic senses, and seven states of consciousness. The number seven, denoting the complete gamut of physical life, indicates readiness for transition to a new octave of endeavor. The number of action and completion of form, astrologically it corresponds to Sagittarius; and is explained in symbolical pictograph by the Seventh Major Arcanum of the tarot, which represents the triumph over all temptations and obstacles of the physically perfect man. Upon this tarot arcanum is founded the ancient degree of the Royal Arch.

In its initiatory ritual the candidate is caused symbolically to recapitulate man's involution, and his evolution up to the state of perfect physical manhood. As the result of this perfection, or adeptship, among other priceless treasures obtained, he is given the Omnific Word.

This initiation, to represent that on every plane the soul is vitalized by its ego and functions through some kind of form—there being a trinity of ego, soul and body always present—can only take place when there are three candidates to undergo the ceremony at the same time. To indicate that these three elements of man's constitution are never entirely separated, and that during the Cycle of Necessity through the seven realms to the one where the candidate now functions there has been a constant strengthening of the bond between them, and the unfoldment of seven states of consciousness, the three candidates are tied along a single rope which is wrapped seven times around the body of each.

The Chapter represents the Tabernacle erected near the ruins of the Temple. It is an oblong square divided into separate compartments by four veils. Its square form represents the physical plane where initiation is first conducted.

Significance of the Banners and Three Times Three

The banner of the guard at the outer veil is blue, the color of the planet Saturn, and of the selfishness which must be overcome at the first step. The banner of the guard of the second veil is purple, the color of the planet Jupiter, and of the love of wealth and worldly station, which must be triumphed over at the second step. The banner of the guard of the third veil is scarlet, the color of the planet Mars, and of the hate and passion that must be left behind if the sanctuary is to be reached. The banner of the guard of the fourth, or inner veil is white, the color of the planet Uranus. This indicates that all the experiences of life, represented by the various planetary colors, must be purified and fluxed by the methods of spiritual alchemy and then combined, as the prismatic colors combine, to form the white light of spiritual gold before final adeptship is attained. These four veils also represent the four elemental kingdoms—gnomes, undines, salamanders and sylphs—which the adept of the physical plane is called upon to master.

It is asked how a Royal Arch Mason is known. The answer is that it is by three times three. This symbolizes that he possesses knowledge of the three trines of the soul's pilgrimage. The first trine, with its apex above indicating where the twin souls separated, represents by its separating sides the divergent lines followed in involution by the male and the female monads. Its base represents the mineral realm where the two souls are farthest apart. The second trine starts with the mineral as the base line and the human state of life as the point where the two sides converge. This indicates that it is possible, though only one far spiritually advanced could recognize it if it did take place, for the twin souls to meet as human beings on the physical plane. The third trine has its base in human life, and its apex in the seventh spiritual state where soul-mates are permanently united.

In opening the Chapter all kneel about the altar on their right knees in the form of a circle. The circle represents spirit, and the attitude denotes the willingness to dedicate their services unreservedly to it.

This circle is called a living arch, and is symbolical of the lives through which the soul passes in its cycle of necessity. The High Priest reads from the Bible, then each crosses his arms and gives his left hand to his left-hand companion, as token of the trials and temptations that must be surmounted. They then balance three times three with their arms, permitting them to rise and fall in three series of three, with a pause between each series, indicating the three trines of life: involution to mineral, evolution to man, and final evolution from man to angel. The password, Raboni, signifies to overcome, and indicates the determination to overcome all barriers to spiritual progress.

Because the higher trinity of man's being must be present before soul-union can take place, and because it is the product of the united effort of the ego and its two monads, the Omnific Royal Arch Word can only be given in groups of three. Each of the three companions—the three representing ego and two monads—takes his brother on the left by the right wrist with his right hand, and with his left hand grasps the left wrist of his brother on the right. To indicate the three as functioning in the mineral realm of life they place their three right feet together in the form of a triangle. Their left hands form a trine in the middle region, to indicate the three functioning on the astral plane. And their right hands form a trine above their heads to typify the three functioning on the spiritual plane of life.

They then balance three times three and bring the right hand down upon the left, signifying victory over temptation through wisdom, indicated by the number nine (see Course 6, *The Sacred Tarot,* Chapter 7), in the union of positive (right-hand) and negative (left-hand) forces. Their right hands are next raised above their heads as they give at low breath the word: Jah-buh-lun, Je-ho-vah, G-O-D. Low breath has reference to the spiritual impulse that propelled the monads upon their cyclic journey. The Omnific Word is syllabled and pronounced alternately so that each of the three speak all nine syllables, or altogether twenty-seven. These twenty-seven syllables represent the twenty-seven days it takes the moon to pass through the circle of zodiacal signs and return to its original starting point. This symbolizes the soul's journey from its differentiation back to the spiritual state.

The three candidates personate the three Most Excellent Masters who, at the destruction of Jerusalem, were carried captive into Babylon where they remained seventy years until liberated by Cyrus, King of Persia. They then returned over a rugged road to assist in rebuilding the Temple. Now the number ten represents a complete cycle (see Course 6, *The Sacred Tarot,* Chapter 7) of experience. Multiplied by seven to become seventy it indicates successive cycles during which the perfection of form is attained. This climax of evolution on the material plane, the perfect physical form, is man, who possesses a seven-fold constitution. Thus does the soul, descending into the Babylon of matter, become a captive of sense and seeming. It is only liberated when perfect physical manhood is reached and work is ready to be started in the reconstruction of its physical temple.

The candidates are permitted to enter the Chapter, representing the material world, through a living arch. This is formed by the brethren standing in two lines facing each other, each locking fingers with the brother opposite. It typifies the forms of life through which the soul passes in its cyclic journey, and to represent the struggles in each of these lives the candidates are kneaded by the brothers' knuckles. This punishment is so hard as often to prostrate them on the floor, indicating the dissolution of one form before another is attracted.

The end of the ritual that portrays involution finds the candidates confronted by a burning bush. This is the divine creative fire, by the energy of which the soul ascends through the various forms of physical life, finally to rebuild its spiritual temple, a miniature structure patterned in detail after the universal temple. The destruction of the temple signifies here the fall of spirit, or the involution of the soul into matter. This is brought out by reading the account given in the 26th Chapter of Chronicles, and throwing the candidates on the floor and binding them amid much confusion, and carrying them out into the preparation room. A few minutes later, to indicate that the evolutionary journey has commenced, they are released and told that Cyrus, King of Persia, has issued a proclamation to build another temple at Jerusalem.

The Living Arch

The living arch by which the candidates enter the Chapter is symbolical of the elemental life-forms passed through before the soul incarnates for the first time on the physical plane.

To represent successive existences in the mineral realm of earth the candidates again pass through the living arch. Then, to typify the experiences of the impersonal soul in the astral realm after it has passed through the mineral states of life, they are led over a rugged road around the room and back again to the living arch.

The next time through the living arch—the second time after the destruction of the temple, but the third time through—they are treated more harshly. This indicates that in passing through repeated incarnations in the vegetable kingdom of life the soul awakens to greater sensitiveness, becomes more aware of external conditions. Then again the candidates are led over a rugged road, indicating the period between vegetable and animal existence spent in the astral realm where experiences in the vegetable realm are thoroughly assimilated. To show the completion of this cycle of astral existence they are led around the room to still again confront the living arch.

The third time through the arch since destruction of the temple—the fourth and last time in all—they are treated still more roughly. This denotes in the animal kingdom through which the soul evolves that sensitiveness, consciousness, and suffering become more intense. Then once more they are led over the rugged road, this time to indicate the period of assimilation in the astral realm after completing evolution through the animal forms, and before the soul is competent to incarnate in a human body. They are then led on around the room, but as the living arch composed of numerous brethren indicates a series of lives, and as the soul incarnates but once in the human form, they this time are not confronted by the living arch, but now are in sight of the ruins of the old temple, near the outer veil of the tabernacle. This tabernacle is the body of man, the last dwelling of the soul in physical form before the reconstruction of its spiritual temple.

To conquer the realm of gnomes and pass the veil of Saturn into the first apartment requires unselfishness. The password is "I am that I am." It is said to refer to Moses who was sent by "I AM" to the Children of Israel. This means that the ego, which sends the monad into physical life for the sake of experiencing good and evil that it may reconstruct the spiritual temple, is eternal spirit, enduring forever through time without beginning and time without end. It is the realization of this divine relationship to the ego that first prompts the soul to true unselfishness.

To conquer the realm of undines and pass the veil of Jupiter requires knowledge and sacrifice. The passwords are Shem, Ham, and Japhet. The sign is to cast a rod upon the ground and pick it up again by the end. This indicates that a knowledge of magic is necessary to the adept, and also that the creative energy, typified by the rod, to be of greatest service, must be given a spiral (spiritual) form and made to serve a living purpose, as indicated by the serpent. This sign also refers to the fourth chapter of Exodus: "And the Lord said unto Moses, what is in thy hand? And he said a rod. And the Lord said, Cast it on the ground, and he cast it and it became a serpent."

Noah, of course, personifies the sun. His three sons—the three important visible stations of the sun—are the Ascendant, the Midheaven, and the Descendant. Ham, who beholds the nakedness of his father, the sun, as the latter rises and ascends to the midheaven, growing in illumination, represents the Ascendant. But when the sun reaches the Midheaven its illumination begins to diminish, and as it moves forward the Midheaven and Descendant, corresponding to Japhet and Shem, seem to move backward toward him, finally covering him with the garment of night. Ham, symbolizing the sun rising in the sign Scorpio, indicated by Noah's drunkenness, uncovers the sun after he has yielded to base desire. This represents indulgence and degeneration. He therefore does not receive the parental blessing bestowed upon the other two, who show base desire on the wane, and who are ashamed of depravity. These three passwords, to be understood, imply a knowledge of astrology. To be used in overcoming the realm of the undines they imply that the candidate no longer delights in satisfying base desires, but through his knowledge of generation has become master of his desires.

To conquer the realm of salamanders and pass the veil of Mars into the third apartment requires purity and strength. The passwords are Shem, Japhet, and Adoniram, and the sign is made by thrusting the hand into the bosom and again drawing it out. This sign is said to refer to the fourth chapter of Exodus: "And the Lord said unto Moses, put now thine hand into thy bosom; and he put his hand into his bosom; and when he took it out, behold his hand was leprous as snow." In the passwords here Adoniram, typifying the soul-mate of Hiram Abiff, is substituted for Ham who belongs to the realm of external desires. Adoniram indicates the sun rising in the sign Taurus, the sign of regeneration, instead of in Scorpio. This reference indicates that the candidate is expected to understand spiritual astrology as well as the more physical branches. And it signifies that at this stage of his initiation, regenerate union must entirely supersede generation. The sign indicates the powers that may be exercised by the adept in high magic. It also warns of the frightful penalty that those must pay who fall into the snare of sex magic.

To conquer the realm of sylphs and pass the veil of Uranus into the inmost compartment where adeptship is finally attained requires great self mastery and wisdom. The passwords are Haggai, Joshua, and Zerubbabel. These characters were holy men who came into possession of wonderful powers through the consecration of their lives to the work of God. Only such others, therefore, as likewise consecrate their energies to the performance of the divine will, and strive to assist the progressive evolution of creation, can ever arrive at true adeptship.

The sign is made by holding out a tumbler of water and pouring a little on the floor. This is said to refer to the fourth chapter of Exodus: "And it shall come to pass, if they will not believe in the two former signs, thou shalt take the water of the river and pour it upon the dry land; and the water shall become blood upon the dry land." Thus is signified that when properly understood the creative periods of woman are a source of occult power. Alchemy, as well as astrology and magic must be mastered by the would-be adept. At the point of progression now considered, the grosser energies are transmuted to build up electromagnetic power. The form of the finer bodies, as symbolized by the earth, is subject to the molding influence of the passions and aspirations. The sign, consequently, refers to the transmutation of the emotions, symbolized by the water, into living active energies.

To pass the inner veil it is also necessary for the candidate to present the signet of Truth of Zerubbabel. This is a triangular piece of metal with the name Zerubbabel engraved upon it. Zerubbabel was the chosen of the Lord. In other words, he understood and conformed to the Law. He was present at the building of the first temple and his hand saw the completion of the new one.

Now the trine represents the ego and its twin souls, the metal signifying their most valuable experiences on the physical plane. Zerubbabel being present at the beginning signifies that the differentiation of the twin souls was under law. His being present at the completion of the new temple signifies that the reunion of twin souls is likewise under law. The signet of Truth, therefore, is that the ego and twin souls stand in relation to each other as Life, Light, and Love. Furthermore, those who, like Zerubbabel, understand and obey nature's laws, interiorly recognize the truth, even when external evidence is lacking to substantiate it, that the twin souls of one ego must join to build the new temple of the angelic form.

When they have passed the inner veil the candidates arrive at that portion of the Chapter where they are ready to take the final initiation that confers upon them adeptship on the physical plane. They consequently are examined by the brethren and declared eligible and "just such men as are wanted in building the temple." Asked what work they will undertake, they reply that they will undertake any service, however servile or dangerous. All aspirants to adeptship are given a work, more often than not bringing hardships and the condemnation of the ignorant, and sometimes making them outcasts and subjects of persecution. The neophyte's future progress depends upon the manner in which he accomplishes that which has been given him to do. If he shirks it because of its arduous nature, or because it lends to unpopularity, or because it interferes with worldly interests, he is barred from further initiation.

Next the candidates are directed to go to the northeast corner of the old temple and remove the rubbish preparatory to starting the new building. The northeast is the portion of the mundane sphere where the sun rises in spring at the renewal of the year after it crosses the equinox. It is the point where its regeneration commences. The candidates are furnished, one with a crowbar, typical of the plumb, and the masculine in nature; one with a shovel, in form representing the sun of spirit penetrating the square of matter; and the other with a pick, symbolizing the plumb, or vertical line of the sun's rays, uniting with the moon, or crescent of soul. The crowbar thus symbolizes the ego. The shovel symbolizes the ego sending a ray of itself, the soul, into matter. The pick symbolizes that the result is union of ego and soul. In other words, the product of the soul's experiences in material environment is self-consciousness.

After digging awhile in the rubbish of dogmatic science and religious superstition, the candidates find a ring, typical of their evolving spiritual insight, by which they pull up a keystone of an arch disclosing an entrance to a vault below. This keystone is the one wrought by Hiram Abiff. It signifies, as elsewhere explained, that the key to soul power is union between harmoniously wedded man and woman, and that the key to occult science is the knowledge of astrology.

One of the candidates agrees to descend into the vault. This vault represents the lowest grade of adeptship where treasures of knowledge are concealed. A rope is wound seven times around his body, to typify his possession of the seven states of consciousness, and he is lowered by a companion into the vault. Here he finds three small trying squares which prove to be the jewels of the Ancient Grand Masters, King Solomon, Hiram, King of Tyre, and Hiram Abiff.

Ancient Masonry

First Step Toward Adeptship

These trying squares typify the three planes of adeptship, each having three grades, that are discovered by the worthy neophyte. These on the physical plane are the scientific grade, the lucidic grade and the grade of soul consciousness. In natal astrology they represent the birth-chart, progressed aspects, and cycles, each of which is triune, and taken together as the Hermetic System of Natal Astrology, comprise a perfect system. The birth-chart embraces zodiacal signs, planets and mundane houses, related to each other as spirit, soul and body. Progressions consist of major progressions, minor progressions and transits, related to each other in the same manner. Cycles likewise correspond to man's triune nature, being divided into solar revolutions, lunar revolutions and planetary periods. These three try squares where humanity is concerned signify man and woman united in a common work; functioning on all three planes of life. The recognition of these jewels is the first step toward actual adeptship.

After the discovery of the jewels—the discovery of the methods by which knowledge may be tried and its value proved so that if it is found of correct proportions it may be used as a stone in building the temple—one of the candidates is again lowered into the vault. During this event the sun is at meridian height, and its illuminating rays enable him to discover a small box standing on a pedestal. The light and heat from the sun at this time are so intense that he raises his hand and draws it briskly across his forehead, then drops it again to his side. This is the dieugard of the Royal Arch degree.

The sun is represented as at its strongest position, typical of the virility which if utilized to furnish electromagnetic vibrations that can be used in Intellectual ESP, may result in illumination, signified by the dieugard. The dieugard further refers to the fact that when such illumination is present, the attention has become so absorbed in exploring regions of the inner plane and acquiring from it information of value, that the individual for the time being is quite blinded to all that happens in the physical world.

Ark of the Covenant

The box discovered by the neophyte through his exercise of Intellectual ESP is removed to the external world and examined. The High Priest pronounces it to be the Ark of the Covenant of God.

This Ark is a miniature representation of the universe and contains a condensed copy of both the Oral Law and the Written Law. The square form of the base, as described in the Scripture and in Ancient Masonry, symbolizes the world of matter and the physical body of man. The coffer above the base typifies man's soul and the astral world. The mercy seat which is over the coffer represents man's ego and the spiritual world. These three main divisions of the Ark are the same as the three worlds mentioned in the Kabala. They are: Asiah, the world of action, or physical world; Yetsirah, the world of formation, or astral realm; and Briah, the world of creation, or spiritual realm. Alchemically these main divisions are Salt, Mercury, and Sulphur. Astrologically they are Mundane Houses, Planets, and Zodiacal Signs. Still above the realms mentioned is the Angelic world, the world of Emanation, or Atziluth of the Kabala, represented in alchemy by Azoth, and in astrology by starry constellations. In the Ark of the Covenant it is present as the overshadowing wings of the Cherubims.

Upon the Ark and around it, to represent the zodiac, is a crown of gold. At each corner of the square base is a ring, two on one side and two on the other. Through the two rings on one side, to represent the pillar Jachin there is run a carrying stave; and through the two rings on the other side another stave to represent Boaz is run. Thus is this representation of the universe divided into masculine and feminine, as the zodiac is divided by summer and winter signs into north and south. Each ring with the pole through it has the elements of the number ten. So do astrologers divide the zodiac into spaces of ten degrees each, calling these important sections decanates. Each such decanate is ruled by a planet. Likewise the nine decanates of each quarter are presided over by one of the symbolical forms of the sphinx, that is, by the Bull, Lion, Eagle, or Man. The planetary rulers of the decanates of a quadrant, together with the ruler of the quadrant as a whole—for the symbolical forms of the sphinx are governed by Venus, Sun, Pluto, and Uranus—gives ten planetary rulers to each quarter of the heavens. These are symbolized by the four rings with the poles through them.

The two cherubims are in the two ends of the Mercy Seat, or realm of spirit. They are placed facing each other with their wings covering the Mercy Seat and meeting over it. They represent the highest mystery of man's being, the meeting of soul-mates in the realm of spirit. This attainment of angelhood is the climax of spiritual life, and is symbolized by the meeting of the overshadowing wings. The cherubims represent the angelic progenitors of the human race and the purified souls of previous rounds of humanity who through the union of the two monads have attained to angelhood. It was from this realm of life that Moses was instructed, as revealed by the twenty-fifth chapter of Exodus: "And there I will meet thee, and I will commune with thee from above the Mercy seat, from between the two cherubims which are upon the ark of the testimony, of all things which I will give thee in commandment unto the Children of Israel."

Within the Ark are four emblems: the rod of Aaron that budded, the cup that contains the manna, the tablets of the Law, and the manna contained in the cup. It is these four emblems, slightly altered, that today constitute the four suits of the tarot, and somewhat further altered are pictured as the four suits of common playing cards.

The rod of Aaron in the tarot has become the scepter of power, the clubs of common playing cards. It expresses creative force, the source of human energy; represents the executive attribute, and signifies virility. Astrologically it corresponds to the fiery signs of the zodiac.

The cup by its form represents reception, the feminine in nature. It remains unaltered in the tarot, and not less expresses the emotional nature of the watery signs of the zodiac when represented in modern playing cards by hearts.

The tablets of the Law have been supplanted in the tarot by the sword of retribution by which infringement of the Law is punished. These in common playing cards have given way to spades; the spade, a symbol of toil, being likewise an emblem of affliction. The tablets of the Law were joined to express the union of positive and negative forces, a thought preserved by the form of the cross in both the spade and the sword. Astrologically the tablets symbolize the earthy signs of the zodiac.

The manna held by the cup symbolizes the fruit of the union of positive and negative forces. What this fruit may be depends upon the forces united, but the product is considered as of value. Manna was of value at the time of its use. Money is of value, and the suit of pentacles of the tarot pictures this thought by coins. Intelligence is of even greater value; therefore, upon each coin, as symbol of intelligence, is depicted a five-point star. But in modern times diamonds came to be considered as of more value than silver or gold, and we consequently find diamonds pictured on the playing cards. Astrologically the manna symbolizes the airy signs of the zodiac.

These four emblems represent the four great universal principles everywhere and at all times operative. On every plane positive and negative forces unite in the production of new conditions. Man and woman unite physically in the production of children, they unite in regeneration to accomplish the Great Work, and twin souls unite to become the angel.

The High Priest of the Chapter looking into the Ark discovers the long lost book of the law and says: "You now see that the world is indebted to Masonry for the preservation of this sacred volume. Had it not been for the wisdom and precaution of our Ancient Brethren, this, the only remaining copy of the Law, would have been destroyed at the destruction of Jerusalem."

This is undoubtedly true; for had not the Ancient Masons taken the precaution to conceal their wisdom in the allegories of the various Scriptures, it would have been destroyed by religious fanaticism. And with even greater cunning, and in a manner more easily interpreted because less covered with irrelevant rubbish, they concealed their wisdom, yet perpetuated it with certainty, by engraving it on plates and giving these into the hands of ignorant persons as a means of gambling. They capitalized a popular vice and made it serve a good end; for although the Church has ever been suspicious of playing cards, they have been perpetuated and in the Egyptian Tarot we today possess an accurate copy of the Oral Law as it was understood of old.

Upon finding the manna in the Ark the High Priest says: "Companions, we read in the book of the law, that he that overcometh, will I give to eat of the hidden manna." He then gives each of the candidates a piece of the manna as a token that they have triumphed over their animal natures. Next he finds a stick with some buds upon it, which he proclaims is the rod of Aaron. Then he takes from the Ark four pieces of paper which he places together so as to show a key to the ineffable characters of this degree. Needless to say these pieces of paper represent the scroll of heaven divided into four quadrants, and the characters, which may be translated in terms of the alphabet of any language, are the signs of the zodiac and the planets; for each planet and each sign corresponds to one letter of the alphabet.

By this correspondence between the common alphabet and the alphabet of the skies the vibratory influence of any name may be determined. And through the correspondence of the starry alphabet to numbers, tones, and colors the vibratory influences of these also are known. Then as the thought-cells within the astral body of man mapped in the birth-chart by the corresponding sign or planet pick up, radio fashion, the astral vibrations radiated by name, tone, number or color, and influence the individual's life and destiny accordingly, it is but a matter of comparing it with the birth-chart and progressed aspects to determine the precise influence on the individual of any name, tone, number or color with which there is close association. Those whose vibrations are similar to discordant thought-cells in his astral body increase the power of such thought-cells to attract disaster. On the other hand, those whose vibrations are similar to harmonious thought-cells (see Course 6, *The Sacred Tarot* for details) give added power to attract events which are fortunate.

The Lost Word Recovered

When the Ark is first found the three trying squares, which are the jewels of the three ancient Grand Masters, cover the names of Deity written in three different languages. This proves to be the lost Master Mason's Word which becomes the Grand Omnific Arch Word. It is written in three languages to indicate its application on all three planes of life. Its correct pronunciation is Jod-He-Vau-He but this is not revealed to the candidate until the ineffable degrees are reached, and he is then sworn not to pronounce it more than once in his life. As the word refers to marriage this vow signifies that promiscuity is not countenanced; for high magic depends for its success upon absolute purity. The Master Mason's Word, so long lost, and recovered as Jod-He-Vau-He, denotes that in every sphere and on every plane the spiral of life depends upon the interaction of positive and negative forces.

This Word applied on the plane of generation relates to bringing perfect children into the world. The Ancient Masons believed that children should not be the result of chance, but that they should be religiously prepared for. In the first place a time was selected for union that would bring the child into the world when the planetary influences were favorable to the qualities and fortune it was desired he should have. Then for a period of not less than a lunar month before union great temperance in all directions was exercised that both might be exceedingly virile and capable of great intensity. During this preparatory period the mind was kept lofty and as spiritual as possible through reading and devotional exercises. Also, during this period, the qualities to be possessed by the child were daily and vividly formulated and held in the mind by both, these qualities having been agreed upon. Then during the time of union these qualities were again held in the imaginations of both. The Ancients held that under these conditions, if there was true love between the husband and wife and their energies blended harmoniously, that the child would be conceived who when born would possess the abilities and tendencies so formulated.

On the plane of regeneration the Master's Word relates to the blending of etheric and astral energies by which work is accomplished on the astral plane. Such blending of forces between man and wife only takes place when the energies have been raised to a higher vibratory frequency than that accompanying purely physical desire. Physical desire gives way to the mood of tender affection. And while caresses may assist to bring about the rapport between them, physical contact is not necessary, and they may be thousands of miles apart. Nor are any particular organs concerned in this higher union. It is a complete fusion of the finer forces and a blending of the astral bodies. There is an exchange of energy, a complete sympathy and a mutual understanding without the necessity of the spoken word, an entire absence of selfishness, the mind being lifted to new heights where the soul pants and longs for all that is spiritual and good, and pours itself out in blessings upon others. In this ecstatic union the participants are incapable of any thought that is base or gross or worldly. And because of the exalted vibratory state which they temporarily occupy, their minds are capable both of receiving priceless information from the inner realm and of creating conditions on the astral plane that later will externalize on earth for the benefit of all.

In its highest application the Master's Word becomes the Omnific Word, the union of soul-mates to become the angel.

The grand sign of the Royal Arch degree is made by locking the fingers of both hands together and carrying them to the top of the head, the palms upward. The interlocking hands refer to the union of man and woman. Being carried to the top of the head indicates regenerate union. The palms up signifies the expectation of receiving divine illumination as the result.

The initiation passed, the candidate is crowned by the High Priest. This indicates the natural right and ability of one to rule who has surmounted the trials, received divine illumination, and entered the most exterior grade of adeptship.

In this Royal Arch degree, which we have been considering, the construction of the temple is not attempted. The rubbish is removed and the site of the new temple is purified. During this work the key to the lowest arch of adeptship is discovered. This teaches that those who would entertain celestial visitors must purify themselves and thus have the temple a fit place to receive such exalted beings. When the candidate enters the vault by the light of virile illumination both the Oral Law and the Written Law are discovered and the Master's Word is received. Thus in the seventh degree the Lost Word is recovered. By the law of numbers, then, in the fourteenth degree it should be applied to the reconstruction of the temple, that is, given the correct pronunciation. And the twenty-first degree should see the temple erected.

The particular symbol of the Royal Arch degree is the two interlaced equilateral triangles in the center of which are two clasped hands, one a man's and the other a woman's. It is a symbolical representation of the Lost Master's Word. It means the marriage of man possessing an equally developed body, intellect, and soul with a woman possessing a proportionally developed body, intellect, and soul, by which they evolve the highest potencies of their spiritual and mental natures.

This symbol has a significance not unrelated to the symbol of the password Shibboleth of the F.C. degree. The latter is represented by a sheaf of wheat near a water-ford. The water-ford signifies the emotional nature by which the transition from generation to regeneration is accomplished, and the suspended sheaf of wheat represents the excellent harvest of new powers that are attained when the emotions are lifted to a higher plane of action.

9. Select Master Degree

The Select Master degree is based upon the Ninth Major Arcanum of the tarot, corresponding to Aquarius, which is emblematical of Wisdom gained through experience. It is the emblem of Prudence.

At the building of Solomon's Temple it was feared that should the Children of Israel continue to disobey the Law, the temple would be destroyed by their enemies, and the knowledge of the arts and sciences, as well as that of the Oral Law, and of the models of the temple, would be lost. To prevent such priceless knowledge being lost to the human race, a secret vault was built leading from King Solomon's most retired apartment, or the most interior realm, in a westerly, or material, direction, and ending beneath the Sanctum Sanctorum. It was divided into nine separate arches, or grades, the ninth, or lowest, being a place for holding grand council, and to contain an exact copy of all in the Sanctum Sanctorum above.

This ninth arch represents the most external plane of adeptship, in which, by the Law of Correspondences, the candidate who has reached this state of wisdom recognizes that his constitution contains an exact copy of all that is in the sky above. The vault was built by 24 workmen, representing the diurnal rotation of the earth during 24 hours. This rotation progresses the horoscope and builds the various events into the life. The time for work was from 9 to 12 P.M. At that time the sun was entirely hidden from view, sinking to the lowest portion of the chart and passing from the house of pleasure through that part of the horoscope that rules hidden treasure, mystery, secret things, and the end of all undertakings.

The particular symbol of this degree represents three triangular tables arranged in a row. At each corner of a table is a lighted candle, and in the center a triangular plate of gold. Each table represents one of the three planes, and the three candles of each table represent the light shed by the three grades of adeptship belonging to each plane. The triangle of gold is the symbol of man's higher trinity seeking the golden light of wisdom.

The candidate to this degree is made to enact the part of Izabud, a friend of King Solomon, who through an oversight of the latter, and over zealousness on his own part, entered the ninth arch, and for so doing was condemned to death. He pleads for clemency, but is informed that only three can be employed in each arch, the number being already full. In the work of the adept, it is the higher trinity of his constitution that governs, the lower section having no voice in his doings; therefore, it is represented that only three workmen are able to work in each arch, or grade, of wisdom.

Finally it is decided to execute the guard Ahishar, who was asleep at his post and allowed Izabud to pass unchallenged, and to permit Izabud to live and fill his place. This drama impresses upon the candidate the necessity of prudence, that undue haste in matters of soul development is fraught with peril, and that when found worthy he will be admitted to the inner secrets. Should he, however, stumble unwittingly upon dangerous knowledge, he must never reveal it to the unworthy, and once initiated into its secrets he must ever be awake to his obligations and to his higher self; otherwise he will be found unworthy of such trust and will deserve the fate of Ahishar.

10. Super Excellent Master Degree

The Super Excellent Master degree is based upon the Tenth Major Arcanum of the tarot, presided over by the planet Uranus. This Arcanum is called the Wheel of Destiny, and depicts sudden alterations of fortune.

The degree centers around Zedekiah, the last king of Israel, who is suddenly set upon with innumerable forces by Nebuchadnezzar. They first take the city, then the temple; and pursuing the king into the plains of Jerico whither he had fled by way of the gate which is by the king's garden between two walls, they capture and carry him to Babylon. In the prison of Babylon his thumbs are cut off, his eyes put out, and his body bound in fetters of brass. As a penalty for perjury he is carried captive into a strange land.

In the macrocosm the sun, bounded on either side by the wall of the northern and southern signs, is assailed by the forces of winter and flees through the gate of the autumnal equinox. He is carried captive into the winter signs, where his strength of will, symbolized by the thumbs, is cut off. His light is dimmed—put out—and his body is bound in the icy fetters between Libra and Sagittarius, these signs ruling the metals copper and tin, of which bronze is composed.

In this manner is indicated the fate of those who are weak enough to misuse their powers; for the Bible states Zedekiah did evil in the sight of the Lord, and as a consequence the temple was destroyed. Nebuchadnezzar typifies the forces of evil that beset the neophyte who disobeys the Law. And even when he deserts the temple and attempts by way of the astral world to flee through the gateway of death, bounded by the two external sheaths, or bodies, that encompass the garden of his desires, he is yet pursued by the legions of Lower-Pluto, made their captive, and carried into iniquitous realms. His will is destroyed, symbolized by the loss of thumbs, his spiritual sight is put out, and he is bound to the nether regions by the fetters of his gross desires. Such is the fate of those disobedient to the admonitions of their higher selves.

11. Heroine of Jerico

This degree is based upon the Eleventh Major Arcanum of the tarot, which is a pictorial representation of occult forces and feminine power. It corresponds to the planet Neptune.

The Heroine of Jerico was a woman who protected two spies sent from Israel.

She hid them from the King of Jerico by covering them over with stalks of flax. Flax is a symbol of strength. They made their escape by permitting her to let down a cord through the window; for her house was upon the wall of the city. The house of Neptune is Pisces and is on the wall, or equinoctial colure, dividing summer and winter. By means of the feminine powers of Neptune, the sun and moon, typified by the two spies, make their escape from the city of winter into the region of summer.

The sign of this degree is made by the candidate, who may be the wife of a Royal Arch Mason. She imitates the scarlet line let down for the escape of the spies. Taking a red handkerchief, she places one corner of it in her mouth and lets it hang down in front of her, crossing her hands on her breast over it. The red handkerchief is symbolical of woman's creative periods, which, did she but know it, are the source of her greatest strength. They constitute the index of her magical possibilities, and have been recognized in all ages as a source of occult power. The crossed hands upon the breast signify the use or abuse of the power according to good or evil inspiration.

The word is given by the man placing his right foot inside the lady's foot, his toe to her heel, denoting mutual understanding. He puts his right hand on her shoulder and says, "My life"; to which she replies by putting her right hand on his shoulder—the hands on each other's shoulders symbolizing mutual aid—and saying as she bends forward, "For yours." He then puts his left hand on her shoulder and says, "If ye utter not"; to which she replies by placing her left hand on his shoulder and saying, "This is our business." This is a symbol of mutual reception. Then he whispers the word Rahab. Thus is symbolized by these various actions the interdependence of man and woman for progress.

The brother then says, "It is very dark tonight." The candidate answers, "Yes, but not so dark but that I can see." He then asks, "What can you see?" She answers, "A scarlet line." Then she says, "Because it saved my life in the hour of danger." All of which refers to the life giving powers of woman.

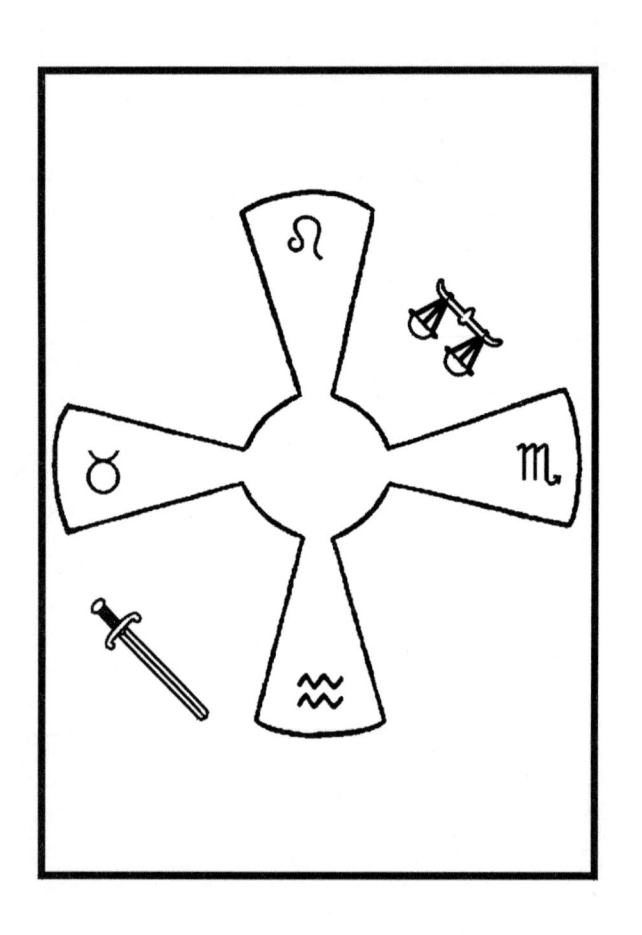

Chapter 11

Degrees of the Cross

THE SIX DEGREES from the Heroine of Jerico to the Ineffable Degrees, as given in Richardson's Monitor of Freemasonry, are each based upon the Thirteenth Major Arcanum of the tarot, which pictures the transition from one life to another through death. They correspond thus to the zodiacal sign Aries; for the sun each year expires on the autumnal cross of Libra and is resurrected in spring on the vernal cross of Aries. One of the chief characteristics of this sign Aries is a warring disposition, therefore its cross is more frequently represented by a sword, the inversion of the cross of peace. This prepares us, consequently, to find in the ritual symbolizing the transition from one cycle to another through Aries, not only the emblem of the cross, but also much military display.

Whether we cross the etheric Boundary-Line symbolically referred to as the River Jordan through death, or temporarily through Extension of Consciousness, we function in a region where, because velocities are greater than 186,284 miles per second, time, gravitation and space take on entirely new characteristics, and the chief motive power is thought. Therefore before considering the rituals associated with the degrees of the cross which imply the individual moves to the inner plane, we should examine in some detail these characteristics of the realm where he will function.

Time on the Inner Plane

What is implied by the different order of time to be found on the astral plane is illustrated by the report of the Zenith Foundation after thirty weeks of research into the gigantic mass of data on little-known mental powers, made available through the co-operation of its millions of radio listeners, from whom it received and tabulated over a quarter of a million pieces of mail in the winter of 1937-38.

Authentic personal experiences indicate that time is not a factor in telepathic communication. Possession of the ability to visualize in detail events which have not happened, a phenomenon science calls precognition, seems but slightly less rare than telepathy itself.

Now a point is a cross-section of a line, a line is a cross-section of a plane, and a plane is a cross-section of a solid. It must follow, therefore, that a solid object is a cross-section of four-dimensional existence, if existence has four dimensions. And certainly we cannot define an object's position completely unless we include time.

Thus in defining the position of an object it is not enough to say it is on the eighth floor of a building located at Second and Hill Streets, Los Angeles. That defines its position in three dimensions. But if the definition is to be complete it must contain the year, month, day and minute. When this fourth- dimensional position is added, then its place in the space-time continuum is completely defined. Furthermore, any solid whose position is thus specifically defined is a cross-section of its existence in time, that is, of the dimension extending from its past into its future.

One of the fundamentals of relativity is that there is no such thing as absolute time. Time, as indicated in chapter 9 in connection with the space-time conditions that express in the day-year progressed aspects in natal astrology, is relative.

The time of our clocks, for instance, is correlated to the velocity of the earth's rotation on its axis. But when, through some means, our consciousness is able to move more speedily to distant points on the earth's surface, we are able to apprehend events in our Now which, relative to a time correlated to the velocity of the earth's rotation, are in the past or in the future. By radio, for instance, on a Thursday evening here in Los Angeles, we can hear broadcasts of news of what is happening in Europe on Friday morning; and we can hear at 1:00 o'clock Thursday morning, a Hawaiian band playing in Honolulu at 10:30 o'clock Wednesday evening.

The soul, or unconscious mind of the individual, is the organization in finer than physical substance of the sum total of his past experiences.

Its own particular movement through the dimension designated as time is called its World-Line. Each entity has its own world-line. And all back of the Now point in each world-line is fixed in time, or the fourth dimension; in other words, the past cannot be changed. Furthermore, the trend of world-lines can be projected into the future. But only in so far as the future is perfectly predetermined and not altered through the intervention of intelligent initiative.

When attention is turned from the physical world to the happenings of the inner plane, where velocities are greater than that of light, consciousness becomes more or less aware of what is happening there. And one of the characteristics of inner-plane consciousness is that in addition to observing happenings in their Now, it can move forward or backward along their world-lines. This it can do by virtue of its velocity, which compared to the velocities of physical life is as much greater, and as effective in altering the relation of time, as radio waves are in comparison to the turning of the earth on its axis. Thus is the inner plane observer able to view what took place in the past as if he were witnessing it in the Now, and able to observe what probably will take place in the future as if it were taking place in the Now. To the extent his faculties are cultivated thus to look along world-lines, his ESP enables him to see in all its details any event that took place in the past, and any event that, unless there is intervention by intelligent initiative, will take place in the future.

Distance on the Inner Plane

The Zenith Foundation reported after digesting the results of its comprehensive tests: "That distance and space are not factors in telepathic communications seems definitely indicated by careful analysis of test returns by geographical divisions."

According to relativity, anything moving with 90% the velocity of light shortens to half its length, and at the velocity of light loses all its length. Now as an object cannot have a minus length, that is, a length which is less than nothing, when its velocities are greater than the Boundary-Line energies where it loses all its length, this matter of length ceases to have significance; for the object then has moved into an order of relations where the common conception of distance no longer obtains.

Yet vibrations are space-time relationships. Vibrations have amplitude and frequency, which means that there are a given number of vibrations within a specified interval of time and that each wave occupies a certain space, or if not of ordinary Boundary-Line wave structure, of that which corresponds to space.

And when, through attaining velocities in excess of 186,284 miles per second, an object exists on the inner plane, where distance cannot be measured in terms of physical length, there is still distance of a new order, the distance between vibratory rates. On the inner plane distances are as vast as on the external plane, even though there are no longer such space relations as we are familiar with on the physical plane. Physical space vanishes, and gives place to a space which is measured solely in terms of vibratory difference.

This means that on the inner plane two people are as close together when one is in Los Angeles and the other is in Hongkong as they are if both are in the same room in Los Angeles, provided their vibrations remain the same when one is in Hongkong as when both are in the same room in Los Angeles. This also means that on the inner plane two people in the same room may be at a vast distance from each other, so far apart that it is almost impossible for one to contact the other.

Gravitation on the Inner Plane

According to relativity supported by many experiments with projectiles shot from radio-active matter, projectiles which at times attain tremendous velocities, not only do objects shorten as they acquire higher velocities but they also acquire mass, so that at the velocity of light their resistance to change of motion due to mass becomes infinitely great.

Yet just as it is impossible to have a length which is less than nothing, so also is it impossible to have a mass greater than infinity. Consequently, when velocities greater than those of the Boundary-Line energies are attained, and due to this high velocity something exists on the inner plane, gravitation no longer has an influence over it, nor can physical things influence it in any way. The attraction of gravitation has lost its significance, and attraction of an entirely different order takes its place. This new order of attraction is the affinity of its dominant vibratory rate for a level of inner plane existence of a similar vibratory rate.

Up and down on the physical earth are directions away from or toward the gravitational center of the earth. But up and down on the inner plane are vibratory rates which are higher or which are lower than those of the level where, because of dominant vibratory rates, something habitually exists. Thus it takes effort, the effort temporarily to increase or decrease the dominant vibratory rate, to move away from the astral level where one commonly functions. The basic vibratory level, which may be compared to the carrying wave of radio, attracts everything else having a similar dominant vibratory rate to it very much as gravitation attracts physical objects to each other. But instead of merely pulling down when an intelligence temporarily has raised its dominant rate above that of its normal level, it also pulls up with equal force when the dominant rate temporarily has been lowered by the intelligence below its normal level.

Knights of Three Kings

It is said that at the dedication of the temple Solomon invited all the Eastern Royalty to attend and assist in the ceremonies. And it so happened that two of the kings were at war. These two kings represent the summer and winter halves of the zodiac, and are spoken of as Eastern because it is the Eastern point of union that is considered. Solomon attempted to reconcile them, but to no avail. Finally he invited them into a small apartment of the temple, locked the door, and informed them that they would be kept in darkness with nothing to eat but bread and water until they would agree to live in peace. Solomon went to the chamber on two consecutive days without receiving a favorable reply, but on the third day he was informed that they had agreed. He then advanced toward them holding a lighted candle in each hand saying: "If you can agree in the dark you can in the light."

Now at the winter solstice the sun sheds least light upon the northern hemisphere of the earth, the home of the Ancient Masons. From the winter solstice to the vernal equinox, through three zodiacal signs, Sol struggles to bring winter and summer together. This is the rainy season of the year during which the earth is in darkness due to obscuring clouds. It is the time when famine pinches hardest; for the food garnered the previous autumn has been exhausted during the tedious barren winter. The frugal fare of bread and water refers to this dearth of food and the prevalent rains.

The sign of the degree is to hold out the arms from the body to form a cross, with a candle in each hand. The outstretched arms form the vernal cross, and the two candidates represent the sun and moon in opposition as stationed at Easter, or the resurrection; for this only takes place after the full moon after the sun has crossed the vernal equinox. Agreeing in the light refers to the reconciliation of winter and summer and the passing of the sun into the light of the summer signs, when the days become longer than the nights. As the two kings kept each other from the light, so man and woman in antagonism keep each other in spiritual darkness. The watch-word is Agreed.

Knights of the Red Cross

This degree originally was called The Order of the Knights of the East, signifying the spiritual illumination of those who willingly sacrifice themselves on the cross of expiation. Astrologically it refers to the rising vernal sun. Later it was changed in Palestine to Knights of the Red Cross, representing the cross of the physical plane rather than that spiritual, and as such symbolizing the effort to administer to the physical ills of humanity, to alleviate suffering, save life, and protect the weak.

The sword, an inverted cross, plays an important role in this degree as do various military maneuvers. The knights count themselves into two equal divisions which stand facing each other to represent the signs of winter and summer, the two halves of the zodiac. In fact, most ancient peoples had years of six months, a custom still followed by the Jews. The sacred Year of the Jews is from the vernal equinox to the autumnal equinox and their Civil Year is from Libra to Aries. The knights go through sword play to indicate the struggle between the two opposing forces and then communicate the Jewish Pass, which is given with three cuts over an arch of steel. The three cuts represent the three months of struggle as the sun comes forth from the tomb of winter, and is also symbolical of united action on all three planes of life.

The arch of steel is made by crossing the swords at the level of the waist line, or Libra, symbolizing the autumnal equinox. Each brother steps forward with the left foot and with the free hand seizes the opposite brother by the shoulder to signify union, and in this position they alternately pronounce the passwords. The Jewish passwords Judah and Benjamin symbolize the two signs in which the sun exerts its greatest power, Leo and Aries. Jacob said of Judah: "Judah is a Lion's whelp, from the prey my son art thou gone up. He stooped down, he crouched as a lion," referring in an unmistakable manner to the sign of the Lion. The wolf equally with the ram is sacred to Aries, denoting its fiercest aspect. Jacob said: "Benjamin shall rave as a wolf, in the morning he shall devour the prey, and at night divide the spoils." These Jewish passwords symbolize the home and exaltation of the sun, and are pronounced over the equinoctial cross to indicate the reign of summer and the predominance of masculine forces.

The Persian Pass is given under an arch of steel. The swords are crossed at the level of the head to represent the vernal equinox, Aries being the sign ruling the head. Under this arch the words are given alternately by each. The words are the names of the Persian governors who for a time contended against permitting the temple to be built. They were Tetnai and Shetharboznai. As alien rulers they represent the sun's detriment and fall, Aquarius and Libra, and the triumph of winter over summer, feminine forces over masculine. They are pronounced below the vernal cross to indicate the sun's weakness when in these signs.

The Red Cross Word is communicated by giving three cuts and then drawing the sword back as if to stab the companion of the opposite division to the heart, the word "Veritas" being spoken by one, and the other answering, "Right." The four signs presiding as rulers of the four quadrants of the zodiac symbolize the One Principle, the One Law, the One Agent, and the One Truth that united sum up all possibilities. The Lion, or Leo, sign of the heart in which the sun exerts its dominant power symbolizes the One Principle. The opposite sign of the zodiac, Aquarius, representing the perfection of intelligence, symbolizes the One Truth. The Red Cross Word, Veritas, means Truth. The Red Cross Sign refers to Leo, and both sign and word symbolize the action of the sun at opposite points in the zodiac; in Leo, the sign of its rulership, and in Aquarius, the sign of its detriment. It emphasizes the truth that man rises to his greatest potency when inspired by his affections. The three cuts typify the three signs of each quarter presided over by each of the emblems, Lion and Man, and to the three planes where truth and affection may be applied.

The sign, grip, and word of a Red Cross Knight are given by first clashing the swords together to denote a struggle between opposing forces, between life and death. Then the thumb and forefinger of the left hand are placed to the lips in the attitude of one blowing a blast on a horn, signifying the trumpet of resurrection sounding the triumph over death. Finally three cuts are made to signify the three signs through which the sun passes from its tomb of winter to the cross of spring, and the fingers of the free hands are interlaced to indicate that it is through union that the triumph will be attained, the union of the sun and moon, of man and woman. In this position, with the swords crossed level with the head, or Aries, the word Libertas is pronounced and the opposing brother acknowledges it to be right. Libertas means liberty. Resurrection is the freeing of the soul from earthly bondage. The powers of the sun are freed by the moon on Easter after passing the vernal cross. Man's occult powers are liberated by woman, their mutual efforts lifting them out of the winter of materialism.

The Chamber of the Order of the Red Cross is divided into two apartments by a veil. The apartments represent the two halves of the zodiac and the veil symbolizes the equinoctial colure. The Council being opened, the companions sit in a semi-circle to represent the signs of one half of the zodiac. They each take their hats and toss them on the floor to symbolize union to be lacking, the positive and negative forces separated. They represent the sun. They place their elbows on their knees and bow forward with their heads resting on and supported by their right hands, this dejected attitude being meant to typify the weakness of the sun in the winter signs and the weakness of man to resist the forces of evil when apart from woman. The Prelate then reads at length how after the death of Cyrus, King of Persia, the Children of Israel were interrupted in the building of the temple by their adversaries on the other side of the river. The river, or dividing line, represents the equinoctial colure, and the adversaries represent the forces of winter. A new King, Darius, having ascended to the throne of Persia—that is, the sun having entered another winter sign—Zerubbabel decides to make a journey to the new king and remind him of his promise to send back to Jerusalem all the holy vessels remaining in Babylon. These holy vessels are the planets remaining in the winter signs of the zodiac, and in man represent his divine potentialities which are hidden and hampered by his material inclinations.

The candidate now personates Zerubbabel and takes his obligations kneeling at the altar on his left knee, his right hand grasping the hilt of his sword and his left hand resting on the Bible, square and compass, on which are two swords crossed at right angles. His attitude signifies not only his willingness to abide by the higher and lower laws represented by compass, square, and Bible, but denotes by the crossed swords his determination to conduct an actual warfare against the forces of evil and death. Then the candidate in his travels comes to a bridge which he is told separates the Jewish from the Persian nation. It is the equinox, which he passes by giving three cuts and the Jewish Pass, indicating the fall of the sun from the summer solstice through the sign of its greatest strength across the autumnal equinox of Libra through the three first winter signs. Its entry into Capricorn is symbolized by the Persian Guards taking him captive, making of him a slave in fetters, and putting sackcloth over his head. This is the furthest point of winter; the point in the cycle of the soul where it has evolved to the lowest state of matter and is ready for evolution back to spirit. As a slave he is led to an audience with Darius, who represents the Man of the heavens, Aquarius, presiding over the last quarter of the zodiac.

The candidate is freed by Darius, the king of the zodiacal quarter symbolizing Truth, and invited to a banquet where it is the custom to propound and answer questions. The question is asked, "Which is of greatest strength, wine, the king, or women?" After a long discussion of the relative strength of each it is decided that Truth is stronger than any of the others. The candidate is commended for this answer and is reinvested with his weapons and insignia which were taken from him when he was made prisoner. The royal sign of the zodiac, Leo, is meant by the king, the bibulous sign Scorpio is signified by wine, and the sign of Venus, Taurus, which is also the Moon's exaltation is referred to as women. Truth is symbolized by Aquarius. The Man of the zodiac is the product of the influence of all other signs, and represents the climax of material evolution. Truth is the highest possible standard, and man through his apprehension of truth is made Free and Immortal.

The particular emblem of the Knight of the Red Cross is a seven-point star in the center of which is a red cross surrounded by a circle in which are the words: "Magna est Veritas et Praevalebit." The red cross is emblematical of the world of physical suffering. The seven-point star represents the seven active principles in nature. The circle is the zodiac. The words mean that Truth is Mighty and Will Prevail. The whole symbolizes the fact that One Indomitable Truth pervades alike the zodiac, the spheres of planetary angels, and the world of mundane suffering; and that man's individual progress depends upon his ability to comprehend that Truth and conform his efforts to it.

Order of Knights Templar

The Encampment of Knights Templar is divided by a veil into two compartments to represent the summer and winter halves of the zodiac. In front of the throne is a triangle, representing man's triune nature; body, soul, and spirit. Above it is a banner with a cross upon it surrounded by rays of light, symbolizing renewed life through death, and light received through union. On either side are sky-blue banners, the color of Saturn, of wisdom gained through earthly experience. The one on the right bears a pascal lamb above which is a maltese cross and the motto: "The Will of God." The lamb is the equinoctial sign Aries, where the sun is rejuvenated in spring. The maltese cross is the emblem of the solstice where the sun crosses from eastern to western or from western to eastern zodiacal signs. Each of its arms represents one quarter of the zodiac. The whole emblem symbolizes the sun sinking to the winter solstice and relinquishing the virile powers conferred by Aries. The Son of Man referred to this waning strength by saying: "Thy Will not mine be done," which is the significance of the motto of the banner. The banner upon the left has upon it the emblems of the order—a sword, a battle axe, trumpet, and shield—symbolizing by their form the signs ruling the zodiacal quarters: Taurus, Leo, Scorpio, and Aquarius. Above these is a crowing cock, representing the triumph of virility over death and the conditions imposed by the stars. It is typical of the sun resurrected into the signs of summer, immortality victorious over mortality. The three banners symbolize the cross of Christ between the two crucified thieves. The cross of Christ is the autumnal equinox, from which the sun sinks into the tomb of winter. The maltese cross dominating the lamb is the solstitial cross of winter, symbolizing the unrepentant thief. The crossed emblems on the right of the cross of Christ being surmounted by a crowing cock represents the vernal cross and the repentant thief to whom the Son of Man promised: "Today shalt thou be with me in paradise."

The knights are dressed in black to indicate the inevitableness of death. A black sash trimmed with silver lace hangs from a black rose on the right shoulder across to the left side, having suspended from it a poinard and a maltese cross. The sash as worn represents the solstitial colure dividing the zodiac into east and west. The western signs are symbolized by the black sash and the eastern signs by the white of the silver trimming. The black rose symbolizes the extinguishment of life and the decline of the sun from the autumnal equinox to the winter solstice. The maltese cross is typical of the solstice, and the poinard represents the vernal equinox; for by its form it is an inversion of the cross of Libra. The particular emblem of the order is worn on the left breast to indicate its dominance over the material motives. This emblem is a nine-point star in the center of which is a golden serpent entwined about a cross and surrounded by a circle in which are the words: "In Hoc Signo Vinces." The nine-point star symbolizes the moon and the eight planets under whose influence experience has been transformed into wisdom. The cross represents the cycle of life completed, and the serpent entwined on it represents wisdom gained through experience with good and evil. The words mean that Under This Sign Thou Shalt Conquer. The whole symbolizes wisdom gained through cyclic experience, by which death will be conquered and a new life gained.

The apron worn by a Knight is black, of triangular shape, trimmed with silver lace, having on it a serpent entwined about a cross, skull with crossbones, and stars placed in triangular form with a red cross in the center of each. The apron symbolizes by the black trine involution, and by the trine of silver lace, evolution. The serpent entwined on the cross means wisdom gained through experience during involution and evolution. The skull and crossbones are a reminder of the inevitableness of death and the following resurrection. The skull is typical of death and transition; the end of the cycle of life, or zodiac, being ruled by Aries, the commencement of a new cycle. The crossed bones signify the equinox, and being Marrow Bones signify renewed life; for it is thought that blood corpuscles, emblematical of life, are formed in the red marrow of the bones. Because of the red cross in the center, each of the three stars represents one of the kingdoms of physical life; mineral, vegetable, and animal; through which, amid suffering, the soul has evolved before arriving at the estate of man.

In this degree the Knights are arranged in the form of a trine to represent the union in a harmonious manner of once opposing forces. The candidate is taken to the chamber of reflection, which is a small room with its walls and furniture painted black to represent the tomb. Upon a table in front of him is a Bible, typifying the Law, skull and crossbones to signify his companionship with the dead, a bowl of water for ablution to represent purification before ascending to higher realms even as the sun must be baptized by the overflowing urn of Aquarius and pass through the waters of Pisces before the resurrection; and a small taper symbolizing his consciousness directly after death. Here he must write and sign his name to the answers to three questions. The first is his affirmation never to draw his sword except in the defense of the Christian religion. It signifies his intent to combat evil only. The second answer affirms he has nothing heavy on his conscience, referring to the expiation of ill deeds in the astral worlds of purification. The third is his avowed intention to abide by the rules of the Encampment, meaning that he will conform his endeavors to whatever laws are necessary for spiritual advancement.

The question being satisfactorily answered he is dressed in pilgrim's weeds and sent on a seven-year pilgrimage to represent man's experiences on the material plane. He is provided with sandals, symbolizing the Oral Law, the traditional writings of men; bread, symbolizing material experience; and water, symbolizing emotions. One after another he passes the guards of the different veils, who each examine his script, give him good advice at some length, replenish his supply of bread and water, and send him on his way. This represents the sun moving past the summer solstice, past the autumnal equinox and winter solstice, and thus through three quadrants of the heavens. Finally the candidate is admitted to the fourth compartment to represent the sun in the last quarter of the zodiac. This symbolizes man triumphing over the four elemental kingdoms of earth, fire, water, and air. Having been found worthy, his sentence is remitted from seven years to three and he is given a sword and buckler to symbolize the sun passing to a new cycle. It also symbolizes the man, arrived at physical adeptship before the allotted span of life has been passed, who undergoes voluntary dissolution so that he may better support the heavens and combat the hells of the astral region.

The candidate has now become a Pilgrim Warrior sentenced to serve seven years in warfare, and has been given the Pilgrim Warrior's pass, Maher-Shalal-Hashbaz, meaning to spoil. This is given with four cuts under an arch of steel, to represent the necessity of conquering the four kingdoms of the astral world, the arch symbolizing the vernal cross of Aries. He now goes on a pilgrimage of warfare and again passes the three guards and comes to a halt before the fourth veil guarding the asylum. This asylum, as the region where the step to a new phase of initiation is taken, refers to the sign Pisces, the last sign of the zodiac, which rules imprisonment and places of refuge. To indicate the candidate's desire to complete the cycle and pass to higher realms the Senior Warden stamps on the floor three times four, referring to the four zodiacal triplicities. Here he gives assurance that he holds no enmity toward any soul on earth. This symbolizes the end of purification, typified in the zodiac by the urn of Aquarius. He is now required to partake of five libations, signifying the synthesis of the four quarters of the zodiac in the form of the fifth emblem represented by the sphinx. The first four are water mixed with wine, material emotions mixed with those spiritual; but the fifth is of pure wine to represent complete transmutation into spiritual life. The first libation is to Solomon, King of Israel, or the ego. The second libation is to Hiram, King of Tyre, the spiritual body. The third libation is to Hiram Abiff, the Widow's Son, the divine soul. The candidate is in front of a triangular table around which are ranged twelve burning candles and twelve cups, symbolizing life and love, the positive and negative aspects of the twelve zodiacal signs. In the center of the table is a black coffin, symbolizing the tomb. Above this is the Bible, representing the Law that progress is made through death, the latter represented by a skull and cross-bones resting on the Bible. The Prelate then reads concerning the betrayal of the Christos by one of the twelve, and orders the candidate to extinguish one of the tapers to signify the apostasy of Judas Iscariot, the zodiacal sign of death, Scorpio.

The skull, which symbolizes the soul-mate of Hiram, and Pluto, ruler of the sign of death, is called Old Simon in memory of Simon of Cyrene who bore the cross of Christ and shared his misfortunes. The history of the trial and crucifixion being read, the candidate is called upon to drink the fourth libation to Simon of Cyrene. His term of warfare is reduced from seven to three years on account of good behavior and he must now pass a year in penance. He takes the skull in one hand and a lighted taper in the other, symbols of life and death, and travels to the sepulchre of the sun. He gains entrance to the sepulchre by means of five cuts, a symbol of intelligent dominion of the four zodiacal quarters, and by means of the password Golgotha, which means a skull, and symbolizes the end of life. At this point is read the portion of the Bible relating how the angel of heaven rolled the stone away from the tomb of the sun. That is, the sun descending from the cross of Libra into the Tomb of Capricorn reascends to summer because the angle of heaven of equinoctial Aries rolls away the stone of winter.

The candidate is now given a black cross, symbolizing the autumnal cross of death. It signifies the stage of the adept's journey representing the second death, the transition of the spiritualized man of the higher astral realms into the realm of pure spirit above the astral. The candidate is shortly admitted to the asylum, or fourth room and requested to drink from the skull the fifth libation of pure wine. This fifth libation symbolizes the spiritual body that survives the second death. It also symbolizes the reunion of soul-mates, the first libation representing the ego, the second the spiritual body of Hiram, the third the divine soul of Hiram, the fourth the soul-mate who shares all spiritual vicissitudes, and the fifth the spiritual body of the soul-mate which blends with Hiram's after the second death. In case the candidate refuses to take the fifth libation as ordered he is charged by six knights with drawn swords. He is the seventh, thus indicating that the septenary of existence compels this spiritual reunion if immortality is to be attained.

Having partaken of life from the cup of Aries, the skull, he is appointed to fill the vacancy caused by Judas Iscariot, and so relights the extinguished taper; for Aries, the sign of life, is presided over by the same planet as the co-ruler of Scorpio, the sign of death. The dieugard is given by placing the end of the thumb under the chin, the fingers clenched. It denotes the Will to conquer death by passing into the new cycle represented by the chin which is the particular portion of the head where Aries exerts its most pronounced rulership. The cross is given by drawing the hand horizontally across the throat and then darting it up before the face. This is the vernal cross of life. The grand hailing sign of distress is given by placing the right foot over the left, representing the solstitial cross, and extending both arms to signify the autumnal cross, the head inclining to the right in dejection to indicate lack of power. The grip is given by interlacing the fingers of the right and left hands with the opposite brother, and as each crosses his arms pronouncing the word Emmanuel. It refers to the reascension through union after transition.

Knights of Malta

This degree is usually given with the Order of Knights Templar. The sign is made by holding out the hands as if warming them, representing the heat of summer. The lower edge of the left hand is then seized near the middle with the thumb and forefinger of the right hand, representing the painful influence of the sun as it crosses the vernal equinox after being attacked by the claws of the Scorpion, and then the hands are raised in this position to a level with the chin, or Aries, and finally disengaged with a quick motion that extends them down at an angle of forty-five degrees, as if the evil influence of death, or Scorpio, has been thrown off. It is said to refer to Paul when shipwrecked on the Island of Melita being bitten by a serpent as he warmed himself at a fire.

The grand word of a Knight of Malta is INRI, said to be the initials of the words, Iesus Nazarenus, Rex Iudaeorum, meaning Jesus of Nazareth, King of the Jews. But all well informed occultists know these initials are of the words, Igne Natura Renovature Integra, meaning All Nature is Renewed by Fire. This refers to the rejuvenating effect of the creative principle when properly applied and transmuted on the rosy cross of spring.

The grip and word of a Knight of Malta are given by interlacing the fingers of the right hand, placing the forefinger in the other's palm, reaching across with the left hand and pressing the fingers into the other's side at the waist line, or Libra. With the arms thus crossed one pronounces the words, "My Lord," and the other rejoins, "And My God." Their union in this fashion forms a maltese cross and an equinoctial cross, over both of which the sun passes annually. The fingers in the palm refer to Jupiter ruling the sign Sagittarius from which the sun crosses the winter solstice into Capricorn. Jupiter is the greater fortune, the planet of generosity, and this emphasizes the necessity of unselfishness in united effort to gain immortality. The exclamation, "My Lord," means all is under Law; and "My God," refers to the ego overshadowing counterpart souls the final reunion of which results in immortality. This sign is said to refer to Doubting Thomas who must feel the nail prints and the spear wound in the Master's side.

Knights of Christian Mark

The ritual of this degree is based upon resurrection and punishment or reward for deeds done upon earth. After prayer each knight, one after another, takes the Bible and waves it four times over his head saying, "Rex Regnantium et Dominus Dominantium," (King of Kings and Lord of Lords), then kisses the book and passes it to the next and so on around the circle. It symbolizes the sun's passage through the four quarters of the zodiac, signifies that all is under law, and that the sun is the source of all physical and spiritual life. The sign is given by each knight interlacing the fingers of his left hand with those of his brother, and pointing a sword towards his heart, at the same time saying, Tammuz Toulimeth, meaning that life is uncertain and transitory. The sign symbolizes the fall of the sun from Leo, or the soul from spiritual realms, across the equinox where summer and winter, or spirit and matter, join. The candidate is dubbed a knight of the Christian Mark by interlacing his fingers with those of the Invincible Knight and placing his other hand over his heart. The Invincible Knight and the Senior Knight then cross their swords on the back of the candidate's neck, to symbolize the equinoctial cross of spring, and give him these words, "Tammuz Toulimeth," an assurance of the certainty of death and the uncertainty of life.

Next, the Senior Knight reads a long passage the purport of which is, "For he that overcometh, the same shall be clothed in white raiment, and his name shall be written in the book of life." Six Grand Ministers, representing the six summer signs of the zodiac, come forward with swords and shields and one with an ink-horn. They are told to execute the judgment of the Lord, whereupon the candidate bewails his fate that his lips are unclean. The first Minister takes a live coal from the altar and touches it to the candidate's lips, representing the purification after the resurrection, and the sun's passage through Aries after its rebirth. The candidate is then marked on the forehead with a signet leaving the words, King of Kings and Lord of Lords, and is told that the number of the sealed is one-hundred-forty-four-thousand. This refers to an ancient tradition that each volute of every round of humanity produces its harvest of immortal souls. A volute is one precessional cycle. The twelve signs through which the sun annually passes while the equinox is in each sign, multiplied by the twelve signs that the equinox passes through in the precessional cycle, make up the one-hundred-forty-four varieties of souls born during one evolutionary volute of time. Those of all the one-hundred-forty-four zodiacal possibilities who find the Law, or Lord, and abide by it become spiritual kings.

The insignia which is worn over the heart is a triangular plate of gold, representing body, soul, and ego. On one side is the letter G in a five point star. It symbolizes that intelligent man is the climax of evolution through generation. On the other side are seven eyes, symbolizing the seven states of consciousness attained by the adept.

Order of Knights of the Holy Sepulchre

This degree is said to have been founded by St. Helen, mother of Constantine the Great in gratitude for her success in finding the true cross. She had made a journey into the Holy Land and found three crosses but was unable to determine which was the right one. Pope Marcellimus made a test by taking them to the bedside of a dying woman. Touching the first cross, the autumnal cross of Libra, did not affect her. The second cross, the solstitial cross of Capricorn, produced no beneficial effect. But on touching the third cross, the life giving cross of Aries, she immediately was restored to perfect health. It is this latter cross which in spring revivifies the whole world.

The most significant ritual of this degree represents the candidate taking up arms, Aries fashion, to "guard the Holy Sepulchre," the body and material possessions; to "defeat our enemies," the negative forces of evil or winter; to "unfurl the banner of our cross," life through union; to "protect the Roman Eagle," transmute the sex forces into constructive channels; to "return with victory and safety," return to spiritual realms consciously victorious over sense and seeming. The candidates first interlace their fingers, cross their arms and say, "de mortuis, nil nisi bonum," meaning that nothing should be said but good concerning the dead, as the so-called dead are often conscious of our thoughts and words. The interlaced fingers indicate union in accomplishing their mission to overcome the forces of evil denoted by the autumnal cross.

They sally forth, going toward the south, even as the sun after the summer solstice moves south to the struggle with winter after passing the autumnal equinox. They meet a band of Turks, representing the feminine forces of winter, with whom they do battle, seize the crescent and victoriously return north to the Cathedral, the summer signs. They triumphantly place the banner, eagle, and crescent before the altar. The Holy Sepulchre is the winter solstice, matter, or when applied to the incarnating soul it is the mother's womb through which it comes into a new life. As applied to incarnate man it is the body in which he is encased awaiting the period when earthly gestation shall be accomplished and he shall be set free from matter. Applied to the departing soul it is the grave. Yet for the righteous death has no sting and the grave has no victory. This is the significance of the Word of the Order, Sepulchrum, meaning sepulchre. The Roman Eagle bears testimony to the thought; for the same sign representing death, the stinging Scorpion, through regeneration becomes the soaring eagle of spiritual life. In this regeneration the sun is not alone; for the crescent moon is also given a place before the altar even as man and woman mutually sustain each other.

Order of the Cross

The Provost reads the following in opening this degree: "It is now the first hour of the day, the time when our Lord suffered, and the veil of the temple was rent asunder; when darkness and consternation were spread over the earth; when the confusion of the old covenant was made light in the new, the temple of the cross. It is the third watch, when the implements of Masonry were broken; when the flame, which led the Wise Men of the East, reappeared; when the cubic stone was broken, and the word was given." The first hour when the Lord suffered refers to sunrise on the day of the autumnal equinox, the veil of the temple which was rent being the equinoctial colure which was passed by the sun. Nights then became longer than the days and the covenant of summer gave place to winter. The sun had passed through three signs since the summer solstice, or now the third watch. The virility of the sun, mace and plumb, are broken on the cross. The cubic stone is the winter solstice, the dividing line of inertia, which is broken by the reappearance of the sun at Epiphany, the word then being given that heralds resurrection.

The sign is made by looking a brother full in the face and touching him on the right temple, the phrenological faculty of construction, meaning the use of constructive effort which is a quality ruled by Aries. The mark is Baal, Sha-Lisha, Lord of the three, meaning control over the three bodies; physical, astral, and spiritual. The candidate must give correctly his name, age, birth place, and residence; the data for erecting his birth-chart. The initials of the mark, IHS. Iesus Homium Salvator, Jesus Savior of Men, are in Hebrew, Jod-He-Shin, man and woman together attaining adeptship. In Latin they are the initials of words meaning, Son of Man Triumphant.

Secret Monitor

This trading degree is founded upon the Twelfth Major Arcanum of the tarot, called the Hanged Man, corresponding to the sign Pisces, ruling universal brotherhood as well as intrigues and secret organizations.

The history of this degree refers to the brotherly love existing between Jonathan and David in the time of Saul. By means of arrows, symbolical of evil news Jonathan warned David to flee the wrath of Saul, or Saturn. David represents the sun, and Jonathan represents Jupiter, the co-ruler of Pisces and the ruler of Sagittarius, the zodiacal sign of the arrows, which is adjoining the sign Capricorn, ruled by Saturn, or Saul.

The signs of this degree are made secretly to assist each other in financial transactions. Yet to use psychic warnings from the invisible brethren for material advantages over our fellowmen is contrary to occult law, and is apt to be punished with the arrows of affliction. Those who proclaim the Piscean doctrine of universal brotherhood should be willing to make the necessary sacrifices to practice their doctrines. Failing to do so the penalty of expiation will fall as indicated by the dieugard, which is made by assuming the attitude of one who shoots an arrow. It is the symbol of vengeance.

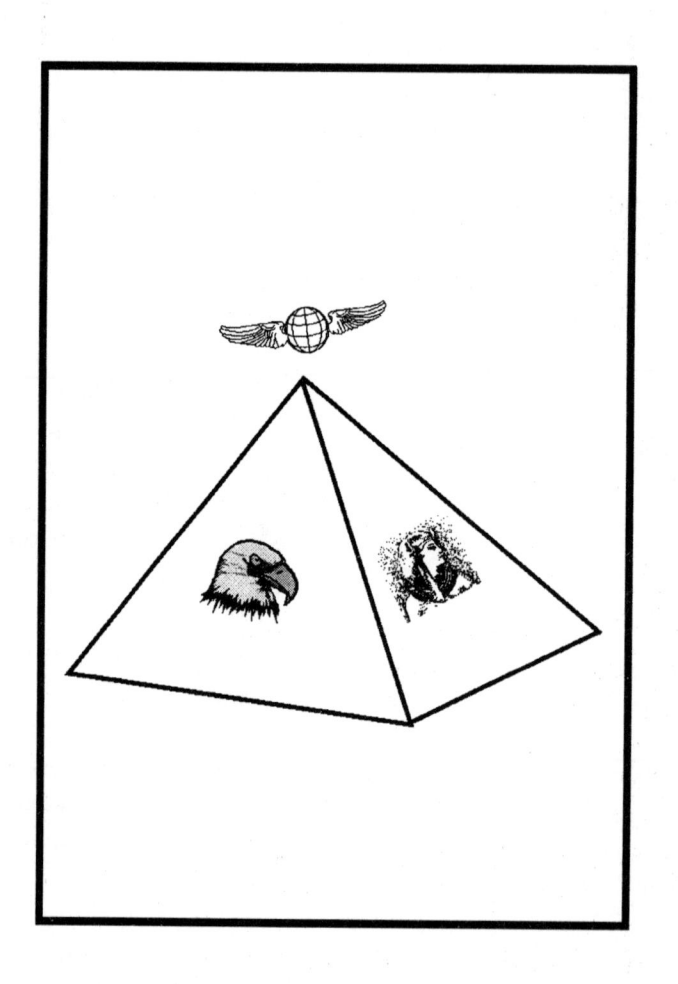

Chapter 12

Ineffable Degrees

OF THE EMBLEMS belonging to the Master's degree, the naked heart symbolizes conscience, and indicates that on the inner planes the motive of any action can never be concealed, and that every impulse is laid bare.

The three steps on the Master's carpet symbolize the three steps in the sun's annual journey; its fall from summer into winter over the autumnal cross, its encasement in the tomb of winter at the southern solstice, and its final resurrection into a new summer by way of the vernal cross. In the cycle of the soul this represents the soul's descent into the mineral realm, its evolution through lower forms of life up to the state of man, and from man, by way of the equinox of regeneration, evolving into the still higher state of angelhood.

The sword pointing to the naked heart signifies remorse for past misdeeds; true repentance followed by penance. It exemplifies the truth that every mistake must be atoned for, and every debt of conscience paid to the last farthing before the spiritual plane is reached. Evil done on earth pursues the soul, as signified by the sword, into the astral. In this realm the conscience is laid bare, as signified by the naked heart, and atonement made through suffering and purification.

The hour-glass is an emblem showing the point where angel and animal meet in the soul and body of man; the up-pointing trine indicating the sands of time through which, in evolving from the animal to the human, there were developed the required initiative and selfish propensities. The down-pointing trine represents not the selfish acquiring of material things denoted by the sand accumulating below; but the evolution of man to angel, which requires giving to society, not receiving from it, well symbolized by the sand of this trine flowing freely away from it.

That Which Determines Control

As the degrees upward from those of the cross, representing transition of the activities to the inner plane, repeatedly refer to ability to control the energies thus contacted and to ability to prevent control by entities thus contacted, this seems to be the place to set forth the principles on which rest such control.

To contact through the inner plane anything belonging to any realm the vibrations must be raised or lowered until they are similar to the vibrations of that which is to be contacted. When such contact is made, the similarity of the vibrations affords opportunity for the exchange of energies. The energy flow is always from the highest potential to the lower potential. This potential difference between individuals and between persons and objects is well illustrated by the Contact Potential Difference between metals discovered by Volta:

> Volta found that when pieces of two different metals, otherwise insulated, are brought into contact, they acquire opposite charges and maintain a difference of electrical potential even while still touching. This potential difference he found to be characteristic of the given pair of metals. Thus when the metals are iron and copper, the iron has a potential about 0.15 volts higher than the copper, while for tin and iron the difference is 0.31 volts, tin being the higher. Volta listed a series of several metals, viz., zinc, lead, tin, iron, copper, silver, gold, such that when any two are put in contact, the one first named is at the higher potential.

I have quoted this principle of Contact Potential Difference from a standard work on electricity because it operates in all action of the mind and is an outstanding factor in ESP and in every variety of psychic phenomena. When we say, for instance, that one person is positive and another is negative, it implies that the one has a high potential and the other has a low potential. Yet, as illustrated by Volta's discovery, such positiveness and negativeness are not absolute, but relative. Iron is in this sense positive to copper, but is negative to tin; and a person who is positive to one individual may be negative to another individual.

In reference to mental and psychic phenomena of all kinds, it is customary to state that the positive controls the negative. In the sense with which positive and negative are thus used this signifies that a higher potential, or voltage, is able to overcome a lower potential, or voltage, and direct whatever action takes place.

From this it will be seen that a positive individual is one who habitually has so high a potential that he strongly resists control from any outside force, and a negative individual is one who habitually has so low a potential that he is easily controlled by outside forces. Also it will be plain from this that a negative thought is one which tends to lower the individual's potential, and a positive thought is one which tends to raise his potential. Fear, worry and anxiety arise from thoughts that rapidly lower the electrical potential of the body, and if intense and persistent enough, after a time can lower the potential differences in the body sufficiently that death results.

The vitality and life of the human body depend upon differences in electrical potential between different organs. The brain has the highest potential—otherwise it could not control the movements—and the liver has the lowest. But when through negative thinking over a long period, or through fatigue, shock, or loss of sleep, the electrical energies are exhausted to a point where there is no difference of potential between the brain and the liver, the body is dead.

In the nervous system there is a continual competition between electrical energies of different potentials, the highest potential always being successful in exercising control over the movements. And there is ever a similar competition between the potentials mobilized by the different thoughts which strive to get attention. The thought having the highest potential at the moment gets the attention.

These competitions between electrical energies of different potentials are mentioned to introduce the principle with which we are here concerned, that when on the inner plane we contact closely another individual, a condition, or a thought-form, there is a similar competition between astral potentials. Whether through hypersensitivity of the nervous system, or through extension of consciousness, we make a close contact with something on the inner plane, some part of us has tuned in on it. In the case of hypersensitivity we have used the electromagnetic energies of the nervous system, or some portion of it, to tune after the manner of a receiving set. In the case of extension of consciousness we have used the electromagnetic energies to give the faculties of the unconscious mind an activity which places them in contact with that to be apprehended. In either instance we have tuned the astral energies associated with our nerves or associated with our intellects to the object, thought-form, personality, or whatnot about which we seek information.

If we acquire the information through hypersensitivity, this means that the astral energies associated with the nerve currents of our nervous system or some part of it have a lower potential, even though temporarily of the same vibratory frequency and vibratory modulation, than the astral energy being radiated by that which is contacted. For the reason the energy it radiates is thus of higher potential, we FEEL it distinctly.

On the other hand if the astral energies associated with the nerve currents and radiated from our nervous system have a higher potential than the vibrations tuned in on, the astral vibratory rates radiated by that which is contacted fail to move in on the electrical currents carried by the nervous system, and they are not felt by any portion of it. There is a competition between the vibrations radiated by that which is tuned in on and the vibrations of the individual who has thus tuned himself to these same vibratory rates.

An individual who has tuned in on something else either as a receiving set or to make an examination by the faculties of the unconscious mind, is as closely in contact with it on the inner plane through this similarity of vibratory rates as are two things on the external plane when they physically touch each other, and the energies as readily flow from the one to the other. The direction of flow of the astral energies when such contact is made is from high potential to low potential.

In Extension of Consciousness properly accomplished, the potential of the individual making the contact is at all times kept higher than the potential of that which is contacted. He does not, therefore, "take on" the condition which he contacts. Instead of being like the individual who, witnessing another in a serious accident sympathetically feels the other's pain, and thus is partially incapacitated from effective action, he is like the skilled surgeon on the scene who has trained himself not to respond sympathetically to the patient's pain, but to keep his intellect alert examining the condition and directing action in the most effective way.

In acquiring information through the positive method of Extension of Consciousness, the individual can recognize sound, colors, thoughts, even the feel of things. But in thus using the senses of the astral body he employs them from the standpoint of intellect, and does not permit energy from that which he contacts to flow to himself. Instead, through his own higher potential, the energy used in the examination is furnished by himself.

Secret Master

The Secret Master degree is based upon the Fourteenth Major Arcanum of the tarot, which symbolizes regeneration and the application of the Master's Word. The latter was recovered in the Seventh, or Royal Arch degree. Astrologically the Secret Master degree corresponds to the zodiacal sign Taurus where, after the resurrection on the cross of Aries, the sun fecundates the earth and brings forth the succulent verdure of spring. It is the positive rays of the sun mingled with the negative nature of Taurus, where the moon is exalted, that regenerates the whole world.

A Secret Master Lodge is said to represent the Sanctuary of Solomon's Temple, the astral plane, which adjoins the Sanctum Sanctorum, or world of spirit. It is hung with black sprinkled with white tears to symbolize the realm of purification entered into after the resurrection from the wintry tomb of Aries. It is lighted by nine candelabra of nine lights each. The nine candelabra represent the nine decanates the sun passes through in its regeneration from the vernal equinox to the summer solstice. The eighty-one lights symbolize the eighty-one days it takes the moon to thrice circle the zodiac, each time being born to new life, to represent the life of the soul and its transition on all three planes. The Master is dressed as King Solomon, and sits before a triangular table to signify his actions on these three planes of life. He is dressed in royal robes to symbolize his authority, and holds in his hand a scepter, symbol of his virile power. A large ribbon of blue indicates knowledge gained through experiences with matter, winter, or Saturn. It extends from the right shoulder to the left hip, indicating knowledge of sex energy; and at the hip is suspended a golden triangle, signifying that this energy may be used on all three planes to gain illumination.

The second officer is Adoniram, representing Pluto and the soulmate of Hiram Abiff. He is clothed in black robe and cap to indicate mourning, and decorated with a white ribbon bordered with black, to indicate the dawning light of hope for immortality. The ribbon has a black rosette on it, representing the autumnal equinox and the triumph of material forces. Also suspended from it is an ivory key, a spiritual key, with the letter Z engraved upon it. Z is a double 7, a union of a positive 7, or physically perfect man, with a negative 7, or physically perfect woman. It is the union of two open trines, an open trine meaning energy expended. But in this union there is compensation, and the energies are directed along the highest lines possible to embodied man, regenerate forces being used for a definite purpose.

The other brethren wear black robes and caps, white aprons with black strings, and white gloves. They represent the union of positive and negative zodiacal signs, the apron strings indicating the equinox. The flap of the apron is blue, denoting knowledge of sex gained through experience. Upon the flap is a golden eye, symbol of spiritual wisdom.

Adoniram, asked if he is a Secret Master, replies, "I have passed from the square to the compass; I have seen the tomb of our respectful Master Hiram Abiff, and shed tears at the same." This symbolizes the moon as well as the sun passing through the rains of winter and crossing the vernal equinox. The winter union with the sun is signified by the square and that of summer by the compass. To the soul the tomb of the missing mate is the material world where both must sojourn, usually separated by its barriers, a cause for mourning. But there is also cause for hope as indicated by Hiram saying, "The dawn of day has driven away darkness, and the great light begins to shine in the lodge." This is the dawn of resurrection, or in physical life illumination through regeneration. The Master raps seven times to signify that the brethren are perfect physical men, and says, "If the great light is a token of the dawn of day, and we are all Secret Masters, it is time to begin our labors." The labor refers to the work of the sun in summer preparing the crops for harvest, and to the work on the astral plane of assisting others less progressed, the assistance being rendered by those who have entered into regeneration; and it refers to the even more strenuous labor performed in that region by those who have consciously passed through the tomb of death.

The candidate when admitted is led to the altar and kneels on his right knee, symbolizing his desire to render positive service. His head is bound, and fastened to his forehead by the bandage is a square, symbolizing the duties and obligations that still bind him to those yet struggling in the throes of matter. In his right hand is a great light, signifying his intention to labor spreading knowledge. On the altar is a crown of laurel and olive leaves, indicating his double victory, that of strife and that of love. The words are Shaddai, Adonai, and Juha, mystically signifying, Praise be to the Lord of the new Light. The password is Zizon, signifying a double triumph; that over the physical and that over the inner nature. The sign is given by placing the two forefingers of the right hand on the lips, indicating silence concerning the mysteries of both planes. The token is given by crossing the legs as the hands join in the Lion's grip. The crossed legs symbolize the solstitial cross, and the grip indicates the power of the sun in Leo by which he raises the moon from the winter signs to be united with him in the regenerate signs of summer. It represents the power of the purified soul to find and rescue its lost mate from the bondage of matter.

In closing, Adoniram is asked his duty, and replies that it is to guard the furniture of the Sanctorum, consisting of the altar of incense, the two tables of shew-bread and the golden candlesticks. The tables of shew-bread signify the result of experiences with good and evil which is assimilated by man's spiritual nature. The candlesticks are placed five on the north and five on the south of the holy place, and thus symbolize man and woman. The age of Adoniram is stated to be three times twenty-seven, meaning the twenty-seven days it takes the moon to complete its circle of life around the zodiac, three times around symbolizing the soul's progress through three planes. The special emblem of the Secret Master degree is a triangle in which are the Hebrew letters Jod-He-Vau-He surrounded by light. This is the Master's Word as revealed to Enoch, applicable alike on all three planes. It is the secret of uniting positive and negative forces to produce the spiral of life.

Perfect Master

The Perfect Master degree is based upon the Twentieth Major Arcanum of the tarot, symbolizing the day of judgment and corresponding astrologically to the moon. The lodge is hung with green tapestry—the color of the moon—on eight columns, four on each side at equal distances, symbolizing perfect equilibrium, and justice received. There are sixteen lights placed at the cardinal points to represent the three signs and the presiding ruler of each zodiacal quarter. A pyramid stands in the north with open compass upon it, symbolizing the earth as an epitome of the universe under the direction of stellar law. The pyramid is the most stable form. The base is typical of the square of matter and the sides represent the four zodiacal triplicities meeting in a common point. Its most important significance is that of the earth being the womb of the universe from which is born, after its period of gestation, the Son of God. The pyramid at the north symbolizes the earth under law, but as yet uninhabited by intelligent life. Another pyramid in the south has a blazing star upon it to represent gestation completed and the earth being delivered of its child, Man, who rules the world while in it, and when born into the realm above may become a god. A table stands before the canopy covered with black to typify the plane of death.

The assistants are decorated with a green ribbon about the neck from which is hung a compass extended to 60 degrees, symbolizing by the green ribbon, love received, and by the compass, harmonious union. The brethren wear black caps and robes, indicative of having passed the tomb of materialism, aprons of white leather with green flaps, signifying the reception of the reward for purity. Upon the apron is embroidered a square stone surrounded by three circles with the letter J in the center, symbolizing the earth surrounded by Mundane Houses, Zodiacal Signs, and Constellations, through all of which penetrates the divine fire, or J. The hour being four, the time when the sun at the equinox enters the first house of the horoscope, or house of life, it is time for the brethren to go to work, or enter upon the duties of the new life beyond matter.

The candidate has a green cord placed about his neck which is finally withdrawn by the Master to symbolize the moon passing out of the spring sign Taurus to a more elevated station, and man ready to be raised to a love higher than that of earth, and to an immortal work signified by the sprig of cassia placed in his left hand. The first sign is given by placing the palm of the left hand upon the right temple and stepping back with the right foot and again bringing it to its first position. It refers to the constructive use of virile energy in recovering the lost spiritual state. The second sign is made by raising the hands and eyes upward and letting the hands fall crossed in front, at the same time dropping the eyes downward, meaning the fall into temptation, from spirit into matter, or the sun across the autumnal equinox. The password is Acacia, symbolizing immortality. The token is that of a Mark Master, given on the five points of fellowship as explained in that degree. The Mysterious word is Je-Vau, meaning divine fire in union. The candidate approaches the East by four times four steps, from a pair of compasses extended from an angle of seven degrees to that of sixty degrees. The four times four refers to traversing the zodiacal circle, twelve signs ruled by the lords of the four seasons, corresponding to the sixteen Court Cards of the tarot. From seven degrees refers to perfect physical manhood, and sixty degrees refers to perfect union.

The tomb of Hiram was of black and white marble, good and evil experiences on earth. It was entered between the two pillars, winter and summer, supporting a stone surrounded by three circles, already explained. The heart of Hiram was enclosed in a golden urn, symbol of spiritual affection. It was pierced by a sword to indicate the afflictions befalling those who attempt to realize their spiritual ideals of affection on earth, and the resurrection of those ideals beyond matter; the sword representing transition over the cross of Aries. It is the action of a luminary in Leo, the heart; in Scorpio, the urn; and in Aries, the sword. On the tomb was engraved the letter J, the virile Hebrew Jod. To the side of the urn was fastened a triangular stone on which were the letters J M B, surrounded by a wreath of cassia. The urn was placed upon the top of an obelisk erected on the tomb, symbolizing the solstitial colure, the foot resting on the tomb of winter, and the top, or summer solstice, being the highest point of heaven where the luminary passing through the tomb will finally be elevated. J is Jachin from which the soul falls. B is Boaz, the winter signs, or material realm where it falls, and M (see Course 6, *The Sacred Tarot*) is Aries where resurrection takes place. The triangular stone represents the experience of body, soul, and ego with material conditions, and the wreath of cassia surrounding the letters denoting the pilgrimage indicates that immortality has been attained. Hiram, the moon, returning to its home in Cancer, the summer solstice, is greeted by Solomon, the sun, who says with joy in his heart, "It is accomplished and complete." The special emblem of this degree is a coffin with a five-point star on the lid, and leaning over it a sprig of cassia. It signifies man enshrouded in the tomb of earth being promised immortal life in other realms.

Intimate Secretary

The Intimate Secretary degree is based upon the Eighteenth Major Arcanum of the tarot, symbolizing false friends and deception. It corresponds astrologically to the sign Cancer. The Lodge is hung with black spangles with white tears to represent the realm of purification after death. There is a triangular table on which is a scroll and crossed swords, representing the record inscribed in the astral light of man's struggles on all three planes of endeavor. The Masters wear long blue robes and caps, symbol of wisdom gained through experience; their aprons are bordered with red, the white symbolizing purity, and the red symbolizing passion of purpose. On the apron is a scroll, and a golden triangle with the letters A P P in its corners. The letter A of the tarot symbolizes will, and P symbolizes hope. The scroll and lettered triangle signify spiritual effort on all three planes is sustained by will and two hopes; hope of future life, and hope of future love. All are recorded in the book of life. They also wear a red ribbon with a golden triangle suspended from it, meaning energy to be used on three planes. Their gloves are white, bordered with red, signifying purity and energy in execution. On the Bible is laid a triple triangle, symbolizing the law of perfect co-ordination between body, soul, and ego on all three planes.

The candidate in this degree takes the part of a spy who listens at the veil, is captured and condemned by Hiram King of Tyre, and is freed by the intercession of Solomon. Astrologically it symbolizes the moon separating from the sun and passing into the captivity of opposite zodiacal signs and finally being rescued from them by its return to the sun. It represents the soul of man after death, in the twilight realms of the astral, undergoing judgment for deeds done in the flesh and being found worthy after some purification to enter more spiritual realms because of the strength of its rapport with the ego.

The first sign is made by closing the right hand and drawing it from the left shoulder to the right hip. It refers to the fall of man through the destructive use of sex. It is also the fall of the sun into winter. The second sign is made by crossing the arms in front and holding them up so the thumbs touch opposite temples, speaking the mysterious word Je-Vau. It refers to constructive use of virile powers in union; astrologically the resurrection of the sun on the vernal cross, the mysterious word signifying its subsequent union with the moon. The grip is given by joining the right hands and turning them downward thrice, saying one of these words at each turn: Berith, Nedir, Shelmoth. These words symbolize the autumnal equinox, the winter solstice, or lowest point, and the vernal equinox, respectively; and each turn of the hands signifies the union of the sun and moon after the sun passes these points. It signifies man and woman united in indulgence, in proper generation, and in regeneration. The password is Joabert, and the response is Terbel. Joabert is the listener, or the soul seeking to be conscious of the inner voice. Terbel is the guard of the inner realms, the dweller on the threshold.

Provost and Judge

The degree of Provost and Judge is based upon the Seventeenth Major Arcanum of the tarot, symbolizing the star of hope, and corresponding astrologically to the sign Gemini. The lodge is hung with red tapestries to represent the energies actuating life. There are five candelabra of five lights each, four being at the corners of the room and the other being in the center. The number five is the symbol of man. Each of the candelabra at the corners symbolizes man evolving through the zodiacal quarter corresponding to one of the four kingdoms, mineral, vegetable, animal, and man; and the candelabrum in the center represents man after his transit to the realm of purification where he recapitulates his past evolution and passes judgment upon his conduct. In the east is an illuminated transparent triangle in which is a circle around which are the letters J A I N, with a blazing star in the center on which are three J's. The triangle represents infinite Life, Light, and Love, the source of all being. The circle is the zodiac, and the letters symbolize the divine influx from above as transmitted through each zodiacal quadrant. J represents the divine fire in Leo, A represents the will in Scorpio, I represents intelligence in Aquarius, and N represents regenerate energy in Taurus. The blazing star in the center is man, the focus of universal forces, retaining a portion for his own use, reflecting the finer essence above, and refracting the grosser portions of the One Life Principle below, as symbolized by the three J's.

The brethren wear black robes and caps to symbolize their passage through the tomb of death; white aprons trimmed with red to symbolize purity sustained by virile energy; with a red and a white rosette on the apron to signify regeneration and translation to spiritual life; and a pocket in which to carry plans, the ideas formulated and vitalized in union. On the flap is a golden key, and another is suspended from a red collar. The red collar is symbol of ardent affections, and the golden key signifies astrological knowledge. The hour is said to be break of day; 8,2, and 7; meaning the entrance into a new life in higher realms has started through 8, Judgment; 2, with the aid of Esoteric Science; and 7, Victory over all temptations. They all combine in seventeen, the Star of Hope for future joy (see Course 6, *The Sacred Tarot*).

The candidate is led to the southwest corner of the lodge where the sun sinks in winter at the close of day, and is there instructed to kneel and pronounce the word Beroke, meaning to descend. The Master then says "Kumi," meaning to rise, signifying a new epoch begun even as the sun rises at break of day. The first sign is to place the first two fingers of the right hand to the side of the nose with the thumb under the chin, symbolizing the will to use the energy of Mars, signified by the chin; to vitalize the etheric body, signified by the Jupiter finger; in the process of breathing, indicated by the nose. The physical body is also to be considered in this process as the finger of Saturn is used as well as that of Jupiter. The second sign is like the first except that one finger only is used, signifying the use of Mars energy to vitalize the etheric body. The token is given by clenching the three first fingers over the thumb and interlacing the little fingers. It means that will is to be subjected to science, as Mercury rules the little finger and also rules science. The password is Tito, the first to draw plans for the workmen. This signifies the formulative power of the intellect. The candidate having given the password and signs is presented with a key to a small ebony box which contains the plans for building the temple, and a key for opening an ebony box containing all the temple keys. The ebony box is man's physical constitution, containing a correspondence to the universe. It is unlocked by practical astrology. The ivory box is man's spiritual constitution and soul, containing the keys to all spiritual mysteries. It is unlocked by the spiritual astrology so carefully preserved in Masonry.

Intendant of the Building

This degree is based upon the Nineteenth Major Arcanum of the tarot. It symbolizes reunion and corresponds to the zodiacal sign Leo. The lodge is lighted with three candelabra with nine lights each, the symbolism of which has already been explained. In addition there are five candles in the east to indicate man rising into another sphere of influence.

The brethren wear white aprons lined with red and bordered with green, symbolizing purity, energy, and receptive capacity. On the apron is a star with nine points, symbolizing wisdom gained under planetary influence; a sprig of cassia, representing immortality; and a balance, emblem of justice. On the corners of the triangular flap are the letters B A J, symbolizing occult science illumined by divine fire, directed by will. The collar is of red to indicate affectional energy, and from it is suspended a golden trine with the letters J A B in the corners, and in the center three J's. The three J's represent the divine fire penetrating the three worlds. On the reverse of the triangle the three J's are in the corners and G is in the center, indicating the divine fire used in generation. As used on the first side they indicate that the divine fire aids the will to remove the veil of Isis.

In this degree, a chief of the five orders of architecture is selected to fill the vacant place of Hiram Abiff. The five orders of architecture are: Tuscan, Doric, Ionic, Corinthian, and Composite. The first four represent the zodiacal quarters and their correspondences. The composite, a combination of the others, symbolizes man. The true soul-mate being lost, a worthy substitute is selected to assist in the work. The obligation is taken while the candidate lies prostrate, and he is lifted under a sprig of cassia by the Lion's grip. The signs and passwords all refer to the separation of sun and moon, of man and woman, to the sorrowful descent into the winter signs, or matter; and to the reascent to spiritual realms, reunion, and consequent immortality. In the closing lecture the Senior Warden says: "I have made the five steps of exactness; I have penetrated the inmost part of the temple; and I have seen the great light, in the middle of which were three mysterious letters." The five steps of exactness refer to evolution through four kingdoms and the entering of the fifth, the kingdom of regenerate man. It also indicates the successive subjugation of the five physical senses leading to illumination and the use of the creative energy to explore the three planes, as signified by the three J's.

Master of Elect Nine

This degree is based upon the Sixteenth Major Arcanum of the tarot, symbolizing catastrophe. It corresponds astrologically to the planet Mars. Solomon had appointed nine Masters to go to the spot where it had been learned one of the assassins of Hiram Abiff was concealed. Mars, one of the nine planets, represented by Joabert, steals ahead of the others and discovers the murderer asleep with a poinard at his feet. This is the equinox at the foot of Pisces. Mars takes the poinard and stabs him first in the head, Aries, and then in the heart, Leo. He then cuts off the villain's head and taking it in one hand and the bloody knife in the other returns to Solomon's home. The place of sunrise, Jubulum, is killed by the vernal cross, wielded by Mars. He is first stabbed in the head to indicate the sun rising in Aries, and later in the heart, in Leo, to which the sun returns. Cutting off the head signified that the rising sun has passed out of Aries. Its influence in the sign of the head has been cut off, and he passes to the rightful place of Solomon, in Leo. The sign is made by striking toward the companion's forehead as if stabbing, and the companion placing his hand to the spot as if feeling of a wound; then striking at the companion's heart crying Nekum, and the companion answering by placing his hand on his breast and saying Necar. These words mean Vengeance, and Vengeance Is Taken. The jewel of the order is a gold-handled dagger with a silver blade. The handle and blade symbolize the summer and winter signs, and the guard symbolizes the equinox.

Masters Elect of Fifteen

The degree Masters Elect of Fifteen is based upon the Fifteenth Major Arcanum of the tarot. It symbolizes the fate of the evil, and corresponds astrologically to the planet Saturn. The two other assassins of Hiram Abiff were not captured and punished with the first. Through one of his Intendants, Solomon learned that two persons answering their description had come to the country of Cheth and were working in the quarries. Cheth is the eighth Hebrew letter and presides over the Eighth Major Arcanum of the tarot, which symbolizes justice and corresponds to the sign Capricorn, the home of Saturn. Capricorn is the winter sign that symbolizes crystallization and has rule over quarries.

In front of each of the two officers that symbolize the sun and moon, one in the east and one in the west, is a candelabrum of five lights; one candelabrum to represent man and one candelabrum to represent woman. The brethren wear white aprons on which is pictured a square city, a form of birth-chart still used by Raphael in his annual ephemeris. It has three gates, and over each a human head impaled on a spire. These represent the three visible angles of the heavens, or assassins. Jubulum was captured in the preceding degree in a cave, that is, in Capricorn, stabbed with the vernal cross at the foot of Pisces, decapitated by passing into Taurus; and finally this representative of the Ascendant at sunrise returns to Leo carried by the strength of regenerate Mars. In the present degree, Jubela and Jubelo, Midheaven and Descendant, are captured in Capricorn and are carried from this region of crystallization into the warm months of summer, or Jerusalem. Their heads are cut off as they pass from Aries; and as they pass the summer solstice into Cancer, which rules the belly, their bodies are cut open. The sign of the degree is to place the point of a poinard under the chin and draw it downward to the waist, speaking the word Zerbul. It symbolizes the passage of the sun from Aries across the solstitial cross to the sign Libra.

Sublime Knights Elected

This degree is based upon the Twenty-second Major Arcanum of the tarot, symbolizing the foolish man. It corresponds astrologically to the planet Pluto. Solomon rewarded twelve of the Masters for their efforts to apprehend the assassins of Hiram Abiff by conferring upon them this degree and giving them command over the Twelve Tribes of Israel. They represent the twelve signs of the zodiac. The zodiacal circle crossed by equinox and solstice is the symbol of the world. By removing the circle, or spiritual portion of the symbol, we have the cross of earth in its most material aspect. If the upper bar of the cross be removed the result is the Tau Cross, or English T, emblem of the Lower-Pluto influence, the primitive phallic symbol of creative energy directed to material ends. The lower bar, or vertical line, indicates the sun in Capricorn at the winter solstice. It represents man spending his energies for material advantage, the worldly wise and spiritually foolish. By reversing the T so that the lower bar is missing we have a representation of the sun at the summer solstice as it enters Cancer, the emblem of the Upper-Pluto influence, signifying the virile energies directed to spiritual construction. And herein lies the paradox of the twenty-second card of the tarot, a card few students have understood; for the man that to the worldly may seem foolish may really have reversed the Tau, come under the Upper-Pluto influence, and being a true sage ignores the things that many spend their energies to obtain.

The candidate in this degree is required to swallow a piece of the heart of Hiram Abiff which is presented to him on a trowel by the Master. He is told that he may swallow it without injury if he is a faithful Mason but that it will not remain in the body of one perjured. This heart is the zodiacal sign Leo, symbol of affection, through the power of which Hiram is again united to Solomon. The trowel is an instrument used to bind together. Its form represents two souls occupying one form and overshadowed by a common ego. The candidate partaking of the heart on the trowel symbolically enacts the permanent reunion of soul-mates; the reward of the spiritually wise, whose efforts are denoted by the reversed T. Astrologically it is the reunion of the sun and moon in Leo, which is the sign that rules the house of love in a natural chart.

Grand Master Architect

This degree is said to have been founded by King Solomon as a school of architects where deserving craftsmen might receive proper instruction. These Grand Master Architects are men who have mastered the various occult and lucidic sciences and have been found worthy to serve as Masters to struggling neophytes. The Chapter is decorated with white hangings, sprinkled with red flames, symbolizing purity combined with fiery enthusiasm. The five orders of architecture are present, symbolizing man who contains within himself the zodiacal quarters corresponding to the four kingdoms of elemental life. Man's rightful place is that of Master Architect directing the four elemental realms of life in their work of cosmic construction. The apron is stone colored, to indicate work to be done upon earth, and has a star on it to signify man as the chief of that work. The jewel is a gold medal with the five orders of architecture, a star, and a case of mathematical instruments, on each side. It symbolizes man measuring planetary angles and positions in the zodiac, and utilizing his knowledge of astrological cycles, forces and angles to direct the elementals in their work of assisting evolutionary progress.

The candidate makes a tour of the room, which represents the zodiac, and draws an exact plan of it to illustrate his ability to compute astrological positions and map the heavens. There is a star in the north with seven other stars around it to represent the Polar Star, the "Rock of Ages," about which swings the septenary of naked-eye planets. It is called the guiding star of the order; for it is symbolical of the immutability of divine law, and is the axis of all mundane reckoning. The Chapter is said to be opened on the first instant, the first hour, the first day, the first year, when Solomon commenced the Temple. This is according to the prescribed rules of astrology; as a chart of the heavens for the instant commencing an enterprise indicates its future success or failure, even as a chart of the instant of physical birth reveals a child's physical destiny.

The sign is made by sliding the right hand into the palm of the left, clenching the fingers of the right hand and tracing a plan with the thumb in the other's left hand, looking at him as if taking dictation. It refers to man and woman united and taking advantage of astrological conditions to promote their interests. It indicates that from their knowledge of astrology they are able to formulate a plan of mutual effort. The token is given by interlacing the fingers of the right hand with those of the brother's left and placing the free hand on the hip. The united hands are at a level with the head. It indicates united transmutation from Scorpio to Aries, or the sun resurrected with the moon on the vernal equinox.

Knights of the Ninth Arch

This degree revolves around a vision of Enoch in which he saw the letters of the Ineffable Name engraved upon a triangular plate of gold which was lowered into the bowels of the earth to the ninth arch. Later he and Methuselah built a temple underground of nine arches and deposited a facsimile of the plate on a pedestal of white in the ninth arch. He also built two pillars on a high mountain nearby; one of brass to withstand water, and the other of marble to withstand fire. On the marble pillar he traced hieroglyphics disclosing the whereabouts of the golden plate; and on the pillar of brass he engraved the principles of geometry, or Masonry. This was before the flood.

In clearing away the rubbish to rebuild the temple the vault is discovered and the plate recovered in the same manner as the vault and Ark of the Covenant were found in the Royal Arch degree. This ninth arch is the lowest grade of actual adeptship, where the mysterious laws are fully revealed to the worthy neophyte. Enoch was the perfect man, representing the natural adepts of the golden age. Methuselah was his son who lived to great age, symbolizing those who through subsequent ages have been found worthy custodians of ancient wisdom and who have proceeded with the work outlined by the Ancient Masons. The Ineffable Name in the lowest grade of adeptship is represented as mounted on a white marble pedestal to indicate that understanding while in the body depends upon purity. The pillar of marble on the high mountain is the physical means adopted by the Magi to preserve their knowledge for posterity such as monuments, sacred allegories, hieroglyphics, and the tarot. This marble pillar is said to have been destroyed by the flood, but a portion is extant as we find in the next degree. The pillar of brass was not destroyed; for it represents the records left in the astral world where is preserved all the wisdom of ancient days. The floods of religious emotionalism and sensualism may destroy the material records of the past, assisted by physical floods due to climatic changes, but neither are effectual to efface the records left by Enoch, the early spiritual adepts, on the brazen astral column.

Degree of Perfection

The degree of perfection is based upon the Twenty-first Major Arcanum of the tarot. This pictures the Crown of the Magi, symbolizing the accomplishment of the great work and corresponding astrologically to the sun. The lodge is represented as a subterranean vault hung with red curtains. It symbolizes the earth from which the adept is departing, the red indicating generated energy. A part of Enoch's marble pillar, found among the ruins, is placed in the west. The pillar of Beauty, or astral records, the Burning Bush, or divine fire, and the triangle of Enoch with the sacred Jod-He-Vau-He engraved upon it are in the east. When the members are not at work the lodge is lighted by the Burning Bush, and when they are at work they are lighted by twenty-four lights. Three are in the north to represent the monad's evolution through the mineral, vegetable, and animal kingdoms; five are in the south to indicate that man is a fruit of material evolution; seven are in the west to symbolize man arriving at physical perfection through the application of the subjective laws of union; and nine are in the east to represent man's wisdom before he is permitted to enter the ninth arch. These twenty-four lights correspond to the twenty-four hours in which the earth completes one rotation on its axis and symbolize all the experiences necessary to man upon the physical earth. Also before each of the officers is a triangular white table, symbolizing the spiritual plane to which the adept is translated.

For the same reason, that is, because it is meant to symbolize the voluntary completion of earthly experience, there can be only twenty-seven working members in a Grand Lodge of Perfection. These twenty-seven represent the twenty-seven days it takes the moon, symbol of the soul, to make a complete transit of zodiacal experience. The work of this degree is a recapitulation of preceding degrees, even as the adept ready to leave the physical plane goes carefully over his past, tabulating experiences for future reference. Here for the first time the candidate receives the true pronunciation of the Word as revealed to Enoch; for Enoch, representing the children of the golden age, walked with God and was not. That is, he was translated consciously without the process of death as we know it. In the golden age when the cycle of life had been run tradition records that there was a gradual voluntary dissolution by which the soul liberated itself from the body and passed consciously to a higher realm. In those days there were neither phantoms nor shades in our earth's electromagnetic sphere. The adept who succeeds in accomplishing the great work while in the flesh understands the law governing translation and is able to pass to his future work in the spiritual world even as did Enoch, without being hampered by death or being detained in the astral worlds for experience and purification.

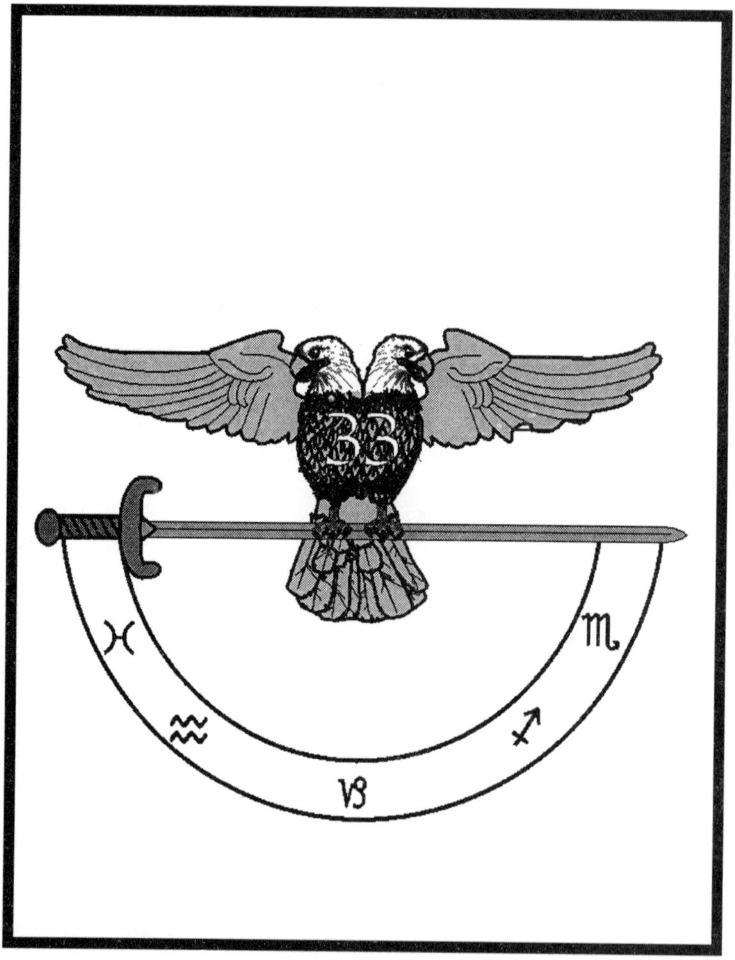
33

Chapter 13

Historical Degrees

IN CONNECTION with the historical degrees, mention should be made of the origin of both Scottish Rite Masonry and York Rite Masonry. I do not wish it implied that I agree with Albert Churchward in archaeological matters. But as he seems to be correct in his opinion of the origin of these two orders of Masonry, and is himself a high degree Mason, I take the liberty of quoting from his Arcana of Freemasonry.

> Chevalier Ramsay stated that modern Masonry had its beginning in the Society of Architects founded in Scotland under the protection of King Robert Bruce, and the title of 'Ancient and Accepted Masons of the Scottish Rite' may have possibly been formed in Scotland there and then; but if that is so, we must trace the origin of this to the Order of Knights Templar, who fled to Scotland, and through them to the ancient Mysteries practiced in the East. From whence did these Templars receive them? It is well known that one of the charges made against Jacques de Molay and his associates was that 'they used sacred rites in their initiation." Their four oaths are well known, but who knew their rites of initiation? The aim of the Society of Architects was to perpetuate the ancient order of the Temple, and they continued to use their initiations of members, symbols, signs, and some parts of the initiatory rites, which had been obtained in the East, but they only knew three degrees out of the seven lesser and ten greater. The next question is: From whence did the Templars receive those symbols, and their esoteric meaning, in which we plainly trace the doctrines of the old Egyptians? No doubt from the Christians, who, like the Emperor Julian, the Bishop Sinnesius, Clement of Alexandria, and

many other philosophers, had been initiated into some of the mysteries by the Priests of Egypt before being converted to Christianity. In this way we can trace how part of the religious mysteries of Egypt, signs and symbols, etc., came to Scotland.

Speaking further concerning the Egyptians he says:

There were also many who crossed over to Europe from Egypt, and spread from Italy into France, who possessed and clung to the true doctrines, endured torture, and some even death, by the early Roman Priests, who tried to usurp the temporal power by destroying the spiritual ideas; and yet these brothers would rather suffer death than give up their secrets and beliefs. Many of these migrations can be traced through Europe and finally to Scotland.

Relative to York Rite Masonry, Churchward continues:

As regards the origin from the Druids, I have given in 'Signs and Symbols of Primordial Man' the proofs of the origin of the Druids, and where they came from. They were High Priests of Egypt, who left the mother country at the early part of the Solar Cult, and were therefore well versed both in the seven Lesser Mysteries and the ten Greater Mysteries; and these practiced their religious rites in England until the edict of Canute prohibited their open worship. Canute reigned from 1015 to 1036. To evade persecution they resorted to private meetings and secret celebrations. I do not entertain any doubt that they formed the first so-called 'Lodges' in England, as a cloak to screen their religious rites and ceremonies, and to keep them as pure as they had received them originally from their parent sources in Egypt. Many of these old Druid Priests joined the Christian Church, and were the so-called Culdees, but although they had joined the Christian Church, they kept themselves very much aloof for a long period, up to the twelfth century.

These were the last remnants of the old Druid Priests—descendants of their Egyptian brethren—who practiced the pure Eschatology of their forefathers. Gradually they all died out as a separate and distinct class, and those who remained were merged into Christianity; but up to the twelfth century at least they brought all their doctrines with them, and practiced them in secret places, in so-called Lodges.

Here we have one source of the origin of Freemasonry, both in the Lesser Mysteries (seven degrees) and in the Greater Mysteries—so-called Higher Degrees in this country.

The Druids, in Gaul, were mostly put to the sword, others fled to this country for protection, when the Roman Christian doctrines were brought to them. In America it was the same. As soon as the Spanish Priests arrived there they persecuted all the Solar and Stellar people, murdered their priests, overthrew their Temples, and scattered them with fire and sword. Yet there is sufficient evidence left in their Signs, Symbols, and writings on the wall which may prove my contention that all these had the same Eschatology, signs, symbols, and rites as the Old Egyptians, from whence they came, and that all these are analogous to our own with really very little innovation, considering the many thousands of years that these have been handed down from country to country, and generation to generation, as we must acknowledge to be the case if we study the history of the human past.

Three Methods of Acquiring Information From the Inner Plane

Ancient Masonry presents not merely a philosophy of life based upon provable information, but also instructions relative to the general principles, applying which an individual can make the most rapid spiritual progress and develop his latent occult powers. More specific instructions in such training should be reserved for those who prove, by tests, that they have sufficient comprehension of occult matters that they will not be likely to misinterpret or misapply the information presented to them. These will find such detailed information presented in the systematic graduate course embraced in the "Not Sold" Brotherhood of Light Award Manuscripts.

However, as reference repeatedly has been made in these Ancient Masonry lessons to Extra-Sensory Perception, it should be clearly understood by anyone contemplating psychic work of any kind that there are three distinct methods of acquiring information from the inner plane, and just what takes place in each. The three methods are: Mediumship, Feeling ESP, and Intellectual ESP.

Mediumship

That which distinguishes mediumship is the partial or complete control of the medium by some intelligence other than his own. Mankind owes a deep debt of gratitude to spiritualistic mediums. I shall be the last to criticize them. Many in the ranks of spiritualism have sacrificed tremendously that the race might advance; many mediums have been martyrs to the cause of demonstrating human survival beyond the grave. But in spite of this debt of gratitude, the very real dangers to those who develop such mediumship cause us to discourage our students from attempting to become mediums. The reason is set forth in detail in Brotherhood of Light Course 1, *Laws of Occultism,* published in 1919. The subsequent years, in which through the many psychics contacted in connection with Church of Light work there has been unusual opportunity to observe the effects of the various types of development and psychic practice among a great many individuals, has but served more and more to confirm the attitude then taken. To sum this attitude up, The Church of Light does not advocate that anyone shall become a medium.

Two Methods of Independent Psychic Work

The Church of Light has found, however, as the result of its own research and observation, that psychic work in which there is no control by some other entity is accomplished in two quite distinct ways. These two methods, even though exercised and directed by the individual using them and not by some outside intelligence, are as different as day and night, positive and negative. The one depends upon hypersensitivity of the nervous system, and is called FEELING ESP. The other is purely an intellectual activity, and is called INTELLECTUAL ESP.

Feeling ESP

At the appropriate place in the "Not Sold" manuscripts I go into the details of these two methods. Here I hope only to bring out their contrasts so clearly that the neophyte will never mistake the one method for the other. The majority of independent psychics employ Feeling ESP. They make use of the hypersensitivity system of mental activity in which the nervous system or some part of it is tuned in on the astral counterpart of the object or person about which information is wanted. The nervous system, or some part of it, becomes a receiving set through which the electrical energies and astral energies closely associated with it pick up, radio fashion, the astral vibrations radiated by whatever is tuned in on. The individual then feels the condition of that which is thus contacted. The energy causing this feeling is furnished by that which is contacted. The individual who is hypersensitive is able to feel so discriminatingly what is received that his unconscious mind can give detailed information about that which is tuned in on, and perhaps about its past and probable future.

A quarter of a century of experience with students all over the world who have developed this Feeling ESP has convinced The Church of Light feels that this method of psychic development should be approached with caution.

Intellectual ESP

The unconscious mind, itself occupying the astral plane, has faculties which, given proper impetus and sufficient energy with which to work, on this inner plane can examine objects and thoughts and communicate with other intelligences. In Intellectual ESP hypersensitivity plays no part. Instead of becoming a receiving set, the electrical energies of the nervous system radiate high-frequency vibrations which afford the faculties of the unconscious mind the energies with which to perform their work. Feeling or hypersensitivity plays no more part in such examination by the unconscious mind on the inner plane than it does in a similar examination on the physical plane, nor are the emotions more active.

The examination is conducted by the unconscious mind reinforced by the astral energies provided by the high-frequency electromagnetic radiations of the nervous system. This examination, which may include past and future as well as all aspects of the present about which information is sought, is an intellectual appraisal the results of which are not communicated to other sections of the nervous system, but, much as something is remembered even though seen but a moment before, is communicated directly to the brain as an Intellectual awareness.

The Brotherhood of Light ESP Research Department has found that the psychics using Feeling ESP can acquire information readily from persons or other living things which radiate strongly, or about people from objects which they have touched, or from their thoughts; but do poorly with the ESP cards. Those among our students who get the highest scores with the ESP cards, and in tests with inanimate objects in which the human vibrations are absent, are those who, perhaps without knowing how they do it, nevertheless, employ Intellectual ESP.

So far in our extensive investigation, and with numerous students who have made tests with it, we have found no danger in cultivating Intellectual ESP.

Age of a Prince of Jerusalem

Zerubbabel, while rebuilding the temple, was interrupted by the Samaritans who finally forced him to abandon work. He thereupon sent an embassy to Darius, representing the ruler of the winter sign entered into by the sun, who issued orders prohibiting all persons from interfering with the work of construction on pain of death on the cross of Aries. The lodge consists of two apartments connected by a hall. The apartment in the west represents the western signs of the zodiac and is hung with yellow, the color sacred to Venus, which rules Libra, the sign of the western equinox where Zerubbabel now holds court. The eastern apartment where the cabinet of Darius is situated represents the eastern equinox of Aries; for Aries is the leader of the eastern zodiacal signs. The hall connecting the two zodiacal divisions is the solstitial colure.

The jewel of the order exemplifies the ritual accurately. It is a golden medal, or zodiacal circle. On one side is a hand holding a balance, symbolizing the human soul involving through Libra into the winter of matter, man entering into generate union, and the five planets descending into the winter signs through the door of the autumnal equinox. On the other side is a two-edged sword with five stars around its blade and over it the letters D. Z. The sword symbolizes the vernal equinox. The five stars represent man evolving into spiritual summer, man entering into regenerate union, and the five planets emerging from the winter signs, victoriously crossing the vernal equinox of spring. D. Z. are the initials of Darius and Zerubbabel, and also have an esoteric significance. Thus the Hebrew letter Z means sword and symbolizes victory. The soul enters matter through Libra, the door to realization, and emerges victorious by means of the sword of intelligence, Aries. Man enters generation by D, corresponding to the sex sign Scorpio, to realize sensation, but frees himself from bondage by means of regeneration.

The candidate with four knights—the five symbolizing man—journey from the court of Zerubbabel in Libra to the cabinet of Darius in Aries, and back to Libra, completely circling the zodiac. Each time they pass through the hall they are attacked by armed ruffians, symbolizing the struggle of the solar forces to become repolarized at the solstitial points of Capricorn and Cancer. The password is Tebeth, which is a Hebrew symbol for Capricorn, the point where the soul descends no lower and becomes incarnated in the mineral. The sacred word is Adar, Hebrew symbol of Pisces, the zodiacal sign in which thanks should be given for the completion of the zodiacal temple. The age of a Prince of Jerusalem is said to be five times fifteen. Fifteen signifies the passage of the twelve signs over the three visible angles, or one diurnal rotation of the earth, which according to the Hermetic System of Astrology measures out to man the events of one year of life. The fourth gate to the temple, referring to the Nadir which is invisible, mythology informs us was always closed. This explains why there were but three assassins. Five times fifteen also points mystically to the sacred cycle of the soul, called Naronia, which governs the expansion and contraction of the psychic forces and thought-cell energies within the constitution of man. The age of a Prince of Jerusalem signifies that the candidate has observed the Naronic cycles of soul development, explained in the 13th Award Manuscript. from month to month and from year to year.

Knights of East and West

This degree is based upon a vision of St. John as given in the Apocalypse. The book of seven seals is the septenary law of nature. The One Universal Principle is refracted from seven sub-centers about the Spiritual Sun, partaking of the quality of each medium through which it passes. As a definite portion of the divine essence under the dominion of one of the planetary angels it bears the seal and is governed by the laws relating to one planet. The twenty-four elders are the twenty-four hours, and symbolize those who have endured through great time. The seven lamps are the seven planetary angels. The four beasts, one with a head like a lion, one with a head like a calf, one with a head like a man, and one with a head like an eagle, are the lords of the zodiacal quadrants; and their many eyes looking within are the stars of these quadrants which look within from the circumference of the constellations. Each beast has six wings and rests not day and night, meaning that due to the earth's diurnal rotation each quadrant flies by in six hours.

The candidate bares his arms and the wardens lance them so as to procure blood on a napkin to represent those who have come out of great tribulation and washed their robes and made them white in the blood of the lamb. The blood of the lamb means the spiritual life of regeneration by which the body is completely purified. The Master then opens the seals of the great book. Opening the first he takes there from a quiver of arrows and a crown. It represents Sagittarius and the planetary seal of Jupiter. Opening the second seal he takes out a sword, signifying the sign Aries and the seal of Mars. Opening the third seal he takes out a balance, representing Libra and the seal of Venus. Opening the fourth seal he removes a skull, indicating the pale horse death, the sign Capricorn and the seal of Saturn. Opening the fifth seal he finds a cloth stained with blood, symbolizing the sign Virgo and the seal of Mercury. As the sixth seal is opened the sun is darkened and the moon is stained with blood to indicate the sign Cancer and the seal of the Moon. Opening the seventh seal he removes incense, symbolizing Leo, the house of love, and also seven trumpets to show planetary dominion, and thus the seal of the Sun. The four winds signify the aspirations of those born in each zodiacal quadrant, and the precessional cycle which governs the spiritual and mental influx received by men during different stages of evolution.

The draft on the floor, a heptagon in a circle, over the angles of which are placed letters, represents the seven planetary angels surrounded by the zodiac. The six elevated canopies in the north and the six in the south are the summer and winter zodiacal signs, eleven of which are occupied by venerable Ancients who are the ascended souls of those belonging to the state of life and degree of emanation of each sign. The vacant seat is that from which Judas, the sign Scorpio, fell, later to be occupied by the elect, or Eagle. The man in the center of the draft is the macrocosmic man of the kabala.

Knight of Rose Cross

This degree is also called Sovereign Prince of Rose Croix de Harodin and Knight of the Eagle and Pelican. There was once a tradition that the pelican feeds its young with its own blood, hence it has been used as a symbol of sacrifice. The rose is the ancient emblem of spring. Upon the cross it signifies the resurrection of the sun after death on the autumnal cross, also signifies man regenerated. The eagle is sex, or Scorpio, spiritualized. The special emblem of this degree is a pelican feeding her seven young, on one side of her a rose and on the other side a sprig of cassia; above her a radiant cross upon which climbs a rose. The pelican feeding her young symbolizes the sacrifice of material aims to spiritual ideals. Each planet has its evil side as well as a spiritual quality. The regeneration of all through sacrifice is indicated by the seven young pelicans partaking of blood, or spiritual sustenance, from their mother, who represents the universal mother Isis. The rose on the right signifies the rejuvenating effect of partaking of spiritual nourishment; the cassia on the left signifies immortality gained; and the radiant rosy cross above is the symbol of the conscious translation to spiritual realms of those who have sacrificed all their lower nature to the higher.

The lodge has three apartments. The first represents Calvary, or the autumn of life. It is lighted with thirty-three candles to indicate full experience under the twelve zodiacal signs and ten planets through the ten kingdoms of universal life, completing the cycle of necessity. The thirty-third candle signifies transition to a new cycle. Eleven lights are placed on each of three pillars six feet high. The number eleven (see Course 6, *The Sacred Tarot*) signifies force. It is the force of the sanctified man on all three planes, corresponding to the sun at the three visible angles, culminating six hours after rising, setting six hours after culminating, and rising six hours after passing the nadir, or material point, or plane below man. The second apartment represents Christ ascending into heaven, and the third apartment represents hell; symbolizing the relative conditions after death of the sanctified and the evil man.

The purpose of this assembly is said to be the recovery of the Lost Word. The means of recovery is indicated by the candidate presenting to each of the brethren one pair of men's gloves and one pair of women's gloves and two sticks of sealing wax, symbolizing united work. The result is referred to as, "The moment when the word was recovered; when the cubic stone was changed into a mysterious rose, when the flaming star appeared in all its splendor; when our altars resumed their ordinary form; when the true light dispelled darkness, and the new law became visible in all our works." The cubic stone is physical gratification, which when the Lost Word is found is transmuted into the rose of spiritual union, revealing the pole star, Truth; illuminating all mysteries, causing oblation to be made to the soul rather than to the senses, and work to be performed harmonious with the new laws thus discovered.

Grand Pontiff

The New Jerusalem as seen by St. John is the foundation of this degree. It is square with twelve gates; and in the midst a tree bearing twelve kinds of fruit. Above the earth, it descends upon the old Jerusalem crushing a three-headed hydra chained on the ruins. The New Jerusalem is the celestial heavens bounded by the twelve zodiacal constellations, or gates. The tree is that of immortal life, and the twelve fruits it yields are the immortal souls of those born under each sign through which the sun passes by precession of the equinoxes. The moon's nodes are known astrologically as the dragon's head and tail. The dragon is the serpentine cycle of the moon; corresponding to the cycle of the soul. The dragon has three heads, which symbolizes that the cycle of necessity embraces three planes. The New Jerusalem, or angelic realm, is attained only after the soul has successfully completed this cycle, leaving the attractions of each realm conquered and chained to the plane of their origin. The mountain at one side of the city indicates that the path to celestial realms lies along the summit of the highest type of physical development and union.

Grand Master of All Symbolic Lodges

The brethren in this degree wear blue and yellow scarfs crossed in front and rear, indicating the union of wisdom with love. The Wardens wear a jewel suspended from the yellow scarf of love. It is a triangular golden plate with the word Secret on one side and the letter R on the other. The Hebrew R symbolizes ascension. The jewel signifies the secret rejuvenation of the soul through the power of love. The same thought is more specifically expressed in the closing lecture: "My Brother, enter into the cave of Silol, work with Grand Rofdam, measure your steps to the sun, and then the great black eagle will cover you with its wings, to the end of what you desire, by the help of the most sublime Princes Grand Commanders." The cave of Silol is union, Rofdam is vibration, the sun refers to the virile power generated, and the eagle is the spiritual plane contacted, by the help of whose denizens will be attained that which is desired.

Chief of the Tabernacle

This degree is based upon the establishment of the Jewish Order of Priesthood, and their work of offering sacrifices. There are two side altars, one on the right in front of a representation of the sun, for sacrifices; and one on the left in front of a transparency of the moon, for incense. Man makes oblation of his animal nature to his ego, and exerts his executive power to direct his energies to noble purpose. To his soul he offers the sweet incense of aspiration and loving thought. Both execution and reception are necessary to propitiate his divine nature. The brethren, representing Levites, wear white robes, symbols of purity. Over each robe is a scarlet sash trimmed with gold fringe, and at the bottom on the right hip is a black rosette from which hangs a golden censer. The black rosette symbolizes death on the physical plane, and the scarlet sash symbolizes virile energies used to build up the spiritual body, as signified by the censer. On the apron is pictured a golden chandelier with seven branches, and on the flap is a violet colored myrtle. The chandelier symbolizes the seven active principles of nature which are consciously utilized by the Magus. Violet is the color sacred to Mercury. Myrtle is evergreen, and emits a sweet-smelling odor. The violet myrtle symbolizes the intelligent use of the creative principle which, typified by the flap, is directed to the construction of the spiritual body, ruled by Mercury, and to the attainment of immortality as indicated by the evergreen.

Prince of the Tabernacle

The main apartment in this degree is made perfectly circular to represent the zodiac. In the middle is a chandelier with seven branches, each branch having seven lights. There is also a round table on which is a cluster of inflamed hearts and some incense. The apartment symbolizes the zodiac as the cycle of life, and the seven branches of the chandelier represent the septenary of planetary influences affecting the physical under which the neophyte struggles. The other planets of the chain affect man more through his mental and astral nature, thus operating indirectly to produce physical conditions and events. The forty-nine lights symbolize seven branches of astrology, seven branches of alchemy, seven branches of magic, man's septenary constitution, seven physical senses, seven psychic senses, and seven states of consciousness; all of which must be mastered before reaching adeptship. The inflamed hearts symbolize the burning desire of the aspirant to learn the great truths concerning life and immortality, and his devotion to the Cosmic Work which has been given him to perform. The incense symbolizes the thoughts and aspirations ascending to higher worlds. The candidate approaches the altar by six equal steps and one long one. The long seventh step symbolizes that in evolution when the six states below man from mineral up are passed, and the seventh state, the state of manhood, is reached, there is offered the possibility of encompassing much in one life and gaining heaven, as it were, in a single bound.

Knight of Brazen Serpent

This degree is founded upon the history of the brazen serpent set up by Moses that those bitten by fiery serpents might look thereon and live. Fiery serpents symbolize impure desires. The brazen serpent entwined on a T, or on a phallic Tau, symbolizes wisdom of good and evil gained through experience with generation. Moses healed his people of their licentiousness by teaching them the truths concerning generation. And it is of equal importance today that proper generation should be understood. No one can truly be regenerate until he has mastered the mysteries of generation. Those who isolate themselves from the other sex in the hope of attaining regeneration without passing through the intermediate grade of generation only deceive themselves, and become bitten by the fiery serpents that infest the astral regions and prey upon the imaginations of celibates.

The lodge is opened at one past meridian, the time when the sun is transiting the house in the horoscope ruling instruction and philosophy. The nature of the instruction is disclosed by the lodge being closed at four past meridian, the sun just having completed its daily journey through the house of death, ruled by Scorpio, the sign of sex. The serpent is of brass, a union of positive and negative metals; and on the flap of the apron is the Hebrew feminine letter He, indicating the importance of both man and woman to produce the serpentine spiral called life.

Prince of Mercy

The Bible speaks of three sacred covenants: one with Abraham by circumcision, one with the Israelites in the wilderness through the intercession of Moses, and one with mankind through the resurrection of

Christ. These are the acts of mercy upon which the degree is founded. Circumcision is a rite symbolizing the passage of the sun completely around the zodiac, and is performed to commemorate his virile strength in triumphing over the forces of evil. Abraham means the father of a multitude, and the first covenant signifies the law of physical union as applied merely to multiplication of the species. Israel means one who wrestles with the Lord, and the second covenant indicates the struggle to subjugate the law of multiplication to the law of generation as taught by Moses; for generation is not confined to the production of physical offspring. The third covenant made through the resurrection of the mystical Christos after crucifixion on the material cross, refers to the laws of regeneration.

The jewel is a golden equilateral triangle, upon which is a heart with the Hebrew He in the center. It symbolizes the receptive quality engendered by the affections resulting in illumination. A special emblem of the Order is an arrow, the feather on one side green, on the other side red, the shaft white, and the point gold. It symbolizes the soul penetrating all mysteries by means of its spiritual illumination supported by purity and guided by the dual attributes of execution and reception.

Sovereign Commander of the Temple

This is a Chivalric Degree. The Wardens wear the order of the degree about their necks. It consists of a white ribbon edged with red, symbolizing purity and energy; and having embroidered on it four Teutonic crosses, each indicating one cycle of the sun past the solstices, and all symbolizing complete realization; the passage through the three planes of the cycle of necessity, after the cycle of involution. From the ribbon hangs a golden triangle upon which is engraved the Tetragrammaton, or sacred name of Deity, meaning that the wearer has complied with the requisites of the divine law on the three evolutionary planes. On the flap of the apron worn by the brethren is a cross encircled by a laurel wreath, signifying victory over death; and on the apron is a key, indicating that the region where the apron is worn is the key to higher life and attainment.

Knights of the Sun

This degree is said to be the key of historical and philosophical Masonry. It is really the key to the history of the world and the philosophy of its inhabitants. Father Adam is stationed in the east to symbolize primitive man, and Brother Truth in the west to represent intellectual man. They signify the alpha and omega of the human race. The lodge is lighted by a sun in the south. There are seven officers called Zaphriel, Zebriel, Camiel, Uriel, Michael, Zaphael, and Gabriel. These are ancient names for the seven planetary angels, who after God actuate the universe. The deific radiance of Life, Light, and Love from the spiritual sun is refracted from these seven sub-centers, and constitutes the source of all life, love, energy, and intelligence manifest on earth. This one universal principle received from the sun enables man to grasp truth, and this truth embraces the law of cycles. The sun's cycles are the key to history and philosophy; for by calculating his precession at the vernal equinox at the rate of 2,156 years through each sign, the quality of mental and spiritual force received by humanity at any date can be determined. A definite section of this precessional influence by sign is under the rulership of each of the planetary forces named above[1], and this directs the channels into which the mental and spiritual forces are turned for its term of power; whether for military, artistic, literary, or other purpose. And as the earth's climatic condition is determined by solar periods it will be seen that the physical environment as well as the intellectual and moral status of the earth's inhabitants at any time past or future can be calculated within certain limits by a true Knight of the sun. The jewel of the degree is a golden sun with a globe engraved upon it, signifying that the earth owes its existence to the sun and depends upon him for all. The sign is made by placing the hand upon the heart, the thumb forming a square. The answer is to raise the hand with the index finger pointing to heaven. It means that as the heart is the source of will and energy to the body, so is the sun the source of all power in the solar system.

Knight of Kadosh

This is a higher aspect of the principle exemplified in Knights Templar work, and is also called Knight of the White and Black Eagle. The eagle is the symbol of sex spiritualized, the power that carries the soul to higher spheres. The white eagle is regenerate and spiritualized man, the black eagle represents woman similarly refined and elevated. Five apartments are necessary, the first four typifying the zodiacal quadrants, symbolizing the completion of the cycle of earthly experience. The fifth represents the spiritual realm to which the adept has been translated. It is hung with red to indicate action and energy. In the east is a throne over which is a crowned double-headed eagle with wings outspread, holding in its talons a two-edged sword. This is the reward awaiting the spiritualized man and woman, the white and black eagles. The two-headed eagle represents the permanent reunion of soul-mates, both intelligences occupying one body. The crown symbolizes the natural right to rule of those who have attained this exalted state. The jewel of the order is suspended from the neck of the eagle to indicate the victory won by love. On its breast is an equilateral triangle bearing the letters of the Tetragrammaton, meaning that the sovereignty was gained through obedience to divine laws on all three planes.

The candidate during initiation must climb a ladder having Two supports and Seven steps. The supports of all initiation are the two pillars, Wisdom and Love. The steps are the seven states from man to angel, the two-headed eagle symbolizing angelhood attained. The crown of human life is the attainment of angelhood through the reunion of the two portions of the ego, the reunion of soul-mates. Human no longer, the angel then occupies a throne at the right hand of Deity.

Sublime Prince of the Royal Secret

The lecture of this degree explains, "That the mysteries of the Craft are the mysteries of religion." The special emblem of the degree figures a human being having two heads, one a man's and one a woman's. It stands on the back of a dragon, the dragon crouched on a winged globe. On the globe is traced a trine, a four-sided square and a cross dividing the globe into quadrants. The human being holds in his right hand a compass, and in his left a square. In a semi-circle over him are the planets, each sending a ray to a cuirass on the front of which is the word Rebis. This figure reveals man's past, and his future destiny. The globe is the earth, and the dragon represents the cycle of necessity that the soul must travel. The globe is winged to indicate its motion. The cross marking the quadrants represents the crossing of the solstice and the equinox. At the lower solstice is the letter Z, indicating the victory over matter. At the upper solstice is the letter I, representing the divine fire that exalts the soul above matter. The trine and square on the earth, and the numbers 3 and 4 accompanying each, symbolize the harmonies and discords through which the soul evolved its septenary constitution and became a microcosm. The feminine hand holding the square indicates the laws of physical union that were obeyed, and the compass in the masculine hand that spiritual laws also have been complied with. The rays of the seven planets converging on the breast-plate bearing the word Rebis means that they have an influence and perfect correspondence within this being. This figure stands on the dragon, having passed triumphantly through the cycle of necessity, and has a man's head and a woman's head to indicate the two halves of the divine soul permanently united. The whole is enclosed in an oval like an egg to convey the idea that every immortal soul when united to its mate is the germ of a future universe. The lodge is always on the top floor of a building, representing the realm of spirit.

Knight of the Sword

The Knight of the sword is intimately connected with the Prince of Jerusalem, and is founded upon the first journey of Zerubbabel to Persia, during which he obtained from Cyrus, King of Persia, permission to rebuild the temple and the freedom of Jewish prisoners who had been held captive seventy years. Ten is the number expressing cyclic duration. The seventy years refer to the seven cycles through the seven states of life from mineral up to and including man during which the soul is imprisoned in matter or the astral realm immediately associated with it. Cyrus typifies the material captor, Saturn, the King of the winter zodiacal signs. He is said to have had a dream as follows: "I imagined I saw a ferocious lion about to throw himself upon me and devour me; his appearance terrified me, and I hastily looked for shelter from his fury; but at that moment I saw my two predecessors, habited as slaves, beneath a glory, which Masons designate by the name of the Grand Architect of the Universe. I was made to understand two words which I saw issuing from a blazing star. They signified, Liberate the Captives, and I understood that if I did not do this my crown would pass from me to strangers."

The lion symbolizes the creative energy which misused destroys. It thus enslaves the soul to the senses, making it a captive of its appetites while on earth, and after death still bound to earth by the magnetic ties of its desires. The creative energy may be used also to free the soul from the senses, even as Leo draws the sun from the domain of Saturn. The blazing star is enlightened man, and the two words that liberate him from bondage to the flesh are Wisdom and Love. The glory spoken of is represented in the lodge by a triangle in which is the ineffable name of Deity. It rests upon a luminous cloud from which an eagle soars, carrying in its beak a banner on which are the words, "Liberate the Captives." It is the eagle of spiritual love freeing the soul and carrying it into brighter spheres than the sub-lunary realms of suffering where it so long has sojourned.

Sovereign Grand Inspector General

The lodge of this degree is painted with skeletons and skulls and cross-bones. This symbolizes association with the dead. The room is lighted with eleven candles, the number symbolizing psychic force, and at the north of the pedestal on which rests the Bible is a skeleton holding in its left hand the banner of the Order, and in its right hand a poinard as in the attitude of striking. This signifies that while members of the Supreme Council on the external plane are the physical instruments through which are governed the lodges of any country, the real Masters have passed the borders of physical life, yet are still potent to enlighten and protect those who have proved worthy neophytes and to strike down any who attempt to desecrate and profane the sacred mysteries. The jewel of this degree is the thirty-third degree emblem.

This emblem is a two-headed golden eagle, wings outspread, holding a sword in its talons. From the two ends of the sword hangs a belt forming an under arc. Below the outspread wings are thirty-two stars. Above and between the eagle's heads is a golden crown surmounted by a Maltese cross. The upper bar of the cross touches an inverted radiant trine having in its center the number thirty-three. The two-headed eagle symbolizes two intelligences occupying one spiritual body, soul mates permanently reunited in one form on the spiritual plane. An eagle is the symbol of sex in its spiritual aspect; the two-headed eagle thus representing the fusion of two spiritually evolved souls who have obeyed the inner promptings of their sexual natures. In this final Masonic revelation is disclosed the reason that prompted the ancients to commence the symbolic cyclic pilgrimage of the soul in the zodiacal sign Leo; for Leo is the sign of that love which springs into existence as the result of natural affinity between soul-mates. These were differentiated at the same moment and constitute the eternal north and south poles of one deific ego.

Leo, the mansion of Sol, well represents the spiritual spheres of the angelic parents; and as the sign ruling the house of love in a natural birth-chart it symbolizes that form of spiritual love resulting from common angelic parentage and identical Cosmic Work. Love, as signified by Venus and her signs, on the other hand, may be the result of planetary affinity, mental compatibility, or other causes.

The belt suspended from the sword on which the reunited souls rest is the zodiacal cycle of necessity from which they are now ready to soar, having risen superior to its attractions by means of the intelligent use of the regenerate sword, the vernal transmutation on the cross of Aries. This means is still further exemplified by the words on the belt signifying, "To me God's Will is Law." And the result of the adoption of the spiritual life is signified by words above the belt meaning that Order has been established from Chaos. The thirty-two stars under the wings represent the twelve zodiacal signs, ten planets, and ten kingdoms of universal life under whose influence the soul pilgrimaged. These kingdoms are: I Celestial, II Spiritual, III Astral, IV Mineral, on the involutionary arc; and V Vegetable, VI Animal, VII Human, VIII Astral, IX Spiritual, X Celestial, on the evolutionary arc.

The crown above the heads of the eagle symbolizes the ego to which both have become united, completing the trinity and conferring upon them the crown of everlasting life. The Maltese cross above the crown indicates the beginning of a new cycle in realms above the spiritual, that they will now enter, which opens up vistas and possibilities undreamed of by man. The ego, as it were, is at the lower solstice of this new cycle; the upper solstice contacting the very presence of the triune God, symbolized by the effulgent trine. Such is the exalted destiny of man. The number thirty-three signifies the cycle of necessity having been completed that the triumphant souls are translated to a new and higher round of life and action. The two threes united as thirty-three indicate the union of two souls having had complete experience on all three planes. And by their union their powers are multiplied as greatly as is the case when the two separate threes are joined in the manner indicated.

Conclusion

The ancient Masons, or Magi, specialized in acquiring knowledge that would enable man to live to his highest and make the most rapid spiritual progress. The information thus gained they passed on to posterity in the language of universal symbolism. In particular they emphasized these four things:

1. That the soul survives physical death and sometimes communicates with those still in the flesh. Also that man has faculties by which, while still on earth, he can explore the inner plane where later he will dwell and prove for himself that personality survives physical death.

They left instructions for the cultivation of such faculties, and for their use in acquiring information. The Brotherhood of Light ESP Research Department is engaged in ascertaining the details of the safest and most effective method of employing these faculties.

2. That energies from the planets exert an influence over human life and destiny. The Brotherhood of Light Astrological Research Department is engaged in acquiring as complete a knowledge as possible of these planetary influences, and of the precise manner in which they influence human life.

3. That love is a powerful constructive agent. The basic vibratory level on which an individual functions, now or in the hereafter, is determined by his own dominant vibratory rate. This dominant vibratory rate is determined by his governing mood, or feeling.

Cold asceticism, intellectual activity, and disregard of the welfare of others cultivate a dominant vibratory rate which enables the individual to contact only lower astral levels. Family life, including the unselfish affections of parents for children, provides opportunity for cultivating a high dominant vibratory rate, through which alone upper astral levels or spiritual realms can be contacted.

Selfishness is the most unprofitable of all things. It chains the individual, until he replaces it with love, to the animal levels of existence. Feelings engendered by parenthood, by caring for the weak and helpless, by harmonious marriage, and by eagerness to contribute to Universal Welfare, raise the basic vibratory rate, and this alone permits spiritual progress.

4. That thought is a powerful influence to shape human life and destiny. The Brotherhood of Light Control of Life Research Department is engaged in determining the most effective way of handling thoughts, feelings and planetary energies to the end of controlling life and destiny.

Note

1. For further information on this subject see Elbert Benjamine, *Astrological Lore of All Ages* (Los Angeles: The Church of Light, 1945/1994).

Study Questions

Ancient Masonry

Chapter 1, **Introduction**

1. Who were the first Masons?
2. In the larger sense what constitutes the Masonic Temple?
3. In what manner was the original Solomon's Temple constructed?
4. For what purpose was astronomy studied by early man?
5. What conditions conduced to development of spiritual giants in ancient times?
6. How were the pictures selected which traced among the stars became the constellations?
7. Of what was the Sun the emblem to the Ancient Masons?
8. Why were two pillars erected in the porch of the temple; one on either side of the great Eastern Gateway?
9. What principle in nature is represented by Boaz, and why is it on the left side of the Gateway of the rising Sun?
10. What principle in nature is represented by Jachin, and why is it on the right side of the Gateway of the rising Sun?
11. In what way was serpent worship related to solar worship?
12. Explain why the plumb is a masculine symbol.
13. Explain why the level is a feminine symbol.
14. Explain why the square is a symbol of union.
15. What is the astrological significance of the square? And of the compass?
16. Of the ten astrological aspects, which one is not measured in the plane of the zodiac?

17. What is the cause of the seasons?
18. What were the seven ancient centers of civilization which at their beginning possessed the doctrines of Ancient Masonry, and from whence it is probable they derived these doctrines?
19. What are two of the chief Masonic doctrines preserved in monuments of stone, but given less emphasis in Ancient Masonic Ritual?
20. Of the four chief tenets of ancient spiritual doctrines embodied in monuments of stone, which two are given special emphasis in the Ancient Masonic ritual?
21. Why did the ancient Masons so strongly emphasize love and the domestic relations?
22. What is the astrological significance of united square and compass?
23. What is signified by the letter G in the center of united square and compass?
24. What is signified by removing the G from the center of the united square and compass?
25. What is signified by the Hebrew letter Shin in the center of the united square and compass?

Chapter 2, **Entered Apprentice and the Planets**

1. What does the word "planet" mean, and from what does it derive this meaning?
2. With one exception, all planets keep within the boundary of a path how many degrees wide?
3. What political period and economic period did the discovery of Uranus usher in 1781?
4. What economic period and what period of religious progression was ushered in by the discovery of Neptune in 1846?
5. What economic period and what period in politics was ushered in when the discovery of Pluto was officially announced on March 12, 1930?
6. How many planets constitute a chain?
7. What was the origin of the thirty-three degrees of Ancient Masonry?

Ancient Masonry 264

8. Why was the disc chosen as the symbol with which to represent the Sun?
9. Why was the crescent chosen as the symbol with which to represent the Moon?
10. Why was the cross chosen as the symbol with which to represent the earth?
11. From what sources were the Coptic alphabet of Egypt, and the Hebrew alphabet derived, and how many characters did each possess?
12. What is a universal symbol?
13. Why, for preserving ideas over long periods of time, are universal symbols more effective than those of some more arbitrary language?
14. Why, in opening a lodge of Entered Apprentices, must there be present one Past Master and at least six apprentices?
15. What is the symbolical significance of the union of cross and crescent as the scythe held in the hands of Old Father Time?

    What lower-octave planet corresponds to each of the following, and what upper-octave planet actually rules each?
16. The etheric body.
17. The astral body.
18. The spiritual body.
19. What is the significance of some officers in the lodge sitting north of the Master, and some sitting south of him?
20. What is expressed through the symbol of Mars being the Venus symbol reversed?
21. What planet symbolizes the soul, and what planet symbolizes the ego?
22. What thought does the symbol of the following planets convey: Uranus, Neptune and Pluto?
23. What is the charter under which a candidate must work?

Chapter 3, **Entered Apprentice and the Signs**

1. Why does the Entered Apprentice lodge represent a ground plan of the temple rather than a plan of some other level?
2. What is symbolized by the common gavel?

3. Why is the common gavel the first instrument used in a Masonic lodge?
4. To the operation of what is all action in the universe due?
5. What is man's only source of will power?
6. What must be available to exercise a spiritual force?
7. What kind of energy is consumed in the use of will on the physical plane?
8. What methods may be employed to increase the kind of energy used by the will on the physical plane?
9. In addition to the transmission of energy in quantity, what else is required to exercise will power?
10. What is the best manner to go about developing will power?
11. Why is it advisable to use the methods of oriental ascetics to develop will power?
12. What is signified by each of the following, and what do each gauge or measure out to man: The 12-inch gauge of Ancient Masonry; the 24-inch rule of Ancient Masonry?

Explain the origin of the constellations picturing the qualities of the following signs, and the origin of the symbol used to designate the sign.

13. Aries
14. Taurus
15. Gemini
16. Cancer
17. Leo
18. Virgo
19. Libra
20. Scorpio
21. Sagittarius
22. Capricorn
23. Aquarius
24. Pisces
25. Did the Ancient Masons teach so-called sex practices?

26. What disastrous condition usually results from sex repression combined with rhythmic breathing, negative diet, and lack of vigorous mental exercise?

Chapter 4, **Numbers and Opening the Lodge**

1. What is memory?
2. What represents the Tyler in the constitution of man?
3. What determines that which is added to the character and what alterations in the character are made?
4. What determines the events which are attracted into a person's life?
5. What is the only way man can change his destiny and make it better than it otherwise would be?
6. What must be used by anything which gets the attention of objective consciousness?
7. To enable an individual to predetermine the kind of thoughts which are to gain the attention of objective consciousness, what must he be able to command?
8. What is the best way to prevent unwanted feelings and thoughts from forcing themselves before the attention?
9. Why does the astral body, symbolized by the Junior Deacon, take care of the door?
10. Why is it the function of the animal soul, symbolized by the Senior Deacon, to welcome and clothe all visiting brethren?
11. In what way does the etheric body, symbolized by the Secretary, make a record of every experience of a person's life?
12. What are the moneys and money bills which the physical body, symbolized by the Treasurer, receives from the Secretary and pays out by the order of the Worshipful Master and the consent of the brethren?
13. Why is it the function of the spiritual body, symbolized by the Junior Warden, to call the craft from labor to refreshment?
14. Why does the divine soul, symbolized by the Senior Warden, have charge of the jewels and implements, and why does it pay the craft their wages?

15. Why is it the function of the ego, symbolized by the Master, to set the craft to work with good and wholesome instructions, or cause it to be done?
16. Why does the Master, in opening the lodge, forbid the use of all profane language, or any disorderly conduct.
17. What does each rap of the gavel indicate?
18. What is the first sign of a Mason?
19. How potent is a thought associated with the emotion of love?
20. What is the trinity possessed by all things having life?
21. What symbol expresses the completion of a cycle?
22. What number indicates one cycle completed and the commencement of a new cycle?
23. What principle is expressed by each of the following numbers: two, three and four?

Chapter 5, **Initiating a Member**

1. What has ever been the purpose of the Mysteries?
2. What psychological effect is obtained by making it difficult to become a candidate for initiation?
3. Who alone is responsible for each soul's destiny?
4. Only through what can freedom be obtained?
5. What is symbolized by the white balls and the black balls used in balloting?
6. Why is the Senior Deacon the proper one to prepare the candidate for initiation?
7. Of what symbolical significance is flannel?
8. Why in the E.A. degree are the drawers red?
9. Why is the shirt not removed?
10. Why is the candidate blindfolded?
11. What is symbolized by the cable-tow?
12. Why does the candidate say he comes from the west and travels to the east in search of light?

13. What type of force unites Jachin and Boaz?
14. What has his first step toward the light to do with these forces?
15. What happens to time as velocities increase?
16. When there is an excess of boundary-line energy, what determines whether the inner-plane is contacted negatively or positively?
17. What relation is there between thought and emotion and breathing on the inner-plane?
18. What is the significance of the candidate taking the oath with the left hand under and the right hand over the Bible, upon which rests the compass and square?
19. What is signified by the clapping of hands when the bandage is removed from the candidate's eyes?
20. What are the three Lesser Lights of Masonry?
21. What is the astrological significance in pronouncing the name of the grip when the word Boaz is halved?
22. Astrologically what represents the six pots of stone in which water is turned into wine?
23. Astrologically, what represents the persecution by Herod?
24. Astrologically, why does the baptism take place at thirty years of age?
25. Astrologically, what is represented by the thirty pieces of silver?
26. When is Easter?
27. Explain the symbolism of the lamb-skin apron.
28. What is the significance of the futile efforts of the candidate to borrow money?

Chapter 6, **Fellowcraft**

1. What characteristic distinguishes astral substance from etheric substance; and what characteristic distinguishes it from physical substance?
2. Why may a lodge of F.C. Masons be opened by five officers instead of seven?
3. To what does the pass-word of the Fellow Craft degree refer?
4. What does the omission of the letter H from the pass-word signify?
5. What is the significance of the 42,000 who perished because they could not properly pronounce the pass-word?

6. Through what means, only, can energy be transmitted from one plane to the substance of the other plane?
7. Can etheric vibrations be produced of greater frequency than the more commonly encountered astral frequencies?
8. Does shrewdness, intelligence and knowledge, or lack of them, indicate the vibratory level of a person or creature?
9. What alone enables an individual to contact an astral level above that where animals and discarnate souls with animal-like propensities reside?
10. Why is it possible to exercise ESP on the lower astral levels and gain information about earthly affairs?
11. Can more spiritual types of information be acquired from such lower astral levels?
12. What is signified in Ancient Masonry by the River Jordan?
13. Why, in Extension of Consciousness, is it unwise to tarry in the so-called River Jordan region?
14. Why, in the F.C. degree, are the drawers no longer red?
15. Why, in the F.C. degree, are the left foot and the left arm still clad?
16. Why are the two knocks upon the lodge door called the Alarm?
17. Instead of killing out desire, what should be done with it?
18. What is symbolized by the square pressed against the right breast?
19. What is signified by one point of the compass being beneath the square and one point being elevated above it?
20. What is symbolized by the cable-tow being placed twice around the neck?
21. Why is it appropriate that the F.C. pass-word should be Jachin?
22. How does an F.C. Mason wear his apron, and what does it thus signify?
23. What is the significance of each of the three jewels?
24. What is the significance of there being no light in the north of the lodge?
25. What does Jacob's ladder symbolize?

Chapter 7, **Lodge Emblems**

1. Why are horses the symbols of thoughts?
2. Why is it more difficult to appraise the true significance of that which is perceived on the physical plane?
3. What is signified when it is said the lodge room is as long as from east to west, as wide as from north to south, as high as from the surface of the earth to the highest heaven, and as deep as from the surface of the earth to the earth's center?
4. What are the three pillars which support the lodge?
5. Why, in the E.A. degree, when a candidate has been reinvested with his clothing is he placed in the northwest corner of the lodgeroom and caused to stand upright like a man?
6. What are signified by the rough ashlar, the perfect ashlar, and the trestleboard?
7. What is signified by the checkered pavement, or mosaic?
8. Where is the Masonic Star located in the sky?
9. What is signified by the east wind that enables the Red Sea to be crossed dry shod?
10. Why are the columns Jachin and Boaz 18 cubits high, 12 cubits in circumference, and 4 in diameter?
11. What is signified by the two globes, one on each column?
12. In what way are these two globes the Archives of Masonry, containing the constitution, rolls and records?
13. What is signified by the long winding Masonic stairway, and why has it three, five, seven or more steps?
14. What is signified by the bee-hive?
15. What is the book of constitutions?
16. What is the significance of the Tyler's sword guarding the book of constitutions?
17. What is symbolized by the all-seeing eye?
18. What is the symbolism of the anchor?
19. What is represented by each of the three stories of the ark of Noah?
20. What is signified by each of the three times Noah sent the dove forth?

21. What relation has the life of Moses to the symbolism of the 47th problem of Euclid?
22. What does the hypotenuse of Euclid's 47th problem symbolize?
23. In what way does incense affect the nervous system in such a way as to increase certain types of energy?
24. What does incense symbolize?
25. What is the symbolical significance of the scythe?

Chapter 8, **Master Mason**

1. Why do three Master Masons comprise a Master Mason's lodge?
2. Why, in the Master Mason degree, is the cable-tow wound three times around the candidate's body?
3. Why, in the Master Mason degree, has the candidate lost two-thirds of his clothing?
4. Why, in the Master Mason degree, are both points of the compass shown above the square?
5. Explain the significance of the apron as worn in the Master Mason degree of Ancient Masonry.
6. Explain the significance of the symbolism of the trowel.
7. Why is it said the craft are at refreshment at high twelve?
8. Who are the fifteen that conspired against Hiram Abiff?
9. Who are the three that did not repent but carried out the crime?
10. What is meant by the blow Hiram Abiff received on his throat from the 24-inch gauge?
11. What is meant by the blow Hiram Abiff received across his breast from the square?
12. What is meant by the blow Hiram Abiff received on his forehead from the gavel?
13. What, in reference to the soul, is symbolized by the Grand Master being buried with the rubbish at low twelve?
14. Why is the grave six feet due east and west and six feet perpendicular?
15. What is symbolized by the sprig of cassia with which the grave was marked?

16. What is signified by Hiram Abiff being discovered at low six?
17. What is the significance of the letter G found on the breast of Hiram Abiff?
18. Why would not the E.A. grip raise Hiram Abiff?
19. Why is the Master's grip called the Lion's grip?
20. What is signified by the union of knee to knee?
21. Do only the good exist on the astral plane after death?
22. Does the personality persist forever on the astral plane?
23. Why, for immortality, is it essential to build a spiritual form?
24. How can a spiritual form be built?
25. Does true Mastership require retirement from contact with others?
26. What is the symbolical significance of the tragedy and resurrection of Hiram Abiff?

Chapter 9, **Mark Master Mason**

1. In what way are Uranus, Neptune and Pluto overseers? Prominence of what planet does the following:
2. Gives facility in using the Inspirational System of mental activity?
3. Maps facility in using Feeling ESP?
4. Maps facility in employing the Inner-plane System of mental activity?
5. What is signified by the Heave-over?
6. Just what is the keystone of psychic development?
7. What happens when by rhythmic breathing or other mans more electrical energy is generated than the nervous system can handle?
8. What condition of electrification should be sought?
9. What must be present if a desired mood is to be sustained?
10. Why is the keystone said to be four by six inches in dimensions?
11. What is the keystone as applied to natal astrology?
12. What evidence is there that major progressed aspects map actual forces and are thus much more than merely symbolic?

13. Explain how on a level where velocities are 365¼ times as great, and therefore time is 365¼ times as slow, that as many events may occur in one day of this slow time as in one year of ordinary calendar time.
14. If the changes which take place in one day on a time-velocity level where time is 365¼ times as slow and velocities are 365¼ times as great as in ordinary physical life, are brought up into the time-velocity level of physical life, over what period of time will they spread?
15. What is signified by the candidate not knowing how to receive wages?
16. What is signified by the candidate being received on the edge of the indenting chisel?
17. What is indicated by the Past Masters wearing hats in the lodge room?
18. What is signified by the unruly conduct of the members when the candidate attempts to conduct the lodge?
19. What is symbolized by the balancing in the Most Excellent Master degree?
20. What is symbolized by the Omnific Word, and why can it only be imparted when all three Masters are present?
21. What is meant in the Royal Master degree by Hiram Abiff answering Adoniram about the Omnific Word: "When I die they will bury it There"?
22. What is meant in the Royal Master degree by stating the beginning of the matter is Alpha and the end Omega?
23. What is the Tree of Life?
24. What commences and what closes the great orbit of the Cycle of Necessity?

Chapter 10, **Royal Arch**

1. Why in the Royal Arch degree, must there be three candidates to undergo the initiation ceremony at the same time?
2. What are the three trines of the soul's pilgrimage?
3. What does the circular living arch symbolize?
4. What is signified by kneading the candidate with the knuckles as he passes through the living arch?
5. Why, each time he passes through the living arch, is the candidate treated more harshly?

6. What is signified by holding out a tumbler of water and pouring a little on the floor?
7. What is signified when the candidate is asked what work he will undertake?
8. What is symbolized by the vault of the Royal Arch degree into which one of the candidates agrees to descend?
9. What do the three trying squares symbolize?
10. What is signified by the sun being at meridian when the small box is discovered and the dieugard is given?
11. By what means is the box, which proves to be a miniature copy of the Ark of the Covenant of God, discovered?
12. What is symbolized by the square base of the Ark?
13. What does the coffer above the base of the Ark symbolize?
14. What is symbolized by the two rings on each side of the Ark through which are thrust carrying poles?
15. What is the astrological significance of each of the four emblems found within the Ark?
16. What is symbolized by the four pieces of paper which are taken from the Ark?
17. What is the lost Master Mason's Word?
18. Why is the Master's Word written in three languages?
19. To what on the path of generation does the Master's Word relate?
20. To what on the plane of regeneration does the Master's Word relate?
21. To what in its highest application does the Master's Word relate?
22. What is symbolized by a sheaf of wheat near a water-ford?
23. What lesson is taught by the drama of Izabud?
24. What lesson is taught by the fate which overtook Zedekiah?
25. What is symbolized by Zedekiah's eyes being put out, his thumbs being cut off, and the bondage in which he found himself?
26. Upon what Major Arcanum of the Tarot is the degree, Heroine of Jericho, based?

Chapter 11, **Degrees of the Cross**

1. Explain why it takes the fourth, or time dimension, as well as the three space dimensions, fully to define the position of an object?
2. Illustrate by the relation of clock time to radio broadcasts from different parts of the world, how we are able to apprehend events in our Now which, relative to a time correlated as to the velocity of the earth's rotation, are in the past or in the future.
3. What is meant by the soul's World-Line?
4. Can any part of the World-Line back of the Now point be altered?
5. To what extent can World-Lines be projected into the future?
6. Why does not the ability thus to project World-Lines into the future imply fatality?
7. What proof is there that many people thus at times do look along World-Lines and perceive future events in detail?
8. What is the chief characteristic of distance on the inner-plane?
9. What report indicated that ordinary distance and space are not factors in ESP?
10. What takes the place of gravitation on the inner-plane?
11. What is symbolized by Solomon's statement, "If you can agree in the dark you can in the light."
12. What is the significance of the pass-words "Judah" and "Benjamin"?
13. What is symbolized by the Red Cross?
14. What is signified by the Red Cross Word, "Veritas"?
15. What is symbolized by the holy vessels which Darius promised to send back to Jerusalem?
16. What is meant astrologically by Truth being stronger than wine, the king, or women?
17. What is symbolized by the Maltese cross?
18. What is symbolized by the serpent entwined about a cross?
19. Of what are the skull and crossbones a reminder?
20. What is the significance of four cuts under an arch of steel?
21. What is symbolized by a black cross?

22. What is signified by the fifth libation being of pure wine and drunk from a skull?
23. What is the occult interpretation of the letters INRI?
24. To what does the statement that the number of the sealed is one hundred forty-four thousand refer?
25. What is signified by the letter G within a five-point star?
26. What is the Holy Sepulcher?
27. What is the significance of the Roman Eagle?
28. What is the cubic stone which, in the Order of the Cross, is said to have been broken?

Chapter 12, **Ineffable Degrees**

1. Astrologically, what are the three steps on the Master's carpet?
2. What is symbolized by a sword pointing to a naked heart?
3. What is symbolized by the point where the two trines of an hour-glass meet?
4. What is the essential condition for contacting, through the inner-plane, anything belonging to any realm?
5. When something is contacted on the inner-plane, what determined the direction of energy flow?
6. Which thought at the moment gets the attention?
7. When, after contacting something on the inner-plane, we feel it distinctly, what does this indicate as to relative potentials?
8. What furnishes the energy used in examining something from the inner-plane through the positive method of Extension of Consciousness?
9. Why, in Extension of Consciousness properly accomplished, does not the individual "take on" the condition which he contacts?
10. What is symbolized by the 81 lights of the Secret Master lodge?
11. What is symbolized by the ivory key with the letter Z engraved upon it?
12. What is symbolized by the crown of laurel and the crown of olive leaves on the altar?

13. What is symbolized when it is stated the age of Adoniram is 3 times 27?
14. What is symbolized by a pyramid in the north with open compass upon it?
15. What is symbolized by a coffin with a five-point star on the lid, and leaning over it a sprig of cassia?
16. What is symbolized by the triple triangle on the Bible?
17. What is symbolized by the golden key?
18. What is symbolized by the small ebony box which contains the plans for building the temple?
19. What is symbolized by the small ivory box containing all the temple keys?
20. What is symbolized by white aprons lined with red?
21. What is symbolized by the poinard at the feet of the sleeping assassin?
22. What is represented by the three gates of the square city, and over each gate a human head?
23. What is symbolized by the Tau Cross, or English letter T?
24. Why is the G.M.A. Chapter opened on the first instant, the first hour, the first day and the first year when Solomon commenced the Temple?
25. Whom did Enoch represent?
26. What is meant when it is stated that Enoch walked with God and was not?

Chapter 13, **Historical Degrees**

1. From whence did the Scottish Rite Masonry probably come?
2. From whence did the York Rite Masonry probably come?
3. What are the three methods of acquiring information from the inner-plane?
4. Why is the method of mediumship not advocated by The Church of Light?
5. What distinguishes the method of mediumship?
6. What distinguishes Feeling ESP?
7. Is Feeling ESP free from all danger?

Ancient Masonry

8. What distinguishes Intellectual ESP?
9. Which one of the three methods only can be fully recommended?
10. What is symbolized by the court of Zerubbabel?
11. What is represented by the eastern apartment where Darius is situated?
12. What is signified by the age of a Prince of Jerusalem being five times fifteen?
13. What is symbolized by the twenty-four elders of the vision of St. John?
14. What is the book of seven seals?
15. What is signified by each of the four beasts of the vision of St. John?
16. What is signified by the pelican feeding her young?
17. What is signified by the New Jerusalem crushing a three-headed hydra chained on the ruins of the old Jerusalem?
18. What is symbolized by a yellow scarf?
19. What is symbolized by a violet colored myrtle?
20. What is symbolized by a round table on which is a cluster of inflamed hearts?
21. What is symbolized by a brazen serpent entwined on a T?
22. What is the symbolical significance of circumcision?
23. What do the seven officers - Zaphiel, Zebriel, Camiel, Uriel, Michael, Zaphael and Gabriel - represent?
24. What is symbolized by the crowned double-headed eagle with wings outspread, holding in its talons a two-edged sword?
25. What is symbolized by the 32 stars under the outspread wings of the eagle?
26. What four things in particular did the ancient Masons emphasize in their teachings?

Appendix

The following natal charts are reprinted here for the use and interest of the student of astrology. The brief biographical sketches are provided to illustrate astrological correspondences to significant life events. The horoscopes of notable personalities were chosen because some aspects of their lives and character are already familiar to the public, and can more easily be correlated with the astrological factors shown.

Permission to freely use and reproduce these charts is hereby granted by the Church of Light.

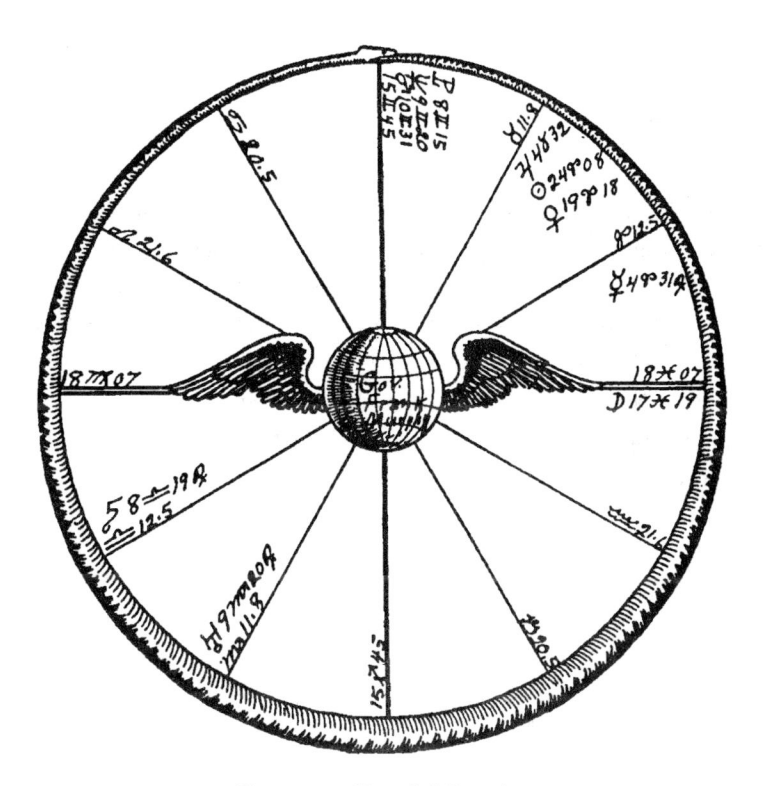

Governor Frank Murphy
April 13, 1893, 3:00 p.m. 82°W40′, 43°N49′.

1917, captain in World War, was assigned to defend doughboys AWL: Mars in ninth (court) semi-square Jupiter ₚ.

1932, had been a judge in Detroit, won fame as a Conciliator put up energetic fight in first election of Franklin D. Roosevelt. Mars square Saturn ₚ, Venus trine Saturn ₚ.

1933, made Governor General of Philippine Islands: Venus conjunction Pluto ᵣ, Mercury (tenth) sextile Moon ᵣ.

1936, resigned Philippine job to fight for Roosevelt's reelection: Mars square Saturn ₚ, Mercury semi-sextile Sun ᵣ.

Jan. 1, 1937, inaugurated Governor of Michigan: Sun trine Saturn ₚ.

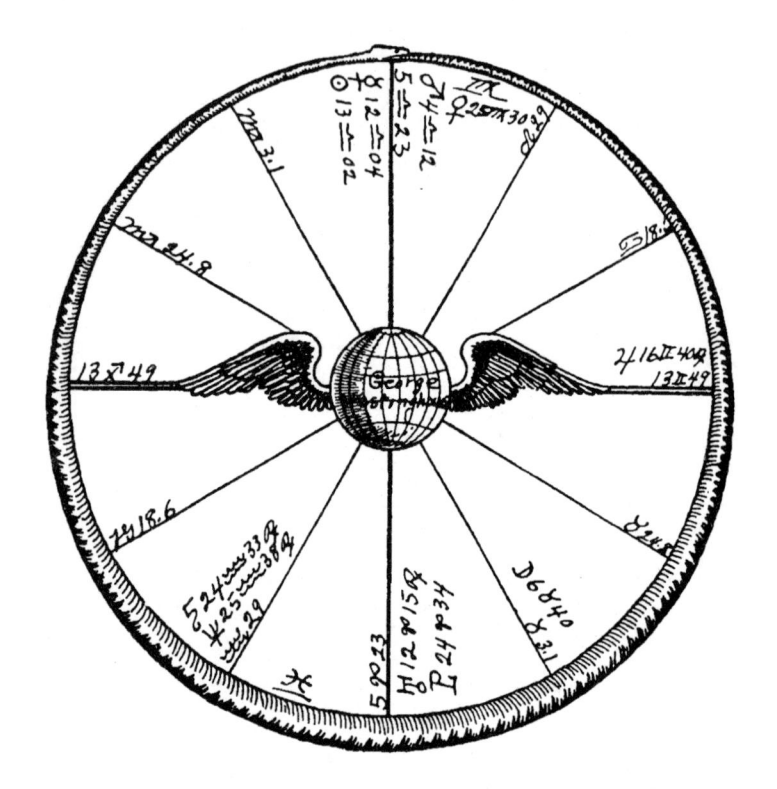

George Westinghouse
October 6, 1846, 11:20 a.m., 74°W20′, 42°N45′

1856, father moved factory and family: Mars sesqui-square Neptune ᵣ.

1862, enlisted in war: Venus conjunction Mars ₚ.

1864, December 1, examination, Acting Third Assistant Engineer on Muscoota: Mars (9th) trine Jupiter ᵣ (ruling 1st).

1865, home (Uranus) again and to school: Mercury inconjunct Uranus ᵣ.

1869, April 13, first air brake patent, organized Westinghouse Airbrake Co.: Venus in tenth, opposition Pluto ᵣ, trine Saturn ᵣ.

1884, bored well for gas and promoted company: Mercury trine Uranus ₚ.

1893, furnished electric lights for World's Fair: Venus square Saturn ₚ, inconjunct Pluto ᵣ, Mars semi-sextile Mars ᵣ.

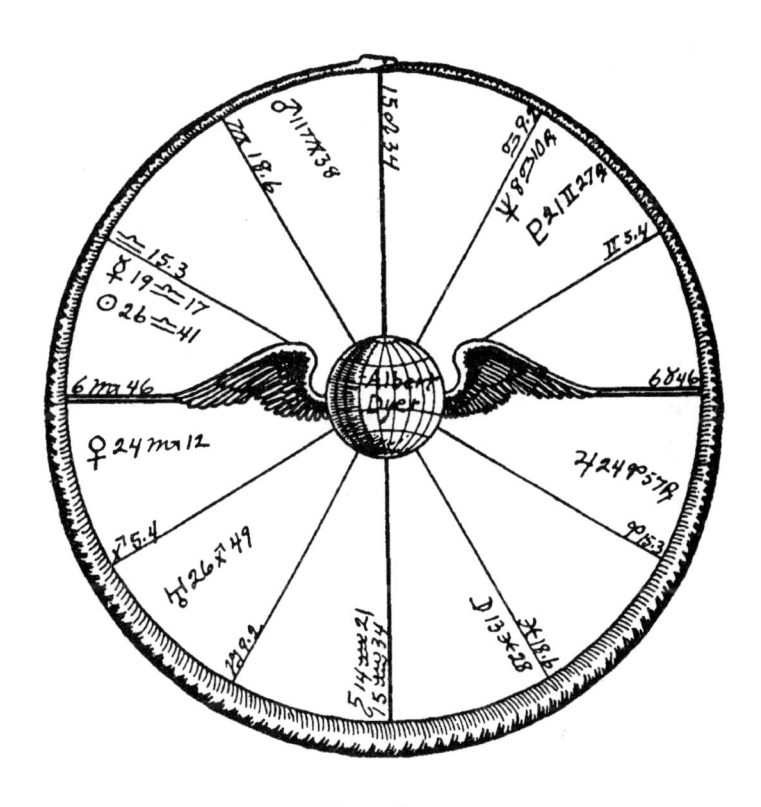

Albert Dyer
October 20, 1904, 7:15 a.m., 74°W15', 43°N45' Data from relative

Adopted as a child: Mars opposition Moon in birth-chart

Insistent sex desires: Mars prominent, Venus rising in Scorpio.

1937, on relief as crossing guard, nothing to do day after day, month after month, but pilot school children safely across the street.

1937, July 26, lured three little girls into hills, attacked and then strangled all three. August 27, convicted of murder and condemned to hang: Jupiter sextile Pluto$_r$ (groups) in house of death (eighth), Mercury square Mars$_r$, applying square Moon$_r$.

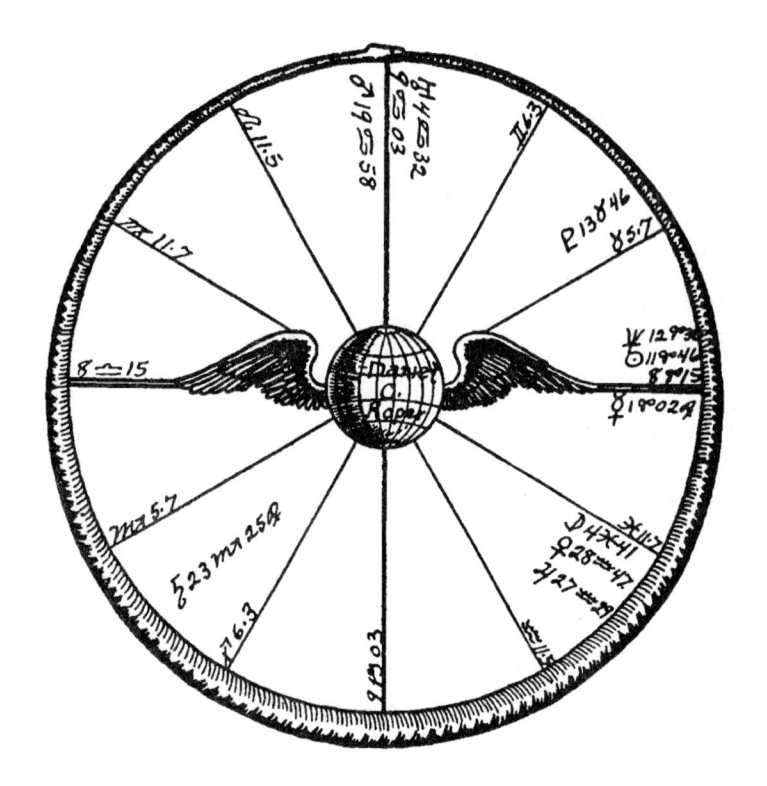

Daniel C. Roper
April 1, 1867, 6:00 p.m., 79°W40′, 34°N37′
Data from Mr. Roper personally

- 1892, two years a member of S. Carolina House of Representatives: Sun sextile Uranus ₚ. Campaigned for election: Sun sextile Moon ᵣ (people), ruler of tenth.

- 1916, chairman organization bureau Wilson presidential campaign: Jupiter conjunction Moon ᵣ, ruler of tenth; Mars (ruling tenth) trine Sun ᵣ, trine Neptune ᵣ (promotion).

- 1933, February 23, appointed Secretary of Commerce: Mars sesqui-square Uranus ₚ, ruling commerce (ninth), Mercury in ninth inconjunct Saturn ᵣ.

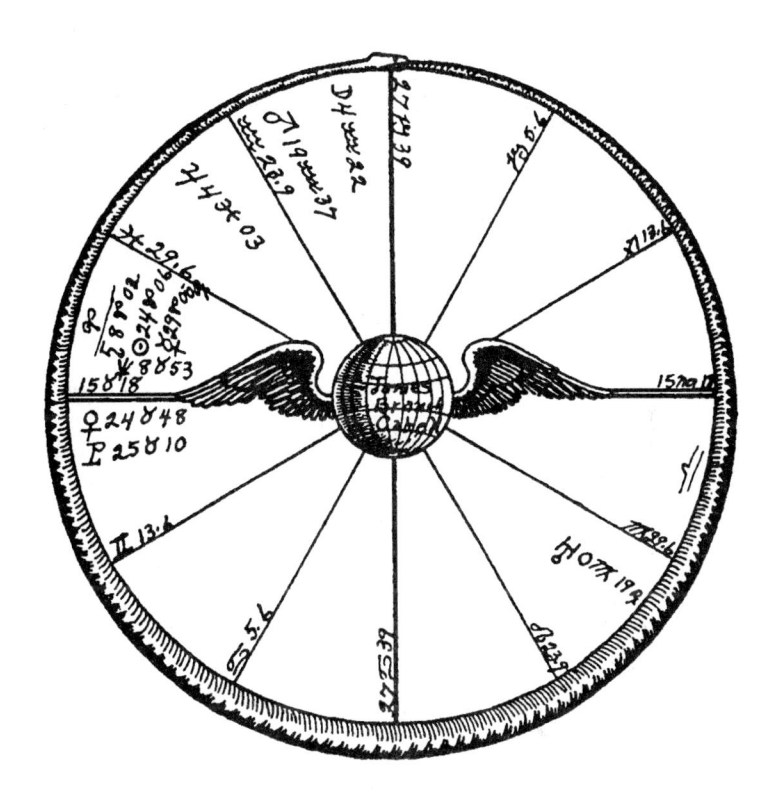

James Branch Cabell
April 14, 1879, 6:30 a.m. L.M.T, 77°W27', 37°N32'
Data from Mr. Cabell personally

1896, instructor of French and Greek: Sun semi-sextile Saturn p, ruler of ninth (teaching)

1898, worked in press-room of Richmond, Va., Times: Mars conjunction Jupiter r, semi-sextile Moon r, ruler of third (newspapers).

1902, started contributing short stories to magazines: Mercury sextile Venus p, then moved to other aspects.

1920, wrote *Beyond Life*: Mercury conjunction Neptune p.

1922, wrote *Jurgen*: Venus semi-square Uranus r (very unconventional).

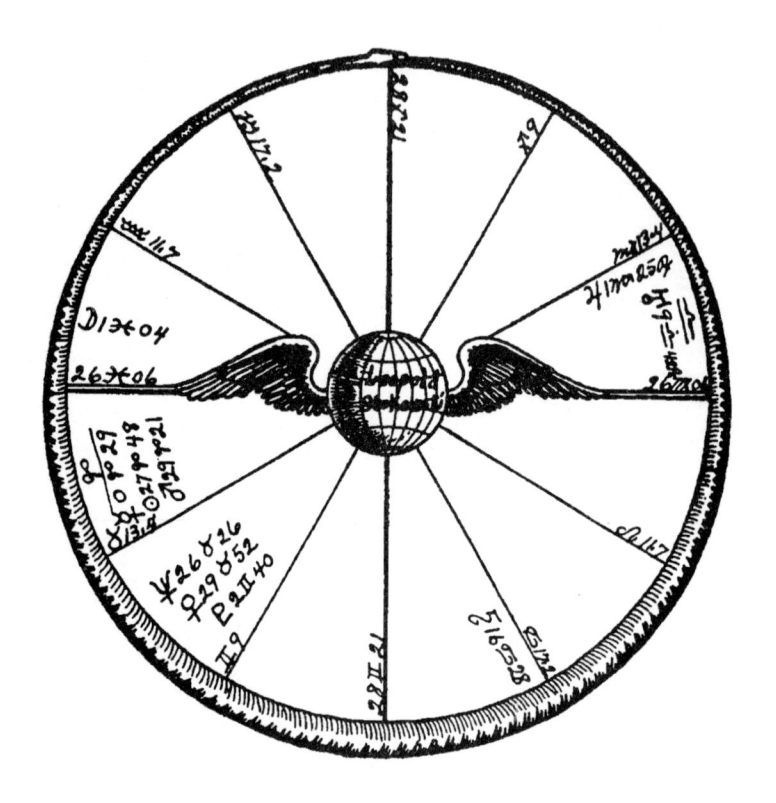

Leopold Stokowski
April 18, 1887, 4:00 a.m., 2°E20', 48°N50'
Data from Stokowski personally

1905, conductor at St. Bartholomew's in New York: Sun sextile Saturn r.

1908, conductor of orchestra concerts in London: Mercury opposition Jupiter p (journey and public), semi-sextile Venus r.

1909, conductor Cincinnati symphony: Mars sextile Saturn r (responsibility), Venus semi-sextile Neptune r (symphony).

1912, conductor of the Philadelphia Philharmonic Orchestra which (1938) he continues successfully to be: Mars sextile Saturn p, Venus trine Jupiter r in seventh (public), Venus sextile Mars r.

Ancient Masonry 286

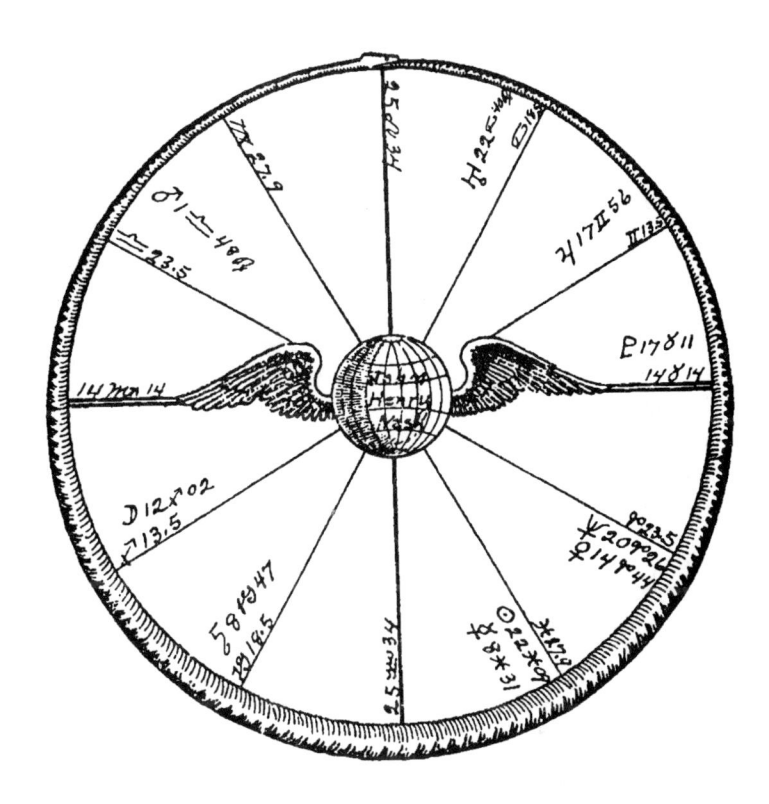

John Henry Nash
March 13, 1871, 10:30 p.m., 79°W45′, 43°N45′
Data from Mr. Nash personally

1916, after working many years for others, began to print books under his own imprint: Sun, ruling house of business (tenth) semi-square Sun ᵣ; Mercury P Uranus ₚ, ruler of house of publishing (ninth). They were artistic editions, Venus inconjunct Saturn ₚ, bringing high prices: Venus ₚ Jupiter ₚ.

1937, issued a catalogue of books he had printed. Catalogue was limited to 500 copies and sold at $5.00. It was seldom an edition of his books exceeded 1,000 copies, and they were much sought by collectors. Mercury sextile Sun ᵣ, sextile Uranus ᵣ.

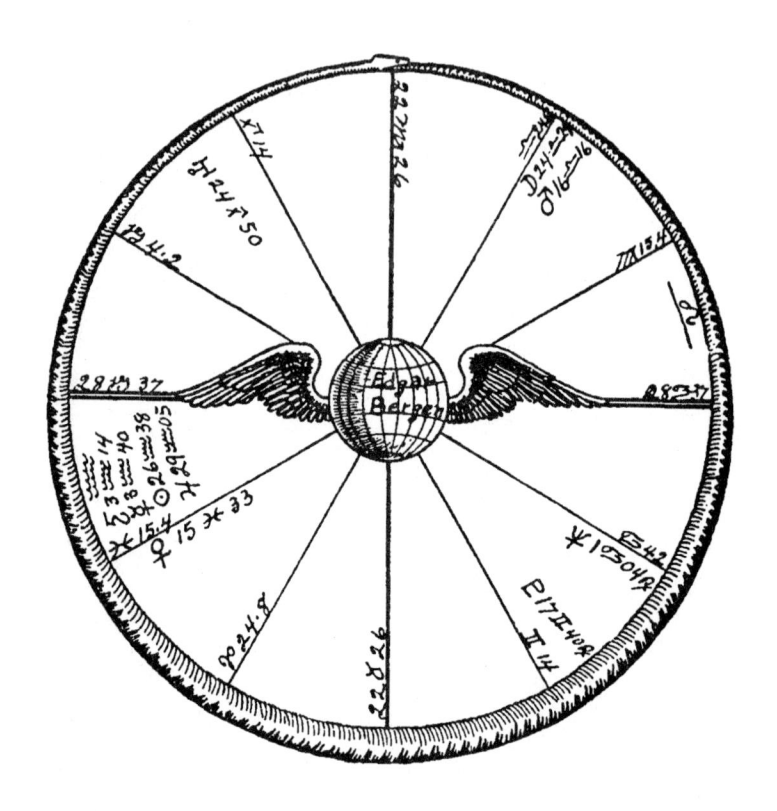

Edgar Bergen

February 16, 1903, 5:30 a.m. 87°W40', 41°N45'
Data, including time of day, Los Angeles Examiner, November 18, 1937

- 1920, July 18, Charlie McCarthy, the wooden dummy with which the ventriloquist was to attain fame, was born, and he was temporarily successful with his act: Mercury trine Pluto ᵣ in fifth.

- 1937, for years Bergen and Charlie had a hard time of it. They were given opportunity to speak over the radio program of a singing star. Their "wise cracks" were quoted everywhere, they skyrocketed to entertainment fame, received enormous salaries for appearance in motion pictures: Sun square Neptune ᵣ in fifth (trine at birth).

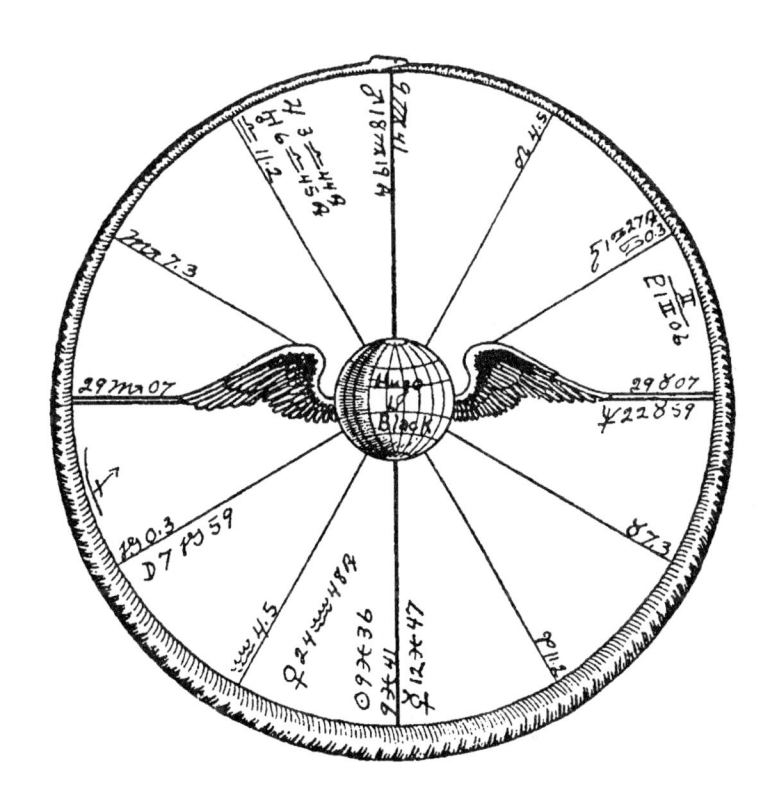

Hugo L. Black

February 27, 1886, 11:57 p.m. CST, 85°W50', 33°N17'
Data, October-November, 1937, Today's Astrology magazine

- 1907, February 12, office and library burned: Mars opposition Sun r, Mercury inconjunct Mars r.

- 1922, joined Ku Klux Klan: Sun semi-square Pluto r, Venus square Pluto r.

- 1925, resigned Klan, prominent in politics: Mars semi-sextile Uranus r, Sun conjunction Mercury p, inconjunct Mars r.

- 1927, took seat in senate: Venus opposition Mars p.

- 1937, appointed Supreme Court Justice amid violent controversy: Sun sextile Saturn r, semi-sextile Pluto r, P Mars r.

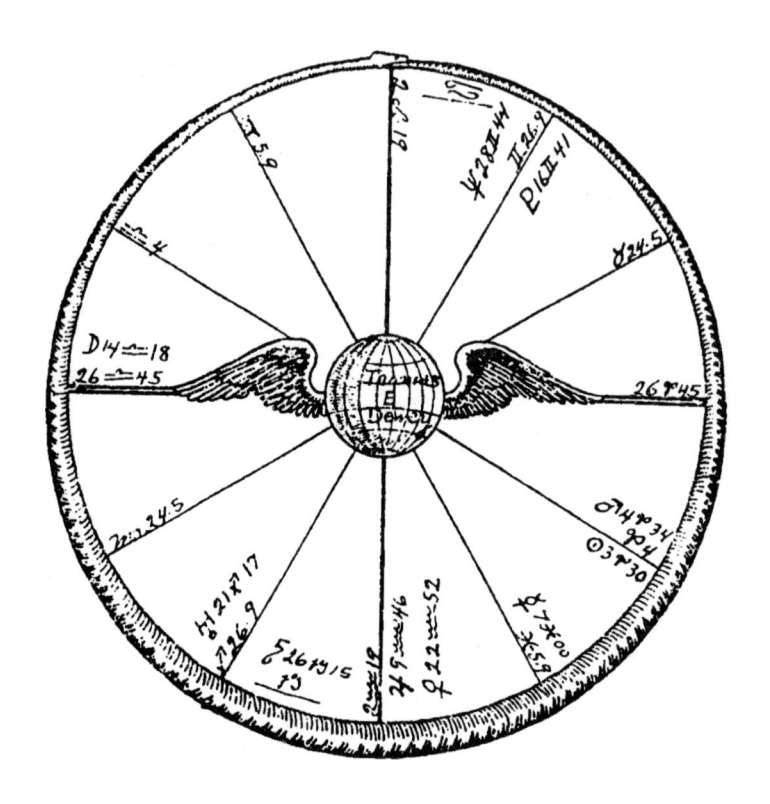

Thomas E. Dewey
March 24, 1902, 7:49 p.m. CST, 84°W11', 43°N
Data, February-March, 1938, Today's Astrology magazine

- 1935, June, appointed Special Prosecutor of racketeers in N.Y.: Sun sesqui-square Uranus ᵣ, Mars semi-square Pluto ᵣ.

- 1936, June, secured conviction of Charles (Lucky) Luciano, and fame: Sun sextile Mercury ᵣ, Jupiter trine Moon ᵣ, Mars semi-square Pluto ᵣ.

- 1937, fame as pioneer "racket buster" grew, mentioned as possible presidential timber: Mercury sextile Mercury ᵣ, Mercury conjunction Sun ₚ.

- 1938, long, highly publicized prosecution of alleged higher-ups in Dutch Schultz mob results in mistrial: Sun square Jupiter ᵣ.

Ancient Masonry 290

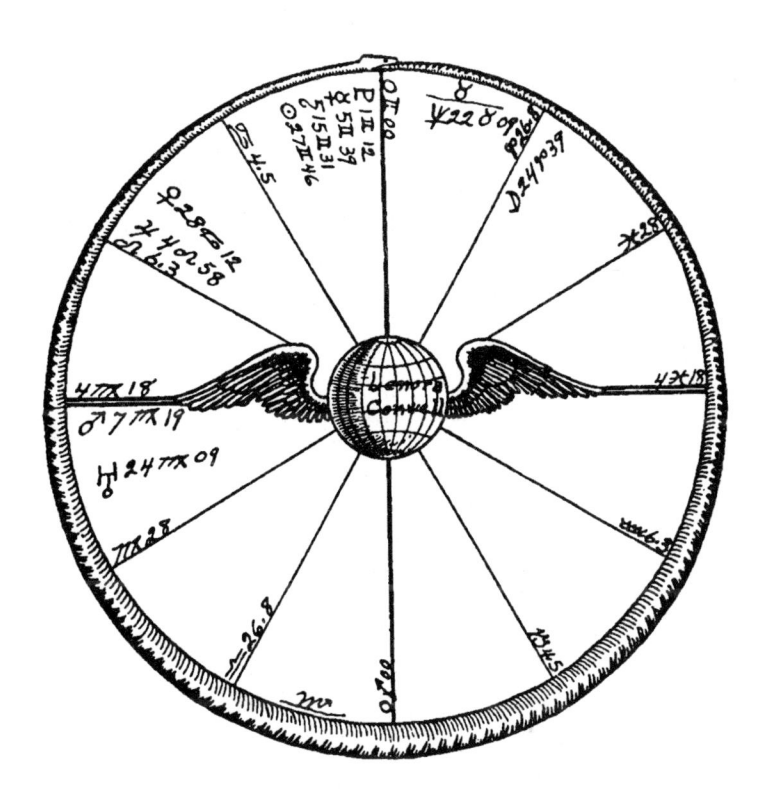

Lenora Conwell
June 18, 1884, 10:35 a.m. C.S.T. 98°W15', 39°N45'
Data from her personally

1912, fall, first serious occult study: Sun sextile Uranus p.

1919, February, joined B. of L.: Sun sextile Pluto r.

1920, organized center, taught astrology: Sun sextile Pluto, p.

1924, April, given charge B. of L. Research Dept.: Sun sextile Mercury r, conjunction Jupiter r.

1934, November, started Hollywood C. of L. Center: sun conjunction Jupiter p, sextile Saturn r.

1935, first magazine articles: Mercury sesqui-square Moon r, Mars semi-sextile Mars r.

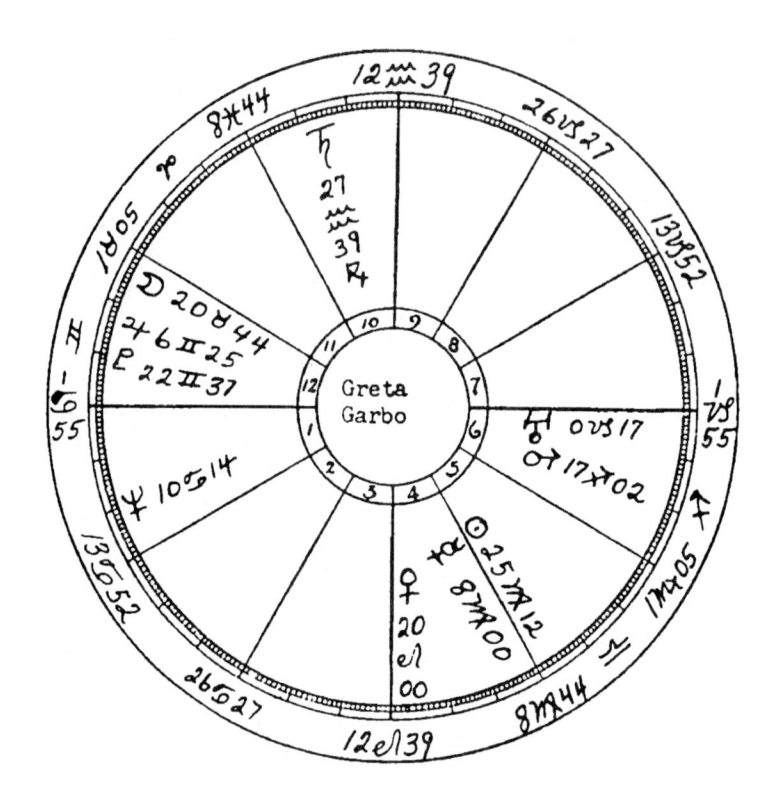

Greta Garbo

September 18, 1905, 9:00 p.m., C.E.T., 59°N20', 18°E03'
Data from passport and personal acquaintance

- 1923, hat advertising led to screen test: Mercury semi-sextile Mercury ᵣ, Mars sextile Saturn ᵣ in tenth.
- 1924, made first picture: Mercury square Neptune ᵣ.
- 1925, signed long term as star with MGM: Venus semi-sextile Sun ₚ.
- 1926, American film debut: Mercury sesqui-square Saturn ᵣ.
- 1927, starred in, *Flesh and the Devil*: Venus square Mars ᵣ.
- 1928, starred in, *The Divine Woman*: Mercury semi-sextile Venus ₚ.
- 1938, vacation abroad with friend Stokowski Sun trine Saturn ₚ, Venus square Uranus ᵣ.

Ancient Masonry 292

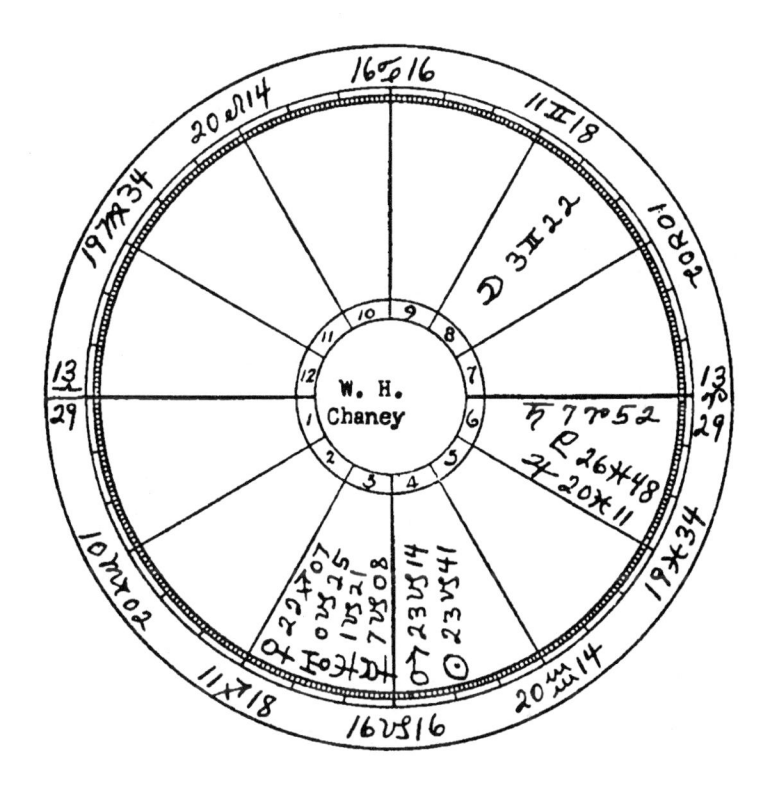

W.H. Chaney
January 13, 1821, 11:31 p.m., 44°N19', 69°W47'
Data given in his Primer of Astrology

1830, father died: Mars semi-sextile Uranus ᵣ

1840, deserted from Navy: Sun semi-square Pluto ᵣ, Mars sextile Saturn ᵣ.

1866, engaged to write book against astrology, but became converted and started lecturing for it: Mercury sextile Sun ᵣ, Venus semi-square Uranus ₚ.

1877, published set of 77 year ephemerides: Sun conjunction Jupiter ᵣ, Venus sextile Uranus ₚ.

1890, published his Primer of Astrology: Sun square Uranus ₚ, Mercury conjunction Jupiter ₚ.

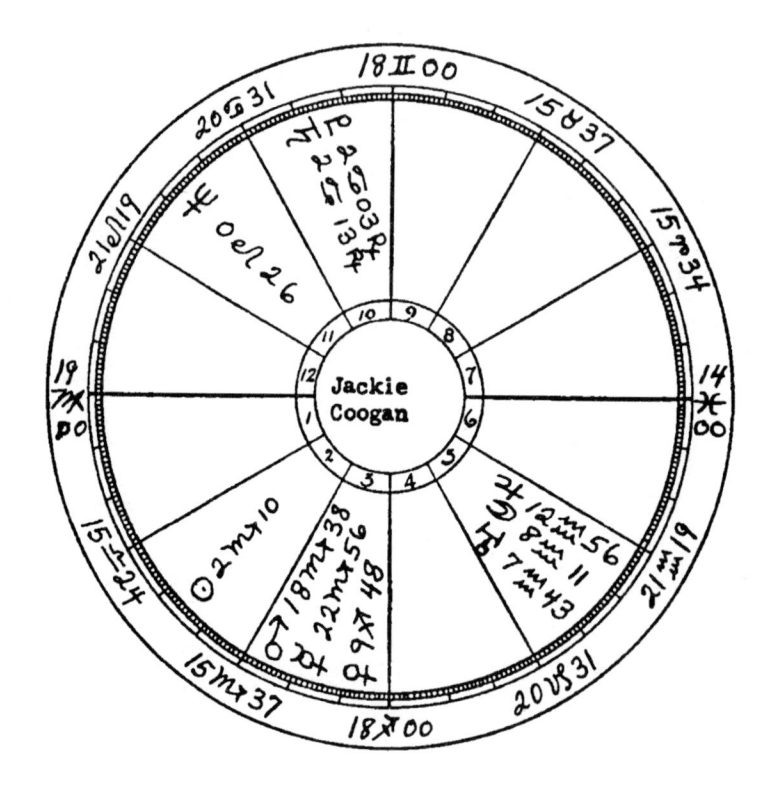

John Leslie (Jackie) Coogan
October 26, 1914, 2:45 a.m. PST, 34°N04′, 118°W15′
Data furnished by mother

1919, gained fame playing the part of the KID in a Charlie Chaplin film: Sun square Uranus ᵣ in 5th, Mercury conjunction Mars ₚ.

1925, left the movies for ten years: Sun square Jupiter ᵣ, Venus sextile Jupiter ᵣ.

1937, vaudeville tour: Venus conjunction Venus ᵣ.

1938, May 15, sued, without avail, mother and stepfather for an accounting of money he had earned: Venus (court) conjunction Venus, Mercury in second, square Uranus ᵣ.

Ancient Masonry   294

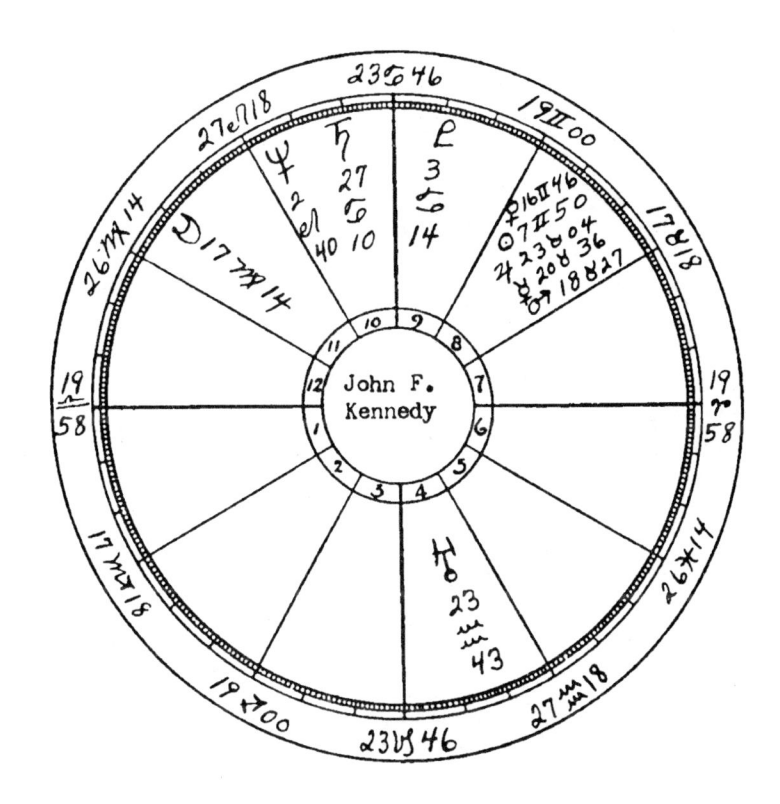

John F. Kennedy
May 29, 1917, 3:00 p.m. 71°W08', 42°N43'
Data, from him personally

1948, 1948 and 1950, elected to U.S. House of Representatives.

1953, Nov. 4, elected to U.S. Senate.

1953, Sept. married Jacqueline Lee Bouvier in Newport, Mass.

1956, just missed nomination for U.S. Vice President.

1958, re-elected to the U.S. Senate.

1960, July 13, nominated for U.S. President.

1960, Nov., elected President.

1962, Nov. 22, assassinated in Dallas Texas.

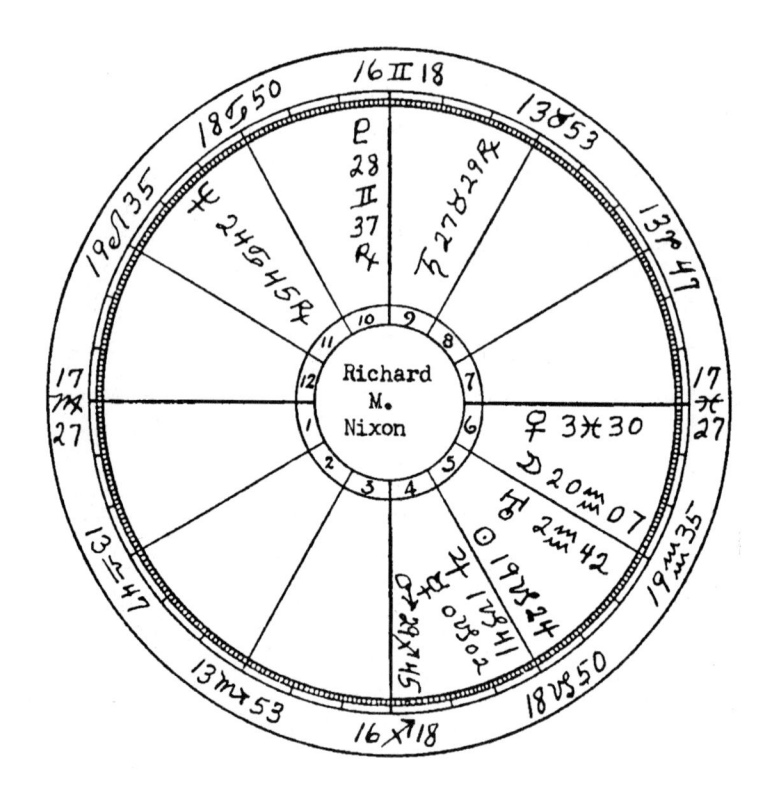

Richard M. Nixon

January 9, 1913, 9:35 p.m., P.S.T., 33°N50', 117°W46'
Data, from him personally

1940, June 21, married Patricia Ryan in Whittier, Calif.

1946 and 1948, elected to the U.S. House of Representatives.

1950, Nov. 7, elected to the U.S. Senate.

1952, Nov. 4, elected U.S. Vice President.

1956, re-elected U.S. Vice President.

1960, July 27, nominated for U.S. President.

1968, November, elected U.S. President.

1972, November, re-elected U.S. President.

1974, resigned as U.S. President amid Watergate scandal.

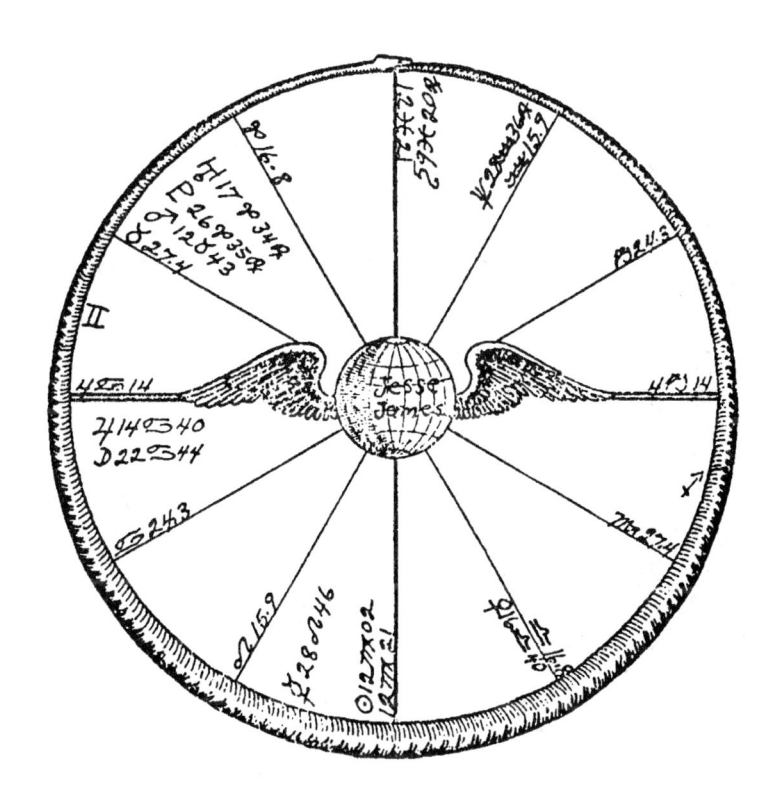

Jessie Woodson James
September 5, 1847, midnight between 4th and 5th, 94°W21', 39°n27'
Data from William B. McElvaney

1851, father went to California and died: Mercury opposition Saturn ₚ.

1861, 1865, Confederate guerrilla: Mars sextile Jupiter ᵣ, Sun sesqui-square Mars.

1866, started to lead bandit band active 15 years; Sun sesqui-square Mars ₚ, Venus inconjunct Mars ₚ, (Mars sextile Jupiter ᵣ all 15 years).

1873, July 21, first train robbery: Mercury opp. Uranus ₚ.

1882, April 3, treacherously shot in back of head and killed by member of own gang, Robert Ford: Sun opposition Uranus ₚ.

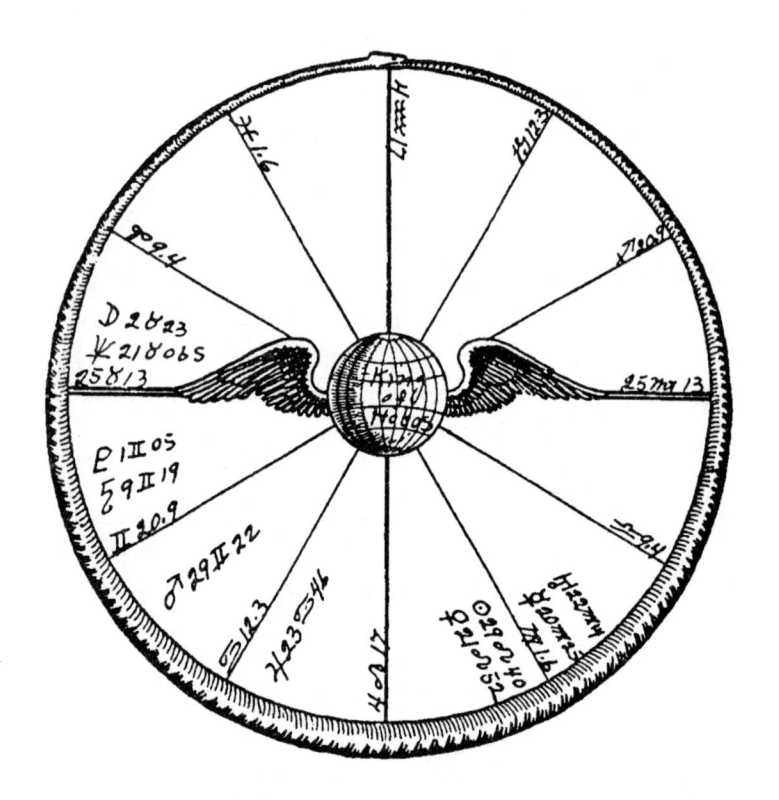

King of Hobos (Jeff Davis)
August 22, 1883, 10:00 p.m. 84°W30', 39°N
Data from him personally

- 1896, ran away form home, sold papers in New York: Mars semi-square Venus ᵣ, Mercury square Mars ₚ, Mars semi-square Neptune ᵣ.
- 1908, charter member, Hobo Fellowship of America: Sun conjunction Uranus ₚ, Venus conjunction Uranus ᵣ.
- 1934, hobo king Lazarowitz abdicated in his favor: Venus semi-sextile Uranus ₚ, Sun semi-sextile Mercury ᵣ.
- 1936, great publicity and gain in membership: Sun trine Neptune ᵣ.
- 1937, April big convention in St. Louis, proclaimed king, given diamond pin, claimed over a million in his Itinerant Migratory Worker's Union, including 40,000 hobettes: Sun semi-sextile Uranus ᵣ.

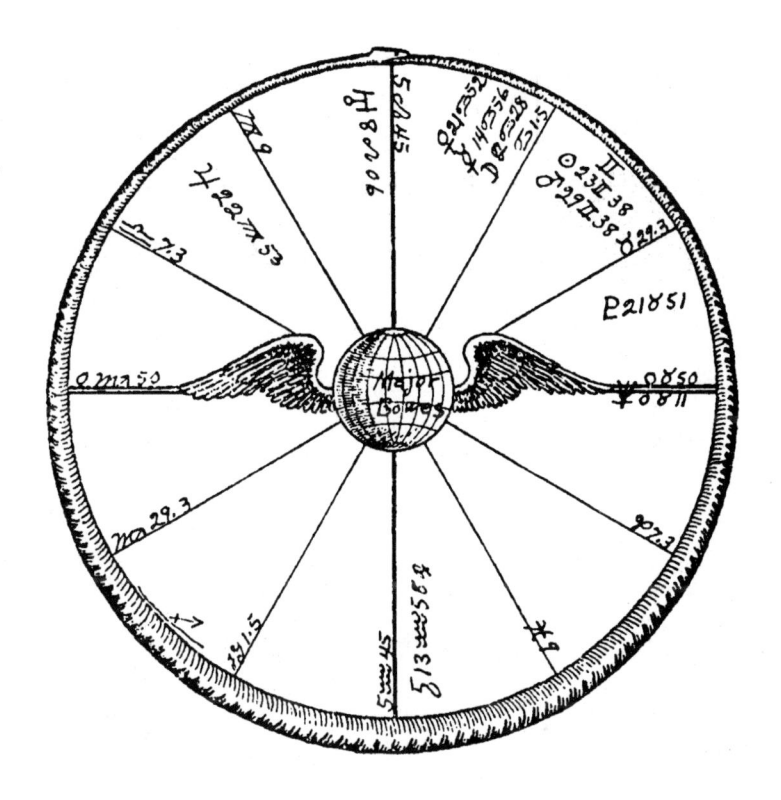

Major Edward Bowes
June 14, 1874, 3:00 p.m. 122°W30', 37°N45'
Data from sister

1908, married, became part owner of several playhouses, including the Cort Theatre in New York and Park Square Theatre in Boston, previously had sold real estate: Mercury conjunction Uranus, Mars conjunction Venus, Venus sextile Moon ᵣ, Sun sextile Jupiter ₚ.

1925, put oldest non-commercial broadcast on air, first broadcast from any theatre: Mars semi-sextile Moon ᵣ, Venus conjunction Jupiter ᵣ.

1935, amateur program, resulting in discovery and encouragement of talent, voted most popular on air: Mars opposition Saturn ₚ, Sun semi-sextile Jupiter ᵣ, Mercury sextile Venus ₚ.

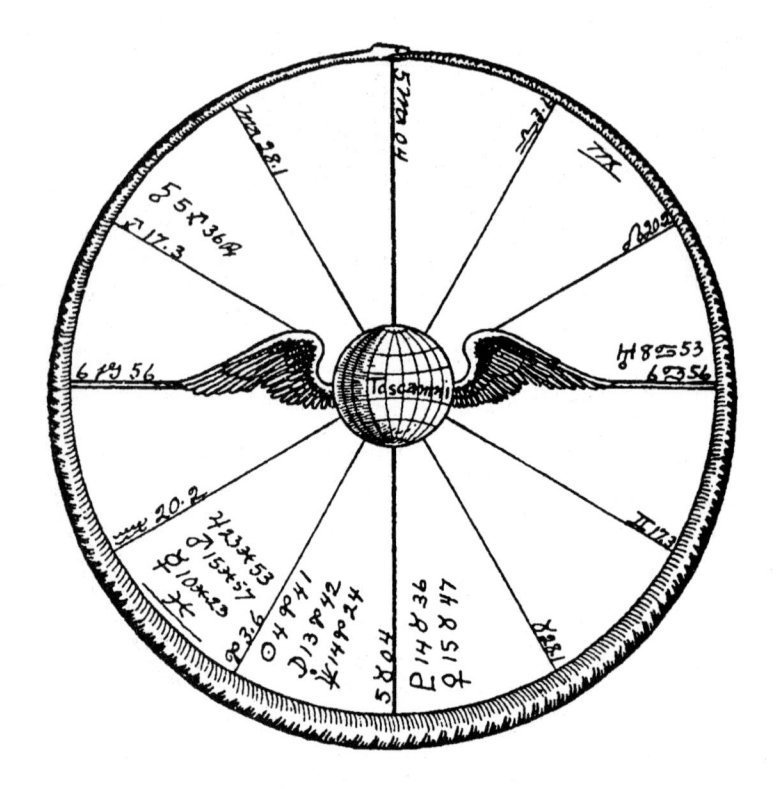

Arturo Toscanini
March 25, 1868, 2:00 a.m. 10°E15′, 44°N45′
Data from letter giving it and written by his own hand

1886, regular director absent, took over direction Rio Opera: Mars semi-square Venus ᵣ, Mars semi-square Pluto ᵣ.

1888, Metropolitan Opera, New York, as director: Sun semi-sextile Sunᵣ, inconjunct Saturn ₚ, Mercury semi-sextile Pluto ᵣ.

1908, 1915, Metropolitan Premiers: Sun conjunction Pluto ᵣ.

1915, residence in Italy, patriotic tours: Mercury conjunction Venus ᵣ and Pluto ₚ.

1937, 1938, after retiring was persuaded to return to give ten NBC radio concerts, acclaimed greatest orchestra conductor in world: Sun sextile Moon ᵣ.

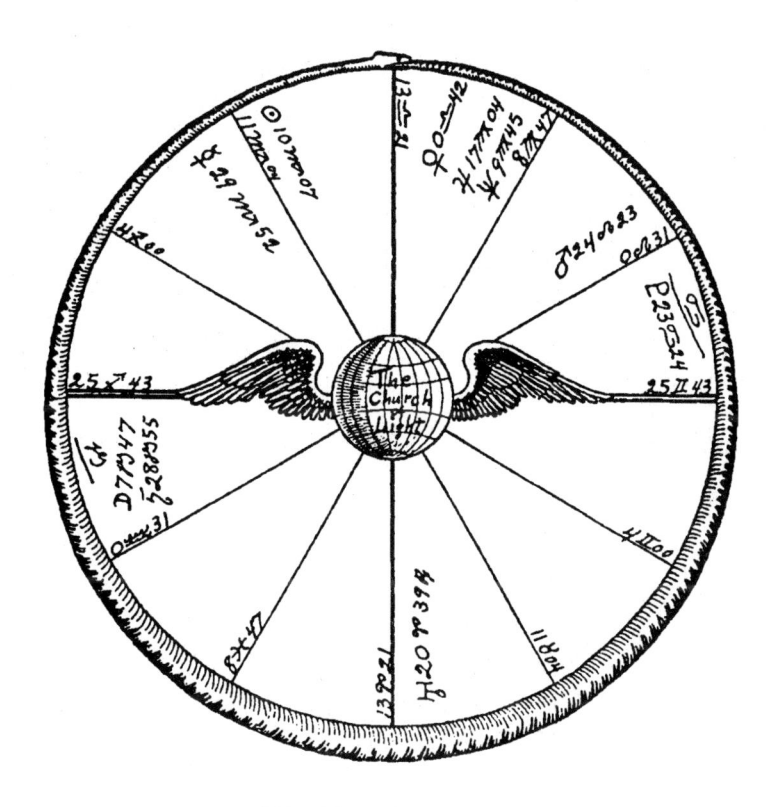

The Church of Light
November 2, 1932, 9:55 a.m. 118°W15', 34°N

The three chief functions of The Church of Light are: to acquire a comprehensive knowledge of nature, including occult force and planes other than the physical; to use this knowledge in teaching as wide a number of people as possible the best way to live; and in all other ways to help as many people as possible.

In electing a time for its birth, during the time available, as favorable a house of preaching and teaching (ninth) as could be had was selected. Uranus and Pluto in angles insures ample research. And the Moon, ruler of the populace, well aspected in the house of membership, gives assurance a vast number will be benefited.

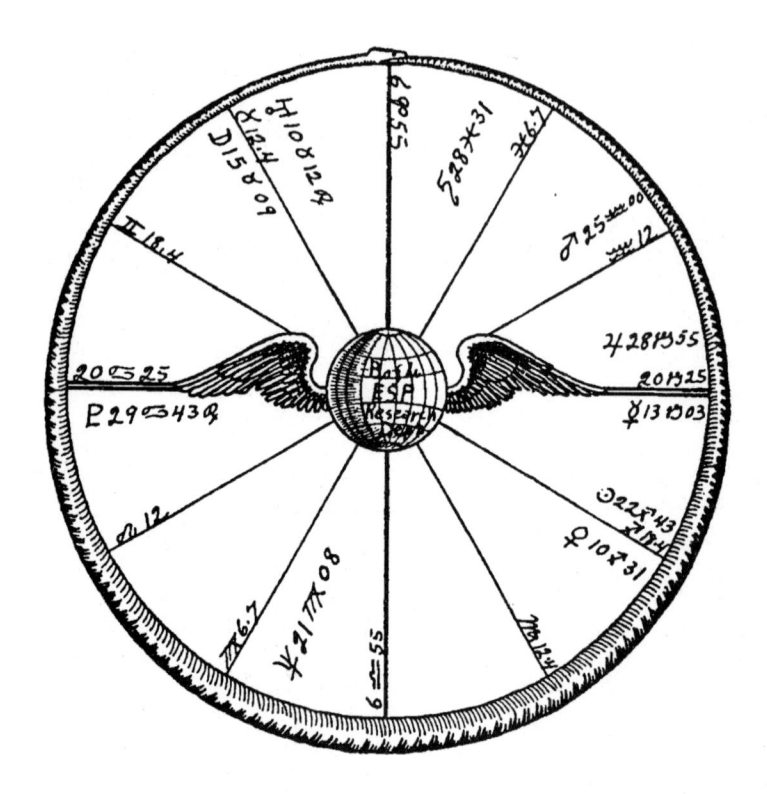

The Brotherhood of Light ESP Research Department
December 14, 1937, 6:45 p.m., 118°W15', 34°N

The Brotherhood of Light ESP Research Department has set itself the task of finding the safest and most effective method of developing efficient Extra-Sensory Perception, to the end that people may be able to use it not alone to their benefit in the more practical affairs of life, but also to the end that as many as possible may be able to explore the inner plane and thus prove to themselves that personality survives physical dissolution. Such widespread firsthand knowledge is deemed the best of all protections against atheistic materialism.

Index

Ancient Masonry

Aaron, 74
  rod of, 191, 193
Abel, Cain and, 139
Abiff, Hiram, 167, 174, 177-78, 179, 188, 226, 233
  assassins of, 151-52, 234, 235
  heart of, 229, 236
  jewels of, 189
  libation to, 213, 214
  resurrection of, 155, 157
  Solomon and, 236
  soul-mate of, 186, 225
  tomb of, 158, 229
  tragedy of, 146-55, 157, 158-59
Abraham, 150
  covenant with, 252
Adeptship, 181, 212, 219
  aspiring to, 151, 187, 188, 189-90, 251
  grades of, 189, 195, 196, 237-38
  magic and, 186
Adoniram, 177-78, 225-26, 227
Affections, 194, 232, 233
  negative, 175
  spiritual, 229
Affinity, law of, 84
Age of a Prince of Jerusalem degree, 246-47
Ahishar, execution of, 197
Alarm (rapping), 109
Alchemy, 187, 251
All-Seeing Eye, 133, 134
All-Wise Intelligence, astrology and, 9
Alphabet

  early, 27-28
  letters of, 25
  numerical value of, 25
  planets and, 22, 193
  zodiacal signs and, 193
  See also Numbers
Amos, quote from, 110-11
Anchor, 133, 134
Ancient Masonry, 6-7, 11, 15
  magic and, 71
  message of, 56-59, 82, 83
  Modern Masonry and, 5, 6, 61
  symbols of, 16
  See also Masonry
Ancient Secret Doctrine, 2
Angel of the Blest, 82
Angel of the Lord, 96
Animal kingdom, 128, 185, 258
Animal soul, 65, 66, 84, 85, 107, 136, 139, 142, 173
  domination by, 107
  sacrifice of, 82
  transformation of, 44, 48, 109-10, 141
Apron, 115, 211
  lamb-skin, 97-98
Aquarius
  Boaz and, 94
  origin of, 53-54
  Truth and, 209
  urn of, 212, 213
  water from, 95, 96
Arcana of Freemasonry (Churchward), quote from, 241-43
Aries

cross of, 201, 213, 214, 217, 225, 229, 246, 258
energy from, 85, 96
equinoctial colure and, 123
letter for, 147
origin of, 49
Ark, 133, 134-36
symbol of, 177, 191-92
three divisions of, 190
Ark of the Covenant, 190-91, 237
Ascendant, 136, 147, 186, 235
Asiah, 190
Aspects, description of, 14
Aspirations, 156, 176, 187
Astral body, 55, 61, 65, 66, 73, 105, 137
forces of, 45, 131
function of, 135
spiritual body and, 144
symbolization of, 141-42
thoughts and, 71
Astral energies, 63, 106, 119, 224, 244, 245
releasing, 168
Astral plane, 87, 122, 143, 153, 194, 256, 258
boundary for, 106-8
entering, 109-13, 115, 144
existence on, 128, 141, 155
nourishment on, 92
physical plane and, 59
records in, 238
velocity on, 101
Astrological Signatures, 72, 123
Astrology, 8, 11
branches of, 251
horary, 168
magic and, 187
practical, 232
science of, 9-10, 24
spiritual, 232
See also Natal astrology
Astronomy, study of, 8
Atlantis, existence of, 15
Atoms, sexed, 42
Atonement, 144, 221
Attainment, keystone of, 167-68
Attraction, 83, 84, 137, 163, 164
decline of, 194

symbolism for, 87
Atziluth, 190
Autumnal equinox, 209, 211, 212, 214, 217, 218
cross of, 96, 210
symbolization of, 206, 221
Azoth, 134, 190
Baal, Sha-Lisha, Lord of the three, 219
Balancing, 176, 177, 183, 233, 246
Balloting, 83-84
Banners, 182-84, 210
Beauty (pillar), 124
Bee-Hive, 133
Benjamin, 207
Bible, 56, 83, 209, 212
chastity and, 103
Oral Law and, 93, 118, 213
Birth-charts, 72, 124, 127, 131, 237
astrologers and, 169
Black magic, 176
number of, 147
Blazing star, 127
Boaz (grip), 153
Boaz (pillar), 12, 115, 130, 190, 229
Jachin and, 90-92
realm of, 91
symbolism of, 94, 97-98, 176
zodiac and, 95-97
Book of Constitutions, 133-34
Book of the Holy Scriptures, 117
Boundary-Line energies, 101, 155, 156, 201, 203, 204
uniting with, 90-92
Braham, golden egg of, 136
Breast, symbolism of, 109, 110, 113
Breast to breast union, 154
Breathing, 232
dynamic, 47, 58, 59
nourishment from, 92
rhythmic, 45, 58, 165
Briah, 190
Brotherhood of Light
Astrological Research Department, 259
Control of Life Research Department, 259

ESP Research Department, 245, 259
   permission of, 4-5
   See also Church of Light
Brother Truth, 253
Burning Bush, 184, 238

Cable-tow, 86, 113, 141, 142, 162
Cain
   Abel and, 139
   Mars and, 139, 142
   Scorpio and, 142
Calvary, 249
Camiel, 253
Cancer, 118
   origin of, 50
Candidates
   clothing for, 84-88, 108-9
   entrance of, 110
   voting for, 83-84
Canute, 242
Capricorn
   Boaz and, 94
   origin of, 53
   raven and, 135
   Saturn and, 95
   solstitial cross of, 131, 217
   tomb of, 96
Cassia, symbolism of, 150, 151, 158
Castor, 50
Caution, importance of, 116, 117
Celestial bodies, maps/charts of, 131
Celestial globe, 9, 14
   quadrants of, 131
Celestial influences, 28, 161
   effects of, 8, 25, 31
   types of, 30
Celestial kingdom, 258
Celestial Longitudes, 14, 123
Celibacy, 57, 58
   advantages of, 102-4, 164-65
   forced, 104-6, 115
   See also Sex, repression of
Cepheus, 127
Chaldeans, Masonry and, 6, 22
Chalk, symbolism of, 128-29
Charcoal, symbolism of, 128-29

"Chariot of Triumph, The," 97
Checkered pavement, 127, 128
Check-words, 116-17
Chemistry, 24, 42
Cherubims, 190, 191
Cheth, 234
Chief of the Tabernacle degree, 250-51
Children, planetary influences on, 194
Chivalric Degree, 253
Christ
   ascending, 249
   betrayal of, 213
   cross of, 210
   resurrection of, 252, 253
   youth of, 95
Chronicles, quote from, 184
Church of Light, 38
   psychic development and, 244, 245
   Research Department, 24
   See also Brotherhood of Light
Churchward, Albert: quotes of, 241-43
Circumcision, symbolism of, 252
Clay, symbolism of, 128-29
Clement of Alexandria, 241
Clothing, 84-88, 108-9
Columns. *See* Pillars
Compass, 112, 228
   higher laws and, 87
   square and, 16-18, 145, 208-9, 226, 255
   symbolism of, 14-15, 17, 93
Confidences, exchanging, 155, 157
Consciousness, 61, 64, 68
   cosmic, 152
   development of, 108, 129, 224
   inner plane and, 157, 203
   magic and, 72
   objective, 61, 63, 64, 66
   seven states of, 129, 171, 181, 189, 217
   symbolism of, 221
   velocities and, 172
Constantine the Great, 217
Constellations, 121, 135, 228
   construction of, 22
   spiritual meaning of, 118, 130-31
Constitution, 181

seven-fold, 101, 138, 161, 184, 251, 255
Contact Potential Difference, 222
Control, determining, 58, 222-25
Co-operation, 106, 111, 115, 116, 128, 134, 156
   husband-wife, 167-68
   lack of, 152
Cosmic Work, 251, 257
Court Cards, 229
Cowans, excluding, 62, 64
Creative energies, 12, 73, 108, 142, 157, 163, 186
   abuse of, 158
   sacrificing, 150
   spiritualization of, 98, 145
   symbolism of, 133, 144, 146, 198, 256
   using, 85, 233
Creative principle, 151, 215
Cross
   emblem of, 201
   inverted, 206
   symbolism of, 25
Crown of the Magi, 238
Cryptic cycles, unlocking, 79
Crystallization, 234, 235
Cup, manna-containing, 191, 192
Cycle of Necessity, 83, 178, 181, 253, 258
Cyrus, King, 183, 184, 208
   Saturn and, 256

Darius, King, 208, 209, 246
David, 219
   as high degree Mason, 75
Deacons, 84, 101
Death
   astral plane and, 155
   defeating, 214, 215, 218
   disintegration following, 141
   preparing for, 144, 210, 211
   scorpion and, 218, 252
   second, 141, 156, 214
   soul and, 259
   symbolization of, 96, 139, 214, 251
   zodiacal sign of, 213
Declination, 14, 17

Dedications, 117-19
Degree of Perfection, 238-39
De Molay, Jacques, 241
Descendant, 136, 147, 148, 186, 235
Desire, 163, 164
   controlling, 93, 109-10
   decline of, 194
   normal, 105
   spiritual laws and, 87
   symbolism for, 87
Destiny, 81
   responsibility for, 82-84
Dieugard, 189, 219
   making, 113-14, 145, 175, 179, 214
Distress, sign of, 69-75, 214
Divine fire, 184, 228, 233, 238
Divine soul, 69, 87, 136, 145, 174, 177
   influence of, 141, 143
   libation to, 214
   separation from, 157, 158
Double Sextile, 17
Double Square, 17
Doubting Thomas, 216
Dragon, 256
   symbolism of, 250, 255
Dreams, 171
   language of, 121
   symbolism of, 122
   velocity of, 172
Druids, 242-43

Eagles, 248
   double-headed, 254-55, 257
   Roman, 97, 217, 218
Earth, symbol for, 31
Easter, 96, 206, 208
Eastern Gateway, 12, 90
Eavesdroppers, excluding, 62, 64
Ecclesiastes, quote from, 143
Ecliptic, 13-14, 15
Ego, 82, 86, 87, 116, 128, 136
   coordination with, 230
   function of, 135, 141, 143, 154
   infinite, 11
   libation to, 214
   separation from, 145, 148, 152

soul and, 113, 162, 188
Eight, meaning of, 78, 111
Einstein, Albert, 59, 90, 101, 170
Electrical energies, 63, 66, 244, 245
   control over, 223
   depletion of, 163, 164, 223
   emotion and, 91, 166
   endocrine glands and, 164
   generation of, 58, 64, 138, 165
   nervous system and, 165
   personal magnetism and, 46
   proper, 163-67, 167-68
   sex factor and, 46, 164, 165, 166
   thought-cells and, 63
   will and, 45-46
Electromagnetic energies, 45, 161, 166, 187, 189, 223-24
   velocity of, 171-72
   See also Magnetic forces
Eleven, symbolism of, 249
Emanation, 190
Emotion
   energy and, 91, 166
   symbolism for, 87
Encampment of Knights Templar, 210
Endocrine glands
   electrical energies and, 164
   secretions by, 103-4
Energy, 75, 76, 254
   controlling, 222
   exchange of, 45, 46, 89, 90, 194, 222
   symbolizing, 233, 253
   unbalance of, 106
   universal, 43, 45
   utilizing, 43, 46, 47, 238
   will power and, 46, 47
   See also Various energies by type
Enoch, 147
   vision of, 237-38, 239
Entered Apprentice degree, 30, 41, 70, 110, 118, 175
   physical plane and, 101
   significance of, 54-56
Entered Apprentice lodge, 37-39, 41, 54-55, 69
   description of, 30-37

Entered Apprentice Mason, 34, 39, 55, 61, 161
   grip of, 94, 153
   jewels for, 116
   soul knowledge and, 30
Ephraimites, 102, 106
Epiphany, 95, 132, 218
Equilibrium, 176, 177
Equinoctial colure, 123, 124, 198, 208
Equinoctial cross, 215, 255
Esoteric wisdom, 86, 94, 232
ESP. *See* Extra-Sensory Perception
Etheric body, 105, 106-8, 115, 137
   vitalizing, 232
Etheric energy, 42-43, 45-46, 58, 64, 66, 106, 138
   abundance of, 59, 101, 102
   Boundary-Line, 155, 156
   generating, 47
   influence of, 107, 108
   sexual fluids and, 105
Euclid's Square, 14
Evolution, 66
   assisting, 236
   climax of, 183, 217
   symbolization of, 211
Exodus, quote from, 186, 187, 191
Extension of Consciousness, 201, 224-25
Extra-Sensory Perception (ESP)
   exercising, 75, 108, 161, 163, 170, 203, 222,
   Feeling, 162, 243, 244-45
   Intellectual, 162, 167, 189, 190, 243, 244, 245

Father Adam, 253
Fellowcraft degree, 101, 113, 115, 147
   initiation for, 108-10, 117
   pass-word of, 195
Fellowcraft lodge, 101-2, 109
Fellowcraft Mason, 161
   Abiff and, 152, 153
   grip of, 114, 153
   jewels for, 117
   oath of, 111
   sign of, 113

Index

Fellowship, five points of, 154-55, 155-59, 229
Feminine principle, 15, 42, 111
Feminine symbol, 13
Fifteen, symbolism of, 147
First House, 124-25
Five, symbolism of, 77, 155, 231
Flammarion, Camille: on intelligence, 43
Foot to foot union, 154
Forty-Seventh Problem of Euclid, 133, 136-38
Four, symbolism of, 77, 137, 161, 255
Fourth dimension, 202, 203
Fox Sisters, 23
Freemasonry. *See* Masonry

G (letter), 152
  meaning of, 18, 133, 217
Gabriel, 253
"Gate of the Sanctuary, The," 97
Gavel, 41, 42, 75
  rapping with, 69, 72, 177
  significance of, 44, 45, 55
  will power and, 46
Gemini, origin of, 50
General Theory of Relativity (Einstein), 59, 90, 101, 170
Generation, 18, 145, 152, 168, 186, 195
  evolution and, 217
  mysteries of, 88, 93, 111, 133, 144
  plane of, 194
  truths about, 252, 253
Geometry, principles of, 136, 237
Gestation, 136, 218
Gestures, 28-29
Gimel, 17
Gnomes, 182, 185
God, 13, 136, 183
  Infinite Mind and, 11
  separation from, 145
Golden Fleece, symbolism of, 97
Gonad glands, 103, 104
  electrical energies and, 164, 165, 166
Grand Architect of the Universe, 11, 64, 65, 256
Grand Lodge, 30, 39, 148, 239
Grand Master Architect degree, 236-37

Grand Master of All Symbolic Lodges degree, 250
Grand Masters, 7, 148, 178, 193
  burial of, 149, 150
  check-word of, 116
  jewels of, 189
Grand Ministers, role of, 216-17
Grand Omnific Arch Word, 193
Grand Pontiff degree, 249-50
Grand Rofdam, 250
Grand Stellar Lodge, 39
Gravitation, 91
  on inner plane, 204-5
  velocity of light and, 90
Great Work, 18, 192
Grips, significance of, 113-16

Hailing sign, 144
Ham, 186
Hands, symbolism of, 111, 145
Hanged Man, 219
He (feminine letter), 136, 137, 138
Heave-over (sign), 162, 163
Hermetic System of Astrology, 95, 169, 247
Hermetic System of Names and Numbers, 75, 102, 137, 147, 154
Hermetic System of Natal Astrology, 189
Heroine of Jericho, 198-99, 201
Hieroglyphics, 2, 237, 238
High Priests, 183, 190, 195, 242
  on manna, 192
Hiram, King, 177
  Abiff and, 146
  jewels of, 189
  libation to, 213
Historical degrees, 241-59
Holy Ghost, 51, 96, 137
Holy Sepulchre, 218
  guarding, 217
Holy Shekinah, 18, 54, 93, 147
Hope, 94, 230
Horizontal sign, 69, 70
Horses, symbolism of, 121
Horus, 138
Hour-Glass, 133, 221

Human experience
  preparing for, 27, 85
  symbolization of, 125
Hypersensitivity, 224, 244, 245

IHS, mark of, 219
Illumination, 82, 93, 225, 226, 253
  reaching, 97
Imagination, 6, 7
Immaculate conception, mystery of, 51
Immortality, 153, 167, 209, 210, 214, 226, 233, 249, 250
  attaining, 16, 27, 146, 148, 157, 158, 229, 251
  eternal progression and, 155
  secrets of, 21
  Self-Conscious, 27, 70
  symbolism of, 150, 229
Incarnation, 85, 128
Incense, description of, 138-39
Incompletion complex, 89
Individuality, 48
  sun and, 31
Infinite Mind, 10-11
Initiation, 4, 65, 84-85, 87, 162
  desire for, 83
Inner plane, 91, 162, 167, 170, 221, 245
  consciousness and, 157, 203, 224
  distance on, 203-4
  exploring, 163, 190, 222, 259
  gravitation on, 204-5
  information from, 243
  nutrition on, 92-94
  time on, 201-2
  velocities on, 203, 205
INRI, 215
Intelligence, 46, 75, 76, 254
  developing, 59
  symbolization of, 132, 192
  See also Knowledge; Wisdom
Intendant of the Building degree, 232-33
Intimate Secretary degree, 230-31
Invincible Knight, 216
Involution, 184

  cycle of, 253
  symbolization of, 211
Isis, 36, 51, 136-37, 233, 249
  Osiris and, 158
Ives, Herbert E., 90-91, 170
Izabud, 196, 197

Jabal, 147
Jachin (grip), 114, 153
Jachin (pillar), 12, 115, 130, 190, 229
  Boaz and, 90-92
  symbolism of, 97-98, 176
  zodiac and, 95-97
Jacob, on Judah, 206-7
Japhet, 186
Jehovah, 41, 183
Je-Vau, 229, 230
Jewels, 116-17, 253
  discovery of, 189
  movable, 126-27
Jewish Order of Priesthood, 250
Jewish Pass, 206, 209
Joabert, 234
Jod (letter), 136, 137, 146, 229
Jod-He-Shin, 219
Jod-He-Vau-He, mystery of, 18, 41, 134, 193, 227, 238
Jonathan, David and, 219
Jubal, 147, 148
Jubela, 147, 148, 235
Jubelo, 147, 148, 235
Jubelum, 147, 149
Jubulum
  capture of, 235
  death of, 234
Judah, Jacob on, 206-7
Judas Iscariot, 96, 214, 248
  apostasy of, 213
Julian, Emperor, 241
Junior Deacon, 34, 55, 56, 61, 62
  function of, 64-65, 86
Junior Overseer, 162
Junior Warden, 36, 55, 69, 114
  Master Masons and, 141
  role of, 67-68, 110, 142-43
  signs by, 72
  as spiritual body, 87
Jupiter, 38

color of, 182
influence of, 174
number of, 155
qualities of, 32-33
symbol of, 32-33
Jupiter finger, 94, 114, 232
Justice, 174, 177
   emblem of, 233
   meting out, 178

Kabala, 54, 93, 147, 190, 248
Keystone, 163, 166, 167
   natal astrology and, 168-73
King Solomon's Temple. *See* Solomon's Temple
Knee to knee union, 154
Knight of Kadosh degree, 254-55
Knight of Rose Cross degree, 248-49
Knight of the Brazen Serpent degree, 252
Knight of the Eagle and Pelican, 248
Knight of the Sword degree, 256-57
Knight of the White and Black Eagle, 254
Knights of Christian Mark degree, 216-17
Knights of East and West degree, 247-48
Knights of Malta degree, 215-16
Knights of the Ninth Arch degree, 237-38
Knights of the Red Cross degree, 206-10
Knights of the Sun degree, 253-54
Knights of Three Kings degree, 205-6
Knowledge
   dangerous, 197
   gaining, 98, 117, 134, 148, 177, 258-59
   preserving, 227, 238
   symbol of, 232
   treasures of, 189
   See also Intelligence; Wisdom
Kundalini, 165, 166

Lamb, creative energy of, 95, 96
Language
   ancient, 121
   profane, 69
   symbols in, 28
Law
   obedience to, 177
   tablets of, 191-92
Law of Association, 121
Law of Correspondences, 196
Law of Sex, 42
Law of spiritual construction, 139
Laws of Occultism, 90, 244
Left hand to back union, 154-55
Leo, 54
   origin of, 51
Libations, series of, 213, 214
Liberate the Captives, 256, 257
Libra, 17
   Boaz and, 94
   cross of, 95, 96, 201, 214, 217
   origin of, 52
   power of, 97
   scales of, 52, 124
   Venus and, 55
Life, 94, 187, 231, 254
   prolonging, 56
   secrets of, 21
   stages of, 128, 256
   trines of, 183
   trinity of, 75-76
Light, 94, 117-19, 187, 231, 254
   laws of gravitation and, 90
   moving toward, 88-90
   velocity of, 203, 204
"Lightning Struck Tower, The," 97
Lion's grip, 153, 175, 227, 233
Living arch
   entering through, 184-89
   symbolism of, 182-83
Lorentz transformation, 171
Lost Word, 134, 148, 225, 227
   recovering, 146, 193-95, 249
   revelation of, 137
   searching for, 152
Love, 83, 94, 187, 231, 256, 257-58
   experiencing, 82, 88, 93, 96
   growth of, 16, 89
   higher, 93, 96, 113
   kinds of, 163
   pillar of, 255

power of, 56, 73, 74, 84, 86, 116, 227, 254, 259
retaining, 88, 164
spiritual, 257
suppression of, 57
violation of, 148
Lower-Pluto realm, 108, 178, 179
influence of, 235
legions of, 198

Machine Period, Uranus and, 23
Magi, 7, 9, 238, 251
Infinite Mind and, 10-11
knowledge acquiring and, 258-59
observation of, 46
Oral Law and, 119
Magic, 6, 159
adeptness and, 186
astrology and, 187
black, 147, 176
consciousness and, 72
destructive, 71, 171, 176
practical, 132
seven branches of, 251
sex, 187
white, 73, 176
will and, 47
Magnetic forces, 46, 84, 89, 103
See also Electromagnetic energies
"Magus, The," 97
Mah-Hah-Bone, 153
Maltese cross, 210, 211, 215, 257, 258
Manhood
seventh state of, 151
sixth state of, 152
Manna, 191, 192
Marcelliums, Pope, 217
Mark Master, 168, 229
pass grip of, 173-74
sign of, 162
Mark Master degree, 161, 162, 174
Mark Well, 173-74
Marriage, 102, 195
chemical, 42
cooperation in, 72, 74, 84, 88, 167-68, 177

higher phases of, 73, 74
importance of, 16, 56, 73, 88, 89, 116
sex and, 57
symbolization of, 93, 132
zodiacal sign of, 124
Marrow Bones, 211
Mars, 70
Bee-Hive and, 133
Cain and, 139, 142
color of, 182
energy of, 169, 232
influence of, 85
Jubelo and, 148
Jubulum and, 234
letter for, 147
Red Sea and, 130
symbol of, 34-35
Masculine principle, 14, 43, 111
Masculine symbol, 13
Mason (word), 6, 15
Masonic lodge, 7-8, 72, 122-23
Masonry, 7
archives of, 131
astrology and, 10
fourth degree of, 161
investigation of, 4, 5
origin of, 242
persecution of, 3-4
symbolic forms of, 2, 29
thirty-three degrees of, 27-28
See also Ancient Masonry; Modern Masonry
Master, 36, 54-55, 56, 61, 62, 65
abdication of, 175
Abiff and, 234
balancing and, 176
death of, 149
F.C. degree and, 101, 114, 115
role of, 68-69, 87, 143, 225
sign of, 72, 152
Worshipful Master and, 67
Master Magicians, 73
Master Mason, 161, 177
grip of, 145, 153
sign of, 145
tools of, 145
Master Mason degree, 118, 146, 153, 156

attaining, 157
candidates for, 141
emblems of, 133, 221
spiritual plane and, 101
Master Mason Lodge, 141, 174
Master of Destinies, 27
Master of Elect Nine degree, 233-34
Master Overseer, 162
Masters Elect of Fifteen degree, 234-35
Materialism, 96, 137, 148, 151, 208
spirituality and, 150
tomb of, 228
Material plane, 88, 111, 126, 144
Material Universe, 10
Mathematics, 8, 25, 136, 137
Meditation, 58, 157
Mediumship, 243-44
Melville, Henry, 4, 5
Memory pictures, 144
Mental forces, 12, 59, 61, 175, 223
deterioration of, 104
gauging, 48, 116
sacrificing, 143
Mercury, 38, 69
Abiff and, 146
influence of, 24
letter for, 147
speech and, 116
Sun and, 65
symbol of, 35-36
Mercury finger, 174, 232
Mercy Seat, 191
Metal tools, 125-26
Methuselah, 237
Michael, 253
Midheaven, 136, 147, 148, 150, 186, 235
Mineral realm, 128, 183, 258
existence in, 184-85
Mission of the Soul, 4
Modern Masonry, 1
Ancient Masonry and, 5, 6, 61
symbolic ritual and, 82
See also Masonry
Monads, 182, 183, 191
Money, 192
borrowing, 98-99
Moon, 14, 17, 39
cycle of, 250

femininity of, 36, 198
influence of, 8, 24, 94
mentality and, 31
sun and, 65, 154, 158, 168, 174, 236
symbolism of, 13, 25, 26, 31, 36
Moses, 138, 185, 186, 191
generation and, 253
intercession of, 252
tabernacle and, 129
Most Excellent Master degree, 175-77, 183
Mother of the Universe, 13
Mount Moria, 150, 152
Mouth to ear union, 155
Mu, existence of, 15
Mundane Houses, 118, 123, 124, 135, 150
Mysteries, 150, 166, 238
knowledge of, 99
learned, 81, 82-83
spiritual, 232

Naked heart, 133, 221
Natal astrology, 69, 124, 189, 202
keystone and, 168-73
on mental capacity, 116
Saturn and, 32
National Academy of Science, 90
Nature
attributes of, 12
chastity and, 102
septenary law of, 247
NAUTICAL ALMANAC (1939), 38
Nebuchadnezzar, Zedekiah and, 197
Negative, positive and, 183, 192, 193-94
Negative foods, 57-58, 59
Neptune, 34
discovery of, 23
influence of, 24, 38, 75, 161, 162, 198
mythology of, 22
symbol of, 38
Nervous system, 171-72
electrical power and, 165

hypersensitivity of, 244
planets and, 162
New Jerusalem, 249, 250
Nine, meaning of, 76, 78-79
Noah, 136
  ark and, 134-35
  sons of, 186
Northeast Corner, description of, 124-25
NOT SOLD lessons, 243, 244
Numbers
  Arabic, 26, 75-79
  deific, 78-79
  foundation of, 26, 136
  function of, 76-79
  Roman, 26
  science of, 161
  symbols of, 25-26
  See also Alphabet

Occult power, 208, 233
  abuse of, 198
  source of, 198
Ointment, symbolism of, 74
Old Simon, death and, 213
Om, 7
Omnific Word, 177, 178, 181, 183, 193, 195
On, 7
One, meaning of, 76
One Agent, 41, 77, 207
133rd Psalm, 75, 87
One Law, 12, 41, 77, 207
One Truth, 77, 207, 209-10
One Universal Principle, 42, 77, 207, 231, 247, 254
  gavel and, 45
  symbolism of, 41
  transmitting, 44
Oral Law, 72, 190, 192, 195, 196
  Bible and, 93, 118, 213
  Book of Constitutions and, 133
  Magi and, 119
  symbolizing, 212
  violation of, 134
Order of Knights of the Holy Sepulchre degree, 217-18

Order of Knights Templar degree, 210-15, 241, 254
Order of the Cross degree, 218-19
Order of the Knights of the East, 206
Order of the Red Cross, Chamber of, 208
Oriental doctrines, 57-58
  celibacy and, 164
Ornaments, description of, 127-28
Orphic Mysteries, egg of, 136
Osiris, 37, 136, 157
  Isis and, 158
Overshadowing Intelligence of Egypt, 137

Passwords, significance of, 113-16
Passion, 12, 87, 107, 163, 187
  incense and, 139
  lightning of, 135
  regeneration and, 105
  vibrations of, 84
Past Master, 30, 37
  grip of, 175
Past Master degree, 174-75
Penance, 213, 221
Perfect ashlar, 126
Perfect Master degree, 227-29
Period of manufacture, Uranus and, 23
Period of oil and gas, Neptune and, 23
Period of republics, Uranus and, 23
Perpendicular sign, 70
Persian Guards, 209
Persian Pass, 207
Personality, 31, 48
Phoebus, 7
Physical body, 115, 135, 137
  death of, 156
  spiritual body and, 142
Physical Laws, obeying, 18, 93
Physical plane, 55, 86, 87, 98, 122, 143, 172, 189, 204
  adeptship on, 188
  astral plane and, 59
  boundary for, 106-8
  death on, 251
  Entered Apprentice degree and, 101
  existence on, 138, 155, 203
  initiation on, 124

leaving, 239
  spiritual plane and, 151
  symbolization of, 151
Physical senses, 94
  master of, 181
  subjugation of, 233
Pictographs, language of, 161
Pike, Albert: work of, 4
Pilgrimage, 212, 213
Pilgrim Warrior, 212-13
Pillar of Beauty, 238
Pillars, 123-24, 255
  brass, 237, 238
  description of, 130-32
  marble, 237, 238
Pisces, 96
  Boaz and, 94
  origin of, 54
  waters of, 212
Planetary angles, measuring, 236
Planets
  alphabet and, 22
  chain of, 24-25
  colors of, 182
  discovery of, 22-24
  energies of, 155, 259
  influence of, 13, 14, 16, 21-26, 31, 32, 75, 118, 127, 128, 138, 144, 169, 194, 259
  letters and, 193
  lower-octave, 30
  symbols of, 25-26
  upper-octave, 24, 161, 162
Playing cards, 191-92
Plumb, 110, 111, 115, 136, 218
  level and, 137
  symbolism of, 13, 188
Pluto, 21, 36, 178, 225
  death and, 213
  discovery of, 23
  influence of, 24, 38, 75, 162
  mythology of, 22
  oversight by, 161
  sphinx and, 191
  symbol of, 38-39
  See also Lower-Pluto realm; Upper-Pluto realm
Pluto Period, 23-24

Points, 117-19
Pole Star (Polaris), 127, 237, 249
Pollux, 50
Positions
  change of, 137
  defining, 202, 236
Positive
  negative and, 183, 192, 193-94
  transference of, 175
Potential
  lowering, 223, 224
  raising, 223, 224, 225
Precessional cycle, 217, 254
Prelate, 208, 213
Priests of Egypt, 57, 242
Prince of Jerusalem, 246-47, 256
Prince of Mercy degree, 252-53
Prince of the Tabernacle degree, 251-52
Progressed aspects, 72, 168, 169, 170, 189
Provost and Judge degree, 231-32
Prudence, 196, 197
Psychic development, 82, 244, 245
  keystone of, 163-67
Psychic forces, 43, 57, 94, 164, 181, 222, 223, 247, 257
  measure of, 158
  seed and, 103
Purification, 144, 212, 221, 225, 230, 231, 239
  end of, 213
Purity, 236, 238
  reward for, 228
  spiritual illumination and, 253
  symbolizing, 233, 251, 253
Pyramids, 2, 228

Queen of Sheeba, sign of, 176

Ramsay, Chevalier, 241
Raphael, ephemeris of, 235
Rapping, 55, 69, 72, 88, 109, 143, 177
Realization, 137
  number of, 161
Reason, 54, 62, 94
Rebis (word), 255, 256

Red Cross Sign/Word, 207
Red Sea, symbolism of, 129-30
Regeneration, 74, 114, 168, 186, 188, 192, 195, 218, 225, 226, 231, 246, 248
   aspiring to, 102, 103, 109, 252
   mysteries of, 111, 112, 133
   passion and, 105
   plane of, 194
   understanding, 104, 144, 145
Relativity transformations, 172-73
Religion, derivation of, 11
Repressions
   effects of, 104-5
   releasing, 74
Reproduction
   energy for, 104
   trinity and, 76
Repulsion, 83, 84, 137
Resurrection, 155, 206, 208, 212, 216, 226, 248
   promise of, 150
   symbolization of, 150, 221
Richardson's Monitor of Freemasonry, 5, 201
Right angles, 70, 88, 93
Ritual, 1
   emphasis of, 15-18
   mystery and, 82
River Jordan, symbolism of, 106-8, 131
Robert Bruce, King: Masons and, 241
Robertson, H.P.: quote of, 170
"Rock of Ages," 237
Rough ashlar, 126
Royal Arch, 181-99
Royal Arch degree, 225, 237
   dieugard of, 189
   grand sign of, 195
Royal Arch Mason, 198
   three times three and, 182
Royal Master degree, 177-79
Royal Sun, 12

Sacrifice, 144, 150
   number of, 143
   symbol of, 248-49

Sages of Chaldea, 57
Sagittarius
   Boaz and, 94
   origin of, 52-53
   solstitial colure and, 123
   symbolism of, 121
St. Helen, Holy Sepulchre and, 217
St. John, 247, 249
St. John the Baptist, 117, 118
St. John the Evangel, 117, 118
Salt (Vau), 134, 190
Samaritans, Zerubbabel and, 246
Sanctum Sanctorum (world of spirit), 141, 147, 158, 196, 225, 227
Satan
   number of, 147
   sign of, 95
Saturn, 35, 38
   Capricorn and, 95
   qualities of, 32, 135
   symbol of, 32, 139
   vibrations of, 169
Saturnalia, 132
Saturn finger, 114, 145, 232
Saul, wrath of, 219
Scales of Libra, 52, 124
Science of the Soul and the Stars, 10
Scientific American Magazine, quote from, 170
Scientific Encyclopedia (Van Nostrand), 38
Scorpio, 98
   Boaz and, 94
   Cain and, 142
   constructive power of, 163
   death and, 96, 213, 218, 252
   defeating, 215
   origin of, 52
   Virgo and, 52
Scottish Rite Masonry, 241
Scythe, 133, 139
Secretary, role of, 66-67, 101, 115
Secret Doctrine, 3, 15
Secret Master degree, 225-26, 227
Secret Monitor, 219
Seed, retention of, 103, 104
Select Master degree, 196-97
Self-Conscious Immortality, 27, 70

Self-consciousness, 82, 83, 128, 188
Semi-Sextile, 17
Semi-Square, 17, 127
Semites, Masonry and, 6
Senior Deacon, 35
   as animal soul, 85
   candidate clothing and, 84, 85
   role of, 65-66, 86-87
Senior Knight, 216
Senior Overseer, 162
Senior Warden, 34, 36, 55, 69, 114, 162, 173, 213, 233
   as divine soul, 87
   Master Masons and, 141
   role of, 68, 110, 128, 143
   signs by, 72
Sensualism, 73, 87, 166, 238
   energy for, 85
   symbolization of, 135
   vibrations of, 150
Sephir Yetzirah (Book of Formation), 27
Serpents, 12-13, 17, 83, 186, 211
   brazen, 252
Sesqui-Square, 17
Seven
   perfection of, 76
   symbolism of, 78, 110-11, 181
Seventh degree, 75, 225
Sex, 12, 73, 74
   destructive use of, 230
   inanimate objects and, 43
   marriage and, 57
   meaning of, 43
   repression, 58, 59, 102-4, 105, 106
   spiritual aspect of, 254, 257
   See also Celibacy
Sex activity, 56, 163
   electrification and, 166
   prohibiting, 104
   selfish, 115
   special, 57
Sex energy
   knowledge of, 225, 226
   transmuting, 217
Sex fluids
   fallacy about, 104
   retaining, 105

Sex magic, 57, 187
Sextiles, 17-18, 127
Sex worship, 13
Shem, 186
Shetharboznai, 207
Shibboleth (pass-grip), giving, 114
Shibboleth (pass-word), 102, 108, 109, 195
Shin (letter), 18
Signs, symbols of, 25-26
Simon of Cyrene, libation to, 213
Sinnesius, Bishop, 241
Six, symbolism of, 78, 106, 138
Skull and crossbones, 211, 212, 213, 257
Sky, symbology from, 13
Sleep, function of, 67-68
Society of Architects, 241
Sol, 7, 205, 257
Solar disc, symbolism of, 31
Solar religion, 11, 13
Sol-Om-On, 7
Solomon, King, 131, 151, 177, 196
   Abiff and, 146, 152, 153, 234, 235, 236
   beneficence of, 174
   Eastern Royalty and, 205
   Grand Master architects and, 236
   intercession of, 230
   jewels of, 189
   libation to, 213
   Master as, 225
Solomon's Temple, 9, 30, 37, 64, 82, 94, 102
   building, 10-12, 17, 115, 125, 126, 129, 173, 177, 196
   columns of, 12
   Masonic Brethren and, 7
   representation of, 117
Solstitial colure, 118, 119, 123, 124
Solstitial cross, 214, 255
Song of Degrees (133rd Psalm), 75, 87
Son of God, 138, 228
Son of Man, 210, 219
Soul, 7, 202-3
   coordination with, 230

death and, 259
ego and, 113, 162, 188
journey of, 82-84, 101, 128, 146-55, 158-59, 178, 184, 209, 227, 239, 250, 257, 258
stars and, 117-18
transformation of, 39, 73, 82, 89, 112, 128-29, 134, 136, 146, 149, 158, 181, 184, 197
union of, 168, 178, 183, 258
vitalization of, 86, 89
See also Divine soul
Soul consciousness, 30, 189
Soul-mates, 233, 257
reunion of, 191, 214, 236, 255
spiritual body of, 214
union of, 177, 179, 182, 195
"Source of Strength," 12
Sovereign Commander of the Temple degree, 253
Sovereign Grand Inspector General degree, 257-58
Sovereign Prince of Rose Croix de Harodin, 248
Special theory of relativity, 170
Sphinx, 213
four fold, 41, 77, 161
symbolical forms of, 191
Spiritual Alchemy, 43, 125, 126, 129, 156
Spiritual body, 69, 73, 87, 105, 137, 145, 156, 177, 179, 257
astral body and, 144
building up, 251
function of, 135, 141, 143
incense and, 139
libation to, 214
physical body and, 142
symbolization of, 133
two souls in, 146
Spirituality, 81, 112, 213, 214, 231
acquiring, 88-90, 94, 97, 101, 108, 151, 157, 212
birth of, 23
encouraging, 151
materialism and, 150
Spiritual laws, 142, 255

desires and, 87
obedience to, 18, 93, 145
Spiritual plane, 55, 87, 126, 141, 148, 152, 183, 191, 254, 257
approaching, 111, 143-45
function of, 129, 156
Master Mason's degree and, 101
nourishment on, 92, 249
perceiving, 145
physical plane and, 151
symbolizing, 150, 239
travel on, 142, 144
Spiritual power, 46, 86, 104, 126, 156
creative forces and, 235
Spiritual progress
barriers to, 183
making, 113, 243, 258
Spiritual Sun, 11, 247
Spiritual temple
destruction of, 184
reconstruction of, 184, 185
Spiritual wisdom, 15-16
aspiring for, 130
symbolization of, 226
Spiritual world, 190
constellations and, 118
descent from, 148
Square, 98, 115, 127
compass and, 16-18, 145, 208-9, 226, 255
oblong, 88, 111
passive, 97
physical plane and, 112
symbolism of, 13-14, 17, 93, 109, 111
Staircase, symbolism of, 131-32
Star and Garter order, 97
Star of Hope, 232
Starry Constellations, 135
Stars
currents from, 45
soul and, 117-18
Strength, 12
dynamic, 71
gauging, 48
symbolization of, 198
Strength (pillar), 124

Sublime Knights Elected degree, 235-36
Sublime Prince of the Royal Secret degree, 255-56
Substance, 75, 76
Sulphur (Jod), 134, 190
Sumerians, Masonry and, 6
Summer solstice, 209, 212, 217, 218, 235
Sun, 14, 17, 55
  assistants to, 65
  bursting of, 136
  feminine powers of, 198
  journey of, 15, 131, 158
  moon and, 154, 158, 168, 174, 236
  seasons and, 8
  symbolism of, 7-8, 11-12, 13, 25, 26, 30, 31, 36-37, 94
Sun finger, 176
Sun-God, names of, 7
Super Excellent Master degree, 197-98
Supreme Architect, workmanship of, 125
Supreme Council, 257
Swords
  crossed, 209
  naked heart and, 221
  symbolism of, 133-34, 206
Sylphs, 182, 187
Symbolism, 1, 2, 89
  ancients and, 81
  importance of, 4, 116, 122
  investigating, 3, 29
  language of, 16, 121
  universal, 27, 28-29, 70, 258
Symbols
  communicating with, 28-29
  meaning of, 16, 27, 122
  origin of, 25-26
  universal, 27, 28-29, 70

Tablets of Aeth, 4
Tantrics, 57
Tarot (Royal Path of Life), 16, 27, 28, 121
  Major Arcana of, 75
  suits of, 191
Tau, 236

symbolism of, 252
Tau Cross, 41, 235
Taurus
  dove and, 135
  influence of, 49-50
Telepathic communication, 202
Temple
  building, 187, 188
  destruction of, 185
  purification of, 195
Temple of King Solomon. *See* Solomon's Temple
Temple of the Sun, building, 9-10
Temptation
  symbolization of, 138, 175
  victory over, 176, 177, 183, 232
Ten, 76
  symbolism of, 79, 154, 256
Terrestrial bodies, maps/charts of, 131
Tetnai, 207
Tetragrammaton, 136, 161, 253, 255
Theories, proving/disproving, 3
Theory of Relativity. *See* General Theory of Relativity
Thirty-third degree emblem, 257
Thirty-three, symbolism of, 258
Thirty-Three Degrees of Masonry, origin of, 27-28
Thirty-Two Paths of Wisdom, 27
Thor
  gavel and, 42
  quality of, 33
Thought-cells, 61, 62, 69, 71, 193, 247
  constructive, 73
  energy for, 63
Thoughts, 224
  astral bodies and, 71
  degrading, 71-72
  energizing, 63, 71, 164
  handling, 48, 156, 259
  incense and, 139
  magical, 71
  negative, 222-23
  positive, 222-23
  power of, 259

Ancient Masonry

Three, symbolism of, 77, 255
Three Great Lights, 93-94
Three Lesser Lights, 93-94
Three steps, 133
   symbolization of, 221
Three Steps on the Master's Carpet, 133
Three times three, significance of, 182-84
Time, 91, 203
   boundary-line, 172
   evolutionary volutes of, 217
   on inner plane, 201-2
   slowing, 172
   speeding up, 172
   symbolism of, 158
   velocity of, 170
Tomb of Capricorn, 214
Tower of Babel, 2
Treasurer, 35
   role of, 67, 101, 115
   Secretary and, 66
Trestleboard, 126, 127
Trine, 17, 127, 146, 182, 183, 187
   down-pointing, 221-22
   up-pointing, 221
Trowel, 236
   significance of, 145-46
Truth, 249
   adherence to, 127, 210, 254
   higher, 93, 109, 134
   learning, 81, 99, 150
   realization of, 93, 109
   signet of, 187
   strength of, 209
   symbolization of, 209
Truth of Zerubbabel, 187
Tubal-Cain, 145
Twelve, symbolization of, 143, 147
12-inch Gauge, 54
   significance of, 48-49
24-inch Gauge, 148
   significance of, 48-49
Twin souls, 178, 187, 188
   influence of, 50
   uniting of, 192
Two, meaning of, 76-77
Tyler
   role of, 55, 56, 62-64
   sword of, 133, 134

Unconscious mind, 62, 202-3
   astral plane and, 245
   inner plane and, 224
   language of, 121
Understanding, 109, 156
   negative, 86
   restrictive, 86
   symbolization of, 88
   sympathetic, 89
Undines, 182, 185-86
Union, 116, 250
   higher, 194
   proper, 167-68
   spiritual, 144, 147, 148
   symbolism of, 13, 17-18, 176
Universal Creative Principle, symbol of, 41
Universal Welfare, 156, 259
Upper-Pluto realm, influence of, 236
Urania, 61
Uranus, 33, 38
   color of, 182
   discovery of, 22-23
   influence of, 24, 38, 75, 161, 162, 191
   mythology of, 22
   symbol of, 37-38
   vibrations of, 169
Uriel, 253

Vegetable kingdom, 128, 185, 258
Velocities, 106, 155, 156, 203-4
   consciousness and, 172
   increase in, 170, 171
   slowing down, 171
Vengeance, 234
   symbol of, 219
Venus, 56, 69, 70, 113, 135, 175
   hair and, 158
   Holy Ghost and, 96
   influence of, 24, 38, 86, 94, 258
   letter for, 147
   Libra and, 55
   number of, 106
   sphinx and, 191
   Sun and, 65

symbol of, 33-34
　throat and, 148
　vibrations of, 169
Veritas (Melville), 4
Vernal cross, 96, 206, 208, 221, 234, 235
Vernal equinox, 205, 206, 207, 211, 215, 226
Vibrations, 48, 74, 79, 84, 106, 131, 245, 250
　astrological, 139
　intensity of, 90, 107-8, 126, 193, 194
　lowering, 222
　planetary, 138, 155
　raising, 222
　space-time relationships and, 203-4
Vibratory rate, 46, 107-8, 109, 155, 194
　astral, 224
　dominant, 204, 205, 259
　range of, 156
Virgin, sign of, 95
Virgin Mary, 137
Virgo
　origin of, 51
　Scorpio and, 52
Virile energies, 44, 96, 231, 235, 251
　constructive use of, 228, 230
　generation of, 250
　positive, 167
Volutes, 217
Vulcan, 34
　gavel and, 42

Wages, receiving, 167, 173, 174
Wardens, 64, 65, 101, 250
Wheel of Destiny, 197
Will, 12, 43, 230
　developing, 47-48, 59, 88, 156-57
　electrical energy and, 45-46
　proper culture of, 46-48
　symbolization of, 88
Will of Deity, 3, 9, 11

Will power, 77
　energy and, 46, 47
　exercising, 46, 47, 58
　source of, 43-45
　symbolism of, 94
Winter solstice, 205, 211, 212, 231, 235
　Holy Sepulchre and, 218
　symbolism of, 131
Wisdom, 83, 196, 256
　acquiring, 82
　symbolizing, 233
　See also Intelligence; Knowledge
Wisdom (pillar), 124, 255
Wise Men of the East, 218
World-Line, 203
Worshipful Master, 37, 64, 65
　assisting, 68
　Jachin grip and, 114
　role of, 66, 67, 110
Written Law, 72, 93, 190, 195

Year of the Jews, 206
Yetsirah, 190
Yogis, 45, 47
York Rite Masonry, 241

Zaphael, 253
Zaphriel, 253
Zebriel, 253
Zedekiah, capture of, 197
Zenith Foundation, 201, 203
Zerubbabel, 208, 256
　Samaritans and, 246
Zodiacal signs, 10, 22, 135, 190, 228
　astral plane and, 118
　esoteric meaning of, 25-26
　influence of, 25, 28, 48-49
　letters and, 193
　union of, 226

Other Brotherhood of Light Books

The following pages present brief descriptions of the 21 Brotherhood of Light courses, written by C. C. Zain. The information contained therein represents the ancient wisdom of the Hermetic Tradition, transmitted orally in earlier ages only to initiates of The Brotherhood of Light. It was the life's work of Elbert Benjamine, under the pen name of C. C. Zain, to present this complete system of esoteric knowledge in an organized format, available for the first time to the public.

Course 1, Laws of Occultism
Inner Plane Theory and the Fundamentals of Psychic Phenomena
$16.95   6x9   192pp

The word "occult" means hidden or unseen. This course or book focuses on the study of the unseen energies affecting every persons life. The reader will come to understand how the concept, "character is destiny" is at the basis of all events attracted into their life. By learning about these energies and learning how to work within the boundaries of these undeviating natural laws one may exercise more control over the amount of success, happiness and prosperity that will be attracted. In this course various types of psychic phenomena are examined and explained. The nature of the inner plane and how it affects human life and activities is revealed.

39. Occult Data 40. Astral Substance 41. Astral Vibrations 42. Doctrine of Nativities 43. Doctrine of Mediumship 44. Spirits 45. Phenomenal Spiritism

Course 2, Astrological Signatures
Evolution of the Soul and the Nature of Astrological Energies
$16.95   6x9   256pp

This is our best book for those beginning their study of astrology. The signs of the zodiac, the planets, the mundane houses and the aspects are all discussed in detail. Also discussed is the nature of the soul and how it makes progress here and hereafter. Explanations of how the experiences of everyday life are necessary to prepare each person for a higher destiny. Of special interest are the chapters concerning reincarnation and the ancient ritual of Egyptian Initiation.

2. The Two Keys 46. The Zodiac 47. Mundane Houses 4. The Mission of the Soul 3. Physiology and Correspondence 5. Doctrine of Signatures 20. Facts and Fancies About Reincarnation 21. Facts and Fancies About Reincarnation - 2 1. The ritual of Egyptian Initiation

Course 3, Spiritual Alchemy
The Hermetic Art of Spiritual Transformation
$16.95   6x9   128pp

The ancient alchemist sought transmutation and immortality. For the soul to be immortal it must build for itself an imperishable spiritual body in which it can function after the dissolution of both the physical and astral forms. The experiences of life are symbolized by the metals of alchemy. Through proper mental attitude we purify the metals, develop our character and create our destiny. The various states of consciousness available to man are set forth and analyzed.

49. Doctrine of Spiritual Alchemy 50. Seven Spiritual Metals 51. Purifying the Metals 53. Transmutation 54. Higher Consciousness

Course 4, Ancient Masonry
The Spiritual Meaning of Masonic Degrees, Rituals and Symbols
$16.95   6x9   336pp

In this course the rituals and symbols of Ancient Masonry are revealed. For the modern Freemason this is an unprecedented work enabling him to perceive the esoteric and spiritual significance of the symbols and everything done in the lodge room. The astrological significance of the symbols and their relationship to soul development are thoroughly discussed.

6. Ancient Masonry Introduction   7. Entered Apprentice and the Planets   8. Entered Apprentice and the Signs   9. Numbers and Opening the Lodge   10. Initiating a Member   11. Fellowcraft   12. Lodge Emblems   13. Master Mason   14. Mark Master Mason   15. Royal Arch   16. Degrees of the Cross   17. Ineffable Degrees   18. Historical De-

Book 5, Esoteric Psychology
Success Through Directed Thinking and Induced Emotion
$16.95   6x9   320pp

Of all the energies that influence people, none have a more powerful effect than their own thoughts. Directing one's thinking is the most potent of all forces to control one's life and destiny. Commonly, efforts to exercise control are hindered by faulty concepts or repression resulting from environmental conditioning. Whether this conditioning expresses in a subtle way or one that is more obvious, the consequence hinders progress. *Esoteric Psychology* contains information which will assist in identifying and eliminating obstacles to progress.

Serial Lesson Numbers: 56. Doctrine of Esoteric Psychology   57. Reason and Intuition   58. Language and the Value of Dreams   59. Desire and How to Use It   60. Why Repression is Not Morality   61. How to Rule the Stars   62. How to Apply Suggestion   63. Correct Use of Affirmations   64. How to Think Constructively   65. How to Cultivate Subliminal Thinking   66. How to Develop Creative Imagination   67. How to Demon-

Course 6, The Sacred Tarot
The Art of Card Reading and the Underlying Spiritual Science
$16.95   6x9   336pp

The Sacred Tarot is a favorite of metaphysics students everywhere and companion to *The Brotherhood of Light Egyptian Tarot Cards*. With this book the student may readily determine the astrological correspondence of any number, name, color, gem or other object. In this book The Religion of the Stars system of numerology is set forth, and divination by means of numbers is explained. This book is also one of the most complete, detailed synthesis of the Tarot archetypes as they manifest in different areas of occult science and spiritual truth. Each of the 78 cards is elucidated and 11 tarot card spreads are illustrated.

48. Doctrine of Kabalism   22. Foundation of the Science   23. Scope and Use of Tarot   24. Involution and Evolution of Numbers   25. Reading the Meaning of Numbers   26. Making an Astrological Chart   27. Influence of Changing the Name   28. Reading Names in Detail   29. The Color of a Name   30. Natural Talismans and Artificial

Book 7, Spiritual Astrology
The Origins of Astro-Mythology and Stellar Religion
$16.95   6x9   352pp

This course describes the outstanding attributes of those born under the influence of each of the 48 ancient constellations. Also revealed are the specific doctrines associated with each of the constellations. These ancient spiritual doctrines, formulated by the most wise of prehistoric times, later found their way into ancient mythology, the Bible and other sacred writings. This course or book sets forth the most significant of the stories associated with these doctrines and reveals their true meaning.

Serial Lesson Numbers: 71. Our Spiritual Legacy 72. The Foundation of Youth 73. Knights of King Arthur 74. Story of the Three Bears 75. The Ladder to Heaven 76. Is there a Santa Claus 77. Why Eve Was Tempted 78. The Marriage in Heaven 79. The Scorpion and the Eagle 80. The Bow of Bright Promise 81. News From the Summerland 82. In the Reign of Aquarius 83. The Tree of Life

Course 8, Horary Astrology
How to Erect and Judge a Horoscope
$16.95   6x9   224pp

This course is often chosen by beginning students of astrology for its technical lesson "How to Erect A Horoscope", as well as for its clearly organized system for judging any horoscope. More advanced students refer to this volume for horary chart interpretation. The section on horary astrology is of special interest for its explanation of how and why this branch of astrology can solve a problem relating to events past, present and future. Also included for beginning students are C.C. Zain's chart erection short-cuts, for which he designed the Church of Light #2 Chart Pad.

86. How to Erect a Horoscope 87. Strength and Aspects of the Planets 88. First Seven Steps in Judging Any Horoscope 89. The Doctrine of Horary Astrology 90. Questions Relating to First Six Houses 91. Questions Relating to Last Six Houses 92. How to Select the Best time for Any Undertaking 36. Chart Erection Short Cuts and Examples

Course 9, Mental Alchemy
How thoughts and Feelings Shape Our Lives
$16.95   6x9   224pp

The astrological energies mapped by a birth chart are not the cause of the conditions and events that come into one's life - it is the character of the individual. Character is composed of thought cells built and organized on the inner plane. Course 9 explains how these thought cell groups, which constitute man's unconscious mind, have been formed before his birth, and how they are modified after birth by experience. Of importance is an explanation of how these thought cells can be reconditioned to work for the things the individual desires.

95. The Inner Nature of Poverty, Failure and Disease 96. Just how to Find the Thought-Cause of Any Condition 97. How to Find a Mental Antidote 98. How to Apply a Mental Antidote 99. Just How to Heal Yourself 100. Just How to Attain Realization 101. Just How to Give Absent Treatments

Course 10-1, Natal Astrology: Part One
Delineating the Horoscope
$16.95   6x9   224pp

In a step by step fashion, *Delineating the Horoscope*, presents the Hermetic system of natal astrology along with the unsurpassed "Outline of a Complete Astrological Reading". Beginning and advanced students will enjoy the explanations of the 36 decanates, illustrated with examples of renowned persons having Sun, Moon or Ascendant in each of the described decanates.

103. First Eighteen Decanates Analyzed   104. Last Eighteen Decanates Analyzed   105. Stature, Temperament, Disposition and Mental Ability   106. Vitality, Health and Disease   107. Business, Finances and Vocational Selection   108. Friends, Enemies and Associates   109. Love, Marriage and Partnership   110. How to Delineate a Horoscope.

Course 10-2, Natal Astrology: Part Two
Progressing the Horoscope
$16.95   6x9   224pp

A technical manual on the Hermetic system of major and minor progressions. The progressed aspects of natal astrology reveal probable future events through indicating the manner in which an individuals thought cells will work to attract events. With this information the individual can learn to take precautionary actions and learn to recondition the energy so that a more desirable outcome can be achieved. To round out the study of natal astrology, a lesson on the Hermetic system of rectifying the horoscope is included for use in erecting a birth chart when the exact birth time is unknown.

19. Hermetic System of Progressions   111. Major Progressions of Sun and Angles   112. Major Progressions of the Moon   113. Major Progressions of the Planets   114. Minor Progressions of the Sun and Angles   115. Minor Progressions of the Moon and Planets   116. Transits, Revolutions and Cycles   117. Rectifying the Horoscope

Course 11, Divination & Character Reading
Tools and Techniques for Enhancing ESP
$16.95   6x9   192pp

Divination is a means to assist extension of consciousness on the inner plane to acquire the information desired. By understanding the nature of and learning about the various methods of divination one may begin to use these technique more effectively. Clairvoyance, precognition, telepathy, the divining rod, teacup and coffee cup methods, among others are discussed in detail. The last four lessons are devoted to learning to read character based on physical characteristics.

118. Doctrine of Divination   119. Teacup and Coffee Cup Divination   120. Divining Rod and Other Divination   121. Instantaneous Character Reading   122. Significance of Body and Head   123. Instantaneous Reading From Profile   124. Instantaneous Vocational Analysis

Course 12-1, Natural Alchemy: Part One
Evolution of Life
$16.95   6x9   224pp

We live in kinship with all life forms, animate and inanimate. For humans to understand their place in nature, and thus what their relation can be to other life forms, to other people and to God, the individual needs to know how the various life forms including that of the human, have developed to the state they now occupy. Course 12, Part 1 offers *The Religion of the Stars* unique interpretation of how natural selection and adaptation is influenced by Psychokinesis, ESP and inner plane influence.

125. Origin of the Earth   126. Origin and Development of Plants   127. Progress of Invertebrate Life   128. Fishes and Amphibians   129. Reptiles and Birds   130. Development Among Mammals   131. Development of Man   132. Development of Knowledge

Course 12-2, Natural Alchemy: Part Two
Evolution of Religion
$16.95   6x9   224pp

This course deals with the evolution of those ideas which constitute various religions. Part 2 begins with the most primitive religions and shows how these, and the cultures coincident with them, gradually developed into the more complex systems of belief of today. The tenets of each important present day religion are explained, and finally there is set forth the basic tenets of *The Religion of the Stars*.

133. The Foundations of Religion   134. Early Religions of the World   135. Religion in Historic Times   136. Tao, Confucianism, Zoroastrianism and Mohammedanism   137. Hinduism and Buddhism   138. Judaism and Christianity   139. The Stellarian Religion   140. Astrology is Religion's Road Map

Course 13, Mundane Astrology
Interpreting Astrological Phenomena for Cities, Nations and Groups
$16.95   6x9   272pp

Astrological energies influence the trend of world events. When a natal chart isn't available, these influences can be determined through the mundane cycle charts of nations, cities, groups etc. This course is one of the few technical manuals on the erection of mundane cycle charts and their delineation. Such information is valuable because it enables one to take precautionary actions and arrange personal affairs to take most advantage of city, national or world conditions. It also helps one to foresee conditions and thus exert political influence in support of those measures which insure peace and give people freedom from want, freedom from fear, freedom of expression and freedom of religion.

141. Doctrine of Mundane Astrology   142. Cycles of Pluto and Neptune   143. Cycles of Uranus   144. Cycles of Saturn   145. Cycles of Jupiter   146. Cycles of Mars   147. Major Conjunctions of the Planets   148. Cycles of the Sun   149. Cycles of the Moon

Course 14, Occultism Applied
How to Increase Your Happiness, Usefulness and Spirituality
$16.95   6x9   320pp

Just how to use occult knowledge and occult energies in everyday life is considered in detail in this book. The reader will learn about how he/she is being trained for a unique mission and about how they have a special job to do in God's Great Evolutionary Plan. It points out the advantage of living the completely constructive life. One of the most critical lessons to learn is that to gain the things we desire from life usually requires that some of our habit systems be changed. Changing habits is not easy but the three fundamental principles given in Course 14 will give the quickest and surest success.

151. Finding One's Cosmic Work 152. Living the Completely Constructive Life 153. Diet and Breathing 154. How to Keep Young 155. How to Be Attractive 156. How to Have Friends 157. How to Get Employment 158. How to Make Money 159. How to Achieve Honors 160. How to be Successful in Marriage 161. How to Have a Pleasant Home 162. How to be Happy

Course 15, Weather Predicting
The Hermetic System of Astrological Weather Analysis
$16.95   6x9   192pp

Astrological energies have a profound influence over the weather conditions of earth. They indicate changes from the normal trends in a given locality. With practice, one can determine trends in temperature, moisture and wind quite precisely. This is particularly useful information for those involved in agriculture, aviation, travel or planning a social event. It is an aspect of astrological studies that should not be neglected by anyone seeking a complete, working knowledge of astrology. *Weather Predicting* is a complete treatment of the subject and the only text available entirely devoted to astrological influences on the weather.

190. Astrological Weather Predicting 191. Reading Astrological Weather Charts 192. Astrological Temperature Charts 193. Astrological Air Movement Charts 194. Astro-

Course 16, Stellar Healing
Astrological Predisposition, Diagnosis and Treatment of Disease
$16.95   6x9   320pp

Health is a valuable asset. The positions of the planets in the birth chart indicate the diseases toward which an individual is predisposed. *Stellar Healing* gives the birth chart and progressed constants of 160 diseases. It also sets forth a most effective method of drugless healing and indicates specific Stellar Treatments. In addition, it shows how to calculate in terms of ASTRODYNES, HARMODYNES and DISCORDYNES the precise power and harmony of any planet, aspect, sign or house. ASTRODYNES are the unsurpassed mathematical formula for the measurement of astrological power.

197. Stellar Anatomy 198. Basis of Stellar Diagnosis 199. Principles of Stellar Healing 200. Technique of Stellar Healing 201. Stellar Healing in Practice 202. Diagnosis and Treatment 203. Abdominal Troubles - Bleeding 204. Blindness - Coronary Thrombosis 205. Cyst - Hay Fever 206. Headache - Mumps 207. Nervous Breakdown - Scarlet Fever 208. Sciatica - Yellow Fever

Course 17, Cosmic Alchemy
The Spiritual Guide to Universal Progression
$16.95   6x9   256pp

Man is not an isolated unit. Instead he is a member of world society and can be an energetic worker in the realization of God's Evolutionary Plan. This course indicates how each person can become active in achieving the realization of this plan. Each person can act to insure that there will be no more wars; that poverty will be abolished; and, that educational facilities and the widest possible access to information will be available to all. Most importantly, this course unmasks the much misunderstood word spirituality. It shows exactly what spirituality is, and the three general methods of gaining it by learning to: (1) View events from the standpoint of spiritual alchemy, (2) Cultivate thoughts, feelings and actions that arise from the desire to benefit others, and (3) Raise the vibratory rate through a heightened intellectual and emotional appreciation.

164. Conquest of War 165. Abolition of Poverty 166. Cosmic Politics 167. Heredity and Environment 168. How to Be Spiritual 169. Spiritual Value of Education 170. How to Appraise Spiritual Values 171. Minor Aids to Spiritual Advancements 172. Major Aids to Spiritual Advancements

Course 18, Imponderable Forces
The Wholesome Pathway
$16.95   6x9   192pp

Course 18 explains the extent to which reliance should be placed on transits, minor progressed aspects, major progressed aspects and other astrological conditions as well as explains the proper attitude toward such astrological weather. It indicates how sympathies and antipathies work, and how much importance to attribute to birthstones, numbers, names and environmental vibrations. Since the greatest enemy of fear and superstition is thorough understanding, this course explains in detail ceremonial magic, sorcery and witchcraft, and how to protect oneself against black magic of any kind. It shows how we are influenced by suggestions and inversive propaganda and how to avoid thus being influenced. This book gives the reader a comprehensive survey of the wholesome pathway and how to follow it.

183. How to Act Under Adverse Progressed Aspects 184. Sympathies and Antipathies 185. Ceremonial Magic 186. Sorcery and Witchcraft 187. Ritual and Religion 188. Press, Radio and Billboard 189. The Wholesome Pathway

Course 19, Organic Alchemy
The Universal law of Soul Progression
$16.95   6x9   192pp

To take advantage of nature's laws we must understand them. Man is not set apart from other living things, but all forms of life come under one uniform and universal law. This course explains in detail how the polarity of the soul, as indicated by its astrological signature, multiplied by the energy of its ego, plus pleasure and pain results in progression of the soul. Nature uses pleasure not as a reward but to inform the organism when it is successfully adapting itself to its environment — pain when it fails to adapt. This course gives a great deal of information about the problems and habits of other life forms, why there is no unpardonable sin, how the cosmos is managed, and its sets forth an outline of the general cosmic plan.

209. The Ceaseless Surge of Life 210. Every Life Form Manifests a Soul 211. The Universal Law of Soul Progression 212. The Uses of Pleasure and Pain 213. The Universal Law of Compensation 214. The Universal Moral Code 215. Discerning God's Great Plan

Course 20, The Next Life
A Guide To Living Conditions on the Inner Plane
$16.95   6x9   272pp

Life on earth is but one phase of existence. Physical life constitutes necessary schooling so that the soul can function effectively on a higher plane where it will be less restricted. By understanding the nature of the life to come, the individual is better prepared to live this life and the next. Course 20 gives a great deal of information about the conditions to be met and the activities of life after physical death. It tells about the various levels of the inner plane world, about the three methods of birth into the next life, about the influence of desires there, of the effect of sorrowing for those who have passed to the next life and how they may be helped, of the work to be done there and how education is handled. *The Next Life* is not only interesting, but the information it contains will be a highly valuable guide to anyone when passing from the physical plane.

173. Turning the Dial to Inner Planes   174. Properties of Life On The Inner Plane   175. Birth Into the Next Life   176. Astrological Influences in The Next Life   177. Occupations of the Next Life 178. Education and Progress in The Next Life   179. Earth Bound Souls and the Astral Hells   180. Domestic Relations of the Next Life   181. Social Contracts and Amusements in the Next Life   182. Through Astral and Spiritual to

Course 21, Personal Alchemy
The Neophyte's Path to Spiritual Attainment
$16.95   6x9   272pp

The student who has gained the knowledge contained in the first 20 *Brotherhood of Light* courses is apt to decide to develop himself and his powers to the very best advantage. Consequently, *Personal Alchemy* gives precise instructions on the steps such an individual should take and the order in which he should take them.

216. Three Things Every Neophyte Should Know   217. The First Three Habits a Neophyte Should Adopt   218. Avenues to Illumination   219. Spiritual Hindrance by Family and Friends   220. Spiritual Trends in Personal Conduct   221. How to Keep Mentally and Physically Fit   222. What to Eat When Mercury or Uranus is Afflicted   223. What to Eat When sun, Moon or Pluto is Afflicted   224. What to Eat When Saturn, Jupiter or Neptune is Afflicted   225. What to Eat when Venus or Mars is Afflicted

To Order Brotherhood of Light Books:

Qty	#	Item	Price	Amt

Please include shipping & handling charges: $6.00 first item, $1.00 for each additional item. USA only please.

☐ YES ! Please send me a free catalog.

Subtotal	
Shipping	
TOTAL	

Ship To: _____

Address: _____

_____

City: _____

State & Zip Code: _____

Telephone: _____

For ☐ **MasterCard** ☐ **Visa** Orders Only:

Card No. _____ **Exp Date** _____

Card Holder Signature _____

Send your check or money order to:

The Church of Light
111 So. Kraemer Blvd., Suite A
Brea, CA 92821-4676